Peace versus Justice?

Peace versus Justice?

The Dilemma of Transitional Justice in Africa

Edited by Chandra Lekha Sriram and Suren Pillay

 UNIVERSITY OF KWAZULU-NATAL PRESS

Published in 2010 in the UK and US by James Currey
an imprint of Boydell and Brewer Ltd, PO Box 9, Woodbridge, Suffolk IP12 3DF, UK
and 668 Mount Hope Avenue, Rochester NY 14620, USA
www.jamescurrey.com
www.boydellandbrewer.com

Published in 2009 by University of KwaZulu-Natal Press
Private Bag X01
Scottsville 3209
South Africa
E-mail: books@ukzn.ac.za
Website: www.uknpress.co.za

ISBN: 978-1-86914-173-8 (University of KwaZulu-Natal Press paper)
ISBN: 978-1-84701-021-6 (James Currey paper)

British Library Cataloguing in Publication Data
Peace v. justice? : the dilemma of transitional justice in Africa.
1. Transitional justice--Africa. 2. Reconciliation--
Political aspects--Africa. 3. Truth commissions--Africa.
4. War crime trials--Africa.
I. Sriram, Chandra Lekha, 1971- II. Pillay, Suren.
303.6'9'096-dc22

Managing editor: Sally Hines
Editor: Juliet Haw
Typesetter: Patricia Comrie
Indexer: Nora Buchanan
Cover design: Kult Creative
Cover image adapted from photograph by Sven Torfinn / Panos Pictures

Printed and bound in Great Britain by
CPI Antony Rowe Ltd, Chippenham and Eastbourne

Contents

Abbreviations

AFRC	Armed Forces Revolutionary Council
AGP	Mozambican General Peace Agreement (*Acordo Geral de Paz*)
AMETRAMO	Mozambican Association of Traditional Practitioners
ANC	African National Congress
APC	All People's Congress
APRM	African Peer Review Mechanism
AU	African Union
AUC	United Self-Defense Groups of Colombia
AWB	Afrikaner Weerstandsbeweging
CAR	Central African Republic
CAVR	Commission for Reception, Truth and Reconciliation
CCR	Centre for Conflict Resolution
CDD	Centre for Democratic Development (Ghana)
CDF	Civil Defence Forces
CLO	Civil Liberties Organisation
CODESA	Congress for a Democratic South Africa
CPP	Convention People's Party
CSO	civil society organisation
CSSDCA	Conference on Security, Stability, Development and Co-operation in Africa
CSVR	Centre for the Study of Violence and Reconciliation
CVR	Comisión de la Verdad y Reconciliación
DA	Democratic Alliance
DDR	disarmament, demobilisation and reintegration
DRC	Democratic Republic of the Congo
ECOMOG	Economic Community of West African States Military Observer Group

ECOMOG	Economic Community of West African States Monitoring Group
ECOSOCC	Economic, Social and Cultural Council
ECOWAS	Economic Community of West African States
ELN	National Liberation Army
ERC	Equity and Reconciliation Commission
EU	European Union
FARC	Revolutionary Armed Forces of Colombia
FMLN	Farabundo Marti National Liberation Front
FRELIMO	Liberation Front of Mozambique
GEAR	Growth, Employment and Redistribution
HRC	Human Rights Commission
HRVIC	Human Rights Violations Investigation Commission
ICC	International Criminal Court
ICTJ	International Center for Transitional Justice
ICTR	International Criminal Tribunal for Rwanda
ICTY	International Criminal Tribunal for the Former Yugoslavia
IDP	internally displaced person
IER	Instance Equité et Réconciliation
ILC	International Law Commission
IMF	International Monetary Fund
LRA	Lord's Resistance Army
MARWOPNET	Mano River Women's Peace Network
MRTA	Movimiento Revolucionario Tupac Amaru
NATO	North Atlantic Treaty Organisation
NCD	National Commission for Democracy
NCP-SL	Network for Collaborative Peacebuilding in Sierra Leone
NDC	National Democratic Congress
NEPAD	New Partnership for Africa's Development
NGO	non-governmental organisation
NLM	National Liberation Movement
NMJD	Network Movement for Justice and Development
NPA	National Prosecuting Authority
NPFL	National Patriotic Front of Liberia
NPP	New Patriotic Party
NRC	National Reconciliation Commission (Ghana)
NTA	National Television Authority

NURC	National Unity and Reconciliation Commission
OAU	Organisation of African Unity
OHCHR	Office of the High Commissioner for Human Rights
ONUMOZ	United Nations Mission in Mozambique
PBC	Peacebuilding Commission
PMDC	People's Movement for Democratic Change (Sierra Leone)
PNC	People's National Congress
PNDC	Provisional National Defence Council
PNU	Party of National Unity
PP	Progress Party
PSC	Peace and Security Council
RDP	Reconstruction and Development Programme
RENAMO	Mozambican National Resistance
RPA	Rwanda Patriotic Army
RPF	Rwandan Patriotic Front
RUF	Revolutionary United Front
SADF	South African Defence Force
SCSL	Special Court for Sierra Leone
SL	Sendero Luminoso (Shining Path)
SLPP	Sierra Leone People's Party
SLTRC	Sierra Leone Truth and Reconciliation Commission
SNC	Sovereign National Conference
TCRP	Truth and Community Reconciliation Project
TIG	community service (*travaux d'intérêt général*)
TRC	Truth and Reconciliation Commission
UNAMSIL	United Nations Mission in Sierra Leone
UNCHR	United Nations High Commission for Human Rights
UNCOI	United Nations Commission of Inquiry on Darfur
UNDP	United Nations Development Programme
UNICEF	United Nations Children's Fund
UNIFEM	United Nations Development Fund for Women
UNMIS	United Nations Mission in Sudan
UNTAET	United Nations Transitional Administration in East Timor
UPDF	Uganda People's Defence Forces
WACSOF	West African Civil Society Forum
WNC	Women's National Coalition

Acknowledgements

This book would not have been possible without the assistance and co-operation of many people. First and foremost, we thank the authors for their contribution to the seminar organised by the Centre for Conflict Resolution (CCR) at the University of Cape Town, South Africa, on 'Peace versus Justice? Truth and Reconciliation Commissions and War Crimes Tribunals in Africa' in May 2007. We appreciate the authors' tireless contributions and their patience during the process of bringing this project to fruition. We would further like to thank the other participants at this seminar – too numerous to list – who provided insight into the historical and current roles and impact of truth and reconciliation processes and war crimes trials around the globe and in Africa.

We, the editors, extend a special thanks to Dr Adekeye Adebajo, the CCR's Executive Director, for inviting us to co-edit this project, and for his support in shepherding this challenging project through to completion. We also acknowledge the work of individuals at the CCR who helped to ensure the successful completion of this volume: Dawn Nagar, Pippa Segall and Elizabeth Myburgh provided excellent support throughout the process. Ken McGillivray provided excellent copy-editing on the text in the final stages of the manuscript, for which we are also most appreciative. We would also like to thank the University of KwaZulu-Natal Press for editorial support.

The CCR extends its appreciation and grateful thanks to the primary funder of this project, the government of Denmark, as well as its other Africa Programme funders: the governments of the Netherlands, Sweden, Norway and Finland as well as the United Kingdom's Department for International Development (DFID) and the Swiss Agency for Development and Cooperation.

We hope that this book will contribute significantly to the understanding among both specialists and the general public of the importance and role of truth and reconciliation processes and truth commissions in Africa, particularly although not exclusively, in countries emerging from violent conflict. The rapid proliferation of these mechanisms in Africa and the attention of international institutions such as the International Criminal Court to crimes in Africa make this volume particularly timely.

Chandra Lekha Sriram, London, and Suren Pillay, Cape Town
October 2008

Introduction

Transitional Justice and Peacebuilding

Chandra Lekha Sriram

PEACE VERSUS JUSTICE?

The so-called peace versus justice dilemma arises following violent conflict, in which victims and their families, local and international non-governmental organisations (NGOs), and other actors in the international community often demand that some form of accountability be imposed on the perpetrators of gross human rights violations and war crimes. Those calling for accountability frequently insist that it must be pursued for the sake of the victims, their survivors, society at large, deterrence and the (re)building of democracy and the rule of law. Those seeking to promote peacebuilding (a broad range of activities to ensure that conflict does not re-emerge) may concur that there is value in seeking accountability, but raise concerns that it may destabilise fragile post-conflict states. These two positions often form the poles of the so-called peace versus justice debate, which deals with the critical policy decisions made about accountability in the context of peacemaking and peacebuilding. This dichotomous dilemma is often overstated. In reality the choice is seldom simply 'justice' or 'peace' but rather a complex mixture of both. The practice of transitional justice, as it has emerged over the past 25 years or so, offers a range of options to states emerging from conflict, including truth commissions, domestic trials, international and hybrid tribunals and traditional justice mechanisms. Much can be learned from earlier experiences of transition in southern Europe and Latin America that may help to inform African countries considering transitional justice processes.[1] This volume takes account of those prior transitions, while focusing on the challenges and practices of pursuing peace and justice in Africa.

CHALLENGES AND DEVELOPMENTS IN AFRICA

African countries face dilemmas similar to those faced by democratising states before them, but these are exacerbated by the fact that many are emerging not from dictatorships but from violent conflicts, many of which were protracted, recurrent and regional.[2] Transitional justice mechanisms may contribute to peacebuilding processes but may also serve as impediments to peacemaking, particularly where conflicts are regional and the pursuit of justice in one locale may impact upon peacemaking or justice in another.[3] Nonetheless, despite the risks and frequently strong opposition from current and former state officials, transitional justice mechanisms are becoming increasingly common in Africa. While many senior government officials were effectively immune from national and international human rights law during much of Africa's post-colonial era, the last decade has seen a reversal of this trend. The International Criminal Tribunal for Rwanda (ICTR) prosecuted some of those responsible for the 1994 Rwandan genocide, and war criminals in Liberia and Sierra Leone have been pursued by the Special Court for Sierra Leone (SCSL). International accountability mechanisms have been developed to respond to wide-ranging crimes in conflicts involving massive casualties but are often only able to pursue a small number of perpetrators. The International Criminal Court (ICC) in The Hague is engaged in investigations of situations in four African countries – Uganda, the Democratic Republic of the Congo (DRC), the Sudan and the Central African Republic (CAR) – and there has been a proliferation in the use of national truth and reconciliation commissions to document human rights violations.[4] Occasionally domestic processes have more success in pursuing perpetrators.[5]

Prosecutions

Domestic trials and more internationalised war crimes trials and tribunals have become relatively common tools of transitional justice. International or hybrid tribunals were created for Rwanda and Sierra Leone. The mandate of these tribunals is to prosecute individuals alleged to have perpetrated gross human rights violations but only those who bore significant responsibility. However, tribunals have often been criticised for promoting 'victors' justice'. For example, Liberian President Ellen Johnson-Sirleaf helped to facilitate the arrest of Charles Taylor, a former political rival, in 2006. The Sierra Leonean court has been viewed by some as a tool of the United States both in its battle against the ICC and in its pursuit of the global war on terror (see Chapter 11 in this volume). These tribunals are also often accused of overlooking the victims' need for restitution or reconciliation as well as the broader needs of society to heal and rebuild. This has particularly proved to be the case when tribunals are considered to be either too remote from the location of the crimes, such as the Rwandan tribunal or an unnecessary drain upon resources that should instead have been devoted to rebuilding national judicial capacity, as with the Sierra Leonean court. Concerns have also been raised that the ICC has focused excessively on African cases.

Truth commissions

In the last two decades there have been over 25 truth commissions or truth and reconciliation commissions (TRCs) globally, with at least seven of these based in Africa.[6] The South African TRC is often held up as a model to be emulated, both in Africa and in other countries emerging from conflict or serious repression. Countries such as Ghana and Liberia have created such bodies in the absence of official trials, while Sierra Leone's truth commission operated contemporaneously with the Special Court during 2003–2004. The nature of truth commissions may differ but they generally perform two key functions: Firstly, they attempt to document human rights abuses that were perpetrated during a specified timeframe; secondly, they often make recommendations regarding institutional reforms that may help to prevent future violations and, less frequently, regarding reparations to victims. Truth commissions can help to promote not only truth-telling or reconciliation but also nation-building and peacebuilding. However, in countries such as Uganda, the 1986 truth commission was seen as a tool used by the government of Yoweri Museveni to discredit the previous regime rather than as a transparent mechanism to facilitate reconciliation.[7]

Traditional mechanisms

In Africa a range of traditional mechanisms to promote reconciliation also exists.[8] For example, among the Acholi of northern Uganda, indigenous reconciliation processes involve truth-telling and requests for forgiveness to achieve both reconciliation and to challenge perpetrators of human rights abuses. Traditional approaches to conflict resolution and justice may differ significantly from western legal systems that emphasise prosecution and retributive justice.[9] In Rwanda, the *gacaca* process has been used not as an alternative to western-style justice but to complement it when the ICTR and the Rwandan courts have been unable to address the alleged perpetrators, who may number 100 000 or more.

Chandra Lekha Sriram

While tribunals and TRCs have their proponents and detractors, they have come to play an important role in peacebuilding processes in both Africa and globally. Thus it is timely, given the almost unprecedented proliferation of such mechanisms in Africa, to consider the role that these commissions have played in addressing gross human rights violations and war crimes on the continent, as well as the impact they have had, both positive and negative, on countries and regions facing entrenched conflict cycles. This volume seeks to do so through an examination of peace and the politics of justice in Africa, and through examining specific processes such as TRCs, tribunals and traditional justice as well as through a consideration of the emerging role of the ICC.

THE DEVELOPMENT AND OBJECTIVES OF THIS BOOK

In May 2007, the Centre for Conflict Resolution (CCR) at the University of Cape Town, South Africa, held a workshop on 'Truth and Reconciliation Commissions and War Crimes Tribunals in Africa'. The meeting brought together experts and practitioners from across the continent as well as from outside Africa to review and analyse the experiences and lessons learnt from recent case studies of transitional justice on the continent, building on earlier work by the CCR in assessing the development of peacebuilding initiatives in Africa. The studies examined experiences in South Africa, Sierra Leone, Ghana, Uganda, Rwanda, Mozambique, Sudan, the DRC and the CAR.[10] The approaches examined in the meeting encompass a range of judicial and non-judicial processes adopted by post-conflict societies to address human rights abuses of the past, ranging from United Nations (UN) tribunals to 'hybrid' criminal courts, domestic trials and truth and reconciliation commissions.

The Cape Town workshop focused on five key questions, some of which were elaborated on, challenged and even rejected in the course of the meeting as well as in the chapters presented in this volume:

- What have been the African experiences of transitional justice?
- Should justice or truth be prioritised when dealing with post-conflict reconstruction in Africa?
- What are the challenges for nation-building posed by granting amnesty to perpetrators of war crimes?
- How effective have recent war crimes tribunals and truth commissions in Africa been at targeting human rights perpetrators?
- Do the current models for addressing truth and justice overlook indigenous African methods of post-conflict reconstruction?

Participants presented papers on various aspects of these questions, which were discussed extensively and are presented in revised forms in this volume. The workshop and this volume benefited immensely from the participation not only of scholars and analysts but genuine insider-practitioners. Many of the authors in this volume were important participants in the processes they discuss, whether as members of the Sierra Leonean or South African truth commissions, as legal practitioners in the ICTR or the SCSL, or as critical civil society advocates during transitional processes. Their hands-on perspectives provide new insights on familiar institutions.

KEY LESSONS AS WELL AS RECURRING AND CROSS-CUTTING THEMES
The peace versus justice dilemma is oversimplified
An obvious lesson that has emerged, and one that cannot be stressed enough, is that the peace versus justice dilemma is grossly oversimplified. Countries often pursue peace agreements that include accountability mechanisms or TRCs, or pursue the creation of accountability mechanisms while implementing peace agreements. The pursuit of justice is thus not always an obstacle to peacemaking.[11]

Secondly, many countries may variously pursue amnesty and accountability approaches over the course of time. There is also a wide range of truth commissions and accountability processes: transitional regimes may grant amnesties and later revoke some and impose accountability; other regimes may pursue accountability followed by amnesty or pardon; and transitional arrangements may grant amnesty to many while prosecuting a few.

While the richness of practice and the literature analysing practice clearly demonstrate the above, there is a persistent belief in the sharp dichotomy between peace and justice that needs to be continually challenged. However, in practice, many of these transitional challenges and opportunities do merit closer inspection and a number of recurring and cross-cutting themes emerge from these chapters.

Timing and sequencing
It has become increasingly clear that the timing and sequencing of peacemaking and accountability activities is important. However, it is not always clear precisely what the timing and sequencing should be. Furthermore, there is often more than one 'bite at the apple': accountability processes that are not feasible at one point in time may become feasible at a later time or in another location. Debate continues as to whether accountability mechanisms must be put in place early to

help bolster democratisation and the rule of law or whether they should emerge after a prudent delay, to allow the consolidation of peace and the stabilisation of the new regime. Similarly, it remains debatable whether truth commissions and trials should occur simultaneously and support each other or whether they are necessarily in competition with one another.

The evidence presented in the following chapters suggests that the appropriate timing and sequencing of mechanisms is context-specific. Moreover, choices about accountability may be made several times in, or for, post-conflict or post-authoritarian regimes. For example, prosecutions in Argentina in the 1980s that ended with pardons have been revived through the exercise of universal jurisdiction in Spain as well as domestic trials. On the African continent, Charles Taylor, granted exile in Nigeria in 2003, and thus given protection from prosecution by the SCSL or while in Liberia, now faces trial before the SCSL, which has relocated to The Hague. Ghana's National Reconciliation Commission was established in 2002, some nine years after that country's transition from military to civilian rule.

What is it all for?

Another cross-cutting theme that emerges from the following chapters is the need to question seriously the purpose and legitimacy of any institution that is being created. It is important to be certain that an institution, whether tribunal or TRC, has local support and that it is not purely an external imposition. While there is almost always, if indeed not always, a local demand for justice, there is not necessarily a demand for the specific institutions created. The local–international dynamic is a separate cross-cutting theme discussed below. However, any process must be designed to serve, and should be expected to serve, specific goals and interests. These include the demands of victims, the need for reconciliation, the criteria of retributive justice, deterrence and rebuilding the rule of law. There is a lively debate about whether the institutions examined here can or do serve any or all of these goals. For example, can an international or hybrid tribunal serve to support or build the capacity of the local judiciary? Should it be expected to do so? In Sierra Leone, many expected the SCSL to promote the development of the national judiciary and some judges also embraced the 'legacy' agenda but as an institution this was not a role the Court was well suited to play. It is therefore important not only to be clear about what an institution is designed to do but to ensure that these goals map to real demands, whether they be the

local support not external imposition

demands of the population or the international community. Otherwise there is a risk that a 'cookie-cutter' or template approach to institutions will lead to the creation of certain bodies simply because this is what is done in other post-conflict situations, without consideration of any demand for it or its purpose and legitimacy.

The large footprint of South Africa

In several chapters it becomes clear that the South African 'model' has a large footprint and that many truth commissions created after 1994 have sought to emulate the South African TRC, at least in part, and are frequently compared to it. Specifically, the model is understood to entail an exchange of truth for justice of sorts, in which individuals who testify to their politically motivated criminal acts may receive amnesty for their crimes, while individuals who do not testify may face prosecution. However, this model was and remains contentious within South Africa itself, and several chapters draw attention to the unfinished compromise of the TRC: many issues of social justice such as economic reform and reparations, which were part of that compromise, remain unaddressed. Further, any amnesty granted during a transitional process is contentious within international legal and policy circles. The conditional or limited amnesty, although considered less distasteful than the blanket amnesty created by the 1999 Lomé Peace Accord for Sierra Leone, still remains problematic.[12] Furthermore, the South African experience, like the experience of most countries in transition, is not necessarily transferable either to countries emerging from protracted violent conflict or to those with little or no history of electoral politics and the rule of law, a situation which characterises many of the African countries facing the 'peace versus justice' dilemma today. This is by no means to deny that the challenges that South Africa faced were great or to suggest that it had a history of genuine democracy but rather to distinguish some of the specific challenges that it did *not* face.

Local and international: Decisions, processes and politics

Most chapters in this volume demonstrate the complex interplay between local and international politics and local and international law in the formulation of peace and justice strategies and mechanisms. International politics has clearly shaped some of the responses to past abuses: arguably the use of a hybrid model in Sierra Leone came as part of a backlash against the slow and costly ad hoc

Chandra Lekha Sriram

tribunals for the former Yugoslavia and Rwanda, and the United States' persistent opposition to the ICC and its preference for hybrid and ad hoc responses. International legal imperatives may demand prosecutions that are out of step with local law or peacemaking processes; this is arguably the case with the insistence of the Prosecutor of the ICC that the negotiating processes between the Ugandan government and the Lord's Resistance Army (LRA), as well as any Ugandan legal amnesties, will not impede the prosecution of LRA leader Joseph Kony and other top figures in the LRA. The Prosecutor is clearly within his mandate and the legal norms that oppose or limit amnesty are increasingly being developed. Nonetheless, the Prosecutor does have the discretion to refrain from pursuing cases and some suggest that this is an instance in which he should do so, particularly if the local population most affected by the LRA advocates it. The importance of local decisions and participation, whether or not accountability processes are local, is emphasised in many of the chapters. Thus the transfer of the Charles Taylor trial from Freetown to The Hague, which limited local access to the trial, has been strongly criticised. Local attitudes concerning the appropriate targets of justice may also differ from international attitudes: in particular, opinions regarding who 'bears the greatest responsibility' for past crimes may differ significantly. Finally, international processes may be perceived as having been externally imposed and there may be particular concerns that they focus so extensively on Africa, given the establishment of the ICTR and the SCSL, as well as the fact that all four of the ICC's current investigations are into situations in African states.

Insider-analysts versus armchair critics

Finally, an unusual theme and set of insights emerge from this volume's many insider-analysts. Many of the chapters reflect upon the criticisms that were levelled at the institutions in which they worked and the ways in which external 'armchair' analysts frequently misunderstood the difficult choices that practitioners faced. Particularly when analysts measure institutional performance against idealised standards it is not surprising that it often falls short. Participants in such institutions are particularly well placed to remind us of the very real challenges they face. Many of these challenges arise precisely because of the tensions between achieving peace and promoting justice: there are logistical challenges in obtaining custody of defendants or securing testimony before truth commissions, as well as having to deal with tight budgets with many competing demands, not to mention the challenges of access and publicity of activities in war-torn countries. It is not surprising perhaps that in such circumstances institutions are subject to the criticism that they are too distant from the populace, or simply unknown to them, that they have limited impact in actually doing justice, or that they have little impact on the rebuilding of broader state structures. Such strong criticisms have been levelled at the ICTR and the SCSL in particular.[13]

Insider-analysts can also provide an important response to valid external criticism by elaborating upon practices that were successful and by identifying instances in which mid-course corrections were developed. Insiders may note successes that outsiders take insufficient note of, such as the degree to which bodies such as the ICTR and the SCSL have developed important new jurisprudence on international crimes, particularly with respect to crimes relating to women and children in conflict. They may also be able to identify significant challenges that outsiders have yet to take note of, such as the challenge of dealing practically with individuals who are acquitted of charges of serious abuses but are nonetheless unwelcome in any location. The chapters written by insider-analysts therefore provide important correctives and new insights into the challenges of pursuing peace with justice.

THE STRUCTURE OF THE VOLUME

This volume comprises five parts. Part I considers the challenges to peace and justice in Africa. In this section the critical conceptual and political debates surrounding the search for a balance between peace and justice are addressed and the challenges faced in Africa are put in comparative perspective. The section leads with a chapter by Yasmin Louise Sooka, perhaps the quintessential insider-analyst, having been a member of both the South African and the Sierra Leonean TRCs. In 'The Politics of Transitional Justice', she provides a *tour d'horizon* of the competing demands for peace and justice in countries emerging from violent conflict or repressive rule. She offers an overview of a number of key Latin American transitional justice processes and reminds us that the South African TRC, although a current benchmark for reconciliation processes, was not the first truth commission. Her discussion of Argentina also offers a stark reminder that the quest for justice may take decades. Sooka develops an insightful analysis of both the successes and the failures of the TRCs of which she was a part. She notes, in particular, challenges that have yet to be fully addressed by such institutions, such as the specific needs of women and child ex-combatants.

In 'Inclusive Justice: The Limitations of Trial Justice and Truth Commissions', Charles Villa-Vicencio, a former member of the South African TRC, develops an insightful analysis of the limits to both prosecutions and truth commissions. He notes in particular that amnesty may not always promote reconciliation but may sometimes foster resentment. While not advocating the rejection of either prosecutions or truth commissions or, for that matter, amnesties, he argues that these tools are simply not sufficient. Rather, he suggests, more must be actively done to overcome the animosity, mistrust and embedded inequalities that have emerged during protracted conflict. He proposes that what is needed is a national conversation, as through a TRC, that genuinely seeks to address the needs and viewpoints of all, whether victim or perpetrator, winner or loser. He argues that the South African TRC continues to be the model against which many commissions are measured and that it can provide significant guidance for other processes, despite the differences between the South African experience and those in other African countries emerging from conflict.

In 'Prosecute or Pardon? Between Truth Commissions and War Crimes Trials', Kingsley Chiedu Moghalu, a former spokesperson for the Rwanda tribunal, examines the political factors that shape a country's decision to prosecute or pardon. He argues that while there is no single prescription, in general, judicial processes have a better track record than other transitional justice mechanisms. He maintains a healthy degree of scepticism about legalistic approaches and argues that amnesties should be the exception rather than the rule. Nonetheless, he notes a number of countries in which amnesties appear to have been successful. These are instances where the country moved forward without, apparently, a great demand for accountability: for example, South Africa, Spain and Mozambique. Many countries that have used amnesties or terminated prosecutions have eventually revisited past abuses: Chile and Argentina are notable in this regard. Nigeria's 30-year policy of silence on abuses was broken with a 2001 truth commission. TRCs, he observes, are often viewed as useful compromises but he questions whether they have the significant and lasting effects that many of their advocates claim they have.

Sheila Meintjes, a gender commissioner at the South African Commission on Gender Equality, is another insider-analyst. Her contribution, 'Gender and Truth and Reconciliation Commissions: Comparative Reflections', offers a critical feminist analysis of TRCs. She argues forcefully that a pure human rights approach can never develop a full historical account of past conflicts and struggles, and in particular may overlook key aspects of race, ethnicity, class and gender. She suggests that the mandate of the South African TRC was thus limited and overlooked critical ways in which women were affected during the apartheid struggle, their active role in that struggle and the problematic representation of 'women's' interests by a limited set of elite women. She also critiques the treatment of 'gender' as code for 'women', which she believes excludes the gendered experiences of men in conflict situations.

Mireille Affa'a Mindzie's chapter, 'Transitional Justice, Democratisation and the Rule of Law', discusses the interconnected relationship between democratisation and the rule of law in peacebuilding. She argues that particular challenges arise in African states where there is neither a clear war-to-peace transition nor a transition from authoritarian rule to democracy. In such contexts, she maintains, there are limits to the degree that transitional justice can support democratisation and the rule of law. However, she sees some promise in good governance, conflict resolution and accountability principles and mechanisms being developed on and by the continent, particularly through the African Union (AU).

Part II examines specific truth and reconciliation processes on the African continent. The first chapter is by the consummate insider-analyst Alex Boraine, formerly vice-chair of the South African TRC and founder and chairperson of the International Center for Transitional Justice (ICTJ), a think-tank that provides policy advice and support on transitional justice. In 'South Africa's Truth and Reconciliation Commission from a Global Perspective', Boraine discusses three truth commissions that built in significant part upon the South African model: in Sierra Leone, the Democratic Republic of Timor-Leste and Peru. He elaborates on the ways in which each commission sought to improve upon, or make more appropriate to the local context, the South African approach. For example, in Sierra Leone both national and international commissioners were utilised in an attempt to assuage concerns about partiality. The commission in Timor-Leste uses limited amnesties, allowing them only for the least serious offences and requiring a visible act of remorse, whereas Peru's commission did not offer amnesties for political crimes. As an insider Boraine is able not only to note where these commissions adapted the South African commission model but also to identify for future commissions some of the limitations of that approach, such as its failure to secure justice or accountability for those who designed apartheid policies.

Thelma Ekiyor focuses upon one of the TRCs influenced by the South African model in 'Reflecting on the Sierra Leone Truth and Reconciliation Commission: A Peacebuilding Perspective'. She notes that although the Lomé Peace Accord notoriously failed to end the conflict in Sierra Leone it did provide an important framework for post-conflict peacebuilding by addressing issues of the disarmament, demobilisation and reintegration (DDR) of ex-combatants, as well as providing for the creation of the TRC. She recognises that the commission had a difficult start, with both its independence and local ownership being questioned, and that it had a tense and at times combative relationship with the SCSL. She, like Meintjes, notes the particular challenge for the TRC in addressing crimes against women and children. She argues finally that several key lessons may be learned from this experience, including the need to ensure that TRCs and trials, where operating contemporaneously, do not conflict with each other. Her chapter also notes the need to recognise that the operation of the TRC is the beginning rather than the end of a peacebuilding process.

Father Matthew Kukah is also an insider-analyst of processes in Nigeria, having been a member of the Human Rights Violations Investigation Commission (HRVIC, or the Justice Oputa Panel, named for its head) and chairperson of the Ogoni-Shell Reconciliation Committee. In 'Peace versus Justice? A View from Nigeria', Kukah discusses the genesis and work of the HRVIC, which was appointed in 1999 and conducted hearings from 2000–2001, but whose report has never been officially released. He describes from an insider's perspective the challenge and process of creating an investigative methodology, eliciting information from multiple sources and seeking submissions or memoranda. He argues that criticisms of TRCs are often unfair, and are levelled by analysts who lack an understanding of the challenges of such institutions. Indeed, the HRVIC worked with significant limitations, including the refusal of former generals to appear before it. Moreover, Kukah believes that the refusal of the country to release the report officially was a great disservice, although the report can be found online.[14] The weaknesses of the commission, he argues, must be understood in this context.

Kenneth Agyemang Attafuah is another insider-analyst, having been the executive secretary of Ghana's National Reconciliation Commission. In 'A Path to Peace: Ghana's National Reconciliation Commission in Retrospect', he discusses the operation of the commission, which was created in part because key provisions of the 1992 Ghanaian Constitution prohibit judicial inquiry into the past. The commission was modelled on the South African TRC and its operations emphasised reconciliation and healing as well as public education. Atypically, it was not created as part of a transitional process but some nine years after a return to civilian rule, in 2002. Attafuah notes that the delay between the transition and the TRC is important, suggesting that TRCs may still have a role to play even if they are temporally distant from the events that they excavate. Supporters of former president Jerry Rawlings nonetheless view the TRC with suspicion, believing that it may be an attempt to embarrass him.

John L. Hirsch is an insider-analyst with extensive experience as a diplomat in Africa, including as US Ambassador to Sierra Leone from 1995–1998. In his chapter, 'Peace and Justice: Mozambique and Sierra Leone Compared', he examines the distinct paths chosen by these two countries. While Mozambique chose to pursue an official policy of not looking back, traditional and religious processes were utilised, he argues, to promote significant reconciliation. By contrast, in Sierra Leone, the overlapping processes of transitional justice promoted by the international community, the Special Court for Sierra Leone and the Truth and Reconciliation Commission, have had relatively little significance for most Sierra Leoneans. Hirsch thus argues that decisions about whether to prosecute or not are context-dependent, and should be made through domestically rather than internationally driven processes.

Part III discusses the war crimes tribunals that were created for Sierra Leone and Rwanda. In 'Sierra Leone's "not-so" Special Court', Abdul Tejan-Cole provides insider insights as a former defence counsel at the Court. He begins with the Lomé Peace Accord, which he describes as a triumph of the prioritisation of peace over justice, albeit a failed one that he suggests enabled renewed violence. While highly critical of the Court, Tejan-Cole argues that it has developed important case law surrounding the issues of child soldiers and gender-based crimes. He questions, however, its ability to serve the interests of justice or peacebuilding and argues in particular that, because Sierra Leoneans had relatively little input, it was not a truly hybrid court. He argues that it failed to develop its legacy because it failed to offer genuine support to Sierra Leone's domestic judicial system or to reach out sufficiently to the population. These criticisms, often made by outsiders, are given depth and force when Tejan-Cole's role within the Court is considered.

In 'Charles Taylor, the Special Court for Sierra Leone, and International Politics', Abdul Rahman Lamin also criticises the Court, although from a political

Chandra Lekha Sriram

perspective. In particular, he argues that the Court has been politicised, both in terms of its being influenced politically and in terms of it having political ramifications, in ways that undermine its legitimacy. He focuses upon two controversies to make this point. The first is the timing and content of the indictment (and its unsealing) of Charles Taylor, which generated diplomatic unease and might have undermined peacemaking not in Sierra Leone but in Liberia. The second is the indictment and/or trial of members of the Civil Defence Forces (CDF), including, until his death, the head of CDF, Sam Hinga Norman. Lamin believes these actions of the Court were unduly influenced by the United States or other external forces and in turn alienated it from the Sierra Leonean people.

Wambui Mwangi, a former employee of the ICTR and current legal officer of the UN, offers an insider analysis in 'The International Criminal Tribunal for Rwanda: Reconciling the Acquitted'. She emphasises the tensions that can flare up as a result of the differences between justice as promoted by the international community and justice as locally experienced, particularly in the light of local needs for peacebuilding. She focuses upon a little-known but significant problem: the fate of individuals who have been acquitted by international criminal tribunals such as the ICTR. Many are not welcome in their home communities and yet may be excluded by law from claiming refugee status in many European countries because of the charges previously laid against them. Should they return to unwelcoming homes they have the potential to disrupt peacebuilding and news of their acquittals has been greeted with large-scale protest. This problem is not unique to the ICTR.

Part IV takes up the matter of the practice of traditional justice. In 'The Politics of Peace, Justice and Healing in Post-war Mozambique: Practices of Rupture by *Magamba* Spirits and Healers in Gorongosa', Victor Igreja provides a fascinating analysis of the ad hoc use of a traditional conflict-resolution mechanism to address violent incidents that occurred during Mozambique's conflict from 1975–1992. Because the post-conflict government of Joachim Chissano insisted upon the path of silence and forgetting, Mozambique had neither trials nor a truth commission. For a decade after the end of the conflict the episodic use of a ritual involving spirits and healers appears to have been a localised attempt to fill the gap or address the imposed silence. Igreja's chapter, based upon participant-observation in the rituals themselves, offers important insight into a little-known practice and suggests that where no public discussion of the past is permitted or endorsed it may be created through alternative means.

Helen Scanlon and Nompumelelo Motlafi consider just whose justice is being served in the use of traditional justice mechanisms in their chapter on 'Indigenous Justice or Political Instrument? The Modern *Gacaca* Courts of Rwanda'. They consider the context in which *gacaca* was created – an overwhelmed domestic legal and prison system coupled with a genuine need for reconciliation within the nation – and question whether *gacaca* has lived up to its promise or operated as a genuinely traditional process. Current *gacaca*, they argue, is almost unrecognisably different from the traditional forms of *gacaca*. Further, it may itself violate standards of due process and create violence and reprisals through its operation. It also, to date, appears to be biased in excluding abuses committed by the Tutsi- ✓ dominated Rwandan Patriotic Front (RPF), which took power at the end of the genocide and now presents itself as liberators. They argue that the *gacaca* courts are therefore ill-designed to do what they promise, which is to facilitate wide-scale reconciliation in Rwanda.

The final section in the book, Part V, addresses the emergent role played by the ICC on the African continent. In 'The International Criminal Court Africa Experiment: The Central African Republic, Darfur, Northern Uganda and the Democratic Republic of the Congo', Chandra Lekha Sriram considers a range of criticisms that have been levelled at the ICC, beginning with the concerns that, because the only cases under formal investigation at this time are in Africa, the Court is excessively Africa-focused or that Africa is being used as a guinea pig. She suggests that this is not the case as three of the four cases were brought to the Court by the states themselves. Further, she argues, the high percentage of African states that have ratified the ICC Statute, many of which are experiencing or emerging from violent conflict, helps to explain the Africa-dominated caseload of the Court. She does state, however, that there is cause for concern in that the aggressive pursuit of some cases, such as those against Joseph Kony and other LRA members, may undermine peacemaking in Uganda or peacebuilding in other countries.

Dumisa Ntsebeza's 'The International Criminal Court in Darfur' examines one of the ICC's four cases. An advocate at the High Court of South Africa and a former TRC commissioner, he examines the situation in Darfur and in light of his experiences with the above, considers the appropriateness of a TRC there. He is also a former member of the International Commission of Inquiry into the situation in Darfur, where an estimated 200 000 people have been killed and millions displaced. He emphasises the commission's recommendations that prosecutions were imperative and that a TRC could not be created as a substitute but as a complementary measure might have had some utility. However, he notes that such a body would only be appropriate once hostilities ceased, as part of efforts at peacebuilding and reconciliation.

Finally, Suren Pillay's 'Conclusion' draws out the key insights of the book and considers prospects for the future.

The volume offers several critical contributions that distinguish it from the vast literature on truth and reconciliation processes and tribunals. Firstly, as already noted, this book benefits from the insights of many insider-observers. Secondly, the ways in which these processes and institutions have developed in Africa are emphasised. While these mechanisms have drawn heavily upon lessons learned elsewhere and been designed both for and by Africans, they have often failed to take account of the particular needs of Africans. They have also been fundamentally changed in the process. Thus it is important to assess the unique ways in which truth-telling and accountability processes have developed on the continent, as well as how they have interacted with local, national and international politics. The volume is further strengthened by the extensive contributions of African scholars and practitioners, as the majority of contributions here come from Africans rather than outsiders. Given these unique features, it is hoped that the volume will be of use to both African policymakers and scholars and will provide insights to those working on these complex issues globally.

NOTES AND REFERENCES

1. Books dealing with global practice in transitional justice include P. Hayner, *Unspeakable truths: Confronting state terror and atrocity* (London: Routledge, 2001); C. Hesse and R. Post (eds.), *Human rights in political transitions: Gettysburg to Bosnia* (New York: Zone Books, 1999); N.J. Kritz (ed.), *Transitional justice: How emerging democracies reckon with former regimes*, 3 vols. (Washington, DC: United States Institute of Peace Press, 1993); J. Malamud-Goti, *Game without end: State terror and the politics of justice* (Norman, OK: University of Oklahoma Press, 1996); R. Mani, *Beyond retribution: Seeking justice in the shadows of war* (Cambridge: Polity Press, 2002); M. Minow, *Between vengeance and forgiveness: Facing history after genocide and mass violence* (Boston: Beacon Press, 1998); A. Neier, *War crimes: Brutality, genocide, terror, and the struggle for justice* (New York: Times Books, 1998); M. Osiel, *Mass atrocity, collective memory, and the law* (New Brunswick, NJ: Transaction Books, 1997); N. Roht-Arriaza (ed.), *Impunity and human rights in international law and practice* (Oxford: Oxford University Press, 1995); R.I. Rotberg and D. Thompson (eds.), *Truth v justice: The morality of truth commissions* (Princeton: Princeton University Press, 2000); C.L. Sriram, *Confronting past*

human rights violations: Justice vs peace in times of transition (London: Frank Cass, 2004); C.L. Sriram, *Globalizing justice for mass atrocities: A revolution in accountability* (London: Routledge, 2005); P.R. Williams and M.P. Scharf, *Peace with justice? War crimes and accountability in the former Yugoslavia* (Lanham, MD: Rowman and Littlefield, 2002).

2. C.L. Sriram and Z. Nielsen (eds.), *Exploring subregional conflict: Opportunities for conflict prevention* (Boulder, CO: Lynne Rienner, 2004) discusses the challenge of regional conflicts and the risks of return to conflict.

3. C.L. Sriram and A. Ross, 'Geographies of crime and justice: Contemporary transitional justice and the creation of "zones of impunity"', *International Journal of Transitional Justice* 1(1), 2007: 45–65.

4. A similar dynamic was observed earlier in Latin America, with a suggestion that it was a 'justice cascade'. See E. Lutz and K. Sikkink, 'The justice cascade: The evolution and impact of foreign human rights trials in Latin America', *Chicago Journal of International Law* 2 (Spring), 2001: 1–33.

5. The genocide in Rwanda killed at least 800 000, while the conflict in Sierra Leone killed 50 000–75 000 people, yet the internationally-mandated tribunals for each have tried just over 40 and under 10 defendants respectively.

6. See generally Hayner, *Unspeakable truths*; see also the database compiled by the United States Institute of Peace, http://www.usip.org/library/truth.html#tc (accessed 20 January 2008).

7. J.R. Quinn, 'Constraints: The un-doing of the Ugandan Truth Commission', *Human Rights Quarterly* 26(2), 2004: 401–427.

8. K. Avruch, *Culture and conflict resolution* (Washington, DC: United States Institute of Peace, 1998).

9. H. Assefa, *Peace and reconciliation as a paradigm* (Nairobi: Nairobi Peace Initiative, 1993).

10. CCR, 'African perspectives on the UN peacebuilding commission', CCR/FES Seminar Report (November 2006), www.ccrweb.ccr.uct.ac.za (accessed 12 February 2009).

11. See L. Vinjamuri and A.P. Boesenecker, 'Accountability and peace agreements: Mapping trends from 1980 to 2006', Centre for Humanitarian Dialogue, 2007, www.reliefweb.int/rw/lib.nsf/db900SID/EVOD-77MERJ/$FILE/Full_Report.pdf?OpenElement (accessed 12 February 2009); C. Bell, *Peace agreements and human rights* (Oxford: Oxford University Press, 2000).

12. The guiding principles developed for the UN on this issue state clearly that amnesty may not be offered until the state has prosecuted, or other parties have sought to prosecute, perpetrators. Report of the independent expert to update the Set of Principles to Combat Impunity, Diane Orentlicher, UN Doc E/CN.4/2005/102/Add.1 (8 February 2005), Principle 24.

13. I have raised some of these criticisms elsewhere, albeit with full recognition of the challenging circumstances of operation. Sriram, *Confronting past human rights violations*.

14. See summary and links provided by the Centre for the Study of Violence and Reconciliation, www.justiceinperspective.org.za/index.php?option=com_content&task=view&id=23&Itemid=57 (accessed 20 January 2008).

PART I

Peace and Justice in Africa

1

The Politics of Transitional Justice

Yasmin Louise Sooka

INTRODUCTION

In recent decades there has been an increased focus on transitional justice and the rule of law in both conflict and post-conflict societies. Transitional justice strategies have become necessary to promote justice for past abuses and to build national unity and reconciliation. Justice, peace and democracy are not mutually exclusive objectives but are mutually reinforcing imperatives. Advancing all three objectives in fragile post-conflict settings requires strategic planning, careful integration and a sensible sequencing of events.[1]

The reality for most transitional societies is that the new government may have achieved political power but may not have achieved control over either the security forces or certain perpetrators of gross human rights violations. Attempting to hold the latter accountable may result in the destabilisation of that society,[2] and this fragility has characterised most transitional governments in recent times. Thus the overriding paradigm for some has been 'transitional politics' and the question whether prosecutions may imperil a transition to democracy and whether the risks may outweigh the potential gains.

The dilemma of 'peace versus justice' can therefore present a real challenge as perpetrators will always argue for impunity and blanket amnesty under the pretext of 'national unity'.[3] The argument for 'national unity' usually results in the rights of victims being compromised for the sake of national reconciliation. Some argue that South Africa is a case in point, where the amnesty provisions resulted in the rights of victims being set aside for the sake of national unity and reconciliation.[4]

My experiences while serving as a human rights lawyer in South Africa during the apartheid years and, subsequently, as a commissioner in the Truth and

Reconciliation Commissions set up in both South Africa and Sierra Leone have strengthened my conviction that peace cannot come with the expense of creating further impunity. However, it is absolutely critical that measures of accountability are consistent with, or contribute to, the building of democracy and are premised on the rule of law and respect for internationally recognised human rights.

These challenges are not unique to any one post-conflict society but have emerged in every region of the world: Latin America, eastern and southern Europe, South Africa and West Africa. Legal scholars have upheld the principle that the only appropriate response to human rights violations is to hold those responsible criminally accountable; the state is obliged to punish and to hold accountable those who have committed human rights violations, irrespective of whether they have the de facto political power or the ostensible positivist legal authority to do so.[5]

Peace requires warring factions to lay down arms so that they can participate in the building of democracy. This is an important consideration and may require some form of amnesty.

However, the real issue is that impunity is one of the primary causes underlying gross violations of human rights.[6] Impunity arises from a failure by states to meet their obligations to investigate violations or to take appropriate action in respect of perpetrators, particularly in the area of justice, by ensuring that:

- those suspected of criminal responsibility are prosecuted, tried and duly punished;
- victims are provided with effective remedies and receive reparation for the injuries suffered;
- the inalienable right to know the truth about violations is honoured; and
- necessary steps are taken to prevent a recurrence of violations.[7]

The challenges of dealing with post-conflict environments necessitate an approach that balances a variety of goals which include the pursuit of accountability, truth and reparation, the preservation of peace and the building of genuine democracy and the rule of law.[8] Thus any transitional justice approach should include both judicial and non-judicial mechanisms and should seek to encompass broadly the various dimensions of justice that can heal wounds and contribute to social reconstruction based on a fundamental belief in universal human rights.

INTERNATIONAL LEGAL STANDARDS

Ever since the Nuremberg Trials, the international community has elaborated treaties that prohibit and punish international crimes such as genocide, serious breaches of the Geneva Conventions and torture. Certain human rights violations and violations of international humanitarian law are violations of *jus cogens* obligations. States are obliged to prosecute or extradite individuals suspected of perpetrating these crimes.[9]

The political bodies of the United Nations (UN) as well as human rights bodies have, in the words of the UN Security Council, affirmed the responsibility of states to 'end impunity and to prosecute those responsible for genocide, crimes against humanity and serious violations of humanitarian law'.[10] The only exception to this rule arises in situations where amnesty would bring an end to armed conflict. The UN Secretary-General summarised the UN policy in a 2000 report in the following way:

> While recognizing that amnesty is an accepted legal concept and a gesture of peace and reconciliation at the end of a civil war or an internal armed conflict the United Nations has consistently maintained the position that amnesty cannot be granted in respect of international crimes, such as genocide, crimes against humanity or other serious violations of international humanitarian law.[11]

The additional architecture of the International Criminal Court (ICC), as well as the decisions that have been made in many regional human rights systems, has created new reticence towards the granting of amnesties. The impact of this is already being felt in negotiations that are currently taking place because mediators no longer have the luxury of offering immunity or amnesty for serious crimes. This poses new challenges as to how to get warlords and dictators to step down from power and consequently presents an even greater challenge to the transitional justice community: how do we ensure peace when we can no longer offer immunity from prosecutions for serious crimes? What will our leverage be? The arrest and trial of Charles Taylor has implications for other leaders who are responsible for committing atrocities. Human rights activists should be concerned with ending conflict and restoring peace, as it is this that may help to ensure an end to the violations that take place during conflict.

In this chapter, I consider a range of transitional justice processes that have occurred, from Latin America to Africa, with an emphasis on my personal experiences in South Africa and Sierra Leone.

TRANSITIONAL JUSTICE

Transitional justice involves the political choices that are made by states when confronting the pattern of human rights violations committed by former governments. Important questions to ask are: 'Where is the transition leading?'; 'When does the transition begin and when does it end?'; and 'Is an end to the conflict enough?' In response to these questions, conflict-resolution practitioners highlight the difference between 'negative' peace and 'positive' peace.[12] The term 'positive peace' refers to lasting solutions that both address the root causes of conflict and also seek to ensure that the conflict does not recur. Real democracy is considered to be the prime objective of positive peace.[13] 'Negative peace' secures only an end to the immediate violence and does not address the root causes of the violence, nor does it provide lasting and durable solutions to ensure that the conflict does not arise again. 'Negative peace' only creates a democratic deficit that permits old divisions and tensions to flare up again. Many commentators have argued that there is a risk that conflict will flare up again if there is the perception that past injustices have not been addressed.[14]

A demand for punishment undoubtedly affects any negotiations intended to bring a conflict to an end. However, a peace process that concentrates only on ending the conflict almost always compromises the rights of victims and the opportunity to address systematic atrocities (see Chapter 11 in this volume).

Diane Orentlicher has argued for the emergence of a general state duty to punish certain serious human rights violations.[15] Her argument is based on the presumption that a state has the power to do this. New states are thus confronted with having to make decisions concerning whether to punish perpetrators and hold them accountable even though doing so may result in a political coup or encourage further violence. Policy questions that confront new states include:

- Who should be punished? What crimes should be punished?
- Should everybody responsible for the perpetration of a human rights violation be punished?
- Is there a set of principles or human rights standards in international law which can be applied in such situations?

José Zalaquett, the Chilean human rights lawyer, has said that any policy that is intended to deal with past human rights abuses should have two overall objectives: to prevent the recurrence of such abuses and to repair the damage they have caused, to the maximum extent possible.[16] Zalaquett argued that, whatever the policy, a new government will need to keep in mind the larger objective, the aim of which is the achievement of a measure of national unity and reconciliation, and particularly so when the human rights violations of the past took place in a context of extreme political polarisation and civil strife that included an armed struggle. He termed this goal the 'depolarization of society'.[17] He emphasised the need for the rebuilding or reconstruction of institutions that are conducive to a stable and fair political system and the procurement of the economic resources needed to achieve those ends, particularly when the transition period is marked by fragility and when a measure of economic stability is necessary for political stability.[18] He also outlined the conditions and principles that need to exist for the policy to have legitimacy: the truth must be known, officially proclaimed, officially acknowledged and publicly exposed. Any policy that is adopted must represent the will of the people, should not violate international law related to human rights and must include reparative measures such as compensation for victims and their families, symbolic reparations and a public acknowledgement by the perpetrators of the deeds committed. Zalaquett went further and said that any policy should ensure that a framework for 'preventative measures' was also put in place.[19]

Transitional justice practitioners have begun to speak of a holistic transitional package that should include an accountability mechanism in the form of a truth commission and a judicial mechanism for prosecutions, with both mechanisms existing side by side. In addition, there should be vetting, security sector reform, disarmament, demobilisation and reintegration (DDR) programmes as well as institutional reform programmes.[20] In fact, the tick-box approach that has come to characterise the way in which transitions are being dealt with has its own dangers. Each situation is unique and, in order to legitimise the process, requires the direct input and participation of the affected citizens.

AMNESTIES

A key challenge is the appropriateness and legality of creating amnesties during the transitional process. Many politicians, diplomats, academics and civil society groups argue that formal international or domestic prosecutions may be unlikely to contribute to reconciliation between previously antagonistic groups and, by contrast, amnesties may have the potential to reduce the violence and create a climate in which a move towards reconciliation is encouraged. Those in favour of amnesty in transitional states usually contend that peace can never be achieved without some form of amnesty because it would then be unlikely that combatants would surrender their weapons and dictators transfer power to democrats.[21]

A recent study conducted on amnesties,[22] based on a database created by Louise Mallinder, concluded that more than 420 amnesty processes have been introduced worldwide, many of them occurring since the establishment of the ad hoc tribunals and more than 66 of them having been introduced between January 2001 and December 2005.[23] Mallinder demonstrates that amnesties have continued to be a political reality despite international efforts to combat impunity. She argues that international courts should focus their limited prosecutorial resources on combating the more egregious forms of impunity and should recognise that where amnesties are introduced with democratic approval in an effort to promote peace and reconciliation, they also take into account the needs and rights of victims.[24] According to these criteria South Africa's amnesty deal would probably pass muster as it had the goals of national unity and reconciliation as well as being focused on the rights of victims. South Africa's amnesty deal was, of course, introduced with democratic approval and was upheld by the Constitutional Court of South Africa, the highest court in the land.[25]

Prior to Latin American transitions the blueprint for legal scholars had been 'victor's justice' akin to that seen during the Nuremberg Trials after the Second World War. Even then the prosecutions were selective. Many argue that the actions of the Allied forces, particularly with regard to the bombing of Dresden, should have ensured that somebody was held accountable for that too. The experiences in eastern Europe are inconsistent, especially when considering the execution, without due process, of the Ceaucesceaus in Romania or the prosecutions of Stasi members in reunified Germany.

LATIN AMERICAN EXPERIENCES
Argentina

Latin American countries that were experiencing a transition from military rule to democratic rule began to explore new options in the 1980s, the most well-known transitions being those in Argentina, Chile and El Salvador. The most ambitious attempt to deal with abuses of the past took place in Argentina under the leadership of President Raul Alfonsín, who came to power in December 1983.[26] His first act was to annul the amnesty that had been rushed through by the military junta just before it fell. He established a civilian commission, under the leadership of Ernesto Sabato, to conduct a comprehensive investigation into the disappearances that had taken place during the preceding seven-and-a-half years. Thousands of people had been abducted, tortured and murdered and their bodies had been clandestinely disposed of. The military government had refused to provide any information about the fate of the disappeared.

It was the report of the Sabato Commission that helped to consolidate public support for the government's initial prosecutions. President Alfonsín ordered the prosecution of nine military commanders who had led the junta during its reign from 1977–1983. The prosecutions, although announced before the Sabato Commission was established, took place only after its report was published. In addition to the junta members, some 500 middle-ranking officers were prosecuted, and it was this that led to a military revolt. Many of these officers claimed that they were only following orders. In an attempt to calm the military, the government first passed a 'full stop' law and then a 'due obedience law' which limited the prosecutions and allowed most of the accused to go free. Many commentators suggest that had Alfonsín limited the prosecutions to high-level junta leaders his decision might have been accepted by all, including the military. Aryeh Neier has argued that, by giving in, Alfonsín encouraged rebel officers to make further demands and to launch further revolts, thus preparing the way for Carlos Menem, Alfonsín's successor, to grant pardons to 277 of those already convicted or indicted, including nearly 40 generals.[27] Argentinean human rights activists never relented in their quest for justice. Their activism was rewarded when Argentina's Supreme Court ruled the 'full stop' law and the 'due obedience' law unconstitutional in 2005.[28] This paved the way for the prosecution of other junta crimes. Argentina is set to have many trials in the years to come, and the trials have the backing of the government of Nestor Kirchner. In opinion polls undertaken in 2007, more than 70 per cent of the respondents polled approved of the Court's decision to set aside the amnesty laws.[29] It took Argentina more than twenty years to annul the laws which prevented the prosecution of the military. What is striking about Argentina is the Argentine human rights community's relentless quest for justice.

Chile

After taking office in Chile in March 1990, President Patricio Aylwin established a National Commission for Truth and Reconciliation to investigate abuses that had resulted in the death or disappearance of individuals over the previous seventeen years of military rule. However, the mandate of the commission precluded the investigation of torture, which was roundly criticised by civil society, victims and their families. The commission, chaired by Senator Raúl Rettig, issued what was known as the 'Rettig Report'.[30] The report was received by President Aylwin, who apologised to the victims and asked the army to acknowledge its role in the violence. However, three weeks after the release of the report, there were three assassinations in Chile that effectively ended the public discussions on the report. It was reported that thousands of copies of the report were subsequently stored in warehouses in an attempt to avoid the political divisions that would ensue over the issue of past human rights abuses. Nonetheless, the report was significant in that, unlike those of many commissions, its recommendations were implemented. The government also established a National Corporation for Reparations and Reconciliation to follow up on the work of the commission and oversee reparations to victims. Despite these efforts many Chileans felt that justice had been compromised in Chile. Former dictator General Augusto Pinochet had escaped accountability because before stepping down he had ensured that both he and the military were covered by an amnesty. Although the truth commission had done its work in an exemplary fashion it had not been able to bring the perpetrators to justice. It was not until 1998 that, in an extraordinary turn of events, General Pinochet was arrested in London, in response to an extradition request from Spain. The British House of Lords ruled that under international law Pinochet lacked immunity.[31] This emboldened the judges in Chile who, in a series of landmark rulings, removed most of the obstacles to prosecuting Pinochet.[32] In 1999, the Supreme Court of Chile ruled that a 'disappearance' is a continuing crime until death is proved.[33] This ruling meant that the 1978 amnesty did not cover disappearances that had not been solved. In December 2006, the Supreme Court also ruled that because Chile had been in a situation of internal conflict after the 1973 coup, the Geneva Conventions applied. In early 2007, the Court ruled that serious violations could not be subject to amnesty. More than 148 people, including 50 military officers, have since been convicted of human rights violations committed during the seventeen-year dictatorship. To date, more than 400 officers have been arrested or are under investigation for their part in the violations. The Chileans had waited for more than sixteen years for justice. General Pinochet died in Chile while facing several charges for murder, torture and tax evasion.

El Salvador

In El Salvador, the truth and reconciliation commission was established by the UN in 1991 as a result of the peace accord signed by the Salvadoran government and the Farabundo Marti National Liberation Front (FMLN), following the end of a bitter civil war that left much of the country polarised.[34] Due to concerns that a national commission was not feasible, the commission was run by the UN. The commission's subsequent report named over 40 individuals it believed had been responsible for human rights violations. The Salvadoran military went into revolt.[35] Within five days of publication a general amnesty was passed by the legislature.[36]

The experiences of Chile, Argentina and El Salvador demonstrate that the work of truth commissions is often only the first step in the pursuit of accountability, which may take decades. While a number of other truth commissions have been set up in places such as Chad, Uganda and the Philippines, it is the work of the Latin American commissions that has set the benchmark for the commissions that have followed.[37] The Latin American commissions emphasised the following norms: the right of victims to the truth; the right to have the truth known and acknowledged; the right to reparations; and the necessity of institutional reform in order to strengthen the rule of law and democracy. These experiences were instrumental in the decisions to establish truth commissions in both South Africa and Guatemala.[38]

SOUTH AFRICA

The amnesty compromise

The unbanning of the liberation movements in 1990, the subsequent release of Nelson Mandela and the lifting of the state of emergency paved the way for a negotiated peace settlement that brought to an end the struggle against colonialism and apartheid which had lasted for more than 300 years. The negotiations resulted in a date being set for the first democratic elections and for an interim Constitution to be enacted.[39] A major obstacle to finalising the interim Constitution was the question of amnesty. At the time, the right wing and the security forces who were not loyal to the then President F.W. de Klerk posed a threat to stability in the country.[40] Mandela stated privately that if he were to announce a series of criminal trials he could well wake up the following morning to find his home ringed by tanks.[41] The liberation movements were divided on the question of prosecutions and whether prosecutions would be successful.

Representatives of the former apartheid regime insisted that a guarantee of amnesty be written into the interim Constitution. Without it, it is unlikely that the white government would have given up power. The clause which gave effect to the compromise was contained in the postscript to the interim Constitution, which entered into force on 27 April 1994, the first day of the first democratic elections in South Africa. The strength of the South African process was that it was part of a package of initiatives that were intended to set the country on the road to democracy. The interim Constitution contained 34 constitutional principles that formed the basis for South Africa becoming a constitutional state.

When giving effect to the constitutional requirement of amnesty, the new government linked amnesty to truth-telling and reparations for victims, thus ensuring that no 'general amnesty' would be granted. Each individual would have to apply for amnesty and would be required to make a full disclosure of their activities in return for amnesty, in the process proving that the crimes committed had been carried out with a political motive or objective. In making its decision, the Amnesty Committee would weigh up six factors:

- the motive for the crime;
- the objective;
- the context;
- whether the deed was officially authorised;
- its legal and factual nature; and
- its proportionality to a political goal.[42]

To the dismay of most South Africans, applicants were not required to display remorse or make reparations for the crime committed. Once granted amnesty they would be immune from prosecution and a civil claim for damages. If perpetrators failed to come forward and apply, or if they were denied amnesty, they could be prosecuted.[43]

Public participation

The great strength of the South African process was the public participation that led to the legislation that established the Truth Commission. Dullah Omar, the newly elected Minister of Justice, established a working group to assist with the drafting of the relevant law. Civil society, which included human rights lawyers, the religious community and victims, formed a coalition of more than 50 organisations in order to participate in the public dialogue on a truth commission.[44] The coalition strategised on how to make the amnesty process accountable and to ensure that the rights of victims were protected. They made submissions to the working group, participated in the parliamentary hearings and opposed attempts by the former National Party to hold the hearings of the future commission behind 'closed doors'. South Africans were also able to take account of the experiences in Latin America and eastern Europe.[45] The consultative process lasted a year and culminated in legislation that established the Truth and Reconciliation Commission (TRC).[46]

Promotion of National Unity and Reconciliation Act

In 1995, the government of South Africa passed the Promotion of National Unity and Reconciliation Act 34 of 1995.[47] It provided for the establishment of a Truth and Reconciliation Commission made up of seventeen commissioners. The commission was tasked with investigating human rights abuses of the past, granting victims the opportunity to tell their story, granting amnesty, constructing an impartial historical record of the past and drafting a reparations policy. To ensure a degree of impartiality, the commissioners were selected through a countrywide process by a selection panel that was representative of all of the political parties and the major groups in civil society. The commission was made up of three committees: Human Rights Violations, Reparations and Rehabilitation, and Amnesty.

The amnesty provisions were challenged in the newly established Constitutional Court of South Africa by family members of victims who had been murdered and tortured.[48] The applicants argued that the victims had a constitutional right to have justiciable disputes settled in a court of law and the granting of amnesty infringed upon this right and thus obliterated their right to claim the protection of the law for being wronged. The Constitutional Court upheld the granting of amnesty on the basis that it was sanctioned by the Constitution itself.[49] The Court's reasoning was that the Act allowed the victims to unburden their grief publicly, to receive from the new nation the collective recognition that they had been wronged and, most importantly, to help them to discover the truth about what had happened to their loved ones, under what circumstances it had happened, and who was responsible. It went on to say that without the incentive of amnesty, the truth would not emerge and that a negotiated settlement would not have been possible without the incentive of amnesty. By adopting a broad view on reparations, the Court justified the new regime being exempted from liability for acts committed by persons in the course and scope of their employment. It stated that the new state was entrusted with the task of reconciliation and reconstruction, and that the resources of the state would have to be deployed imaginatively so as to encourage the potential of its people. A choice would need to be made concerning whether or not to address the rights of the victims through reparation as this could well divert funds that were desperately needed for the provision of food for the hungry, roofs for the homeless and facilities for education. It was therefore considered legitimate for the state to favour a form of reconstruction of society that involved a wider concept of reparation.[50]

The initial focus of the commission was on victims. It received more than 22 000 statements from victims and held public hearings at which victims could come forward and give testimony. Victim after victim testified about the violations they had suffered at the hands of the state.[51] The commission received more than 7 000 amnesty applications, held more than 2 500 amnesty hearings and granted 1 500 amnesties for thousands of crimes committed during the apartheid years. The perpetrators' testimonies shocked white South Africa. When victims testified, white people who were interviewed said that the victims were exaggerating and when the perpetrators testified, white South Africa claimed that it had not known.[52]

An important feature of the South African commission was its openness and transparency. The public hearings held by the TRC ensured that South Africans became aware of the atrocities that had been committed during the apartheid years. Nobody could deny that the apartheid state had been responsible for committing crimes against humanity in order to preserve white privilege and power.[53] Whereas in other nations a few high profile cases were highlighted, in South Africa thousands of victims were heard. The hearings were broadcast on radio and television and millions heard the testimonies that emerged before the TRC. Hundreds of perpetrators came forward to admit to the crimes they had committed on behalf of the former state.[54] It was the most convincing blow to the myth of apartheid.

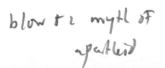
blow to the myth of apartheid

The TRC was confronted by a number of challenges, however: it was not accepted by all the parties that had been involved in the conflict.[55] The top levels of the military did not co-operate with the commission; it was mostly foot soldiers of the apartheid state who applied for amnesty. Senior politicians in the former government and senior leaders in the security forces did not apply for amnesty. They argued that, in terms of the liberation movements, they had conducted a just war and were therefore not required to apply for amnesty as their actions did not constitute gross violations of human rights. It took considerable persuasion to convince them to participate in the amnesty process.

A crucial weakness of the commission was that it did not focus sufficiently on the policies of apartheid, the beneficiaries of apartheid and the political economy of apartheid. It also failed to demonstrate sufficiently to those who had benefited from apartheid and the economic, social, political and legal consequences of colonial and apartheid policies, the legacy that will continue to haunt South Africa for decades. Mahmood Mamdani, a Ugandan scholar who taught at the University of Cape Town during this period, has argued that the TRC produced a 'diminished truth' in that it allowed the beneficiaries of apartheid to escape scrutiny.[56] Mamdani argues that by adopting the Latin American analogy the TRC obscured the link between conquest and dispossession, between racialised power and racialised privilege, between perpetrator and beneficiary.[57] In its failure to examine the effect and impact of apartheid's policies, the TRC allowed only the 'trigger-pullers' to bear the collective shame of the nation.

The government of South Africa took more than five years to begin implementation of the reparations that had been recommended by the TRC. To date few of the commission's recommendations have been implemented. Further, under new prosecution guidelines, former Minister of Law and Order Adriaan Vlok was given a suspended sentence through a plea bargain. These actions of the National Prosecuting Authority (NPA) have strengthened the views of victims that the guidelines should be set aside in order to launch a new legal challenge. Many black South Africans take the view that the beneficiaries of apartheid escaped any accountability for their actions.[58] It is in these ways that the legacy of the commission was compromised.

On the positive side, the South African TRC established the importance of public participation in the decision-making process that led to the establishment of a truth commission, which had in effect democratised the process.[59] It also affirmed the right to the truth for victims and the entire society, as well as the need for a public acknowledgement of the truth. The hearings of the TRC attracted global attention as it was the first commission to hold public hearings in which both victims and perpetrators were heard. It established new norms for truth-seeking bodies: public participation, transparency in the selection of the commissioners, and public hearings. While amnesties are generally considered inconsistent with international law,[60] there may be reason to consider conditional amnesties as a useful compromise, particularly if they help to secure perpetrator confessions.[61]

Lone

SIERRA LEONE[62]

Sierra Leone shares similar characteristics with South Africa and many other countries in Africa that are emerging from conflict: no clear victor in the conflict, a negotiated peace agreement, a government of national unity, and an amnesty deal (see Chapters 7 and 11 in this volume). Sierra Leone emerged from a brutal decade-long civil war in 2000. The conflict between the government of Sierra Leone and the Revolutionary United Front (RUF) resulted in tens of thousands being maimed and killed. Thousands of women were raped and more than a million people are said to have been displaced. Thousands of children were 'abucted' and forced to become child soldiers, with girls forced to suffer ongoing sexual assaults through forced 'marriages'.[63] Many of these children were maimed during the long conflict.[64]

The Lomé Peace Process and Accord illustrate a situation where ending the hostilities was perceived to be more important than ensuring a 'positive or lasting peace'. The Lomé Peace Accord[65] provided an unconditional amnesty for all crimes committed by the combatants during the conflict period, including the RUF in the Government of National Unity, and made rebel leader Foday Sankoh Vice-president (see Chapter 11 in this volume). Moments before the signing of the agreement, the Special Representative of the Secretary-General, Francis Okello, entered a reservation on the peace agreement indicating that the amnesty provisions would not be applicable to crimes against humanity, war crimes and genocide.[66]

In addition to the amnesty provisions, the 1999 Lomé Peace Accord provided for the establishment of a truth and reconciliation commission within 90 days of the agreement being signed. However, legislation establishing the truth commission was not passed until nearly two years later (see Chapter 7 in this volume). The RUF violated the accord and returned to fighting. With the close of conflict and the arrest of Sankoh, President Ahmed Tejan Kabbah asked the UN to assist Sierra Leone with setting up a mechanism to prosecute the RUF. The UN Security Council passed a resolution which mandated the establishment of a Special Court for Sierra Leone (SCSL) to 'prosecute those who bear the greatest responsibility'.[67]

The delay in establishing the Sierra Leone Truth and Reconciliation Commission (SLTRC) meant that the Court and the TRC operated contemporaneously. In my opinion – one shared by many Sierra Leoneans – this was completely unexpected and had a huge impact, often negative, on the operations of both institutions.[68] The omission of any reference to the TRC in any of the enabling instruments establishing the SCSL is quite surprising, given that the UN Secretary-General in his statement to the Security Council said: '[C]are must be taken to ensure that the Special Court for Sierra Leone and the Truth and Reconciliation Commission [SLTRC] will operate in a complementary and mutually supportive manner, fully respectful of their distinct but related functions.'[69]

Challenges experienced

The commission experienced a number of challenges before it even began work. An interim secretariat was established before commissioners were appointed, and many felt that the appointment of its executive secretary was politically motivated.[70] The secretariat had also managed to alienate most of the stakeholders involved in the process.[71] The commissioners, when appointed, thus first had to address the legacy of these mistakes before they could focus on their mandate. The commission was also severely hampered by the fact that it was totally dependent on international funding, and in particular on funds raised by the Office of the High Commissioner for Human Rights (OHCHR) in Geneva.[72] It also competed with the SCSL for funds from the same sources. It had not been envisaged that both institutions would find themselves operating contemporaneously and as a result little thought had been given to the challenges both institutions would face.[73] While this issue requires a discussion on its own, a number of challenges emerged. Firstly, the SCSL received significant international funding and this may have affected the commission's ability to raise funds. Secondly, confusion also existed amongst victims and perpetrators about the role of both institutions as many believed that the TRC was an investigative arm for the Court. Thirdly, the question of which institution had primacy and whether this affected confidentiality also became an issue.[74] Finally, while the SLTRC's relationship with the SCSL was originally cordial, this changed when it sought access to the detainees in the custody of the Court (see Chapter 11 in this volume).[75] The Court's refusal of access was unexpected.

Successes

The SLTRC was one of the first truth commissions to have had a specific mandate[76] to deal with issues of gender justice and child soldiers. Large numbers of women and girls had been raped and forced to become 'bush wives' and many children had been forced into sexual slavery and forcibly recruited by the different sides.[77] The SLTRC's mandate provided that the commission should pay special attention to the 'subject of sexual abuses and to the experiences of children within the armed conflict'.[78]

As part of fulfilling its mandate, the commission ensured that it employed women in key positions in the commission.[79] It also enacted a policy to document gender violence. More than half of the statement-takers employed were women. It also held special hearings for women in all of the fourteen provinces of Sierra Leone and arranged a thematic hearing on violations suffered by women, in which many women's organisations participated. The TRC's final report had a special chapter on women, in which the experiences of women during the conflict period were recorded and discussed.[80] This work was influenced by the fact that a number of women's organisations, deeply conscious of the massive violations that women had suffered during the conflict period, pressurised the commission at the outset to ensure that 'gender issues' received special attention.[81] The work of the TRC was nonetheless severely affected by its limited budget: it was not able to establish a unit on gender because of these constraints. The commission entered into a partnership with the UN Development Fund for Women (UNIFEM) which led to the launch of the 'Initiative for the Truth and Reconciliation Commission' under the UNIFEM's Peace and Security Programme.[82] Despite these limitations, the commission's work on gender has received great praise (see Chapter 7 in this volume).

Like women, children were abused by all of the armed factions involved in the Sierra Leonean conflict and suffered abductions, forced recruitment, sexual slavery and rape, amputations, mutilations, displacement, drugging and torture.[83] Child soldiers were also compelled to commit atrocities.[84] In their submission to the commission the UN Children's Fund (UNICEF) made the following submission: '[P]articularly vulnerable to abuse were children, as they were violated in deep and lasting ways, some too awful to be adequately described . . . In some ways, it is as if a new level of cruelty has been attained in this war, setting the bar lower than ever imagined . . . .'[85] Thousands of children were killed during the conflict in Sierra Leone. UNICEF estimates that more than 6 000 children were conscripted into the fighting forces over the years.[86] Many children were used as soldiers and forced labour by the armed groups. Although the RUF was the first to abduct and forcibly recruit children as soldiers and forced labour in Sierra Leone, all the armed factions recruited children.[87]

The legislation establishing the SLTRC directed it to give special attention to the experiences of children in the armed conflict.[88] The Lomé Peace Accord also provided that the government of Sierra Leone would take into consideration the special needs of children in the DDR process.[89] Thousands of young people, including girls and children, have been demobilised. Many have acquired new skills and have gone on to make new lives for themselves. UNICEF and the Child Protection Agencies have sought to reintegrate them with their families and ensure that they receive education.[90]

The SLTRC worked closely with UNICEF in seeking to document the experiences of children and deal with the experiences of child soldiers.[91] It held special hearings for children in all of the provinces and a thematic hearing on the issue in which many organisations participated. The TRC's final report also contained a special chapter on children. Its recommendations on advancing the rights of children have received great acclaim (see Chapter 7 in this volume).

A major challenge was that the DDR programme was not designed to address adequately the needs of women and girls.[92] Male commanders wanted to appropriate for themselves and their friends the benefits of the programme. They confiscated women's weapons and thus effectively excluded them from the programme.[93] Furthermore, the demobilisation process failed to recognise the different roles that had been played by women and girls in the conflict.[94] Women and girl victims also faced huge difficulties if they had been abducted by any of the rebel groups as, given the stigma of having been associated with such groups, their families were not prepared to take them back into the community.[95]

The SLTRC concluded that the leadership of Sierra Leone should promote reconciliation and ensure that the recommendations of the commission be carried out.[96] It warned that if it failed to do so, then it might face the risk of a civil war breaking out again as the peace was still a fragile one.[97]

Many agree that the commission was successful despite its troubled beginnings (see Chapter 7 in this volume). Its report and recommendations have been widely commended. However, the failure to implement the recommendations more than four years after the report was submitted indicates the lack of commitment by the government of Sierra Leone to addressing the root causes of the conflict, which is necessary for an enduring and sustainable peace.[98]

Sierra Leone was unique in that the two transitional justice institutions, the SCSL and a TRC, operated simultaneously. Abdul Tejan-Cole is illuminating about the impunity gaps that Sierra Leone still faces (see Chapter 11 in this volume).

CONCLUSION

The Latin American and African experiences illustrate the need for a holistic transitional justice approach. The struggle for peace and justice cannot be achieved through the establishment of a truth commission or criminal justice option alone. A holistic transitional justice approach would consider the local context by incorporating a range of measures such as truth-seeking, institutional transformation, vetting, security sector reform, reparations for victims, and DDR programmes which are not at odds with reparation programmes for victims. Any process must have democratic approval and must address the root causes of the conflict, taking into account the democratic deficit that existed before and during the conflict. Any process must seek to restore civic trust in the institutions of government, with every citizen believing that these institutions will work for them, irrespective of their political affiliation, race, religion, gender, or ethnic persuasion or difference. Victims' voices need to be heard. If there is to be lasting peace, uppermost in the minds of those who make decisions on peace and justice should be the need to incorporate justice for victims into any peace and justice mechanism.

I conclude by quoting Diane Orentlicher:

International legal norms affirming that atrocious crimes ought to be punished have provided a powerful antidote to impunity. While there are of course times when those same norms cannot be enforced, it has seemed preferable to say 'not yet' than to reframe global norms in terms that suggest prosecuting atrocious crimes is nothing more than an option. For if we were to move entirely away from the language of legal obligation, we would take from those operating on the frontlines of their countries' struggle for decency one of the most potent weapons in their arsenal.[99]

NOTES AND REFERENCES

1. Report of the Secretary-General, 'The rule of law and transitional justice in conflict and post-conflict societies', UN Doc S/2004/616 (3 August 2004), www.un.org/Docs/sc/sgrep04.html (accessed 4 January 2006).

2. J. Sarkin, *Carrots and sticks: The TRC and the South African amnesty process* (Antwerp: Intersentia, 2004), pp. 32–33.

3. J. Méndez (2006), 'Peace, justice and prevention: Dilemmas and false dilemmas', in *Dealing with the past and transitional justice: Creating conditions for peace, human rights and the rule of law*. Conference Paper 1/2006: Dealing with the Past Series, Schweizerische Eidgenossenschaft, p. 15.

4. Postscript to the Constitution of the Republic of South Africa Act 200 of 1993 (the interim Constitution), www.constitutionalcourt.org.za/site/constitution/english-web/interim/index.html (accessed 10 January 2008). See *Azapo v President of South Africa* 1996 (4) SA 671 (CC).

5. J. Zalaquett, 'Confronting human rights violations committed by former governments: Principles applicable and political constraints', in N.J. Kritz (ed.), *Transitional justice: How emerging democracies reckon with former regimes, vol. 1: General considerations* (Washington, DC: United States Institute of Peace Press, 1995), pp. 3–31.

6. Méndez, 'Peace, justice and prevention', p. 16.

7. Report of Diane Orentlicher (Independent Expert to update the Set of Principles to Combat Impunity), 'Combating impunity: General obligations, promotion and protection of human rights, Principle 1', E/CN.4/2005/102/ADD.1 (8 February 2005), ap.ohchr.org/documents/dpage_e.aspx?si=E/cn.4/2005/102/Add.1 (accessed 10 January 2008).

8. 'The rule of law and transitional justice in conflict and post-conflict societies', para. 25.

9. Updated Set of Principles to Combat Impunity, Principle 21.

10. Statement by the President of the Security Council, UN Doc S/PRST/2002/41 (20 December 2002), para. 4, daccessdds.un.org/doc/UNDOC/GEN/N02/753/01/PDF/N0275301.pdf?OpenElement (accessed 10 January 2008).

11. Report of the Secretary-General on the establishment of a Special Court for Sierra Leone, UN Doc S/2009/915 (4 October 2000), para. 22, daccessdds.un.org/doc/UNDOC/GEN/N00/661/77/PDF/N0066177.pdf?OpenElement (accessed 10 January 2008).

12. W. Thompson and R. Tucker, 'A tale of two democracies peace critiques', *Journal of Conflict Resolution* 41(3), 1997: 428–454.

13. See International Centre for Transitional Justice (2007), 'Peace vs justice'. Unpublished Concept Paper for Workshop on Peace and Justice, May 2007, International Centre for Transitional Justice.

14. Méndez, 'Peace, justice and prevention', p. 17.

15. D. Orentlicher, 'Settling accounts: The duty to prosecute human rights violations of a prior regime', *Yale Law Journal* 100, 1991: 2537–2615.

16. Zalaquett, 'Confronting human rights violations committed by former governments', p. 3.

17. Zalaquett, 'Confronting human rights violations committed by former governments', p. 6.

18. Zalaquett, 'Confronting human rights violations committed by former governments', pp. 6–9.

19. Zalaquett, 'Confronting human rights violations committed by former governments', pp. 6, 7.

20. See Updated Set of Principles to Combat Impunity.

21. R. Alfonsín, 'Never again in Argentina', *Journal of Democracy* 4(1), 1993: 15–19.

22. Figures obtained from a database constructed by Louise Mallinder documenting all amnesty processes since the Second World War. The database will be made available online during 2008. See L. Mallinder, 'Can amnesties and international justice be reconciled?', *The International Journal of Transitional Justice* 1, 2007: 209.

23. Mallinder, 'Can amnesties and international justice be reconciled?'

24. Mallinder, 'Can amnesties and international justice be reconciled?', p. 210.

25. The interim Constitution; see also *AZAPO v President of South Africa* 1996 (4) SA 671 (CC).

26. C.S. Nino, 'The duty to punish past abuses of human rights put into context: The case of Argentina', in Kritz (ed.), *Transitional justice, vol. 1*, 1995, p. 420.

27. A. Neier, 'What should be done about the guilty?' in Kritz (ed.), *Transitional justice, vol. 1*, 1995, p. 179.

28. 'Argentina amnesty laws struck down', 14 June 2005, www.hrw.org/english/docs/2005/06/14/argent11119.htm (accessed 10 January 2008).

29. 'Argentina amnesty laws struck down'.

30. Report of the Chilean National Commission on Truth and Reconciliation, 9 February 1991, www.usip.org/library/tc/doc/reports/chile/chile_1993_intro.html (accessed 10 January 2008).

31. *Commissioner of Police for the Metropolis and others, Ex parte Pinochet* [1999] UKHL 17 (24 March 1999). The House of Lords ruled that Pinochet could be extradited to Spain to face charges but not for offences that allegedly occurred before 1998. On 28 May 2004 the Court of Appeals voted 14 to 9 to revoke Pinochet's dementia status and consequently his immunity from prosecution.

32. *R v Bartle and the Commissioner of Police for the Metropolis and others, Ex parte Pinochet* [1998] UKHL 41; [2000] 1 AC 61; [1998] 4 All ER 897; [1998] 3 WLR 1456 (25 November, 1998).

33. 'Slaking a thirst for justice', *The Economist*, 12 April 2007, www.economist.com/displayStory.cfm?story_id=9017531 (accessed 14 January 2008). In 1999, the Supreme Court of Chile ruled that a 'disappearance' is a continuing crime until death is proved. This ruling meant that the 1978 amnesty did not cover disappearances that had not been solved. In December 2006, the Supreme Court also ruled that because Chile was in a situation of internal conflict after the 1973 coup, the Geneva Conventions applied. In early 2007 the Court ruled that serious violations could not be subjected to amnesty.

34. 'Peace Agreement in the Castle of Chapultepec, Mexico', UN Doc 1992/730 (16 January 1992), www.un.org/documents/sc/res/1992/scres92.htm (accessed 14 January 2008).

35. The Commission's report was called 'From madness to hope'; see T. Buergenthal, 'The United Nations Truth Commission for El Salvador', in Kritz (ed.), *Transitional justice, vol. 1*, 1995, p. 292.

36. 'Slaking a thirst for justice'.

37. P.B. Hayner, 'Fifteen truth commissions 1974–1993: A comparative study', in Kritz (ed.), *Transitional justice, vol. 1*, 1995, p. 261.

38. Hayner, 'Fifteen truth commissions 1974–1993', p. 226.

39. The interim Constitution.

40. During the negotiations, the right wing had been responsible for several bombs and had invaded the place where negotiations were taking place.

41. M. Meredith, *Coming to terms, reconstructing the past* (New York: Public Affairs, 1999).

42. The term 'act associated with a political objective' is defined in sec. 20(2) and (3) of the Promotion of National Unity and Reconciliation Act 34 of 1995.

43. The Promotion of National Unity and Reconciliation Act.

44. I was part of the working group together with George Bizos, Graeme Simpson, Paul van Zyl, the South African Council of Churches and the South African Catholic Bishops Conference.

45. Meredith, *Coming to terms, reconstructing the past,* p. 19.

46. The Promotion of National Unity and Reconciliation Act.

47. The Promotion of National Unity and Reconciliation Act.

48. The *AZAPO* case (n. 27).

49. See the interim Constitution.

50. See Judge Didcott, *AZAPO* case (n. 27).

51. See *Truth and Reconciliation Commission of South Africa Report*, vol. 6, www.doj.gov.za/trc/report/index.htm (accessed on 29 August 2008).

52. See Y. Sooka, 'Race and reconciliation', in A. Adebajo, A. Adedeji and C. Landsberg (eds.), *South Africa in Africa: The post-apartheid decade* (Pietermaritzburg: University of KwaZulu-Natal Press, 2007), pp. 78–91.

53. T. Rosenberg, Foreword, in M. Meredith, *Coming to terms: South Africa's search for truth* (New York: Public Affairs, 1999).

54. Rosenberg, Foreword, pp. xi–xii.

55. The Inkatha Freedom party, a major role-player in the conflict refused to participate in the work of the TRC.

56. M. Mamdani, 'A diminished truth', in W. James and L. van de Vijver (eds.), *After the TRC: Reflections on truth and reconciliation in South Africa* (Athens: Ohio University Press, 2001), pp. 60–63.

57. Mamdani, 'A diminished truth'.

58. Sooka, 'Race and reconciliation'.

59. See *Truth and Reconciliation Commission of South Africa Report*, vol. 6.

60. See 'Combating impunity'.

61. Mallinder, 'Can amnesties and international justice be reconciled?', p. 226.

62. The author was appointed a commissioner to the Sierra Leonean Commission by OHCHR.

63. D. Francis, *Torturous path to peace: Lomé Peace Accord and post-war peace building in Sierra Leone, security dialogue* (London: Sage Publications, 2000); see SLTRC (2004), 'Women and the armed conflict'. *Report of the Truth Commission of Sierra Leone*, vol. 3B, para. 281, p. 159.

64. A. Tejan-Cole, 'Human rights under the Armed Forces Revolutionary Council (AFRC) in Sierra Leone: A catalogue of abuse', *African Journal of International and Comparative Law/RADIC* 10(3), 1998: 481–495.

65. Peace Agreement between the Government of Sierra Leone and the Revolutionary United Front of Sierra Leone (Lomé Peace Agreement), UN Doc. S/1999/777 (7 July 1999), www.reliefweb.int/rw/RWB.NSF/db900SID/MHII-5ZSB6A?OpenDocument&rc=1&cc=sle (accessed 14 January 2008).

66. The reservation of Okello does not appear on the agreement as published by the UN.

67. Security Council Resolution 1315 (2000), UN Doc S/RES/1315 (14 August 2000); The Report of the Secretary-General on the Establishment of a Special Court for Sierra Leone, UN Doc S/2000/915 (4 October 2000), www.un.org/Docs/scres/2000/sc2000.htm and www.un.org/Docs/sc/reports/2000/sgrep00.htm (accessed 14 January 2008).

68. See paragraph on challenges experienced in this chapter; also A. Tejan-Cole, 'The complementary and conflicting relationship between the Special Court for Sierra Leone and the Truth and Reconciliation Commission', *Yale Human Rights and Development Law Journal* 6, 2003: 139–159.

69. See Letter from Secretary-General to the President of the Security Council, UN Doc. S/2001/40 (12 January 2001) para. 9, www.un.org/Docs/sc/letters/2001/sglet01.htm (accessed 14 January 2008).

70. *Report of the Truth Commission of Sierra Leone* (2004), Administrative Management Report.

71. This observation is based upon the author's personal knowledge.

72. See *Report of the Truth Commission of Sierra Leone*.

73. See Human Rights Watch, Policy Paper on the Inter-relationship between the Sierra Leone Special Court and the Truth and Reconciliation Commission, 18 April 2002, www.hrw.org (accessed 14 January 2008).

74. See *Report of the Truth Commission of Sierra Leone*, vol. 3B, p. 379.

75. The TRC and Special Court had held meetings with each other. The Prosecutor had also assured the commission that he respected the independence of the commission. See *Report of the Truth Commission of Sierra Leone*, vol. 3B, pp. 376, 382.

76. The Lomé Peace Accord specifically provided, under the article dealing with post-war rehabilitation and reconstruction, that 'given that women have been particularly victimized during the war, special attention shall be given to their needs and potential in formulating and implementing national rehabilitation, reconstruction and development programmes to enable them to play a central role in the moral, social and physical reconstruction of Sierra Leone'.

77. Lomé Peace Accord and the Truth and Reconciliation Commission Act (TRC Act).

78. TRC Act, art. 6(2)(*b*).

79. 'Women and the armed conflict', *Report of the Truth Commission of Sierra Leone*, vol. 3B, para. 16, p. 88.

80. 'Women and the armed conflict', *Report of the Truth Commission of Sierra Leone*, vol. 3B, pp. 83–230.

81. 'Women and the armed conflict', *Report of the Truth Commission of Sierra Leone*, vol. 3B, para. 33, p. 92.

82. 'Women and the armed conflict', *Report of the Truth Commission of Sierra Leone*, vol. 3B, para. 31, p. 90.

83. 'Women and the armed conflict', *Report of the Truth Commission of Sierra Leone*, vol. 3B, para. 10, p. 235; see also C. Makeni, 'Submissions to the Truth and Reconciliation Commission on the occasion of TRC thematic hearings on children' (16 June 2003), p. 3; The UN Assistance Mission in Sierra Leone (UNAMSIL) (2003), 'Submission to the Truth and Reconciliation Commission on the occasion of TRC thematic hearings on children' (16 June 2003); and UNICEF: Child Protection Programme Report (February 2003), p. 2.

84. See UN Children's Fund (UNICEF) (2003), 'Submission to the Truth and Reconciliation Commission on the occasion of TRC thematic hearings on children' (17 June 2003); and *Report of the Truth Commission of Sierra Leone*, vol. 3B, p. 234.

85. *Report of the Truth Commission of Sierra Leone* (UNICEF submission), vol. 3B, para. 6, p. 234.

86. UNICEF (2003) Child Protection Programme Report (February 2003), p. 2.

87. 'Children and the armed conflict', *Report of the Truth Commission of Sierra Leone*, chap. 4.

88. *Report of the Truth Commission of Sierra Leone*, vol. 3B, p. 235.

89. Lomé Peace Accord, art. 30.

90. National bodies working on child protection issues, that is, Caritas Makeni, Children's Forum Network (CFN), came together under umbrella body; see *Report of the Truth Commission of Sierra Leone*, vol. 3B, para. 20, p. 237.

91. 'Children and the armed conflict', *Report of the Truth Commission of Sierra Leone*, p. 237.

92. 'Women and the armed conflict', *Report of the Truth Commission of Sierra Leone*, para. 215, p. 141.

93. See Executive Secretariat of National Committee for Disarmament, Demobilisation and Reintegration (NCDDR), Monitoring and Evaluation Unit (2003), Report on numbers of children and women that went through disarmament, demobilisation and reintegration process, 9 September 2003.

94. 'Women and the armed conflict', *Report of the Truth Commission of Sierra Leone*, p. 220.

95. 'Women and the armed conflict', *Report of the Truth Commission of Sierra Leone*, para. 546, p. 222.

96. *Report of the Truth Commission of Sierra Leone* (Reconciliation), vol. 3B, para. 15, p. 436.

97. *Report of the Truth Commission of Sierra Leone* (Reconciliation), vol. 3B, paras 15–19, p. 436.

98. Human Rights Watch (2007), Letter to HE Ernest Bai Koroma of Sierra Leone, 14 November 2007, hrw.org/english/docs/2007/11/13/sierra17321.htm (accessed 16 January 2008).

99. D. Orentlicher, 'Settling accounts revisited: Reconciling global norms and local agency', *International Journal for Transitional Justice* 1(2), 2007: 22.

2

Inclusive Justice

The Limitations of Trial Justice and Truth Commissions

Charles Villa-Vicencio

INTRODUCTION

The Rome Treaty of July 1998, which resulted in the establishment of the International Criminal Court (ICC), has placed prosecutions firmly on the transitional justice agenda. Charles Taylor faces trial in The Hague, having been indicted by the Special Court for Sierra Leone (SCSL). The ICC has indicted Thomas Lubanga in the Democratic Republic of the Congo (DRC) and issued arrest warrants for the Lord's Resistance Army (LRA) leaders Joseph Kony, Vincent Otti, Okot Odhiambo, Dominic Ogwen and Raska Lukwiya. These developments, not least the warrants that coincide with the Ugandan peace initiatives and the ICC's focus on Africa, have not gone unnoticed in peacebuilding circles on this continent and elsewhere.

In addition, the South African Truth and Reconciliation Commission (TRC) continues to be seen as a model against which to measure, adjust and improve transitional justice mechanisms around the world. The judicial infrastructure of countries in transition is invariably such that not all alleged perpetrators can be prosecuted in the wake of conflict and it is frequently essential to ask whether it is politically wise to attempt to do so. Indeed, history has taught us that amnesty, qualified or otherwise, is among the more powerful political instruments in the peacebuilding toolbox. Amnesty often comes not as a result of dialogue, goodwill or reconciliation but rather as a calculating tool that is used for political benefit. Amnesty can promote tolerance and peace; it can also polarise and embitter. It can be interpreted as an ingredient in a restorative justice process; it can also be seen as impunity.

My argument is that whether past offences are dealt with via prosecutions, tribunals, national courts, the ICC or amnesties, more is required to overcome the animosity, mistrust and historical inequalities wrought by decades of oppression and war. By augmenting what can be accomplished through prosecutions what possibilities and limitations exist for TRCs and other related historical clarification mechanisms that will enable former enemies and adversaries to deal with the past at emotional, social, economic and political levels?

A primary responsibility of TRCs (one that is often neglected in the transitional justice debate) is the initiation of a process that seeks to draw all parties that have been involved in a conflict, from grassroots to leadership levels, into a national conversation that is honest and thoughtful and motivated by a desire to maximise truth-seeking, truth-telling and acknowledgement. The purpose of the conversation is to break the silence that surrounds the suffering of the victims and survivors of past oppression and to instigate acknowledgement from the perpetrators.

Another relevant question is whether TRCs have the capacity to persuade the benefactors of the past to recognise and acknowledge the privileges that they carry with them into the new society. Clearly these ambitious goals cannot be accomplished in a one-off exercise but require a gradual and cyclical process that operates at different levels of society. These ambitions are usually well beyond the scope of many TRCs but if they were correctly designed and carefully instituted then they could potentially initiate and promote such a process.

Underlying the motivation of TRCs is the conviction that a nation can only begin to reconcile itself once the past has been fully acknowledged and a process has been enacted that allows the nation to understand the causes, motives and perspectives of those responsible for the gross violations of human rights. In order to be more than a sincere hope or romantic ideal, a TRC process should address the needs and demands of victims, survivors and perpetrators, as well as the beneficiaries of the old order and the heirs of the new. I propose that this level of reconciliation and nation-building requires deep and sincere conversation that is aimed at the emergence of a new social contract. On the basis of this, specific policies and programmes can be designed and implemented that will satisfy the basic needs of as many people as is realistically possible. This process will mean prioritising what can be accomplished immediately and projecting a carefully managed national agenda regarding important issues that can only be resolved later. Immediate priorities would be the cessation of hostilities, the setting up of democratic institutions and the affirmation of basic human rights. Other needs such as socio-economic rights will naturally take longer to be implemented. In the words of Adam Habib, these needs are, however, 'more than an irritant to political reconciliation'. Nevertheless, the minimising or suspension of socio-economic justice may assist in achieving a breakthrough in negotiations between the elite and the oppressed and in facilitating the change from authoritarian rule to the beginning of democracy. The danger is that, if not dealt with in a timely manner, this lack of focus on socio-economic imperatives is likely to undermine the process of democratic consolidation.[1]

The South African TRC is an important case study, especially considering that in the 1980s people around the world predicted a bloodbath in South Africa. Instead there was a negotiated settlement that captured the attention of many countries in conflict. In the words of the South Africa interim Constitution, the settlement provided a 'historic bridge' that was designed to take the nation from a deeply divided past 'characterised by strife, conflict, untold suffering and injustice' towards a future 'founded on the recognition of human rights, democracy and peaceful coexistence and development opportunities for all South Africans, irrespective of colour, race, class, belief or sex'.[2] In pursuit of these ideals the government developed new policies and established several commissions, including the TRC.

The South African 'solution' is clearly not the answer to all conflicts around the world. It is important to recognise that the capacity of South Africans to forge peace in the face of threatened anarchy does not mean that South Africans are a 'race apart'. However, the desire of the majority of human beings to co-exist with others suggests that there is political value in considering instances where some human beings get it more or less right. South Africa is one of the few places on earth where there might just be a chance of that happening.

A NATIONAL CONVERSATION

The work of the South African TRC has been variously described as a national conversation, theatre, tragedy, epic storytelling, liturgy or drama. It involved words spoken – words that needed to be heard, words that begged for a response and words that waited for action. It was an attempt to invite citizens to talk and an attempt to generate a new or additional vehicle for democratic participation.

Good conversation, whether in theatre, storytelling or debate, has a way of focusing the mind. It generates ideas. It unleashes new energies. At times it shocks. It silences. We are confronted with a new frontier.

The TRC conversation happened at three levels: conversations within the commission were intense and not always amicable. The tensions inherent in the South African conflict manifested themselves in the attitudes of commissioners and staff. Issues of race, identity, social class and political persuasion impacted on the work of the commission and contributed to the inability of the commission to reach consensus on the nature of reconciliation or the relationship between truth-finding and reconciliation. There were those who equated reconciliation with interpersonal reconciliation and forgiveness. This position was promoted primarily through the passionate and persuasive voice of Archbishop Desmond Tutu, Chairperson of the TRC. A second group argued that it was inappropriate for a state-sponsored commission to promote interpersonal forgiveness. This group advocated the promotion of a national framework for co-existence and civility within which individual healing and forgiveness could eventually take place. The third group had a still more limited view on the role of the TRC. It wanted to focus exclusively on truth-finding, arguing that this would provide a basis for both future co-existence and reconciliation.[3]

Outside the commission the public conversation was often extremely heated and yet this was also an important part of the national conversation. Afrikaans-language newspapers were relentless in their condemnation of the commission, believing that it was engaging in a witch-hunt against white Afrikaners and the former government. Both English-language news media and black-based newspapers gave a more balanced perspective, although here too controversy raged, for example, around the public hearings involving Winnie Madikizela-Mandela, the killing of Chris Hani and other high-profile people and events. The extent of the national debate regarding the work of the TRC was huge. Few if any South Africans failed to have an opinion on the TRC. Most importantly, the silence on the past was being broken.

The breaking of the silence through the work of the commission was varied and multi-layered. Some perpetrators denied or blamed while others confessed; most are likely to take their unspoken words to the grave. Victims remembered and many chose, without success, to forget. Most bystanders denied and looked the other way although some tried to be a part of the new order. The nation continues its conversation encumbered with the struggle of remembering against that of forgetting. Silence persists, however and conversation often merely beckons. Perhaps this is inevitable, if Yael Danieli is correct when he attests to the inability of many individuals and communities to deal adequately with trauma: 'They can find no words to narrate the trauma story and create a meaningful dialogue around it.'[4] This silence renders victims unable either to 'move on' or to grasp the opportunity to repair or restore their lives.

Although the conversation with perpetrators and victims was of a different kind and at a different level, these conversations shaped the identity of the South African TRC. Philippe Salazar suggests that perpetrator testimony was in the genre of the tragic. The voices of victims constituted an epic tale.[5] In the case of the former, a distance was maintained between the person of the perpetrator and his (rarely 'her') staged voice as narrator or actor; perpetrators spoke through lawyers. Often perpetrators said little more than a standard oath, carefully scripted and cautiously uttered. Where there was personal testimony it was rehearsed so that it might comply with the requirements of the legislation that governed the TRC. Amnesty applicants needed to be heard as 'perpetrators with integrity'. It was required that their testimony reflected a political motive for having committed a gross violation of human rights, narrowly defined in the mandate of the TRC as 'killing, torture, abduction or severe ill-treatment'.[6] When applicants could not show that they had been politically motivated they failed to receive amnesty. They were not required to show remorse and most failed to do so. When remorse was expressed it is possible that this too might have been scripted.

Perpetrators spoke to multiple-faceted audiences. The primary audience was the amnesty panel that consisted of judges and lawyers. Perpetrators also indirectly addressed family members and friends, former colleagues, the media and, in some instances, the victims and survivors. This posed the question as to precisely who was on the stage addressing which audience at any one time. When interviewed by researchers two years after appearing before the TRC, several successful and unsuccessful amnesty applicants expressed regret that they had not felt free (often because of pressure from their lawyers) to make the kind of disclosure that, in retrospect, some felt they ought to have made.

'I never told *my* story. There was a gap between what I wanted to say and what I ultimately said,' a high-ranking former military officer observed. 'If I [had] said too much I could have endangered former colleagues. I did not want to embarrass my family. I simply wanted to put the past behind me. The easiest way was to play by the rules of the game. I felt I would be damned if I said too much and I knew I was damned for not saying enough.' Another referred to the sensationalism that often surrounded the amnesty hearings: 'I am a soldier. Soldiers don't cry. They do their job and take the consequences. My day of judgement lies ahead when I meet my God.' Some perpetrators responded remorsefully and as best they could in both their amnesty applications and in their subsequent attempts to contribute to the healing of their victims. Most callously seemed to use the amnesty law to get away with as much as possible.[7] This said, no process – retributive or restorative – could compel perpetrators either to show remorse, to tell the unequivocal truth as they saw it or to make restitution.

If the amnesty hearings were, in the words of one amnesty applicant, 'over-judicial', the intention of the commission was to facilitate victim hearings in a psychologically and socially supportive manner – although it did not always succeed in doing so. There was no cross-examination of victims. Commissioners were to listen attentively with a view to enabling victims to deal with their suffering in a cathartic and honest manner. Victims were encouraged to speak without reserve. In the words of the TRC report, the 'subjective truth' was encouraged and accepted by the commission as part of an inclusive process of truth-recovery. Tears were frequently shed by victims who testified, by members of the public before whom they testified, by television and radio audiences who looked on and at times by commissioners themselves – not least Archbishop Tutu, who chaired the proceedings. It was this that made tangible the essential difference between the TRC victim hearings and court proceedings. Judges don't cry. This genre of storytelling and testimony is now part of the national memory. The question remains as to how deeply it affected society in general and what kind of responses it evoked beyond those of the victims and those closest to them.

Victims and survivors responded to the commission hearings in different ways. Some of them found solace and catharsis. Others felt their wounds were reopened and left unattended. The commission frequently failed to follow up on requests and promises that had been made by commissioners at these hearings. The state, in turn, was slow to recognise or honour the victims through appropriate forms of reparation and in related ways. Some government officials scoffed at what they suggested was unnecessary public hysteria. The TRC's attempts to 'heal' a nation torn apart by decades of violence and death were caricatured in cartoons and explored through theatre and the visual arts. Maurice Charland mentions the importance of the 'impiety of politics' when dealing with the ambiguities and tragedies of history.[8] 'To mock and to ridicule the attempts of the Commission to heal was in a contradictory way perhaps part of the healing process,' suggests Charland.

Trauma is rarely resolved or overcome in a single cathartic moment. It returns to haunt and plague the victim, requiring time and deep reflection, influenced by the social milieu within which the victim finds him- or herself. This has resulted in heated debate between those who argue that the TRC victims' hearings enabled individuals who appeared before it to overcome their trauma and those who argue that the hearings merely resurrected painful memories that were then left unresolved. At best the TRC hearings could only be part of a longer healing process.

The benefit of the hearings lay primarily at the political level. The TRC confronted the nation with a body of testimony that few could ever again dismiss. It helped South Africans to begin to challenge the systemic denial that in other parts of the world so often characterises situations where there has been violence, abuse, crimes against humanity and genocide.

A DOUBLE CRITIQUE

The purpose of dealing with the past in a restorative way inevitably involves more than verbalising memory as an end in itself. It is primarily an exercise in looking back in order to reach forward.

Govan Mbeki, a veteran leader in the South African struggle and the father of President Mbeki, spoke shortly before his death in 2001 of the need to balance 'having and belonging' in the nation-building process in South Africa and elsewhere on the African continent. 'For political renewal to endure, the economy needs to be restructured in such a way that the poor and socially excluded begin to share in the benefits of the nation's wealth,' he insisted. 'People – all people, both black and white, Hutu and Tutsi, Shona and Ndebele – also need to feel they are part of the new nation. If some do not feel welcome or at home in their respective countries they will not only be reluctant to work for the common good, they can also cause considerable trouble.'[9]

To achieve what Govan Mbeki called 'having and belonging', the nature and the causes of an oppressive past need to be exposed in order to minimise the possibility of their perpetuation. The failure to do so could, as a result of new political alliances, mean that former victims, not least the poor, continue to be excluded and alienated. Alternatively, as is the case in some countries, former victors and victims may simply exchange places. There are those who have made the TRC the whipping boy for failing to address this challenge and believe that it could have done more. The question is whether, on what Chinua Achebe called the first day of creation,[10] it was opportune or possible for it to do so.

The most telling critiques of the South African TRC that capture the insights of Govan Mbeki are those of Wole Soyinka and Mahmood Mamdani. Conscious of the fragility of new democracies that are emerging from oppressive regimes where those on opposing sides of a deadly conflict ultimately need to learn to live together, both authors show an understanding of the need to find an alternative to both Nuremberg-type trials and impunity. At the same time, both believe that the mandate of the TRC failed to take into account adequately the underlying depths of the South African malady. Both further imply that this level of exploration is still possible although it is becoming increasingly more difficult to realise.

Soyinka asks the probing question: How far dare a nation go in seeking to accommodate both victims and perpetrators of past abuse?[11] Affirming the need for a purging of the past through truth-telling and acknowledgement, Soyinka is critical of the South African amnesty process primarily because it allowed perpetrators to be absolved not only of criminality but also of responsibility. He suggests that South Africa ought to move beyond the 'hazy zone of remorse' towards 'a social formula that would minister to the wrongs of dispossession on the one hand, chasten those who deviate from humane communal order on the other, [and] serve as a criterion for the future conduct of that society, even in times of stress – and *only then*, heal'.[12]

Soyinka's plea is that reconciliation and healing be grounded in appropriate forms of reparations and the affirmation of the rule of law. He argues that the roots of apartheid oppression went deeper than the torture, abduction, killing and severe ill-treatment that constituted the TRC's definition of gross violations of human rights. Recognising that apartheid was grounded in material deprivation, social humiliation, naked racism and dehumanisation, Soyinka says reparations need to include material restitution and need to redeem victims from what he defines as a 'slave condition' that undermines the humanity of the oppressed. This, he suggests, imposes a sense of obligation and responsibility on both perpetrators and beneficiaries to engage, understand and respond to the needs of the victims of apartheid. It also requires victims to seize and alter their (own) destiny.

too narrow - def. of injustice

Mahmood Mamdani's critique of the South African TRC is similar to that of Soyinka.[13] His concern is that the TRC reduces injustice from the 'injustice of apartheid' – involving the dehumanisation of the majority of the population through the degradation of apartheid – to a narrower definition of injustice. He sees the defining character of the South African struggle not as a conflict between perpetrators and victims as defined in TRC legislation but as one between all beneficiaries and victims of the apartheid system. With justification, Mamdani suggests that Bantu education and forced removals entrenched generations of black South Africans in a South African gulag that must be confronted for justice and reconciliation to become a reality:

> The violence of apartheid was aimed less at individuals than at entire communities, and entire population groups . . . The point is that the Latin American analogy [from which the South African TRC drew its inspiration] obscured the colonial nature of the South African context: the link between conquest and dispossession, between racialized power and racialized privilege. In a word, it obscured the link between perpetrator and beneficiary.[14]

Locating apartheid within the history of European colonialism in which the native majority needed to be subjugated in order to maximise the privilege of beneficiaries, Mamdani's argument is that truth is not enough to ensure reconciliation. This, he suggests, can be realised only through systematic socio-economic reform, which he defines as 'a form of justice other than punishment'.[15] Without opposing prosecutions, which may well be part of the justice he seeks, he prioritises restitution and structural change. He simultaneously stresses the importance of acknowledgement and apology that, he insists, needs to go beyond the formal 'deep regret' about apartheid that was expressed by former President F.W. de Klerk, which he contrasts with the apology of the post-war German leader, Willie Brandt, who went on his knees in the former Warsaw ghetto.

The former government, its supporters and those who accepted the privileges it bestowed need to accept responsibility for past gross violations of human rights. Recognising that many perpetrators and benefactors were victims of a state ideology that drew bystanders and would-be decent people into its clutches, few, if any, individuals are ever entirely without the resources to resist this kind of propaganda.[16] In *Hitler's Willing Executioners* Daniel Goldhagen's argument that

Germans were under the 'grip of a cognitive model' or 'monolithic conversation' so powerful that few were able to escape its impact goes a long way towards explaining the hideous anti-Semitic behaviour of otherwise seemingly decent people.[17] The reality is that some did act, at great personal cost, against the dominant ideology – in Germany, South Africa and elsewhere. The limitation of the South African TRC was that it had neither the mandate nor the time nor, perhaps, the will to address the underlying problem of racism and privilege that underpinned the gross violations of human rights that it sought to uncover.

The question is how to get those who supported and benefited from a system to say a sincere *mea culpa* and commit themselves to work for the restitution and integration of the victims and survivors of a repulsive past. Nelson Mandela's answer is that this needs to be accomplished gently and in a conciliatory manner. In his State of the Nation speech, delivered two weeks after his inauguration as president on 10 May 1994, he declared that, in engaging the past, South Africans 'must be constrained . . . regardless of the accumulated effect of our historical burdens, seizing the time to define for ourselves what we want to make of our shared destiny'.[18] This, according to him, would need to include the granting of amnesty to perpetrators of the most horrible crimes:

> In this context, I also need to point out that the Government will not delay unduly with regard to attending to the vexed and unresolved issue of an amnesty for criminal activities carried out in furtherance of political objectives. We will attend to this matter in a balanced and dignified way. The nation must come to terms with its past in a spirit of oneness and forgiveness and proceed to build the future on the basis of repairing and healing . . . In the meantime, summonsing the full authority of the position we represent, we call on all concerned not to take any steps that might, in any way, impede or compromise the processes of reconciliation that the impending legislation will address. [19]

The double critique of the TRC in terms of the lack of 'having and belonging' stands. Perhaps the TRC could never have been more than a cautious beginning. It could, however, also have reached deeper into the nation's memory by holding a sharper and more penetrating mirror before the nation, persuading it to reflect with a rigorous, penetrating gaze on the origins of the apartheid system that gave rise to the gross human rights violations.

BACK TO THE BEGINNING

We often forget that the TRC was created in the fragility of the earliest days of the South African democracy.[20] The national conversation was hesitant and constrained. It was also volatile and dangerous. Shortly before the first democratic elections in April 1994 General Constand Viljoen, the former chief of the South African Defence Force (SADF), walked out of the white Afrikaner-based Freedom Front Party, having committed himself to 'building and maintaining the armed potential for the [more militant] Afrikaner Volksfront' and warning that the nation was on the brink of war. He soon became disillusioned with the ill-discipline and violent tactics of the Volksfront and returned to a leadership position in the Freedom Front. After a series of behind-the-scenes meetings with the African National Congress (ANC) and others, he persuaded the Freedom Front Party to participate in the pending elections. In a later submission to Parliament's Joint Committee on Justice he applauded Mandela's 'spirit of reconciliation' but warned that what would satisfy the constituency of the ANC on reconciliation would have the opposite effect on the Afrikaner constituency, arguing that the transition had failed to produce a shared vision for the nation. There were skirmishes and threats of insurrection. In Bophuthatswana, which had been afforded 'independence' by the apartheid government in 1977, an uprising known as the Battle of Bop involved the armed forces of the Bophuthatswana Defence Force, troops of the Afrikaner Weerstandsbeweging (AWB) and the Afrikaner Volksfront, as well as the South African army. This led to Bophuthatswana being stripped of its independence. There was also a bizarre and frightening invasion of the World Trade Centre in Johannesburg where the constitutional negotiations known as the Congress for a Democratic South Africa (CODESA) were being held. Eugene Terre'Blanche, head of the AWB, led the foray on horseback but this led to nothing but embarrassment for those in charge of security. Ultimately, there was no resolute armed confrontation and Viljoen later said he knew of no serious coup plans at any point during the transition. However, the antics of those threatening revolt were enough to alarm the ANC leadership that was waiting in the wings to assume power.

Acknowledging these concerns, President Mandela stressed that 'the majority party must have understanding . . . to ensure confidence in the minority parties . . . and to see to it that their views are fully accommodated'.[21] Dullah Omar, the Minister of Justice at the time, responding to the criticism of Amnesty International and other human rights groups that the amnesty clause in the TRC legislation threatened the integrity of international human rights law, stated: 'We are building a future for South Africans [and if] there is conflict between what the international community is saying and what is in the interests of the people of South Africa then I think that we will have to live with that kind of conflict.'[22] The die was cast. The TRC was to be what Johnny de Lange, an architect of the TRC legislation and later Deputy Minister of Justice, called a 'model in the middle'.[23]

Shortly after the TRC began its work, Deputy Presidents Thabo Mbeki and F.W. de Klerk, together with the Director General in the Office of the Presidency, Professor Jakes Gerwel, requested a meeting with the TRC commissioners. The commission saw this as political interference in the work of an independent commission and they refused this request, although it was later agreed that the chairperson of the commission (Archbishop Desmond Tutu) and the deputy chairperson (Dr Alex Boraine) would meet with the presidential team. The purpose of the meeting was to communicate the government's hope that the spirit of the multi-party talks in seeking accommodation and understanding between the political groups and opponents would be taken into account by the TRC. Gerwel later identified this as the beginning of the tensions between the government and the TRC, which had an impact both on the work of the commission and on the implementation of its recommendations.

Both inside and outside the TRC, there were many who did not readily embrace the rapprochement that existed between the former government and the ANC during the multi-party (CODESA) talks. Many wanted the commission to deal more poignantly with the crimes of apartheid.[24] The daily burdens of those who, for example, had suffered under forced removals, Bantu education and related apartheid crimes were implicit in all that the TRC did. And yet for a variety of reasons – political compromise, the need to be seen to be reconciling the nation and what Kader Asmal called the 'liberal procedures of transition' – the commission did not adequately address the nuts and bolts of apartheid policy and practice. This inevitably had an impact on the extent to which the commission was able and/or prepared to demand the truth from some alleged perpetrators as well as from officials of the former state.

The closest the TRC came to addressing the realities of apartheid policy as a whole was during the political party and institutional hearings. The latter hearings were on business and labour, faith communities, the health sector, media, prisons, the military and the legal fraternity. There were also special hearings on children, youth and women. It was within the context of these hearings that many opportunities to uncover the depths of responsibility and hurt that characterised apartheid were missed. They also opened spaces for truth that are yet to be fully explored.

During the political party hearings, former President F.W. de Klerk, on behalf of the National Party and the former government, expressed a formal regret for the hurt caused by apartheid and yet he failed to show the passion and conviction that both the commission and the public were looking for. He insisted that apartheid had gone wrong, perhaps horribly wrong, while stressing that he had no knowledge of the atrocities committed by the security forces. When questioned by the commission he indicated that he was 'not prepared to accept responsibility for the criminal actions of a handful of operatives of the security forces of which [his] party was not aware and which would never have been condoned'.[25] When individuals and organisations both within and outside the country had drawn his attention to the gross violations of human rights committed by the security forces and related agencies prior to the transition, he had appointed several commissions to look into the accusations but had failed to demonstrate the level of commitment needed to get to the bottom of these accusations that the TRC and many beyond its structures were now seeking. In the words of his Deputy Minister of Law and Order, Leon Wessels: 'It was not that we did not know; we didn't want to know. We didn't talk about it; we whispered it in the corridors of parliament.' In contrast to De Klerk, Wessels observed: 'I cannot condone these violent unlawful acts, but nor can I condemn the persons; I cannot disown them. We were on the same side and fought for the same cause . . . I cannot disown any of those men and women who were on our side.' Acknowledging the positive role played by De Klerk in the political transition, he stated:

> I simply believe it is a pity that there is not a collective political and moral acceptance of responsibility forthcoming from the quarters from which I emanate . . . Apartheid was a terrible mistake that blighted our land. South Africans did not listen to the laughing and the crying of one another. I am sorry that I have been so hard of hearing for such a long time.[26]

Committed to putting his own involvement in the apartheid system behind him, Wessels today serves as a commissioner in the South African Human Rights Commission.

A less publicised submission to the TRC came from the white Democratic Alliance (DA), the official opposition party in the apartheid parliament. The DA initially declined to appear before the TRC but later agreed to do so. The various DA representatives spoke of their role in monitoring and witnessing the 'human rights abuses and construction of the edifice of apartheid' and 'a programme of Afrikaner domination . . . [that was] central to the promoting of white interest, depriving blacks, coloureds and Indians of their basic human rights'.[27] Distancing themselves and the English-speaking community from what they saw as an Afrikaner-imposed ideology, they referred to their role in opposing the 'repression of individual liberties', pointing out that they had warned that government policy would 'inevitably lead to ever more violence and counter-violence'. At the same time they made no reference to their complicity as an opposition party in an all-white parliament or the difficult choice they had had to make in this regard. They revealed no sense of the white privilege or selfish gain that lay at the root of an evil and dehumanising system. Closely aligned to business, they had opposed economic sanctions and the commitment of the black majority to render the apartheid government dysfunctional. Indeed, some years later, a senior DA member, Douglas Gibson, criticised a civil society initiative that called on whites simply to acknowledge that they had benefited from apartheid, and insisted that he had attained no benefits as a white person from the apartheid system who had benefited from the privileges of apartheid. The DA made no attempt to persuade or enable whites either to acknowledge any culpability for having accepted the benefits of apartheid or to take responsibility for any form of reparation.

The ANC's submission was both more candid and more extensive than those made by other parties. It included, for example, disclosure on deaths and torture in the ANC detention camps. Although critics felt that the ANC's level of disclosure was partial and inadequate, the TRC findings on the ANC, as published in the TRC's final report, were significantly shaped by the ANC's own submission. Despite this, the ANC resorted to court action in an unsuccessful attempt to stop the release of the TRC report on the eve of its being handed to President Mandela on 26 September 1998. The fact that this was done before the ANC had seen the report suggests that a member of the commission had leaked an earlier, unedited, less discrete version of the report to the ANC, which heightened the already tense relations between the ANC and the commission.

Despite the many gains that were made as a result of the TRC's political party hearings, the lack of candour in these hearings meant that many opportunities to examine the past in a more complete manner were lost.

The special institutional hearings were, in many ways, as tentative as those of the political parties. They failed to acknowledge or disclose the extent of institutional complicity in the functioning of apartheid. The former security police spy, Craig Williamson, illustrated this when he attempted to justify or mitigate his crimes in his declaration to a commission hearing in Cape Town, in October 1997:

> It is not only the task of the members of the Security Forces to examine themselves and their deeds. It is for every member of the society we served to do so. Our weapons, ammunition, uniforms, vehicles, radios and other equipment were all developed and provided by industry. Our finances and banking were done by bankers who even gave us covert credit cards for covert operations. Our Chaplains prayed for our victory and our universities educated us in war. Our propaganda was carried by the media and our political masters were voted back into power time after time with ever increasing majorities.[28]

It was the legal fraternity's hearing that perhaps best illustrated the TRC's restrained approach to dissecting the malady of the past. In much the same way as business people, journalists and members of the medical and health fraternities in their hearings had expressed regret that they had not done as much as they should have to uphold the moral and professional expectations of their professions during the apartheid years, many judges and lawyers echoed their words yet insisted that they had been merely 'doing their job' within the restraints of what the law permitted. However, members of the Black Lawyers' Association, Lawyers for Human Rights, the Legal Resources Centre and the National Association of Democratic Lawyers, amongst others, were highly critical of the legal community and the judiciary. The judges had initially refused to appear before the TRC at all, arguing that this would call into question their independence and open the way for them to be called to account for their behaviour in future situations. Commissioner Yasmin Sooka insisted that the judges be subpoenaed but this was not supported by the majority of commissioners, who felt this would be interpreted as a hostile act by the commission in what was already an unsympathetic environment in government circles. The compromise was a number of voluntary written submissions by several senior judges, including Justices L.W.F. Ackermann (Judge of the Constitutional Court), Arthur Chaskalson

(President of the Constitutional Court), and M.M. Corbett (Chief Justice of the Supreme Court). These were augmented by submissions from a range of legal scholars and others.

Judge Albie Sachs, commenting on the TRC report that was published in September 1998, commended the commission for its serious reflection 'on how evil behaviour is condoned and spreads itself and on what institutional mechanisms . . . are necessary to prevent its reappearance. But did it go far enough? What restrained it?' He asks:

> Business, where were you? Business was making money, business was co-operating directly with the security forces, supplying explosives, trucks and information. The press, where were you? There were some brave newspapers and wonderful journalists, but by and large the press was racist in its structure and fearful in its thinking. The legal profession, the judges, where were you? We judges, old and new, had hard debates in our ranks. The strongest view was that the judiciary had contributed sub-stantially to injustice by enforcing racist laws and showing an unacceptable lack of vigilance in the face of accusations, torture and abuse.[29]

By committing itself to a TRC, South Africa went further than most nations in an attempt to deal with its past. Its work, and more particularly the work of the nation in this regard, is, however, unfinished. The underlying motivations and causes of the apartheid malady and the culpability and responsibility of the many who benefited from apartheid run deep. Not all whites were guilty of gross violations of human rights. Some whites protested against apartheid but all, in one way or another, benefited from white privilege. They, together with those blacks who collaborated with their apartheid masters, were part of an ideology that imposed exclusion and abuse by means of fear and violence. The question is how to get people to acknowledge their complicity. Sleeping dogs do not lie quietly and in time they smell a forgotten bone that they seek to uncover. Memories slumber but do not sleep.

The point has already been made that the uncovering of the past could never have been concluded in a once-off event. The plethora of books, autobiographies, interviews and the deep conflict within government and political circles could be seen as a de facto continuation of the TRC. Indications are, at the same time, that the disclosure and counter-disclosure that is taking place will engender a level of bitterness that the TRC intended to ameliorate if not avoid. Truth, in different guises and versions, insists on coming out and this is likely to continue for the foreseeable future.

The strained conversation of the TRC process was an important step in the public debate but the hard work of lasting reconciliation still needs to be tackled with a renewed sense of truth-telling and the building of a caring society – one that looks beyond past divisions in pursuit of unity rather than division, harmony rather than contention, integrity rather than corruption, civil and constructive debate rather than confrontation and abuse – as a basis for the creation of an opportunity for subjective and material transformation and renewal.

UNFINISHED CONVERSATION

Central to the South African transition is an unfinished conversation that raises all the questions that are equally pertinent to the international transitional justice debate. There are four pertinent concerns that brood at the heart of the unfinished South African transition that I wish to examine, though each is discussed more fully elsewhere in this publication.

Perpetrator engagement

The late Chief Justice Ismael Mahomed spoke of the South African transition as an 'agonising balance', designed to enable both victims and perpetrators to cross the historic bridge from the past into the future. He warned that this should not be 'with heavy dragged steps [that] delay and impede a rapid and enthusiastic transition to the new society at the end of the bridge'.[30] The invitation, as understood by Mahomed, was for all South Africans without undue restraint to share in the nation-building process – on the basis of restorative rather than retributive justice.

Central to this process was that perpetrators of heinous crimes could be granted amnesty in return for their acknowledgement and full disclosure of the crimes they had committed. This means that at least some perpetrators and all those who benefited from apartheid would be free to share in the new society. They would not be required to pay reparations, undertake community service or face expiation of any kind. There was a realisation that white and other benefactors were here to stay; they needed to be drawn into society, excused for past crimes and allowed to keep the material benefits they had acquired during the apartheid years. The intention was to create space within which all who had the necessary skills and resources could contribute to the building of a new society.

To what extent has this happened? The economy has grown, black empowerment is in place and affirmative action has ensured that many formerly disadvantaged people now have important and lucrative positions. There are, however, many who remain without life's most basic needs. Transformation and rectification is incomplete and if this persists it could have dire consequences for the South African settlement.

Rectification

Rectification and restoration may take different forms: compensation, reparation, restoration, apology, lawsuits and punishment are all important ingredients that can contribute to the realisation of restorative justice.[31] It is, however, the social and political context of rectification and restoration that determines, for example, how much punitive justice or compensation is possible and how much it is wise to impose. Donald Shriver suggests: '[V]engeance however understandable from the perspective of victims ultimately kills politics, if by politics we mean negotiations between groups that permit people to realize their mutual interests without destroying those very interests in acts of violence.'[32] He suggests that in a democratic order a responsible citizen is required to vote for someone else's interests in addition to his or her own and ultimately to vote in the interests of the nation as a whole.

Soyinka, Mamdani and others, by contrast, question whether any sense of victim rectification is possible without adequate material and structural transformation. Soyinka talks of the need for 'a social formula that would minister to the wrongs of dispossession on the one hand, chasten those who deviate from humane communal order on the other, [and] serve as a criterion for the future conduct of that society, even in times of stress – and *only then*, heal'.[33] Mamdani, in turn, stresses the importance of restitution and structural change to the benefit of those escaping the gulag of institutionalised apartheid.[34]

In order to provide more than an imaginary, artificial or hoped-for stability and rectification, both the *material* and the *subjective* needs of the victims and survivors of an oppressive past need to be prioritised. In South Africa the newly elected democratic government's decision was to initiate a truth-telling process through the TRC, to play down the need for retribution and to focus the nation on building a strong economy. It asked the poor to be patient. 'You cannot give away what you do not have' are the frequent words of the South African Minister of Finance even today. But how long will the poor be patient? Clearly the greatest threat to political stability in South Africa is the delay in sufficient poverty relief.

Subjective needs are equally difficult to meet and deeply intertwined with material needs. In the words of the TRC mandate, this requires the 'restoration of the human dignity' of victims. This involves acknowledgement of the suffering endured, recognition of the price that was paid and the inclusion of victims and survivors in their own restoration, that of the communities of which they are a part, and that of the nation as a whole. Nyame Goniwe, whose husband Matthew was killed by the security police in 1985, said

> The TRC and the government helped me to recognise that I have human rights and that those who violated my rights would under normal circumstances be prosecuted. I accept that this was not possible in our situation and so I go along with the amnesty process – and yet it is perhaps only those who have been as deeply violated as I have who are able to understand the deep sense of personal deprivation and sense of helplessness I experience. I need to almost daily regain my loss of dignity and self-confidence. The recognition I have received in society has helped but there is still a horrible sense of worthlessness that continues to raise its horrible head as I attempt to rebuild my life and that of my children. Maybe it will always be there because certain things can never be restored or put right. I sometimes think a sincere apology from the persons who destroyed my life by killing Matthew would help me. But so far I have refused to meet them. I simply don't know how sincere their apology will be. It is so difficult for me to trust anyone. I am not prepared to risk a simple 'I am sorry'. I need to recognise a sense of heart-felt sorrow and grief and a genuine attempt by perpetrators to put right what they destroyed in our lives. They can and they must build our new society or simply go away and leave us to heal ourselves and restore our communities.[35]

The South African TRC is a process that continues to fascinate, bewilder and anger all those who ponder the meaning of restorative justice in situations of political transition. The goodwill that existed in the early stages of the transition between those who benefited from and those who suffered at the hands of apartheid has not materialised into a willingness to add economic and material restoration to the political transition that whites conceded.

It is this that drives some to ask whether trials would not have been a better option for ushering in a new society. 'At least I would not have to see my torturer living a comfortable life while I continue to be excluded from the society I helped see born in 1994,' Sipho Tshabalala, an angry township resident, recently shouted at a conference audience.[36]

Prosecutions

Would Tshabalala be less angry if his torturer had been prosecuted? Does prosecution bring closure? Do most victims want prosecutions? What more than prosecution is needed? These are questions that continue to haunt the transitional justice debate.

Thembi Simelane-Nkadimeng has spent 23 years trying to find out what happened to her sister, Nokuthula, who was abducted by the security police and has not been seen since. Speaking at a public symposium on the tenth anniversary of the TRC, she said: 'I am favouring prosecutions now because it is the only option I have, but if I had an option to sit down and talk [with Nokuthula's abductors] I would choose that.'[37] Victims who resort to prosecutions often do so in an attempt to access some level of truth rather than from a desire for retribution. Others simply want a better quality of life. Their demands are often humble ones – a roof over their heads, medical services, a job and a school for their children. Different victims want different things.

The advent of the ICC, which post-dated the South African transition, has intensified the call for prosecutions – although the demands of the ICC have also evoked an ambiguous response. The Office of the High Commissioner for Human Rights (OHCHR) in Uganda encapsulates this response in a February 2007 publication entitled *Options for accountability for reconciliation in Uganda*.[38] It reaffirms the position of the ICC that 'those responsible for the most serious crimes be held accountable in accordance with international norms and principles' and that 'there can be no amnesty for serious crimes, such as war crimes, crimes against humanity, genocide and gross violations of human rights'. The publication at the same time recognises that 'accountability and justice do not begin and end with prosecution and punishment, but include a variety of other measures aimed at ensuring that victims' needs are properly addressed so that society as a whole can come to terms with what previously divided it and fuelled the conflict'. The 'other measures' cited in the document include truth and reconciliation commissions, other historical clarification bodies and traditional reconciliation practices. It is understood that there is a need to know the truth about past atrocities in order for reconciliation and healing to take place. The OHCHR in

Uganda stresses that, in the case of perpetrators of serious crimes as defined under international law, these initiatives cannot be a substitute for formal judicial process but should rather be complementary options that are considered capable of promoting transitional justice. Their recommendation is that a national, consultative process be set in motion to gather views on appropriate forms of accountability and reconciliation.

Will the prosecution of the LRA leader Joseph Kony and his cohorts stop the war in Uganda? Should arrest warrants be issued for officials and officers of the Ugandan government and the Uganda People's Defence Forces (UPDF)? The same questions that concern the underlying nature of the South African conflict need to be asked of the northern Ugandan conflict. Will the conflict necessarily end with the defeat or prosecution of the Acholi perpetrators? What form of justice is required that goes beyond punishment? How can this be realised?

Truth-telling

Timothy Garton Ash identifies three ways of dealing with past atrocities: trials, purges and history lessons, arguing that it is the third path involving history lessons that is the most promising.[39] Michael Marrus identifies the difficulties inherent in criminal trials, arguing that the process involved undermines the quest for a full historical account of the past.[40] The duty of the court is to prosecute against a limited charge sheet. The duty of the defence team is to produce an array of legal arguments designed to challenge and exclude from the court record some of the basic information used in persuasive storytelling and history writing. Nowhere is this seen more clearly than in the trial of Saddam Hussein. He was convicted of crimes against humanity, for the killing and torture of 148 Shi'ite villagers in Dujail following a failed assassination attempt in 1982. He was sentenced to death and subsequently hanged. The courts did not address the more extensive record of his reign of terror. Questions as to whether the United States and the West had encouraged Hussein to invade Iran in 1980 – an invasion that led to the deaths of 1.5 million people – were not posed. The supply of chemical weapons components with which Hussein drenched Iran and the Kurds, the anarchy unleashed by American and British troops in the aftermath of what was described as a 'mission accomplished' and the use of the Hussein's Abu Ghraib torture chambers by American torturers are not part of the court record.

Hussein is the first ruler to be found guilty and made to pay the ultimate price for his crimes against humanity. There was no impunity – at least not for him.

Yet the truth behind Hussein's reign of terror remains untold; more is required than a trial that found Hussein guilty. Hundreds of thousands of Iraqis, Iranians, Kurds and people in the West still seek to know the causes, motives and perspectives that are part of the monstrous crimes during Hussein's rule. If truth has the capacity to heal it must include this level of disclosure. Historians, journalists and those who suffered most will wrestle with this challenge for decades to come. Saddam Hussein's trial has not brought closure for many people.

Trials are important and play a crucial role in attempts to deal with the past but *additional* means need to be found in order to achieve the level of reconciliation that Africa needs in order to restore itself. I am suggesting that a broad-based national conversation, conducted in both formal and informal ways, is one way of doing so.

Reconciliation and nation-building take time. Different ways must be found to promote what Harold Saunders calls 'a cumulative, multi-level and open-ended process of continuous interaction over time, engaging significant clusters of citizens in and out of government and the relationships they form to solve public problems . . . either within or between communities or countries'.[41] This is a process that probably could not have happened at the time of the South African TRC twelve years ago. Tensions were too high and the cost of failure too great. Negotiators who sat at the table to make peace chose to postpone issues of economic restitution until later. In politics change comes through the assertion of power rather than simply through an attempt to promote moral concern. This sense of power is beginning to manifest itself in South Africa through protests and resistance by those whose social and economic situation has not been adequately addressed following the advent of democracy.

THE LITMUS TEST

Luis Moreno-Ocampo, the chief prosecutor of the ICC, speaking in Cape Town, stated that his aim is a 'zero sum case load', or the absence of trials by the ICC, as a consequence of the effective functioning of national judicial systems and political reconciliation.[42] I suggest that there is an element in African peacebuilding that does not prioritise retribution in the way that it is prioritised in Europe, the United States and elsewhere. Whatever the reason for this may be, it is hard to conceive of a Western society within which a person who had played the role of an Ian Smith in the former Rhodesia or a P.W. Botha in South Africa is able to co-exist with former enemies who are today victors in a new order. Moreno-Ocampo's 'zero sum case load', at least in the sense of Western forms of justice, may be difficult to attain in Africa. Archbishop Tutu has observed: 'Retributive justice is largely Western. The African understanding is far more restorative – not so much to punish as to redress or restore a balance that has been knocked askew. The justice we hope for is restorative of the dignity of people.'[43] He ascribes this to what he sees as an African anthropology and more specifically *ubuntu*; it might just as easily be ascribed to the nature of the priorities that the African continent faces. Chief among these is survival and the need for social and material development.

The litmus test for all transitional justice options, which includes prosecutions, different forms of rectification and national conversation, is whether they ultimately contribute to political reconciliation and nation-building. If political reconciliation, in the sense of social cohesion and institutional reform, does not replace oppressive rule and social polarisation, any attempt to ensure the long-term rule of law is clearly doomed. Peace and justice are inextricably interrelated. It is difficult to get the balance right – and the final adjudicators in such matters are the citizenry of the nation whose task is to weather the storms of transition. The international community can assist but dare not dictate. Local ownership is an imperative.

NOTES AND REFERENCES

1. A. Habib, 'Economic policy and power relations in South Africa's transition to democracy', *World Development* 28(2), 2000: 28.
2. Constitution of the Republic of South Africa Act 200 of 1993, www.info.gov.za/documents/constitution/93cons.htm (accessed 19 November 2007).
3. The author's perceptions from his involvement in the TRC.
4. Y. Danieli, *International Handbook of Multigenerational Legacies of Trauma* (New York: Plenum Press, 1998), p. 678.
5. P-J. Salazar, 'How to recognize evil in politics', Symposium on 'Coming to Terms with Reconciliation', University of Wisconsin-Madison, 10–11 November 2006.
6. Promotion of National Unity and Reconciliation Act 34 of 1995.
7. Interviews conducted by the Institute for Justice and Reconciliation between 2000 and 2003. These interviews culminated in the publication: D. Foster, P. Haupt and M. de Beer, *The theatre of violence* (Cape Town: HSRC Press, 2005).
8. M. Charland, 'Reconciliation, identity and impiety', Symposium on 'Coming to Terms with Reconciliation', University of Wisconsin-Madison, 10–11 November 2006.

9. In private conversation with the author, 23 October 2000.

10. C. Achebe, *Morning yet on the first day of creation* (New York: Anchor Press, 1975).

11. W. Soyinka, *The burden of memory, the muse of forgiveness* (Oxford: Oxford University Press, 2000).

12. Soyinka, *The burden of memory*, p. 81 (emphasis added).

13. M. Mamdani, 'Reconciliation without justice', *Southern Africa Review of Books* 46, 1996: 3–5. See also M. Mamdani, 'The truth according to the Truth and Reconciliation Commission', in I. Amadiume and A. An-Naim (eds.), *The politics of memory: Truth, healing and social justice* (London: Zed Books, 2000), pp. 176–183.

14. Mamdani, 'The truth according to the Truth and Reconciliation Commission', p. 179.

15. Mamdani, 'Reconciliation without justice', p. 5.

16. P. French, 'Unchosen evil and moral responsibility', in A. Jovic (ed.), *War crimes and collective wrongdoing. A reader* (Malder, MA: Blackwell Publishers, 2001), pp. 4–41. See also D. Cooper, 'Collective responsibility, moral luck and reconciliation', in Jovic (ed.), *War crimes and collective wrongdoing*, p. 210.

17. D. Goldhagen, *Hitler's willing executioners* (London: Little, Brown and Company, 1996), pp. 34, 45–48.

18. Nelson Mandela, *Joint sittings of both houses of Parliament*, 1st Session, 1st Parliament, 24 May 1994, col. 1–15.

19. Nelson Mandela, *Joint sittings of both houses of Parliament*, 1st Session, 1st Parliament, 24 May 1994, col. 1–15.

20. E. Doxtader, *With faith in the works of words: The beginning of reconciliation in South Africa, 1985–1995* (Cape Town: David Philip, forthcoming). I am indebted to Doxtader for his detailed account of the debate leading to the establishment of the TRC.

21. Nelson Mandela, *Debates of the National Assembly* (Hansard), 2nd Session, 1st Parliament, 17 May 1995, col. 1349–1350.

22. Dullah Omar, Testimony delivered to Parliament's Joint Committee on Justice with regards to the Promotion of National Unity and Reconciliation Bill, 31 January 1995, p. 55, Archives of Parliament, Cape Town, South Africa.

23. Doxtader, *With faith in the works of words*, chap. 5.

24. Doxtader, *With faith in the works of words*, chap. 5.

25. F.W. de Klerk, Second submission of the National Party to the TRC. Political Party Recall Hearings: National Party, Cape Town, 14 May 1997, www.doj.gov.za/trc/submit/np2.htm (accessed 19 November 2007).

26. Leon Wessels, TRC State Security Council Hearings, Johannesburg, 14 October 1997, www.doj.gov.za/trc/special/security/3securit.htm (accessed 19 November 2007).

27. Democratic Party Submission to the TRC, Political Party Hearings, Cape Town, 20 August 1996, www.doj.gov.za/trc/special/party1/dp.htm (accessed 19 November 2007).

28. C. Williamson, Testimony delivered to the TRC at the Armed Forces Hearings Day 3: South African Police, Cape Town, 9 October 1997, www.doj.gov.za/trc/special/forces/sap.htm (accessed 19 November 2007).

29. A. Sachs, Fourth DT Lakdawala Memorial Lecture. New Delhi, 18 December 1998.

30. D.P. Mahomed, Judgment in the Constitutional Court of South Africa. Case CCT 17/96, 25 July 1996.

31. R.C. Roberts, *Injustice and rectification* (New York: Peter Lang, 2002).

32. D. Shriver, 'Long road to reconciliation: Some moral steppingstones'. Paper delivered at Oxford University, 14–16 September 1998.

33. Soyinka, *The burden of memory*, p. 81.

34. Mamdani, 'Reconciliation without justice'.

35. Nyame Goniwe, speaking at the conference 'Reparations and memorialisation: The unfinished business of the TRC', Cape Town, October 2000.

36. Sipho Tshabalala, speaking at the conference 'Reparations and memorialisation: The unfinished business of the TRC', Cape Town, October 2000.

37. Thembi Simelane-Nkadimeng, speaking at the conference 'The TRC: Ten years on', Cape Town, 20–21 April 2006.

38. OHCHR, *Options for accountability for reconciliation in Uganda*, February 2007.

39. T.G. Ash, 'The truth about dictatorship', *New York Review of Books*, 19 February 1998: 40.

40. M. Marrus, 'History and the Holocaust in the courtroom'. Paper delivered at the conference 'Searching for memory and justice: The Holocaust and apartheid', Yale University, 8–10 February 1998.

41. H.H. Saunders, *Politics is about relationship: A blueprint for the citizens' century* (New York: Palgrave Macmillan, 2005), p. 7.

42. Luis Moreno-Ocampo, speaking at the conference 'Transitional justice and peace', Cape Town, 17–26 February 2006.

43. M. Minow, *Between vengeance and forgiveness* (Boston: Beacon Press, 1998), p. 81.

3

Prosecute or Pardon?

Between Truth Commissions and War Crimes Trials

Kingsley Chiedu Moghalu

With a truth commission, governments make a pact with the devil. Our office looks for ways to send the devil to jail.

Carillo Prieto, Mexican Special Prosecutor

No one was to recall the past misdeeds of anyone except the Thirty, the Ten, the Eleven and the governors of the Piraeus, and not even these if they successfully submitted to an examination . . . Trials for homicide should be held in accordance with tradition in cases where a man had himself performed the act of killing or wounding.

Aristotle, *The Athenian Constitution*

INTRODUCTION

This chapter examines how political considerations condition the choices that states make when confronted with two possibilities, that of prosecuting or supporting prosecutions pardons or political responses that do not invoke criminal trials, such as amnesties and truth commissions. The aim is to demonstrate the tensions, in primarily domestic contexts, between order in its most basic sense as a pattern of social activity that guarantees the provision of the primary goals of social life[1] (in this context, stability) and justice. That occasional basic tension flares up in the context of societal transitions from conflict to peace, with the attendant questions of memory in societal construction. If prosecuting particular persons has the potential to destabilise the polity, should such a course be pursued? That debate is usually framed as one that concerns the choice that exists between holding criminal trials for mass atrocities or creating amnesties and truth commissions, or attempting some combination of all three options.

THE DILEMMA

There is no straightforward answer to the question of whether violators of international humanitarian law should be prosecuted or pardoned, especially when they are the political leaders and their prosecution may lead to a greater breakdown of order. Political exemptions from prosecution are not new. In some circumstances they are, in fact, a frequent approach when attempting to achieve the goal of peace and order. This conundrum goes to the heart of the contest for primacy between order and justice. The question is: Do political exemptions or pardons promote order or do they encourage a culture of impunity?[2] Should justice be done in every deserving case, even though the heavens may fall?

The proposition here is that while there is no 'best way' to tackle the question of justice there is a 'better way', whereby political exemptions from prosecution for violations of international humanitarian law should be the exception and not the rule – although in some circumstances the option of pardons cannot be ruled out. Generally legal accountability has a better track record than most of its alternatives but the real issue involves the kind of legal justice that should be implemented. My proposition is not based on the liberal theory of a Kantian peace but, as I shall seek to establish later, on the perspective of international society that combines the recognition of the sovereignty of states, the value of the individual human life that has been violated by genocide, crimes against humanity and war crimes, and the wishes of a political community, as ascertained either through a democratic process or by consensus.

This challenge demands neither excessive cynicism nor cosmopolitan and overly legalistic formulae. To say that the perpetrators of genocide, crimes against humanity and war crimes should, in the name of order, routinely be put beyond the reach of legal justice is a perspective that denies the evolution of international society. Alternatively, to insist that they must be prosecuted in all cases is to fail to take into account the other factors that frequently complicate the issue in cases where the dilemma is present. Such a position would be a false assumption that the world has entered a Kantian age of universal justice. It has not.

The realist perspective is that the problem of what to do with conquered leaders or those who, with blood on their hands, depart the Olympian heights of power through transition is a problem best left to political settlements and not to law courts. It is clear that, in some cases, insisting on prosecutions can do more harm than good and may mean that a peaceful settlement of a conflict is precluded, either triggering a breakdown of order or an escalation of a breakdown where one has already begun. Defeated parties may renew the conflict or if undefeated and seeing only prosecutions at the end of the tunnel, may lose any incentive to change swords into plowshares and seek instead the 'total victory' – and the sovereign state power that comes with it – that would serve as protection from accountability. In other words, for the sake of peaceful societal transitions or interstate relations, it may sometimes prove necessary to make a sacrifice for the future by sweeping violations of international humanitarian law under the carpet.

Ramesh Thakur has argued: 'Criminal law, however effective, cannot replace public or foreign policy. Determining the fate of defeated leaders is primarily a political question, not a judicial one. The legal clarity of judicial verdicts sits uncomfortably with the nuanced morality of confronting and overcoming, through a principled mix of justice and high politics, a troubled past.'[3] Henry Kissinger, commenting with admiration on the Congress of Vienna's magnanimous dispensation towards France after the Napoleonic wars, stated: 'It is the temptation of war to punish; it is the task of policy to construct. Power can sit in judgment, but statesmen must look to the future.'[4]

The realist argument against legalism, especially that which is dispensed by the international criminal tribunals, can be summarised as follows: legalism may claim jurisdiction over the actions of great powers, complicate global diplomacy and attack the historical concept that only sovereign states may impose criminal justice.[5] The realist perspective is that any attempt to completely isolate legal justice from political context is shortsighted. Legal justice is what a political community is prepared to enforce.[6] I define a 'political community' as a duly constituted society – sovereign, part of a sovereign entity, or a conglomeration of sovereign entities – with a cohesive political consensus on its internal social organisation, including what constitutes legal justice.

Such 'consensus' may be attained through a democratic or other deliberative process. In the international society the degree of legitimacy a political community enjoys depends increasingly on how democratic its political and law-making processes are. In the anarchic international system that I argue preceded the international society, this was not the case. In this definitional context, then, the ad hoc international criminal tribunal and the permanent International Criminal Court (ICC) is, for better or worse, a kind of justice model that groups of sovereign states have decided to create and enforce, thereby fulfilling an impulse that has been a characteristic of the twentieth century. The problem with the ad hoc tribunals is that they are the progeny of a more abstract level of political community, one whose 'agency' and democratic credentials, in the nature of a United Nations (UN) Security Council dominated by a few powerful states, is decidedly weaker than, say, a standing ICC that has been established directly by treaty. Thus, there is frequently tension between that agency, legally valid though it is, and the national or sub-national variants of political community.

As its relates specifically to the conundrum of whether to prosecute or pardon, the realist argument is bolstered by the claim that because international criminal tribunals lack the power to exercise pardons, they thereby lack an important attribute – political prerogative though it may be – of a proper criminal justice system. Such tribunals, the argument goes, cannot, in fact, have pardon power because they pretend to be above politics. Support for the argument in favour of discretionary pardon power as a prerequisite for legitimacy has been found in paper 74 of the United States Federalist papers, where Alexander Hamilton aptly expounded that 'humanity and good policy . . . dictate that the benign prerogative of pardoning should be as little as possible fettered or embarrassed . . . in seasons of insurrection or rebellion, a well-timed offer of pardon to the insurgents or rebels may restore the tranquility of the commonwealth'.[7]

The prerogative of mercy may indeed be necessary for the greater good. It is also an indispensable aspect of sovereign political authority. As Ruti Teitel has suggested, both criminal punishment and amnesties can be used to further the goals of political transition – especially where amnesties are made conditional.[8] However, she also argues that between the two there is a preponderance of forbearance of punishment power in order to advance those transitions.[9] This is a statistical reality but it should not be conflated with the respective impacts of both courses of action, which I address in greater detail below.

Arguments against prosecutions demonstrate the unequal and selective application of legalism in the service of interests that are often narrow and self-interested but which occasionally may be of a loftier provenance, as was the case with South Africa's transition to majority rule. Some great powers may support specific, localised efforts at international justice for reasons of narrow self-interest yet may prove reluctant to give carte blanche to across-the-board legal accountability – at the expense of client states.[10] To illustrate, the United States has not supported the establishment of an international criminal tribunal for East Timor (Timor-Leste) or widespread trials for mass atrocities in Chile because the crimes committed in those contexts, especially during the Cold War, were committed by regimes to which it provided strategic support.[11] This is precisely why international criminal justice, which failed to develop as expected after the Nuremberg Trials, only became possible after the end of the Cold War. The selectivity that accompanies the prosecute-or-pardon dilemma is one of the darker aspects of criminal prosecutions for violations of international humanitarian law and is an inevitable outcome of the nature of international society.

However, the argument that international criminal tribunals lack pardon power is erroneous. Firstly, provisions exist in the rules of procedure of the ad hoc international tribunals for Rwanda and the former Yugoslavia that allow the prosecutors of these tribunals, where permission is granted by the judges, to terminate judicial proceedings against an accused person for a variety of reasons, including those of policy.[12] While this is neither an acquittal (as no judicial finding on guilt or innocence has been made) nor a pardon in the strict legal sense, which can only occur following a conviction, it is a pardon in the 'policy' sense in that a prosecutor may exercise discretion as to whether or not to prosecute.

Secondly, even in its strict legal sense, provision for pardons has in fact been made in the statutes and procedural rules of the International Criminal Tribunal for Rwanda (ICTR) and the International Criminal Tribunal for the Former Yugoslavia (ICTY), the Special Court for Sierra Leone (SCSL) and the ICC. In an important subtlety, a person convicted by these tribunals may be pardoned only by the state in which the convict is serving a sentence, where conditions for pardon in the domestic legal systems of such states have been met. However, a convict cannot be pardoned without the approval of the judges of the international tribunal. This is a vivid illustration of how international criminal justice is constrained by the sovereignty of states. International courts do not have sovereignty, however independent or powerful they may appear to be. Admittedly, it is also the case that in a pure legal sense such courts do not have the direct or exclusive prerogative to exercise pardon power because that would run counter to the logic of their creation, which is to act as an accountability mechanism for egregious violations of international human rights.

Some compromise approaches remain mute on the question of whether to prosecute or pardon and instead seek to reconcile the requirements of peace and justice. A pragmatic approach is to negotiate peace agreements with warlords without sanctioning impunity.[13] A similar but more formalistic definition is that 'impunity means the impossibility, *de jure* or *de facto*, of bringing the perpetrators of human rights violations to account – whether in criminal, administrative, or disciplinary proceedings – since they are not subject to any inquiry that might lead to their being accused, arrested, tried and, if found guilty, sentenced to appropriate penalties and to making reparations to their victims'.[14]

A classic example of a pragmatic approach with a strong ethical component is that of the former Yugoslavia, where the United States negotiated the Dayton Peace Agreement between the warring parties in 1995, with Slobodan Milosevic, president of the rump Federal Republic of Yugoslavia, playing a key role in the negotiations. That agreement explicitly called for the prosecution of war criminals. Milosevic was not indicted at the time but there was no deal that guaranteed his immunity from indictment or prosecution, although the fact that he was a negotiating partner with the North Atlantic Treaty Organisation (NATO) may have led him to believe that he would not meet that fate. Milosevic was subsequently indicted by the ICTY for genocide and crimes against humanity and put on trial.[15]

Inherent in this approach is a deferral to a later stage of the decision to prosecute or pardon, placing the necessity for peace well before that of justice. The timing of the indictment is therefore critical. The cart of justice cannot – and, indeed, should not – be put before the proverbial horse of peace. A warlord may opt to continue a war in the hope of victory rather than come to the negotiating table where there is the threat of an indictment for violations of humanitarian law.

Another factor that must be considered in prosecute-or-pardon situations is the position of the UN, which is involved in most negotiations and settlements of armed conflicts. While the UN must frequently navigate between the idealism reflected in the goals of its Charter and the realism of world politics, it has taken a decidedly principled and ethical position on the prosecute-or-pardon question. Although it does not and cannot derogate from a sovereign political authority's right to pardon crimes under domestic law it has staked out a moral high ground regarding violations of international humanitarian law and refuses to recognise that any amnesties can be valid.[16] This is a position consistent with the UN's interpretation of sovereignty since the end of the Cold War. It supports the view that certain crimes are of international concern and cannot be the subject of purported amnesties by sovereign states, even if said crimes have been committed within their territories.

Having clarified the dilemma, I now turn to an examination of some cases where the question of whether to apply legal norms and prosecute individuals for war and other heinous crimes or whether to seek a political solution in the interests of order, has been acute.

BETWEEN TRUTH COMMISSIONS AND CRIMINAL TRIALS

Countries in transition often face difficult choices when deciding how to deal with the past in order to increase the chances of a better future. The transition may be one from armed conflict (Rwanda, Burundi, Sierra Leone and Mozambique, among others), a political one from dictatorship to democracy (Chile and Argentina, and Nigeria in the 1990s), a combination of both, or South Africa's transition from apartheid to majority rule in 1994. 'Transitional justice' is often a critical component of planning the way ahead. By 'transitional justice' I mean the phenomenon and process by which a society utilises legal and quasi-legal institutions to facilitate *fundamental change* from one political order to another or the construction of a new reality against the background of a profound historical memory.[17] It is a means of repudiating the past or building a bridge between it and the future. In short, transitional justice, like Janus, looks backwards and forwards at the same time. It often involves, but is not limited to, transitions towards democracy and the rule of law. It can also be an attempt by a society, either national or international, to confront a historical memory such as the Holocaust, slavery and the like. Such memories may not involve democratic transitions or rule-of-law issues but in all cases there is a common thread – the use of legal or quasi-legal institutions. The objectives of these institutions may vary, converge or diverge and may concern the establishment of the 'truth', reconciliation, reparation or criminal accountability.

Transitional justice tends to involve choices between prosecution and pardon, the latter sometimes in the form of amnesties, and for this reason it is one of the clearest expressions of the dilemma under examination. It has added relevance to this discussion because although the scope of transitional justice often appears to be limited to the domestic legal and political sphere it frequently deals with violations of international humanitarian law that may legitimately fall under international jurisdiction. For example, according to international law, apartheid is a crime against humanity.[18] Moreover, the Nuremberg Trials, though international, are regarded as an example of transitional justice because they marked the beginning of a shift from a fascist political order to a liberal democratic one.

What, then, is the best path to peace and reconciliation for fractured societies? There is a choice to be made between truth and reconciliation commissions that aim to uncover the past and which sometimes promise amnesty to individuals prepared to confess their crimes, and courts and tribunals – national or international – that aim to have criminal prosecutions. Does legalism unearth truth; does 'truth' lead to reconciliation in the absence of accountability; and is it necessarily the case that legal justice contributes to reconciliation? These are but some of the many questions to which there are no easy answers.

In the 1980s, truth and reconciliation commissions emerged as a middle ground between political exemptions from prosecutions and courtroom trials. Contrary to popular belief, these commissions were prominent in Latin America but did not begin in that region.[19] The commission that was created after South Africa's transition from apartheid to black majority rule is probably now the most famous example. No fewer than 25 countries have used combinations of truth commissions and amnesties to facilitate transitions towards stability.[20] Truth commissions have revealed wide variations in quality and content. Although truth commissions and criminal trials often claim the broadly similar aims of contributing to reconciliation they approach these goals from fundamentally different angles.

However, in some instances no middle ground is sought. After the civil war ended in Nigeria in 1970, and in Mozambique following the Mozambican General Peace Agreement (*Acordo Geral de Paz*) in 1992, complete amnesties were granted for acts committed during these conflicts (see Chapters 10 and 14 in this volume). From a legalist point of view it is fair to say that amnesty – impunity, in effect – was the price paid for peace and reconciliation.[21] Mozambique is worthy of more than a passing mention in this context, for it is a rare example of a country that has healed post-conflict wounds without resorting either to truth commissions or to criminal trials. Its success has been remarkable because, more than a decade after the guns fell silent, there is no indication that the country (both the government and its citizens) entertains any sense of loss or regret at the unique path it has followed.[22] Cultural factors and the strong role of religion and religious leaders in conflict resolution played a major role there, as did a deflection of the desire for retribution by placing the responsibility for atrocities upon the extraordinary circumstances of war rather than on the intentional acts of individuals.[23]

Spain, which adopted a comprehensive amnesty policy and avoided what Ruti Teitel has termed 'successor trials' in the post-Franco era, is another example of success for that policy.[24] Few societies have had a similar experience, however.

We can examine the strengths and weaknesses of truth commissions through the prism of South Africa's experience.

Forgiving and forgetting in South Africa

Nelson Mandela's release in 1990 after 27 years in prison marked the beginning of the end of apartheid. Mandela went from prison to the leadership of South Africa, becoming that country's first black president in 1994 and a symbol of freedom and majority rule. The transition from apartheid to black majority rule was an exhilarating experience for the majority but a traumatic one for most of the minority, who had to adjust to a velvet political revolution that righted one of recent history's most egregious wrongs. The gravity of the crime of apartheid, when considered in relation to the economic, political and social complexities of the 'Rainbow Nation', evoked the conundrum of whether to prosecute or pardon.

Apartheid's ghost had to be laid to rest if the country was to move forward but trials for crimes against humanity – legalism – were considered inappropriate in a situation where the difference between the outcome of a peaceful transition and a bloody civil war with a well-armed white minority government lay in the success or failure of negotiations. The negotiations resulted in the establishment of a Truth and Reconciliation Commission (TRC). The creation of the commission was based on faith in the cleansing power of truth, albeit largely without the accompanying legal culpability either for the crimes against humanity that had been perpetrated against the black majority or the acts of violence by apartheid's victims that were seen by many as a justified war of liberation from brutal tyranny but which were nevertheless violations of the official laws of an officially racist state.

In return for full confessions to the TRC, individuals responsible for major, politically motivated human rights crimes were able to obtain amnesty. As one member of the TRC commented, South Africa did not see retributive justice as an indispensable prerequisite for reconciliation. 'The TRC approach trades justice for truth,' he observed frankly. 'It is surely for every nation to decide its own approach to these kinds of difficult situations.'[25] In a similar vein, Archbishop Desmond Tutu, who served as chairperson of the TRC and as its philosopher-king, has described the statesmanship of both F.W. de Klerk, who was South Africa's last apartheid state president, and Nelson Mandela:

> In our case, FW de Klerk showed remarkable courage in his reforms, but he was blessed not with an intransigent, bitter and vengeful counterpart,

but with the almost saintly magnanimity of Nelson Mandela. The whites wanted to dig in their heels and the liberation movement was hell-bent on demanding every pound of flesh through retributive justice akin to the Nuremberg trials. Neither leader heeded these calls.[26]

The TRC approach that attempted to treat justice and truth as mutually exclusive is problematic. One commentator has attempted to create a subtle but ultimately unsatisfactory distinction between the amnesties that were granted by the South African TRC and blanket amnesties: 'In fact the TRC was the best solution. It ensured that amnesty did not mean what the word literally means in Greek ("forgetting"), but was accompanied by a full revelation of the truth; a blanket amnesty would have allowed the criminals to hide everything forever.'[27] This suggests that the amnesties granted by the TRC ensured a significant degree of accountability, which in fact they did not. This reality is demonstrated by Derrick's apt characterisation of the disappointment some South Africans felt at seeing: 'murderous henchmen of the former regime walking free, with their crimes exposed and recorded but not punished'.[28]

The TRC was officially established by an Act of parliament in 1995.[29] Because the South African TRC provides a good example of the several possible facets of such commissions (which are found to a greater or lesser extent in the variations on the TRC model adopted elsewhere), it is helpful to quote the Act of parliament at some length. The legislation provides, *inter alia*:

> Since the Constitution of the Republic of South Africa, 1993 (Act No 200 of 1993), provides a historic bridge between the past of a deeply divided society characterized by strife, conflict, untold suffering and injustice, and a future founded on the recognition of human rights, democracy and peaceful co-existence for all South Africans, irrespective of colour, race, class, belief or sex;
>
> AND SINCE it is deemed necessary to establish the truth in relation to past events as well as the motives and circumstances in which gross violations of human rights have occurred, and to make the findings known in order to prevent a repetition of such acts in future;
>
> AND SINCE the Constitution states that there is a need for understanding but not for vengeance, a need for reparation but not for retaliation, a need for *ubuntu* but not for victimization;

AND SINCE the Constitution states that in order to advance such reconciliation and reconstruction amnesty shall be granted in respect of acts, omissions and offences associated with political objectives committed in the course of the conflicts of the past;

2.(1) There is hereby established a juristic person to be known as the Truth and Reconciliation Commission ...

4. The functions of the Commission shall be to achieve its objectives, and to that end the Commission shall –

(*a*) facilitate, and where necessary initiate or coordinate, inquiries into –

(i) gross violations of human rights, including violations which were part of a systematic pattern of abuse;

(ii) the nature, causes and extent of gross violations of human rights, including the antecedents, circumstances and factors, context, motives and perspectives which led to such violations;

(iii) the identity of all persons, authorities, institutions and organizations involved in such violations;

(iv) the question whether such violations were the result of deliberate planning on the part of the State or a former state or any organs, or of any political organizations, liberation movement or other group or individual; and

(v) accountability, political or otherwise, for any such violation; ...

(*c*) facilitate the granting of amnesty in respect of acts associated with political objectives, by receiving from persons desiring to make full disclosure of all the relevant facts relating to such acts, applications for the granting of amnesty in respect of such acts, and transmitting such applications to the Committee on Amnesty for its decision, and by publishing decisions granting amnesty, in the *Gazette*; ...

(*e*) prepare a comprehensive report which sets out its activities and findings, based on factual and objective information and evidence collected or received by it or placed at its disposal;

(*f*) make recommendation to the President with regard to –

(i) the policy which should be followed or measures which should be taken with regard to the granting of reparation to victims or the taking of other measures aimed at rehabilitating and restoring the human and civil dignity of victims ...

All things considered, the truth and reconciliation approach to South Africa's democratic transition was the best way forward at the time. Had the victims of apartheid insisted on legal accountability, negotiations between them and the white minority might well have broken down and led to the escalation of an internal armed conflict in which all sides would have been the ultimate losers.

The benefits that result from a particular approach to transitional justice at a specific point in time do not necessarily mean that approach will prove similarly beneficial in every situation. Even the passage of time can lead to a different perspective on the particular situation in question. What, then, are the pros and cons of truth and reconciliation commissions?

The pros and cons

The case for TRCs is appealing. They approach the issue of reconciliation with a strong – and welcome – focus on victims, that is, restorative justice, in which an effort is made to restore the victim's human dignity. When a perpetrator confesses his crimes, the victim, by exercising a moral prerogative to forgive, is empowered and thus restored in a psychological sense. Such restorative justice may also be a contextually apt approach. Archbishop Tutu has noted that victim-focused approaches to justice are more akin to historical concepts of justice in African societies: 'Retributive justice is largely Western. The African understanding is far more restorative – not so much to punish as to redress or restore a balance that has been knocked askew. The justice we hope for is restorative of the dignity of our people.'[30] Moreover, criminal trials in either common-law systems or international criminal tribunals where common-law adversarial procedures are dominant frequently fail to address the victim as a person and focus exclusively on the perpetrator.[31]

A second benefit of truth commissions is that, because they are more accessible to ordinary citizens than criminal trials are, they can have a greater healing effect on the wider society. The public airing of crimes, accompanied by confessions, engenders a greater degree of public participation than the arcane technicalities that are common to criminal trials. Thirdly, the amnesties offered by truth and reconciliation commissions encourage a greater willingness by persons who have been involved in the events in question to participate in the process. In so doing, TRCs tend to yield a far more complete narrative of events.

Fourthly, it is worth noting the 'truth' dimension of truth commissions. Positing that truth commissions are a superior vehicle for eliciting the 'truth' than prosecutions, Priscilla Hayner has argued:

The purpose of criminal trials is not to expose the truth . . . but to find whether the criminal standard of proof has been satisfied on specific charges. A measure of truth may emerge in this process, but trials are limited in the truth they are able to tell as they must comply with rules of evidence which often exclude important information.[32]

Martti Koskenniemi has also questioned the ability of a criminal trial to find or establish the 'truth' of complex events involving the actions of many international players, including the Great Powers and international organisations.[33] In this context, to what degree 'truth' is really established in war crimes trials is limited by the inadequate and selective treatment of context. This happens when one of the parties to the conflict – or a third entity that may or may not be a party to the conflict – establishes the framework for its resolution (including a criminal trial as one possible framework) that excludes the acts of another of the parties. This situation has been described as a '*Differend*'.[34] The party whose acts are excluded from accountability is usually either the victor or an external party that undertook peace enforcement through military action.[35] In this scenario – a common one in international criminal justice – the question is whose 'truth' is established with trials of an individual or a select group of political or military leaders.

Finally, proponents of truth commissions argue that such mechanisms facilitate reconciliation more effectively than prosecutions, and that criminal trials may hinder rather than promote reconciliation.[36] South Africa's Archbishop Tutu has expressed reservations that international criminal tribunals established by the UN:

> . . . risk disrupting fragile situations of transition from repression and conflict to a more democratic dispensation. Such tribunals may well ensure accountability and show there will be no impunity. That is fine as far as it goes. But you need something more than retributive justice for healing. In and of itself, the judicial process is handicapped. It alone cannot be effective in reconciling a society divided by hatred.[37]

In an elegant and forceful articulation of the same argument, Ramesh Thakur has commented:

> The international criminal justice route takes away from concerned societies the right to decide whether, how and who to prosecute for alleged

mass crimes . . . It also takes away from them the options of alternative modes of reconciliation. The purely juridical approach to transitional justice traps and suspends communities in the prism of past hatreds. South Africa, Mozambique and Rwanda have all made deliberate policy choices to escape cycles of retributive violence. The record of 'restorative' justice in bringing closure to legacies of systematic savagery is superior to that of institutions of international criminal justice; the latter's closure is more authoritative but also more partial and premature.[38]

On closer examination, however, the truth and reconciliation model in general, including the 'South African miracle', has significant weaknesses. These shortcomings make criminal trials preferable to the South African model except where unique political circumstances demand it. South Africa's TRC, for example, appears to have been the object of far more international than domestic admiration.[39] Even some thoughtful critics of 'show trials' have a hard time providing evidence that establishes the salutary effects of 'truth-telling' at truth commissions.[40] On the contrary, for all the controversies that attended or still surround them, the Nuremberg and Tokyo Trials of half a century ago have clear, empirical benefits in terms of their influence on the subsequent evolution of the societies that were judged to have perpetrated the crimes. It is possible that the contemporary international tribunals for the former Yugoslavia and Rwanda may ultimately have a similar effect, many years hence. A recent opinion poll in South Africa found that only 17 per cent of those interviewed thought that the TRC process had had a positive impact on that country, while two-thirds of the individuals interviewed were of the view that race relations had actually worsened post-TRC.[41]

If, as I have argued, impunity is the absence of accountability, it follows that establishing a culture of accountability is both normal and desirable. This is not blind legalism but rather the belief that it is necessary to introduce an element of accountability in order to deter the recurrence of impunity, which in itself generates conflicts. In other words, if impunity sows the seed that germinates an actual breakdown of order, is skirting accountability a wise choice in the medium to longer term? Would *habitual* amnesties not then be impunity, and is that a path to order or disorder? Accountability in a complete sense is not – or should not be – altered by subjective definitions such as those advanced by the advocates of truth commissions. Accountability does not mean 'truth-telling' for mass atrocities without the possibility of further consequences. This is so even though other goals, including the establishment of the truth, may be seen as the end result of accountability.

A consequence of this weakness of definition and expectation is that truth and reconciliation commissions, unable as they are to ensure or enforce accountability for mass atrocities, ultimately fail to fulfil the deep hunger that victims often have for justice. Those who favour truth commissions over criminal trials in every circumstance, whether by reason of a realist bent or a genuine belief in the moral superiority of truth commissions over trials, fail to take into account this fundamental human desire for justice. Wole Soyinka, the Nigerian poet and Nobel Laureate, has aptly argued that justice is the first condition of humanity.[42] From Hedley Bull's perspective, order is functionally prior to justice. However, the relationship between the two is an intricate one. While justice should not be done though the world perish, that justice is actually the flip side of order is demonstrated by:

- the central place justice occupies in virtually all the world's major religions, which describe it as a constitutive value; and
- the central place that issues of justice occupy in world politics. Justice has many faces, however, including, even in the Scriptures, forgiveness under certain conditions. The point then becomes that while justice is not always an achievable ideal, avoiding it as a matter of course is not an option.

Experience in several post-conflict societies has shown that where perpetrators of grave human rights crimes are not prosecuted for any number of reasons the banished ghost of the victims' thirst for justice returns years later to haunt these societies, reopening old wounds assumed to have 'healed'. This weakness was famously illustrated by the spate of lawsuits in the United Kingdom, Spain and Chile in the late 1990s that sought to bring former Chilean President Augusto Pinochet to justice for the massive human rights violations that his government had committed decades earlier. The polarisation of domestic public opinion that accompanied Pinochet's eventual return to Chile effectively refutes the argument that truth commissions are a sure path to truth and reconciliation. The contemporary view is that the amnesty that had been granted to Pinochet as part of Chile's transition back to democracy was a straightforward case of impunity.

A similar situation exists in Argentina, where a military coup in 1976 overthrew a democracy and instituted a draconian reign of terror in which an estimated

30 000 Argentines were systematically persecuted, kidnapped, tortured and murdered during an internal conflict (the 'dirty war') with guerrillas until 1983, when democracy was restored. The perpetrators of these state-sponsored crimes were not punished, protected as they were by several decrees in which former President Carlos Menem granted pardons to military officials and former guerrillas.[43] In a policy reversal, Néstor Kirchner, who was elected president in May 2003, initiated a process of investigating and arresting members of the former regime responsible for these crimes, the national legislature has annulled some of the laws that shielded the armed forces from prosecution, and a court ruled unconstitutional two of the ten decrees by which Menem granted pardons to members of the army in 1989 and 1990.[44] A public opinion poll in 2003 showed that a clear majority of Argentines (60 per cent) favoured reopening investigations, and many believe that until justice is done and the soldiers responsible for the crimes are held accountable, Argentina's society will be unable to reach closure and make peace with itself. One Argentine professional put it thus: 'How can you call yourself a democracy if these people are exempt from prosecution? How can people have faith in justice in the future if it hasn't dealt with the past?'[45]

This is the problem with 'forgiving and forgetting'. Just as the Chilean and Argentine dilemmas have become clearer through the wisdom of hindsight, so the South African transition has not remained immune from a reappraisal of the conventional wisdom that the TRC process was a saintly affair. There were those who, although recognising the necessary expediency of South Africa's TRC, were somewhat sceptical of how history would judge the TRC in the longer term. Some years ago I argued that 'South Africa's case may appear unique, but not enough time has elapsed since the TRC to evaluate it more definitively'.[46] By early 2004, a clear split had developed in the ranks of President Thabo Mbeki's government in South Africa over the arrest of a former security police colonel charged with the murder of three anti-apartheid activists – an event that appeared to presage an attempt by some senior security officials in the African National Congress (ANC) government to bring several generals of the former apartheid security force to justice.[47] The incident led to fears that South Africa's 'miracle' might unravel and prompted a flurry of negotiations between apartheid-era white intelligence operatives and the ANC government amidst comments by pro-accountability ANC stalwarts about the possibility of 'Nuremberg-style trials'. The angst has sometimes been mutual: there has been a similar backlash within the minority white community over the ANC government's appointment to senior security posts of individuals considered 'terrorists' under apartheid.[48]

When contemplating societies that opted for the collective amnesia of blanket amnesties, the experience of countries such as Nigeria is also instructive. Thirty years after its civil war, the country moved from a wilful suspension of memory ('no victor, no vanquished' was the phrase used by the country's President Yakubu Gowon when the war ended in 1970) to the establishment in 2001 of a truth commission with a temporal mandate stretching back more than three decades. Had Gowon's policy been more consistently implemented over time, Nigeria might have gone the way of Mozambique and Spain, despite the large-scale war crimes committed during a civil war that was fought to forestall the secession of its eastern region, which declared itself the independent Republic of Biafra. Bad governance, human rights abuses and the perceived political marginalisation of the Igbo and some other ethnic groups have caused serious strains in the body politic.

In June 1999 President Olusegun Obasanjo appointed a Human Rights Investigation Commission headed by the respected former Nigerian Supreme Court Judge Chukwudifu Oputa. The commission, which visited South Africa to absorb lessons from that country's TRC, investigated and received public submissions on numerous human rights abuses, in particular, political assassinations, and submitted its report on 28 May 2002. It was also required to recommend judicial, legislative and institutional measures that could redress past human rights abuses in the country. Thus judicial accountability in the form of full-blown trials for mass crimes is a possibility that, though unlikely, cannot be excluded in the future. The government did not release for public consumption either the report of the commission or its recommendations regarding redress. Nevertheless, it may well be that, for some societies, deferring the day of reckoning might facilitate a stronger ability to cope with the trauma of truth commissions or trials at a later date.

A third weakness of truth commissions is that they tend to make a false distinction between *truth*, as supposedly represented by truth commissions, and *justice*, as represented by criminal trials. It has not been empirically established that criminal trials, despite the inherent clash of interests between the defendants and the prosecutor, are intrinsically incapable of arriving at the truth or indeed that they frequently fail to do so. Certainly there are cases where an accused may be found not guilty on the basis of a technicality or a prosecutor's failure to establish guilt with the required standard of proof while, beyond the courtroom, other individuals or interests 'know' that the accused is actually or probably guilty but the cases where individual responsibility for mass atrocity is factually and judicially established outnumbers the cases where it is not. When it comes to violations of international humanitarian law, crimes such as genocide, crimes against humanity and war crimes are – or can – rarely be kept secret. The planning and commission of such crimes usually involves a significant number of agents and a command structure.

In some cases before the international criminal tribunals, in particular the ICTR, accused persons have pleaded guilty and confessed the details of their crimes.[49] These confessions were just as remarkable as any in a truth commission, and shed light on the Rwandan genocide. In none of these cases was the plea of guilt made in exchange for an amnesty, as courts are bound to impose punishment once the guilt of the accused person is established in a criminal trial.[50]

Moreover, even the extent of the 'truth' that can be unearthed by a truth commission can be circumscribed by the commission's terms of reference. South Africa's TRC did not examine apartheid as a crime in itself – a not insubstantial omission for so historic an exercise.[51] It has similarly been noted that the remit of the TRC did not include acts based on official policies that were not illegal under apartheid but, though not involving violence, were just as powerfully oppressive and discriminatory – race classification, social segregation and forced population movements.[52] That these policies at the core of apartheid did not receive the scrutiny of the TRC lays the 'truth' and substance of the commission's work justifiably open to charges of distortion. Thus truth commissions, like international criminal tribunals, can be influenced by the *Differend*.

Finally, while truth and reconciliation commissions are an option for dealing with some kinds of mass crime, especially crimes against humanity, that approach is of little help when the crime in question is that of genocide. The scope of the genocide that occurred in Rwanda in 1994 was so vast, the timespan of its commission so short and its cruelty so shocking, that the Rwandan government that came to power shortly thereafter decided that justice had to be done for reconciliation to be possible.

The case for criminal trials

Having examined the strengths and weaknesses of truth commissions, I now turn to the case for prosecutions. There are a number of arguments that make prosecutions a necessary component of long-term conflict resolution in strife-torn societies. Firstly, justice (accountability through punishment) has a deep psychological impact on individuals and, by extension, on societies. When justice is done, and is seen to have been done, it tends to provide a catharsis for those who have been physically and psychologically scarred by violations of international humanitarian law. Deep-seated resentments – key obstacles to co-existence – are removed, and people on different sides of the divide can feel that a clean slate has been achieved. This objective is better attained when the justice that is handed down is a complete one, involving not only retribution but restoration.

Secondly, trials establish responsibility for crimes adjudicated, thereby negating the risk of a belief in collective guilt, which can hinder peaceful co-existence. Other members of the group to which the defendant or group of defendants may belong are thus spared the weight and shame of guilt for crimes they did not commit and are therefore free to participate in national life on equal terms. This factor helps answer questions such as: Are all Serbs responsible for the crimes of their extremist leaders in the wars of the former Yugoslavia? Are all Hutus to blame for the genocide in Rwanda in 1994?

In this context, I differ on both legal and policy grounds with Mark Osiel's view of 'administrative massacre' as a possible counterpoint to individual responsibility.[53] According to Osiel, incidents of administrative massacre 'characteristically involve many people in co-ordinated ways over space and time', impeding the necessity of proving the wilful acts of particular defendants.[54] The Holocaust in Nazi Germany and the Rwandan genocide are perhaps the best examples of administrative massacre, involving many people and central co-ordination. It is an appealing argument not because it successfully makes the case for mass amnesia and thus provides a sociological excuse for impunity, but because it demonstrates why a synthesis of criminal prosecutions and truth and reconciliation commissions is often necessary. Another writer, in what is arguably a version of the 'administrative massacre' theory, has criticised the 'individualisation' thesis, noting that individualisation of guilt is not neutral in its effects because it fails to address the political, moral and organisational structures that bred the crime: 'To focus on individual leaders may even serve as an alibi for the population at large to relieve itself from responsibility.'[55]

That may well be but these arguments, in particular Osiel's attempt to suspend *mens rea,* do not address the bald fact that the act of participation in a conspiracy to commit genocide, for example, is ultimately an *individual* decision, regardless of the prevailing pressures of the circumstance in question. From the point of view of legalism, it is only a valid defence of mental incapacity, as established in a court of law, which should exculpate an individual from personal responsibility for his or her acts and omissions. Under the Statutes of the ICTR and the ICTY even the well-known defence of following superior orders offers no relief from individual criminal responsibility but may be considered only in mitigation of punishment.[56] For individuals to hide behind this defence for violations of positive law is a path not to order but to disorder.

From a policy viewpoint, accepting the concept of administrative massacre totally negates any contribution that a juridical approach can make to the prevention of conflict. That the leaders and other active perpetrators of the Rwandan genocide assumed they would evade possible justice by spreading the guilt, by roping in thousands of their fellow-countrymen and -women in the commission of the crime, is an illustration of why administrative massacre is an unsustainable approach to punishing mass atrocities. Leaders who orchestrate mass abuses should pay the price, even if it has the effect of exculpating the masses. This is a necessary price of leadership that allows societies to move on after conflict. It would be an unsupportable argument, for example, to say that the German citizenry at large or all Japanese should bear legal responsibility for the Holocaust or the crimes committed by the Japanese Imperial Army in Asia prior to and during the Second World War.

Thirdly, another point in favour of criminal trials as a contribution to conflict resolution and transitional justice is that trials conducted by international or national courts establish an indisputable, even if incomplete, historical record of events, with legally binding consequences. The problem with this aspect of justice is that courts may not be truly independent or impartial in every instance. Expecting a historical record to be generated through a criminal trial raises some problems because, as has been noted: 'For any major event of international politics – and situations where the criminal responsibility of political leaders is invoked is inevitably such – there are many truths and many stakeholders for them.'[57] Nevertheless, where guilt is established, extremists convicted of violations of international humanitarian law are frequently banished from the political arena, creating room for the growth of a democratic culture. This was certainly the case in Germany following the Nuremberg Trials.

Limitations of criminal trials
There are few perfect options when confronting impunity and attempting to achieve a significant degree of peaceful co-existence. Criminal trials, either national

or international, are not immune from the complex and messy nature of such efforts. The chief limitation of a criminal prosecution approach is that trials in courts of law for crimes committed in a political context are no substitute for political and other processes of reconciliation. Advocates of legalism – often human rights, non-governmental organisations (NGOs) – frequently speak and write as if a courtroom trial were a panacea for all the challenges that face a society broken by war or repression. Trials provide a necessary foundation for additional, alternative processes of conflict resolution. However, they are often perceived as vengeance by the parties to a conflict that are in a relatively weak position at the time that 'justice' is sought, and this is an important limitation. Especially in the case of civil wars, post-conflict peace processes must include political dialogue involving opposing groups, even where trials that determine individual criminal responsibility are major components of such a process.

Pursuant to this critique is the question whether criminal trials result in the oft-touted benefit of reconciliation. Archbishop Tutu makes the point that criminal trials may check impunity but they do not really contribute to reconciliation. He cites the example of the ICTR, where the Hutus argued that the Tutsis instigated the trials against Hutu politics and the military.[58] Tutu's point is valid, though only up to a point, which is that by juxtaposing impunity with reconciliation one deals with two different concepts. This is a distinction that has often escaped policy-makers when they seek to utilise criminal law as an instrument of reconciliation.[59] Hannah Arendt, in her famous critique of the Eichmann trial in Israel, sought a way out of this hazy conceptualisation by trying to keep things simple:

> The purpose of the trial is to render justice, and nothing else; even the noblest ulterior purposes – 'the making of a record of the Hitler regime' – can only detract from the law's main business: to weigh the charges brought against the accused, to render judgment and to mete out punishment.[60]

This simplicity, appealing as it is, remains difficult to realise. The political contexts of the events that give rise to criminal trials for violations of humanitarian law means that trials often have a didactic dimension, which is one reason why the excessive focus on the accused has come under criticism.[61] Such crimes frequently involve large numbers of people who have been victimised because of their identity. For this reason, trials for genocide, crimes against humanity and war crimes go beyond 'pure' criminal trials for ordinary crimes but are inherently political. So while the individual on trial answers for him- or herself and not as a group, the group factor is frequently present in the form of conspiracy or common purpose, as well as in the form of the victim as a member of a group (ethnic, religious, political and so on). And because war crimes trials and tribunals are often part of societal transitions or seek to construct societal order, it is difficult to get away from the 'larger issues' of which the trial becomes a microcosm, although Arendt is surely right about the primary purpose of a trial. If these larger issues are taken into account, why focus solely on the defendant? Justice is surely more complete if the victims as a targeted group are recompensed in some form – hence the argument in favour of restorative justice that is victim-focused, which may be additional to, or outside of, a criminal trial context.

There are two important questions that Archbishop Tutu's critique does not answer. The first is whether reconciliation, certainly a desirable but essentially moral or metaphysical concept, is a necessary condition for peace. The second is whether criminal trials represent 'vengeance'. The answer to the first question depends on the prism through which the challenge is viewed – Hobbesian, Grotian or Kantian? There is no question that Archbishop Tutu's perspective is a Kantian one of universal or permanent peace ('peace on earth'). As Hedley Bull has noted, this aspiratory paradigm stands in stark contrast to actual historical experience.[62] If this is so, it follows that we establish unrealistic expectations of criminal trial processes and then criticise such trials for having failed when they do not transform the world as we expect them to. To say, as Archbishop Tutu does, that trials do not achieve reconciliation but truth commissions do is an artificial comparison, for by so doing we would be vesting in criminal trials the expectation of an unlikely outcome. Rather, trials may, as noted above, support the creation of a historical record, which is more achievable than reconciliation. The expectation of reconciliation has arisen mainly due to the language that has been used in the preambles to the statutes of international criminal tribunals such as that for Rwanda, where reconciliation was explicitly stated to be one of the expected outcomes of the ICTR.

There is no empirical proof of any situation, including the Nuremberg Trials and the trials for the Rwandan genocide, where trials have in and of themselves created reconciliation. The sociological standards against which criminal trials for mass atrocities must be judged, if we are to go beyond their primary purpose of rendering justice, is that of the establishment of co-existence, expressed, for example, through a democratic culture and economic and social integration. In other words, peace must be established in the Grotian sense of the absence of order-destabilising conflict.

Some argue that criminal trials are a form of vengeance. While one response might be that such trials prevent unregulated, vigilante justice that is in itself a threat to order, it must be recognised that trials do indeed represent society's vengeance – organised, sanctioned and controlled though it may be – on individuals who engage in deviant behaviour on a massive scale. This is only a reflection of the current state of evolution of international and national societies. It does not make such trials any less desirable, though 'reconciliation' may be a desirable objective too. Following Archbishop Tutu's line of thought to the logical conclusion it omits, it is worth noting that justice is an essential underpinning of all major religions, just as forgiveness and reconciliation are. In this sense, legal justice and reconciliation are but two sides of a coin, with one much more easily achievable in practice than the other. This is so even if, seen from a certain perspective that attaches a high degree of faith to human character, truth and reconciliation mechanisms create a false impression of their superiority over courtroom trials that, because of their technical processes, do not always bring out the best in human nature.

Synthesis

Truth commissions and criminal trials are not mutually exclusive. Sovereign states may opt for truth commissions without eliminating the jurisdiction of international tribunals or national courts. It is possible, even advisable, that both options be exercised at different points of a continuum. A state may begin with one and bring closure with the other – or use both in tandem. Sierra Leone is an example of a post-conflict society that has used both truth commissions for crimes under its national jurisdiction, and criminal trials for violations of international humanitarian law. In that instance the truth commission approach has been particularly beneficial because it encompassed the experiences of children – who had a uniquely prominent role as protagonists and victims of the Sierra Leone conflict – where legalism could not. The policy decision that children would not be tried before the SCSL despite the role several played as child soldiers, meant that the Sierra Leone TRC provided a forum for them to participate in their country's transitional justice process.

This dual approach is also recommended because the scope of mass atrocities committed in a given case all too often overwhelms either a judicial tribunal or a truth commission where either one has the sole task of addressing these crimes. Moreover, a combined approach better addresses the reality that, as David Forsythe put it in a different context, 'some problems are simply too large for a judicial solution'.[63] Not all perpetrators of human rights crimes can be brought to justice but neither should all such persons escape legal accountability. This is a safe middle ground.

Another approach is to recognise that truth commissions and courts are fundamentally different. Hayner, writing on truth commissions, has argued that they are not a substitute for prosecutions and should not be seen as second best.[64] In theory, he presents an excellent case for truth commissions: they have their place because legalism cannot be a practical response in every situation of mass atrocity. In practice, however, truth commissions have all too often served as an alternative to criminal prosecutions. Such mechanisms are most useful when what they are and what they are *not* is quite clear to the societies in which they are used as part of a political/societal transition. It is when they seek to serve, in effect, as a smokescreen of 'accountability' in which a recounting of history replaces culpability that the limitations of truth commissions are painfully exposed.

NOTES AND REFERENCES

1. H. Bull, *The anarchical society* (New York: Columbia University Press, 1977), p. 83.
2. The word 'pardons' is used in a broad sense to describe not only formal pardons for offences but also policy decisions not to prosecute persons who, *prima facie*, may be guilty of violations of international humanitarian law.
3. R. Thakur, 'Politics vs justice at The Hague', *International Herald Tribune*, 15 August 2002.
4. H. Kissinger, *A world restored: Metternich, Castlereagh, and the problems of peace, 1812–1822* (Boston: Houghton Mifflin, 1973), p. 138.
5. Testimony of Professor Jeremy Rabkin, Hearings on International Justice, Committee on International Relations, United States House of Representatives, 28 February 2002.
6. Testimony of Professor Jeremy Rabkin.
7. Testimony of Professor Jeremy Rabkin.
8. R.G. Teitel, *Transitional justice* (Oxford and New York: Oxford University Press, 2000), pp. 51–58.
9. Teitel, *Transitional justice*, p. 52.
10. See J. Nevins, 'Justice still eludes Indonesia', *International Herald Tribune*, 19 February 2004, p. 7.
11. Nevins, 'Justice still eludes Indonesia'. See also J.A. Winters, 'US media and their ignorance partly blamable for E Timor's misery', *Jakarta Post*, 28 May 2002, discussing United States media

reporting of claims of United States involvement in Indonesia's invasion of East Timor in 1975.

12. See *Prosecutor v Bernard Ntuyahaga*, Case No ICTR-98-40-1, 23 February 1999.

13. I define 'impunity' as the absence of accountability and the rule of law within states or other formal organisations, in which coercive power, not rules, regulations or law, is the organising principle.

14. See 'The Administration of Justice and the Human Rights of Detainees: Question of the Impunity of the Perpetrators of Human Rights Violations (civil and political)', Revised Final Report prepared by Mr Joinet for the Commission on Human Rights, UN Document E/CN 4 Sub 2/1997/20/Rev 1, 2 October 1997, p. 17.

15. K.C. Moghalu, *Rwanda's genocide: The politics of global justice* (London: Palgrave, 2005).

16. Article 10 of the Statute of the Special Court for Sierra Leone provides: 'An amnesty granted to any person falling within the jurisdiction of the Special Court in respect of the crimes referred to in articles 2 to 4 of the present Statute shall not be a bar to prosecution.' The crimes referred to are crimes against humanity, violations of article 3 common to the Geneva Conventions and of Additional Protocol II, and other serious violations of international humanitarian law. See Statute of the SCSL, UN Doc S/2000/915.

17. See Teitel, *Transitional justice*. See also I. Amadiume and A. An-Na'im, *The politics of memory: Truth, healing and social justice* (London and New York: Zed Books, 2000).

18. International Convention on the Suppression and Punishment of the Crime of Apartheid, adopted by UN General Assembly Resolution 3068 (XXVIII) of 30 November, 1073, UN Doc A/9030. Article 7(*j*) of the Statute of the ICC lists 'the crime of apartheid' as one of several crimes that constitute crimes against humanity.

19. The Commission of Inquiry into the Disappearance of People in Uganda since 25 January 1971 was established by President Idi Amin Dada in Uganda in 1974. See P.B. Hayner, *Unspeakable truths: Facing the challenge of truth commissions* (New York and London: Routledge, 2002), p. 51. As Hayner notes without irony, the 1974 Ugandan commission is one of the few in her study that was not part of a fundamental political transition, having been established by Amin in response to external political pressure to investigate the disappearances that were perpetrated by officials of his own regime. When President Yoweri Museveni came to power in 1986 he established another truth commission, the Ugandan Commission of Inquiry into Violations of Human Rights.

20. Argentina, Bolivia, Chad, Chile, East Timor (Timor-Leste), Ecuador, El Salvador, Germany, Ghana, Guatemala, Haiti, Malawi, Nepal, Nigeria, Panama, Peru, Philippines, Serbia and Montenegro, Sierra Leone, South Africa, South Korea, Sri Lanka, Uganda, Uruguay and Zimbabwe. See United States Institute of Peace, Truth Commissions Digital Collection, www.usip.org (accessed 15 February 2008).

21. J. Derrick, 'Reconciliation: Incompatible or inseparable?', *African Topics* (August–September), 2000: 10–12.

22. See H. Cobban, 'Healing lessons from another war-torn society – Mozambique', *Christian Science Monitor*, 8 May 2003.

23. Cobban, 'Healing lessons from another war-torn society – Mozambique'.

24. Teitel, *Transitional justice*, p. 53.
25. Remarks by John Daniel, member of the South African TRC, at the 17th General Conference of the International Peace Research Association held in Durban, South Africa, June 1998.
26. D. Tutu, 'War crimes tribunals may end impunity, but they can't heal hatred' (Interview by N. Gardels), *New Perspectives Quarterly* 20(2), Spring 2003: 90–91.
27. Derrick, 'Reconciliation'
28. Derrick, 'Reconciliation'
29. Promotion of National Unity and Reconciliation Act 34 of 1995, 26 July 1995.
30. Quoted in M. Minow, *Between vengeance and forgiveness* (Boston: Beacon Press, 1998), p. 81.
31. A.U. Okali, 'Note on restitutive justice at the International Tribunal for Rwanda', 1998, on file with the author.
32. Hayner, *Unspeakable truths*, p. 100.
33. M. Koskenniemi, 'Between impunity and show trials', *Max Planck Yearbook of United Nations Law* (Dordrecht: Martinus Nijhoff Publishers, 2002).
34. J-F. Lyotard, *The Differend: Phrases in dispute* (G van den Abbeele trans.), quoted in Koskenniemi, 'Between impunity and show trials', p. 17.
35. The *Differend* is applicable to the Nuremberg Trials, and the role of NATO in ending the wars of the former Yugoslavia.
36. Tutu, 'War crimes tribunals may end impunity, but they can't heal hatred'.
37. Tutu, 'War crimes tribunals may end impunity, but they can't heal hatred'.
38. Thakur, 'Politics vs justice at The Hague'. Including Rwanda in this argument appears odd, as Rwanda's present government is unshakeably wedded to prosecutions for the impunity of its predecessor regime, including with the assistance of an international criminal tribunal. Perhaps the aim was to juxtapose that country, on the one hand, with South Africa (truth commission) and Mozambique (blanket amnesty) on the other.
39. John Dugard, 'Reconciliation and justice: The South African experience', Conference paper quoted in A-M. Smith, *Advances in understanding international peacemaking*, vol. II. (Washington, DC: United States Institute of Peace, 2001), p. 12.
40. Koskenniemi, 'Between impunity and show trials', p. 8.
41. E. Kiss, 'Moral ambition within and beyond political constraints: Reflections on restorative justice', in R.J. Rotberg and D. Thompson (eds.), *Truth v justice: The morality of truth commissions* (Princeton: Princeton University Press, 2000), p. 88, and R.J. Rotberg, 'Truth commissions and the provision of truth, justice and reconciliation', in Rotberg and Thompson (eds.), *Truth v justice*, p. 19.
42. See I. Amadiume, 'The politics of memory: Biafra and intellectual responsibility', in Amadiume and An-Na'im, (eds.) *The politics of memory*.
43. See A. Thomson, 'Kirchner seeks to heal wounds inflicted by Argentina's junta', *Financial Times*, 24 March 2004.
44. Thomson, 'Kirchner seeks to heal wounds inflicted by Argentina's junta'.
45. Thomson, 'Kirchner seeks to heal wounds inflicted by Argentina's junta'.
46. K.C. Moghalu, 'No peace without justice: The role of international criminal and humanitarian law in conflict settlement and reconciliation', Paper presented at a conference 'From Impunity to

a Culture of Accountability', organised by the UN University and the University of Utrecht, Netherlands, 26–28 November 2001.

47. 'The threat to SA "miracle"'. *Africa Analysis*, 20 February 2004.

48. S. LaFraniere, 'A South African journey: Bomb maker to police chief', *The New York Times*, 28 February 2004.

49. Three accused persons have pleaded guilty before the Tribunal to genocide and crimes against humanity: Jean Kambanda, former prime minister of Rwanda, Omar Serushago, a former leader of the *Interhamwe* militia, and Georges Ruggio, a Belgian journalist.

50. Kambanda was sentenced to life in prison, Serushago to fifteen years' imprisonment, and Ruggio to twelve years.

51. Dugard, 'Reconciliation and justice'.

52. Dugard, 'Reconciliation and justice'.

53. M. Osiel, 'Ever again: Legal remembrance of administrative massacre', *University of Pennsylvania Law Review* 144, 1995: 463–504.

54. Osiel, 'Ever again'.

55. Koskenniemi, 'Between impunity and show trials', p. 14.

56. Article 6(4), Statute of the ICTR.

57. Koskenniemi, 'Between impunity and show trials', p. 12.

58. Tutu, 'War crimes tribunals may end impunity, but they can't heal hatred'.

59. See Preamble of the Statute of the ICTR.

60. H. Arendt, *Eichmann in Jerusalem: A report on the banality of evil* (rev. ed) (New York: Penguin Books, 1977), p. 5.

61. See Okali, 'Note on restitutive justice at the International Tribunal for Rwanda'.

62. Bull, *The anarchical society*, p. 17.

63. D.P. Forsythe, 'Politics and the International Tribunal for the Former Yugoslavia', in R.S. Clark and M. Sann (eds.), *The prosecution of international crimes* (New Brunswick and London: Transaction Publishers, 1996), p. 199.

64. Hayner, *Unspeakable truths*.

4

Gender and Truth and Reconciliation Commissions

Comparative Reflections

Sheila Meintjes

INTRODUCTION

This chapter critically examines 'truth and reconciliation' from a feminist perspective through a discussion of initiatives developed in South Africa.[1] In the aftermath of the low-level 'liberation' or civil war that lasted for 30 years until the early 1990s, transitional justice mechanisms steered a middle road between punishment and restorative justice. Although this seemed to be progressive, South African gender activists criticised the process as androcentric and gender-blind[2] and this criticism led to a shift in the praxis of the South African process that attempted to integrate gender concerns. Modelled on the South African processes, the post-war dual process of the Special Court for Sierra Leone (SCSL) and the Truth and Reconciliation Commission (TRC) in Sierra Leone took greater measures to include and address gender-based crimes (see Chapter 7 in this volume). Do these shifts suggest that a focus on gender crimes will improve the outcomes of transitional justice for women generally?

Amongst other objectives, the TRC processes were initiated in order to come to terms with the human rights abuses, crimes against humanity and war crimes that variously characterised the brutal past in both these countries. I will not repeat debates that are examined by other contributors to this book regarding the merits of the choices made between peace and justice, nor those that examine the contradictory roles assigned to the SCSL and the TRC in Sierra Leone, nor those debates concerning the processes in the country that sidelined national judicial personnel and processes. Rather I wish to engage in a feminist theoretical reflection on the implications of particular choices made in establishing the terms of reference of the TRCs. In what ways did the frameworks shape androcentric processes and how did they affect women? Did the more gender-sensitive approach in Sierra Leone alter the experiences of women and lead to better outcomes? The terms of the mandates in both were for the TRCs to hear the confessions of perpetrators and the testimony of victims of human rights abuses in order to provide for the investigation and the establishment of as complete a picture as possible of the 'nature, causes, and extent of *gross violations of human rights* committed during the period from 1 March 1960'.[3]

The accumulation of individual accounts of human rights abuse – whether by perpetrators or victims – was intended to provide both a history and a kind of confessional process that would lead to forgiveness that would potentially settle the past and enable both sides to live and work side by side. In South Africa the intention was to create a new terrain in which whites and blacks might see one another as equals and as part of a single nation.

My argument is that the human rights approach could never, in practice, either provide an adequate *historical* understanding as to why the struggle took the form it did or create a platform for a new national beginning. This is not to deny the importance of protecting human rights but rather to emphasise that historical explanation and understanding is not derived from an accumulation of individual, atomised accounts of human rights abuses. Contextual and historical research is needed to provide a fuller understanding of the systemic aspects of the abuse of a particular political regime or political system. The criticisms of the TRC mandate in South Africa concerned both its limited purview and, from a feminist perspective, the fact that nowhere did it specify the need to probe the intersectionalities of race, ethnicity, class and gender.[4]

What we do acquire from the TRC is the poignant testimony of survivors of terrible human rights abuse and the acknowledgement by perpetrators of what they did. In some cases the remorse and apologies of perpetrators might be an outcome in itself and one that may even be accepted by survivors. However, in other cases there might have been a more complex process of painful recollection that might not have led either to closure or to forgiveness.[5] Individual psychological and spiritual battles to overcome the experience of systemic abuse are hard to measure. The process in general might have enabled those who witnessed and participated in the 'truth-telling' to move closer together and even forgive[6] but the reason these terrible events occurred and how the perpetrators could have enacted such terrible acts against other human beings needs a different kind of analysis. This critique of TRCs does not mean that we should question their purpose, however, for there is much evidence that shows that they do contribute to a sense of restorative justice.[7] Nevertheless, the experience of TRCs suggests that we still need to explore more critically the way in which their processes and terms of reference are conceptualised. A central feature of my criticism is that there can be no complete understanding without the consideration of a gender perspective. Gender shapes all of our lives in constitutive ways. It has a normative function in establishing people's roles and opportunities within their own social milieu. Generally, gender power operates in society to establish that men's subjectivity takes primacy over that of women.[8]

I begin with a brief background to the struggles in the two countries. These were situations in which a community of citizens and subjects went to war with one another. In Sierra Leone, the very social and infrastructural fabric was destroyed. In South Africa, the struggle did not destroy the infrastructure in the same way but in its aftermath the country faced the ravages of a system of domination that had created two distinct worlds: one underdeveloped, the other developed.[9] Here I provide a thumbnail descriptive outline which suggests that it was the different forms of oppressive identity and relationships that formed the basis for conflict. I then reflect on what may have prevented the emergence of a new sense of national unity or identity in these societies. I seek to demonstrate that a failure to address the past in a historically nuanced and gender-sensitive way can only lead to further failures. Individual citizens are not abstracted, autonomous, ahistorical actors but are embedded in a political landscape with a distinctive history. In the case of the two countries under discussion, the unfolding of class or group privilege and oppressive relations in the past was quite distinct. This distinctness must be understood and the aftermath of this political situation must be transformed in ways that ensure that previous privilege, inequality and grievances are not reproduced. At the onset of the peace process each country had quite different forms of social organisation and intervention, yet what they had in common was the gendered inequity that existed in the way in which post-war decision-making unfolded. What differed was the manner in which these processes and inequities were challenged.

CONDITIONS OF CIVIL WAR
South Africa

In South Africa, a racist system deprived black people of political, social and economic rights. The ensuing 30-year, low-level civil war was conducted by the armed wing of the African National Congress (ANC) and other liberation armies for a new political order that recognised equality and civil rights for all. The Freedom Charter of 1955 called for democracy, education, housing and the sharing of wealth, as well as the nationalisation of banks, minerals and industry.[10] This was not so much an ideological blueprint for a post-apartheid society as a rallying call that would bring different class interests into a national fold. A repressive white racial state used a masterly system of racial domination based on spatial, social and political differentiation to maintain power and to ensure a thriving mining and manufacturing economy that was based on the cheap labour of a mainly unskilled black working class. Although class divisions may still have crossed the racial divide, all white members of the society benefited from racial oppression. All black people, whatever their class or capability, suffered oppression as a consequence of their race. Ethnicity was used as a means of dividing the oppressed. As early as 1910, and in response to this system, the national struggle for emancipation from racial oppression and ethnic division began. It is hardly surprising that an educated and talented black elite should turn to armed struggle and were easily able to garner support from the discontented wider populace.

State banning of the ANC and other movements in the early 1960s forced the organisational core of the movement into exile and led to the formation of an army of liberation, *Umkhonto we Sizwe* (the Spear of the Nation). Internally, organised resistance took many forms, both legal and illegal. The complex struggle involved different phases and actors who were organised in different formations which included women, the youth, trade unions and community organisations. It involved both blacks and whites who were in opposition to the government, just as there were also many blacks who could have been considered to be collaborators within the apartheid regime. It was a complex and sophisticated system of racial domination, shaped as much by the oppressed as by the oppressors. A simplistic view of the society as one in which all whites were oppressors and all blacks the oppressed misses the nuances of the existent divisions in society along ideological, class, ethnic, linguistic, regional, religious and racial lines, all of which were thoroughly gendered. Men and women experienced different forms of discrimination – or example, only married men could access housing in black

99

townships because black African women were defined by law as 'minors'. Indeed, the different needs and interests of women were reflected in the different ways that women participated in the struggle against apartheid.[11]

When dealing with the perpetration of human rights abuse from all sides the TRC had to take account of this highly complex history, but its terms of reference did not permit a systematic probing of the apartheid system either as a system or as a crime against humanity, as defined by the United Nations (UN).[12] Instead, the way in which the Act that set up the commission framed the discourse resulted in a focus on individual experience, healing and reparations.[13] Three somewhat different branches of the commission dealt with human rights abuse, reconciliation and reparation, and amnesty. It was a quasi-judicial process, with both restorative and retributive elements. If a perpetrator came clean with the truth he or she might receive amnesty after a probing court-like process.

Sierra Leone

It is difficult to discuss the Sierra Leonean case without making reference to its neighbour, Liberia. In Liberia a complex struggle emerged when, in 1980, a young Krahn soldier, Samuel Doe, ousted the Americo-Liberians, who were an elite ruling class that was supported by the United States. Doe proclaimed the end of corruption and a better deal for all the people but during the ten years of his rule he became as corrupt as his predecessors. With the support of the United States and for reasons of Cold War *realpolitik,* Doe ruled for a decade after the coup. The conditions for a civil war unfolded after a rigged election in October 1985. After opposition leaders were arrested and newspapers banned, Doe won the elections. In November 1985 a failed coup by a Gio tribal leader, Thomas Quiwonkpa, led to terrible reprisals. Despite aid from the United States the economy went into gradual decline. Meanwhile, opponents rallied support and received succour from neighbouring countries and training in Libya.

The civil war was unleashed when Charles Taylor sent an insurgent group into Nimba country in December 1989.[14] This set off a chain reaction of state reprisal and fleeing refugees, creating a pool of ready recruits, especially young boys and men, for an insurgent army. The ensuing civil war lasted for the next fourteen years. In the 1990s the war extended to include regional forces of West African states and the Economic Community of West African States Military Observer Group (ECOMOG), who wanted to limit the effects of the war in the region. This interlude, and the death of Doe, led to a new but short-lived

Government of National Unity. It was in this context that the West African forces became a factor in the civil war and their role added to its ferocity. The civil war was then waged at terrible cost, with boys recruited by both insurgent and state forces and trained in terror tactics, girls kidnapped to become sex slaves and rape and torture used to create a state of fear. The insurgents managed to control much of Liberia outside the capital, and their leaders, especially Charles Taylor, amassed extraordinary wealth through laundering diamonds, gold, iron ore and timber from the region. Taylor, his sights on the diamond fields of Sierra Leone, put his weight behind the Sierra Leone Revolutionary United Front (RUF) led by Foday Sankoh.[15]

The fate of Sierra Leone became closely tied to that of Liberia. When Sierra Leone was led by Siaka Stevens in the 1970s, state assets had been stolen and handed to an elite political class, whilst in the countryside an almost feudal system of tied and dependent labour had bred a rural proletariat that sought work on the diamond fields where they received little compensation.

Paul Richards has explored the impact of this historical division of labour on the political outcomes of the 1980s. He presents a compelling argument that, after the late 1980s, when the corrupt Momoh regime – Joseph Saidu Momoh succeeded Stevens in 1985 – lost the support of the International Monetary Fund (IMF) and structural adjustment made education too expensive for most people, young people in particular turned against the government. They were embedded in what he calls a 'forced division of labour' in which they had little choice between fatalistic acquiescence and civil war. Many young men left their rural homes in an attempt to escape from compulsory forced labour meted out by rural customary courts. For those who joined rebel forces, the war would, in their minds, be against both their dependency and their elders.

Young men either found refuge or were abducted by the RUF rebel movement led by Foday Sankoh. About 80 per cent of the recruits to the RUF came from the historic labour dependency areas that were inhabited mainly by the Mende ethnic group.[16] After 1991, in the RUF forest camps where they had their hideouts, the rebel forces were continually threatened by the South African private army, 'Executive Outcomes', employed by Valentine Strasser, who overthrew Momoh that year.[17] The conditions of existence in the forests promoted a sectarian and introverted military culture. They were continuously harassed by the better-trained and armed South Africans and by 1996 they faced defeat. Richards suggests that this situation unhinged the RUF and its members then 'courted apocalyptic recklessness'. According to a report by Radhika Coomaraswamy, UN Special Rapporteur on the Elimination of Violence against Women, hundreds of thousands of people were affected by the violence, at least 72 per cent of all women in the country experienced some form of human rights abuse and 50 per cent experienced sexual violence. The young militants sought out those who had 'demeaned and disregarded them'.[18] With bush knives as weapons, the young soldiers attacked rural communities, maiming and raping in revenge attacks upon their erstwhile homes.

THE DIFFERENCE THAT GENDER MAKES

In all the formal armies and rebel insurgent groups in Sierra Leone and South Africa, the social, political and economic status of individuals was determined by their gender, their power and authority and their class, as well as by other kinds of identity that shaped their worldview. Ethnic identity, religious beliefs and cultural practices were all gendered and played a significant role in constituting how individuals experienced different conflict situations that was quite apart from the personal histories of individuals. The different ways in which these identities shaped life chances and the lived experience of survivors – both perpetrators and victims – would have to be understood very clearly by those leading the peacebuilding and reconstruction period. If the structuring of a post-conflict society were to be one that opened up a new world and were seen as legitimate by all, then not only would every group have to participate but a focus on women's interests as a fundamental category would also have to be integrated into the thinking of the post-conflict reconstruction. Moreover, sustainable peace would not develop from a situation that merely put people back where they had been in the social hierarchy before the conflict. Thus who comprised different categories – government leaders, rebel leaders, combatants, civil society and civilians – and who participated in decisions about peace and reconstruction and how their needs and interests were met were crucial questions for the gendered nature of post-transition outcomes. The conditions for freedom in the sense that Amartya Sen conceptualised them – as promoting the capabilities of citizens – could not simply be defined in 'gender neutral terms'. While the material wellbeing of society in general was important, the question of the political and civil rights of citizens was equally relevant.

The constitutional process in South Africa tried to address both aspects and the Constitution that emerged from the negotiations was one that embraced both material and political rights. What was unique in the South African case was the strong emphasis in its founding principles on 'non-sexism' as well as non-racism. The inclusion of this idea was a result of the pressure that was brought to bear on the constitutional process by a Women's National Coalition (WNC). Women mobilised around an agenda that demanded recognition of their specific role in society and the specific forms of gender discrimination that made women secondary subjects. Gender as a set of relations that constituted men and women in differential power and authority positions was brought to the fore by the demands of the WNC. In particular, the WNC demanded the inclusion of gender equality in the new Bill of Rights in the Constitution.

The South African TRC reflected these concerns in its efforts to ensure that victims received some recompense for their suffering but also in its emphasis on creating a new human rights culture by dealing with the horrors of the past.[19] With the demands of the WNC, the TRC was faced with a strong lobby that demanded that the 'gendered' experience of apartheid and gendered violations of rights be taken into account. The relative success of this lobby is discussed below.

The new South African democratic state centred its first years of government on interventions that proposed a broad Reconstruction and Development Programme (RDP). This was short-lived, replaced as it was by a less people-oriented Growth, Employment and Redistribution (GEAR) programme.[20] According to the RDP, freedom would come only if everyone could enjoy the fruits of the new democracy in ways that dealt with past deprivation. Thus the period of transition and the first years of the new democracy after the elections of 1994 constituted a period of interim justice in which the truth and reconciliation process dealt with the past but equally looked to the future. This meant that whoever participated in the decisions about the transition from civil war to peace and was involved in the unfolding developmental peace processes would have an influence on the nature of the success or otherwise of the outcomes. Some of these issues are addressed below.

Whether we speak of warlords who recruited and brutalised children or predatory state leaders who acted in their own interests and not in the social and national interest, or of more legitimate liberation heroes, it was their voices that dominated the negotiations that led to the post-conflict settlements. However, other critical voices were either muted or missing and if they were heard, were placed within a context that did not fully understand the significance of their experience. It is to this aspect of the post-conflict situation that I wish to turn. During their transition from war to peace both countries in this discussion adopted a combination of punitive and restorative justice principles. The truth and reconciliation process in Sierra Leone occurred after the South African experience and adopted some of the modalities and lessons of that experience. This had critical significance for how both countries dealt with the question of women's experience. I consider first the South African situation and then turn to the experience of Sierra Leone.

WOMEN'S INTERVENTIONS IN THE TRUTH AND RECONCILIATION PROCESSES

South Africa

The processes that are involved in attempting to find sustainable solutions varied in each country. In South Africa, opposing forces of the liberation movements and the apartheid regime began talks, at first covertly, during the 1980s and, after 1992, openly for some months before real negotiations for a new democratic order began. The context of the negotiations was that of a mobilised society still at war with itself. A peace process that was managed by civil society around the country was initiated to try to dampen the violence – concluding in a peace accord. Nevertheless, between 16 000 and 20 000 people died during this period. In the negotiations the presence and dominance of men was remarkable but as the process unfolded amidst the violence that subsequently proved to be orchestrated by shadowy state *agents provocateurs*, women's voices from across the political spectrum united in a coalition that demanded their presence and participation. In the final phase of negotiations women sat in the negotiating teams and a newly formed WNC carefully monitored the gendered implications of both constitutional and political decisions.[21]

Women's political organisation was critical in shaping the content of the interim Constitution and indeed in constructing an idea of citizenship that was neither neutral nor ungendered.[22] The reforms and reconstitution of the state in South Africa that ensued after 1994 were shaped by the activism of this coalition. So, when we talk of the committed efforts at democratic consolidation and nation-building of the post-apartheid era and the new democratic state, it is important to understand that it was a continually contested process that involved different kinds of struggle – that of women, of different class interests, of different regional interests and of different ideological interests – nationalist, liberal and socialist. This process of contesting has not dissipated over the last fourteen years. One arena where we saw this contested process unfold was in the uneasy compromise regarding the establishment of the TRC and its role in providing a platform on which to confront the violence of the apartheid system.[23]

Elsewhere I have discussed the paradoxical relationship between the state and civil society in the processes of institution-making in the transition period.[24] The TRC was a microcosm of broader struggles. It did not have the capacity to mobilise communities to engage with it yet it was reluctant to allow civil society organisations (CSOs) to play a co-ordinating role in bringing survivors forward. So instead of fostering the development of organisational initiatives, particularly of survivors to form either a social movement or a social coalition of sorts, and thus empowering a sense of civic virtue, the TRC held the organisations at arm's length and turned to legal experts to represent those interests. In doing this it effectively undermined its own objectives of developing democratic agency in South Africa.[25] This may not have been intentional but perhaps reflected some of the internal difficulties in relationships between commissioners, and between staff and commissioners. There was an unintended movement away from the possibility of building important social networks and organisation that could have become an integral part of shaping the outcome of the TRC process.[26] Moreover, the way in which such organisations of survivors were treated as the subjects of gross human rights violations as opposed to actors in the struggle against apartheid, tended to define them as 'victims' and thus masked the way in which they had shaped the response of the apartheid state to their activism. Many of the victim accounts given by women, for instance, described their loss of partners or children and only with difficulty did women speak of their own agency or role in the struggle.

During the formulation of the TRC legislation and its passage through parliament, CSOs – two in particular, Justice in Transition led by Alex Boraine and the Centre for the Study of Violence and Reconciliation (CSVR) – engaged with and influenced the process. Boraine in fact became the deputy chairperson of the TRC (see Chapter 6 in this volume). The CSVR, which had positioned itself to assist the TRC, had begun mobilising survivors in an organisation called *Khulumani* (Speak out). The history of *Khulumani* is complex and contested but the organisation provided a space for survivors to meet and discuss their relationship with the TRC as well as the CSVR and to mobilise others. Indeed, since the TRC closed its doors, *Khulumani* has continued to grow in numbers and to attract survivors who wish to give testimony of their experiences under apartheid. Ironically, too, in more recent years discontented former combatants of *Umkhonto we Sizwe* have also joined the organisation, not only in their search for closure but also in an attempt to find mechanisms through which to engage the state, while others are associated with a project developed by the peacebuilding programme in the CSVR.

The truth, reconciliation, restitution and reparations process is not yet complete. The President's Fund, set up to deal with recompensing 'victims', has more than R650 million still unspent and the claims upon it have not ended, despite the fact that the final report of the TRC was handed to President Thabo Mbeki in 2003.[27]

During the existence of the TRC (1995–1998), the CSVR provided public education about the process but was somewhat sidelined when the formal process took on a life of its own. The CSVR teamed up with a Gender Research Group linked to the Centre for Applied Legal Studies at the University of the Witwatersrand to monitor and comment on the gender implications of both the TRC Act itself and the unfolding of the procedures of the commission.[28] This group provided the commission with expert opinions and research findings on several important issues, including the importance of providing women's hearings. The TRC responded positively to many of the suggestions, holding a workshop with broader gender and women's organisations to develop more woman-friendly spaces for engagement with women deponents. However, the TRC did not heed the group's call for a more integrated understanding of the gendered nature of the struggles and the need for a more nuanced gendered methodology in its research and reporting. The experience of women came to be seen as 'a chapter' in the course of South Africa's history.

Sierra Leone

The aftermath of the civil war in Sierra Leone revealed a country in ruins, bereft of any capacity to confront the enormous task of rebuilding the infrastructure. Human and social capital had been depleted by emigration, war and death. The hope that the hybrid transitional justice experiment in Sierra Leone would lead to growing a national judicial system was never a realistic one, and unsurprisingly this objective did not come to fruition amid accusations that, instead, national expertise had been sidelined by international experts (see Chapter 11 in this volume). Despite these criticisms a number of landmark procedural and legal innovations in the Sierra Leone process constituted a new departure for transitional justice and international jurisprudence that has broader implications for international gender justice. The first pertains to its adopting gender crimes explicitly in its definition of crimes against humanity, although gender crimes were first articulated in the terms of the 1993 Vienna Declaration on Violence against Women and the 1998 Rome Statute that brought the International Criminal Court (ICC) into being. The Rome Statute explicitly recognised rape, sexual slavery, enforced prostitution, pregnancy and sterilisation, and other forms of sexual violence as crimes against humanity and as war crimes. The International Criminal Tribunal for the Former Yugoslavia (ICTY) also provides a very important aspect of international legal practice in its rules of evidence to limit the argument of consent as a defence in sexual assault, to exclude the survivor's past sexual history and to expunge the corroborative rule in a victim's testimony.[29] The Sierra Leone Statute included sexual slavery, a phenomenon common in the conflict in Sierra Leone and Liberia, and indeed in South Africa during the 1980s and 1990s. The addition of sexual slavery to the definition of crimes against humanity made possible the first prosecution on this count in Sierra Leone. This will no doubt form a significant component of future post-war trials and act as a new normative boundary in times of war. It is no longer simply a paper right. Another element of the Sierra Leone process that forms an important precedent is the indictment of a perpetrator for forced marriage, a widespread practice both in East and West Africa. If this prosecution succeeds it will at least signal prosecution for a practice that has been a feature of war since the Middle Ages.

CONCLUSIONS: WHAT CAN FEMINIST THEORY OFFER?

In a recent article that addresses the question of whether 'feminism needs a theory of transitional justice' Christine Bell and Catherine O'Rourke offer a strong argument that feminist theory should investigate 'how transitional justice debates help or hinder broader projects of securing material gains for women through transition, rather than trying to fit a feminist notion of justice within transitional justice frameworks'.[30] Clearly, since the South African TRC was established, criticism has seen a much greater focus on gender justice, especially where the shortfalls in terms of its mandate have identified, firstly, insufficient leeway for the commission to investigate the structural and systemic nature of apartheid as a crime against humanity and, secondly, where the commission integrated a women-sensitive approach to its hearings.[31] Both the Rwandan and the Yugoslavian Tribunals have focused on the differential violations and experience of women and men and highlighted how sexual abuse is used to attack women in specific ways that differ from the way in which men are attacked.[32] The focus on gender violence and women-specific war experiences is reflected in the UN Security Council Resolution 1325 of 2000, which calls 'all parties to armed conflict to take special measures to protect women and girls from gender-based violence, particularly rape and other forms of sexual abuse, and all other forms of violence in situations of armed conflict'.[33] This has been entrenched in the Updated Principles to Combat Impunity, which enjoins commissions of inquiry specifically to address the human rights violations of women in conflict situations.[34]

There has been a broad acceptance of the need to deal with gender-based crimes, to draw women into peace processes and to design programmes that can meet women's needs, all of which deepen the content of what is understood as gendered violence. There are two points that need to be made here, though. The first is that 'gender' is used as a synonym for 'women', which means that the gendered experience of men is not put under the spotlight. None of these TRC processes was enjoined to probe the particular ways in which men engage their sexuality in conflict. We suggested that the South African TRC do so but as far as I know it did not form part of the depositions. Men are also sexually violated in war – sodomy is rape; being forced to watch your wife and daughters being raped is tantamount to a sexual assault. What is the consequence and effect of these experiences? It reduces men's sense of self, as it does women's, but in a different way. Men are 'unmanned'. Attacks on men undermine their feelings of responsibility for protecting their homes and families and undermine their masculinity.

The second point is that the efforts to ensure women's presence assume that there is a direct connection between their presence and their will to represent women's interests. This is not the case and it is important to examine which women are at the peace table and to consider whether they do in fact represent a constituency of women. The presence of women does not naturally translate into the fulfilment of women's needs and interests. In South Africa, the mobilisation of women in the WNC and the post-apartheid integration of women into mainstream politics, with a 30 per cent critical mass in parliament, for instance, have made a difference to the legislative framework and policy focus on women's needs and interests but these changes were driven by women who were linked to broader women's movements. South Africa could be described as a 'woman-friendly' state, a consequence of the strength and mobilisation of women in the struggle for liberation and the particular form of the coalition of interests that interjected into the androcentric deliberations during the transition. However, it is important to scrutinise how far representation has really ensured support for women's rights and improved their quality of life in society.[35] Research undertaken at the University of Witswatersrand has shown that a legislative framework which addresses women's particular experience and needs is significant. The Recognition of Customary Marriages Act 120 of 1998, the Domestic Violence Act 116 of 1998, the Maintenance Amendment Act 2 of 1991, as well as policies that provide women with care grants are changes that have made a substantial difference to women's lives and provided women with critical safety nets. While these may provide material gains, neither the norms nor the values in traditional and customary contexts have changed significantly. In all the diverse cultures that Archbishop Desmond Tutu eloquently described as 'the rainbow nation', patriarchal and male rights have not altered much. The constitutional rights and legal changes have not translated into what we might call 'real material transformation'.

Women have been defined as 'subjects' in some of these policy developments. The easy legislative and policy gains, while giving relief, have not led to a growth in women's capability to develop potential. Women remain trapped in cycles of poverty that grants can only alleviate, not transform. More significantly, perhaps, these amendments have not led to any change in the dominance of men in decision-making in society – patriarchal cultures remain in charge, at both state and homestead level. There is also growing evidence of a 'war against women's autonomy' in the form of domestic violence.

Elsewhere we have identified the continuum of violence against women during the transition from war to peace.[36] An approach that focuses on women alone, that emphasises 'women's empowerment', and which in South Africa became the object of the policy of gender mainstreaming and the chief means of transforming women's self-confidence and capabilities, has alienated men, who feel 'left out'.[37] There is both a backlash against women's empowerment and an emphasis on gender transformation in South African society in the new millennium. If we were to focus on changing women's agency without engaging with the foundations of the social construction of power relations in society we would not in fact engage with the key aspects of gendered social conditions and the social relations that trap women and men in unequal power relations.

Debates about the way in which transitional justice has engaged with gender concerns reveal that it is not so much that the transitional justice mechanisms have tended to give precedence to particular women's concerns and not others (although that might be true), but rather that the form the transition takes in general needs to be questioned and addressed in new ways.[38] International feminism has argued for women's involvement in peace processes without giving adequate attention to who exactly those women were (or are). Ann Orford's argument that imperialist feminist universalism can further hinder women's economic opportunities and obscure the way liberalisation and globalisation undermine the scope for a better life for all is a strong one. There needs to be a much more careful understanding of the international and national limits and opportunities involved in what might be called 'transformation'. The way in which the transition brings international agencies into the process may well undermine the interests of poorer women. However, it could equally be that international interests promote poor women's interests in opposition to those of an elite. These are not predetermined relations of power and interest. Women's interests in general seem to have been taken into account in situations where women have organised across divides, where they have lobbied, or where they have taken to the streets at strategic moments to push their issues, and where they have engaged with male allies who hold power, yet none of these actions has anywhere led to fundamental transformation.

Transformation in gender power relations is a process that requires much deeper reflection and action. Whether social engineering from the top can deliver on such a promise is highly questionable. We need to be more realistic about what we expect from transitional justice and what it can really achieve but there is no doubt that feminists and gender activists need to engage in the process, need to promote a gender perspective and need to be vigilant and critical about how the transition integrates women, which women and the kind of justice procedures that are set in place.

NOTES AND REFERENCES

1. Sheila Meintjes was a member of the Gender Group at the Centre for Applied Legal Studies at the University of the Witwatersrand, Johannesburg, which monitored the South African TRC. With Beth Goldblatt she presented a submission to the TRC that led to significant changes in the way the TRC dealt with women and gender issues.
2. A. Boraine, *A country unmasked: Inside South Africa's Truth and Reconciliation Commission* (Cape Town: Oxford University Press, 2000).
3. Promotion of National Unity and Reconciliation Act 34 of 1995.

4. See B. Goldblatt and S. Meintjes, 'Gender and the TRC: Submission to South African Truth and Reconciliation Commission', at http://sunsit.wits.ac.za/csrv/papkhul (accessed 12 February 2009).

5. Truth and Reconciliation Commission, *Truth and Reconciliation Commission of South Africa Report*, 5 volumes (Cape Town: Juta, 1998).

6. I. Chipkin, *Do South Africans exist? Nationalism, democracy and the identity of 'the people'* (Johannesburg: University of the Witwatersrand Press, 2007).

7. See E. Doxtader and C. Villa-Vicencio, *Through fire with water* (Cape Town: David Phillip, 2003).

8. C. Pateman, *The sexual contract* (Cambridge: Polity Press, 1988).

9. J. Seekings and N. Nattrass, *Class, race, and inequality in South Africa* (Pietermaritzburg: University of KwaZulu-Natal Press, 2006).

10. R. Suttner and J. Cronin (eds.), *30 years of the Freedom Charter* (Johannesburg: Ravan Press, 1986).

11. S. Hassim, *Women's organizations and democracy in South Africa: Contesting authority* (Pietermaritzburg: University of KwaZulu-Natal Press, 2006).

12. See Promotion of National Unity and Reconciliation Act.

13. Goldblatt and Meintjes, 'Gender and the TRC'.

14. M. Meredith, *The fate of Africa: A history of fifty years of independence* (Johannesburg: Jonathan Ball, 2005).

15. A. Adebajo, *Liberia's civil war: Nigeria, ECOMOG, and regional security in West Africa* (Boulder, CO: Lynne Reiner, 1996); P. Richards, *Fighting for the rain forest: War, youth and resources in Sierra Leone* (Oxford: James Currey, 1996).

16. P. Richards, 'Forced labour and civil war: Agrarian underpinnings of the Sierra Leone conflict', in P. Kaarsholm (ed.), *Violence, political culture and development in Africa: Congo, Rwanda, Darfur, Liberia, Sierra Leone, Ethiopia, Matabeleland, KwaZulu-Natal* (London: James Currey, 2006), pp. 181–200.

17. Richards, 'Forced labour and civil war'.

18. Richards, 'Forced labour and civil war'.

19. See *Truth and Reconciliation Commission of South Africa Report* (5 volumes).

20. Seekings and Nattrass, *Class, race, and inequality in South Africa*.

21. S.W. Meintjes, 'Gender, nationalism and transformation: Difference and commonality in South Africa's past and present', in R. Wilford and R.L. Miller (eds.), *Women, ethnicity and nationalism: The politics of transition* (London: Routledge, 1998), pp. 62–86.

22. G. Fick, S. Meintjes and M. Simons (eds.), *One woman, one vote: The gender politics of South African elections* (Johannesburg: Electoral Institute of Southern Africa, 2002).

23. See D. Posel and G. Simpson (eds.), *Commissioning the past: Understanding South Africa's Truth and Reconciliation Commission* (Johannesburg: University of the Witwatersrand Press, 2002).

24. S. Meintjes, 'Fostering political accountability through "truth and reconciliation": Civil responsibility and engagement between state and society in South Africa's post-apartheid democracy', in R. Coomaraswamy and D. Fonseka (eds.), *Women, peacemaking and constitutions* (New Delhi: Women Unlimited, 2004).

25. Meintjes, 'Fostering political accountability through "truth and reconciliation"'.

26. Meintjes, 'Fostering political accountability through "truth and reconciliation"'.

27. Meintjes, 'Fostering political accountability through "truth and reconciliation"'.

28. Meintjes, 'Fostering political accountability through "truth and reconciliation"'.

29. C. Bell and C. O'Rourke, 'Does feminism need a theory of transitional justice? An introductory essay', *The International Journal of Transitional Justice* 1, 2007: 23–44.

30. Bell and O'Rourke, 'Does feminism need a theory of transitional justice?'.
31. See Goldblatt and Meintjes, 'Gender and the TRC'.
32. Bell and O'Rourke, 'Does feminism need a theory of transitional justice?'.
33. See UN Security Council Resolution 1325 (2000).
34. Orlenlicher quoted in Bell and O'Rourke, 'Does feminism need a theory of transitional justice?'.
35. Symposium, 'Feminism and democracy: Women engage the South African state', *Politikon* 32(2), 2005.
36. S. Meintjes, M. Turshen and A. Pillay (eds.), *The aftermath: Women in post-conflict transformation* (London: Zed Books, 2002).
37. S. Meintjes, 'Gender equality by design: The case of South Africa's Commission on Gender Equality', *Politikon* 32(2), 2005: 259–276.
38. A. Orford, 'Feminism, imperialism and the mission of international law', *Nordic Journal of International Law* 71, 2002: 275–296.

5

Transitional Justice, Democratisation
and the Rule of Law

Mireille Affa'a Mindzie

There are times when we are told that justice must be set aside in the interests of peace. It is true that justice can only be dispensed when the peaceful order of society is secure. But we have come to understand that the reverse is also true: without justice, there can be no lasting peace.[1]

INTRODUCTION

Violent conflict and authoritarian regimes originate and flourish on the denial of democracy and the rule of law, which, at the same time, are essential elements for ensuring long-lasting peace. At the end of a conflict and during the transition to peace and democratically functioning institutions,[2] peacebuilding and post-conflict reconstruction offer opportunities to re-establish governance, participation, institutional reform and justice, all encompassed in the notions of democracy and rule of law. Transitional justice is the key to peacebuilding and post-conflict reconstruction. It has been defined as 'the formal and informal procedures implemented by a group or institution of accepted legitimacy around the time of a transition out of an oppressive or violent social order, for rendering justice to perpetrators and their collaborators, as well as to their victims'.[3]

From the mid-twentieth century onwards, transitional justice developed in three main phases, beginning with a focus on international criminalisation and subsequent criminal prosecutions in 1945 and the Nuremberg Trials (phase I), the inclusion of innovative and isolated mechanisms and measures of restorative justice during the post-Cold War wave of transitions (phase II), and the broadening of transitional justice and the fight against impunity towards the end of the twentieth century (phase III).[4] After a period when dealing with past atrocities was seen as 'an optional exercise', it is now admitted that transitional justice initiatives should play a key role in building a sustainable peace.[5]

Transitional processes encompass both judicial and non-judicial responses to violations of international human rights law and international humanitarian law. These may include prosecutions of individual perpetrators, the establishment of truth-seeking mechanisms to throw light on the nature of past abuse, reparations offered to victims of violence, the reform of institutions such as the police and the courts and vetting or removing perpetrators from positions of power.[6] In countries shifting from repression to democracy, transitional justice is seen as the first test for the establishment of democracy and the rule of law.[7]

After a wave of political transitions that were implemented through national conferences in several African countries from 1990 onwards,[8] transitional justice processes were proposed or implemented in Burundi, Côte d'Ivoire, the Democratic Republic of the Congo (DRC), Ghana, Liberia, Morocco, Nigeria, Rwanda, Sierra Leone, South Africa, Sudan and Uganda. Other countries such as Angola, Chad, Ethiopia, Mozambique and Namibia also went through particular transition processes in order to address legacies of past abuse that had the potential to 'undermine future reconstruction by fuelling resentment, triggering revenge, and reinforcing a message of impunity'.[9]

Established by national laws or included in peace agreements or other official documents, transitional mechanisms have known relative success in Africa. This chapter considers a number of critical questions:

- Considering the different processes that have recently been implemented on the continent, how has transitional justice been able to restore democracy and the rule of law in African countries emerging from violent conflict or repression?
- How successful have these processes been?
- What challenges have held the democratisation process back?
- What opportunities exist for transitional justice in Africa to re-establish democracy and the rule of law, especially with reference to the standards and institutions developed under the African Union (AU) to protect human rights and strengthen democracy and the rule of law on the continent?

AN OVERVIEW OF TRANSITIONAL PROCESSES

Although the number of armed conflicts has generally decreased in recent years, more countries have been torn by internal violent conflict, especially in Africa, where several states are either in conflict or are now in a post-conflict phase. In 2002, it was estimated that almost half of the African countries, and over one in three African people were directly or indirectly affected by armed conflicts.[10] This trend, characterised by a general breakdown of government, economic privation, civil strife and common human misery, corresponds to the failure of nation-states.[11] In Africa, structural factors that have been specifically identified as fuelling conflicts are: limited political participation and the exclusion of minorities from governance; exploitation and discrimination; socio-economic deprivation combined with inequity; limited access to resources; and the state's lack of institutional capacity to manage conflict constructively.[12] In order to assist 'failed states' in overcoming the impact of conflict on their human and economic resources, it is necessary to engage in a process of reconstruction that also addresses these root causes of conflict.

Post-conflict reconstruction is based on four main tenets: security, social and economic wellbeing, justice and reconciliation, and governance and participation.[13] It is understood that no single best way exists for post-conflict societies to address past abuses. Though numerous factors have conditioned and determined societies' responses to human rights violations, the manner in which a protracted conflict is brought to an end is considered to have a crucial impact on the choice of any transitional tool. According to Yasmin Sooka:

> A military victory by one side over the other will usually allow for a criminal justice mechanism. A negotiated peace agreement that initiates a transition to democracy on the basis of a voluntary transfer of power will result, in most instances, in a truth commission being established.[14]

In recognition that one size will not fit all, recent transitional processes in Africa have featured a wide range of transitional justice mechanisms, such as truth commissions, international or hybrid tribunals as well as traditional justice mechanisms, regardless of whether the end to the conflict was brought about through military or more consensual means (see Chapter 1 in this volume).

Transitional justice measures generally follow clear instances of regime change, as was the case in countries such as Chile, Argentina and South Africa.

However, in Africa, several transitional processes were implemented without a clear break from the past and/or from ongoing conflicts. For example, the Lomé Peace Accord of 1999 for Sierra Leone followed two previous peace agreements that were aimed at ending the conflict and establishing democracy. In Ghana, after the establishment of an Armed Forces Revolutionary Council (AFRC) set up in 1979 to carry out a house-cleaning exercise in the armed forces and society at large, a 1984 National Commission for Democracy (NCD) charged with formulating a programme to study ways of establishing participatory democracy in the country, and forums organised from 1990 in the country's ten regions for Ghanaians to air their views as to their preferred form of government,[15] the 2002 National Reconciliation Commission (NRC) completed various accountability measures that had been implemented by earlier successive governments. In the DRC and Uganda, different degrees of conflict continue, although various transitional justice measures have been initiated. Specifically, while violence still erupts regularly in eastern DRC, a Truth and Reconciliation Commission (TRC) was among five transitional institutions established following the 2002 Pretoria Agreement to support the country's democratisation process; prosecutions were also initiated before the International Criminal Court (ICC) in 2004 for crimes committed since 2002. In August 2006 the DRC held its first democratic elections since its independence in 1960. In Uganda, besides an Amnesty Act passed by the government for demobilised rebels in 2000, first referrals of the situation in the north were made to the ICC in 2003, while pockets of violence persist in different parts of the country.

Despite what was labelled as a 'lack of clarity about when to implement transitional justice', transitional mechanisms in Africa have had the potential to re-establish and strengthen democracy and the rule of law in countries emerging from protracted armed conflict or willing to depart from long-term repressive regimes.[16]

Democracy and the rule of law are elements of governance that may foster multi-ethnic consensus and promote reconciliation after violent conflict.[17] Defined as 'a process of gradually introducing more participatory politics, including elections and the creation of a civil society supportive of tolerant, pluralistic politics through adherence to constitutional rules of the game',[18] democratisation is an important element of post-conflict reconstruction. It is a complex and iterative process that must take account of national conditions and which often relies upon power-sharing. South Africa is often cited as an example of a successful home-grown democratisation process that helped to end apartheid, avoided a race war, and laid the basis for democracy and reconciliation. In the DRC, while many rejoiced over the first elections, organised after 46 years of independence, the path to democracy, as defined and closely monitored by the international community, is believed to have led to the endorsement of pre-known and pre-accepted political leaders. Sustainable transition from violent conflict and authoritarian regimes to peace and democracy must involve popular support and the involvement of civil society, respect for human rights and gender equality, as well as constitutional processes and institutional reform, all of which are essential to democracy and the rule of law.

Specifically, overall public support – not merely support from the political elite – is necessary to achieve a successful transition to peace. Ownership of a truth-seeking process is an essential element required to ensure its acceptance and, consequently, that the recommendations formulated by such a transitional mechanism are implemented.[19] For instance, the credibility of the truth commission in the DRC was weakened due to a lack of adequate consultation prior to its establishment. Proposed by members of the Inter-Congolese Dialogue as part of the peace negotiations, the commission was born out of limited consultation in which victims were not broadly involved. Its members, some of whom were associated with various armed groups or nominated by their political parties, were also seen as partisan.[20] In neighbouring Burundi, the establishment of transitional justice mechanisms has been stalled by a national consultation process that aims to address issues such as the role of the government, the participation of the United Nations (UN), civil society organisations (CSOs) and the people of Burundi, the question of amnesty and its non-applicability to the crime of genocide, crimes against humanity and war crimes and the relationship that exists between the proposed Truth and Reconciliation Commission and the Special Tribunal.[21] While the delays may be important to enable consultation, there is reason to be concerned about undue delay.

A democratic transitional process further calls for vulnerable groups to be empowered and allowed to play their part in the process. In Sierra Leone, the Truth and Reconciliation Commission (SLTRC) was inaugurated in 2002 to promote reconciliation through a process of truth-telling, apology and pardon. Despite initial concerns generated by its co-existence with the Special Court and the limited time available for hearings in most of the provinces, the SLTRC progressively gained the support of major stakeholders, including groups of victims, witnesses and perpetrators. By the end of 2003, although its targets were not fully attained, the commission had held 93 public hearings.[22] Interviews were conducted in 141 of the country's 149 chiefdoms as well as in Gambia, Guinea and Nigeria, where refugees from Sierra Leone were living, and nearly 8 000 testimonies were collected.[23] Women and girls, children more generally, amputees and ex-combatants were given an opportunity to tell their story and take part in the peacebuilding process that followed the brutal ten-year civil war (see Chapter 7 in this volume). In post-apartheid South Africa, awareness of gender specificities within the South African struggle for racial equality created a strong women's movement and led to the inclusion of women's concerns in the new democratic debate.

In addition to its support of, and participation in, any democratisation process, a strengthened civil society serves as 'a guarantee for a sound societal fabric' and its absence is considered to reveal the weight of an oppressive regime.[24] There is a risk of 'romanticising civil society' and its contribution to transitional justice and democratisation,[25] but a vigorous civil society can also play a critical role in designing, implementing, monitoring and improving transitional processes.[26]

In Liberia, civil society was actively able to take part, from the start, in the establishment of the Truth and Reconciliation Commission (TRC). The commission was created under the 2003 Comprehensive Peace Agreement and passed into law by the National Transitional Legislative Assembly in June 2005, before it was inaugurated in February 2006. Civil society groups had the opportunity to influence the formulation of the commission's mandate and the selection of its members. Civil society succeeded in ensuring that all of the commissioners underwent a vetting and public scrutiny process, promising ownership and accountability of the mechanism to the entire nation. Vetting processes are defined as formal mechanisms for identifying and removing individuals responsible for abuses from public office, especially from the police, the prison services, the army and the judiciary.[27] Procedural protections of the rule of law and non-discrimination must be put in place to avoid the abuse of vetting, particularly given the vague description of 'perpetrators', who can, in some countries, constitute more than half the population.[28] If conducted properly, the process of vetting allows for the active participation of civil society, which can monitor the protection of due process and consideration for victims.

Besides popular participation and civil society scrutiny, democratisation processes require mechanisms that allow for power-sharing, control of decision-making and the establishment or consolidation of democratic institutions such as political parties and a functioning parliament. By formulating recommendations that promote political and institutional reform, truth-seeking mechanisms have the potential to restore democracy and the rule of law in post-conflict settings and post-authoritarian regimes.

In Morocco, the Instance Equité et Réconciliation (IER), one of the few examples of a TRC established without a regime change, was set up by King Muhammed VI after only limited consultations with CSOs. Aiming specifically to 'accelerate democratic change by revitalising civil society and political debate',[29] the IER recommended constitutional reforms to guarantee human rights, the diminution of executive powers, the strengthening of parliament and real independence for the judicial branch. Although severely criticised by national human rights organisations for its proximity to the king's palace, the Moroccan TRC is considered to offer a road map for political and institutional change that could lead to the establishment of the rule of law in Morocco and constitute a stimulating and hopeful precedent in the Arab Islamic world.[30]

Democracy and good governance on the one hand and human rights on the other are encompassed in the notion of the rule of law.[31] The rule of law refers to:

> [A] principle of governance in which all persons, institutions and entities, public and private, including the State itself, are accountable to laws that are publicly promulgated, equally enforced and independently adjudicated, and which are consistent with international human rights norms and standards.[32]

The rule of law implies a variety of goals and requires such measures as will ensure adherence to principles of the supremacy of law, equality before the law, accountability to the law, the impartiality of justice, the separation of powers, participation in decision-making, legal certainty, the protection of human rights, and procedural and legal transparency.[33]

Constitutions lay the foundations for the rule of law. In societies that have encountered violence or repression, the end of conflict provides an opportunity to engage in various activities such as drafting new Constitutions and revising legislation. Transitional constitution-making processes must take into consideration historic and cultural values, as well as national and group identities.

Such processes must also break with the past, in the sense that they should not incorporate principles that may hinder national reconciliation and democratic development. For instance, because equality constitutes a central element of peace and development, and because social, political and economic marginalisation, including that of women, is part of the structural violence that is one of the underlying causes of violent conflicts in Africa, addressing past inequalities – including gender inequalities – is a condition for effective post-conflict peacebuilding and reconciliation.[34]

After the 1994 genocide in Rwanda there was a pressing need to rebuild human capital. Thus the new Constitution provided women with considerable opportunities. Rwanda now has the largest female parliamentary representation in the world[35] and the increased numerical and qualitative participation of women has resulted in various legislative reforms, such as the new inheritance and marriage laws.[36] In Sierra Leone, in adherence to the Lomé Peace Accord and the recommendations of the TRC concerning the review of the 1991 Constitution, the government set up a Constitutional Review Commission in September 2006. Amongst its recommendations, the commission advocated the broadening of the criteria for citizenship, legal proceedings in the case of human rights violations, the protection of the environment, the right to collective bargaining and the removal of provisions relating to gender discrimination.[37]

Besides making provision for the more equal participation of both men and women in public affairs, transitional constitution-making processes should be inclusive, resulting from a national dialogue, and should address all the sensitive issues that have led to and could once again lead to further grievances, instability and conflict.[38] From the beginning of negotiations between the African National Congress (ANC) and the white South African government in the late 1980s to the adoption of the 1996 Constitution, the democratisation process was marked by an all-inclusive strategy that helped to identify the main issues pertaining to a very particular transition from the apartheid regime to a democratic regime. This all-inclusive strategy contributed to establishing sustainable peace.[39]

In addition to new constitution-making processes, post-conflict settings allow for law enforcement institutions to be reformed and strengthened, and require that past human rights abuses be adequately addressed.[40] In Sierra Leone, the SLTRC recommended that the Human Rights Commission, called for by the 1999 Lomé Peace Accord, be established to serve as 'both a watchdog and a visible route through which people could access their rights'. That commission, whose members were to be selected after consultation with civil society and other stakeholders, monitors and assesses the observance of human rights throughout the country. Its mandate conforms to the Paris Principles, and it should help to create a national culture of human rights through its various functions, which include advocacy, research, advice, monitoring and investigation, and through its power to secure appropriate reparations where human rights have been violated.

In the aftermath of divisive conflicts the promotion of the rule of law further calls for the establishment of an independent judiciary that can serve as a forum for ensuring accountability and the peaceful resolution of disputes.[41] Essential for the fight against impunity, prosecutions aim to:

- bring to justice those responsible for serious violations of human rights and humanitarian law;
- put an end to such violations and prevent their recurrence;
- secure justice and dignity for victims;
- establish a record of past events;
- promote national reconciliation;
- re-establish the rule of law; and
- contribute to the restoration of peace.[42]

Prosecutions have contributed to the progressive development of international criminal law, including the clarification of legal issues such as rape as a war crime.[43] Criminal trials also have the potential to restore public confidence in the state's ability and willingness to enforce the law. They help to establish detailed and well-substantiated records of particular incidents and events during past conflicts; they may further contribute to deterrence, the removal of extremist elements from the national political process and the restoration of peace.

Post-conflict prosecutions, particularly those in national courts, have the potential to help reconstruct national justice systems that have been undermined by the war and to enhance the capacity of national lawyers, officials and staff. However, due to poor legal capacity and limited political will, only a few trials for past gross human rights abuses have been held in Africa. Where such trials have been conducted, they have been hampered by numerous difficulties. For example, in post-genocide Rwanda it was estimated that only ten Rwandan lawyers were available because most legal professionals had either been killed or fled the country. The situation was further compounded by the fact that local infrastructures had been pillaged or heavily damaged. In 1996, an Organic Law was passed by the parliament in an attempt to restore the judicial system and to put on trial the sheer number of prisoners allegedly involved in the genocide.[44]

In Ethiopia, following the deposition of the repressive Dergue regime, which had been characterised by systematic human rights abuses against perceived opponents, the new Ethiopian government created a Special Prosecutor's Office in 1991. The mandate of the Special Prosecutor was to establish a historical record of abuses and prosecute those responsible for crimes of the prior regime between 1974 and 1991. Prosecutions were undertaken within the national court system of Ethiopia and the trials were not concluded until January 2007.[45]

Where the necessary technical capacity and political will does not exist and the domestic judiciary is unwilling or unable to prosecute, there have been steady calls for international judicial processes that can provide alternative justice. This is what occurred in Rwanda, where the UN Security Council established the International Criminal Tribunal for Rwanda (ICTR) in 1994 to prosecute those bearing the greatest responsibility for genocide and other serious violations of international humanitarian law committed between 1 January and 31 December 1994.[46] Following a period of violent criticism and heavy scepticism, the ICTR has reached a phase where 80 people have been indicted, 27 judgments involving 33 accused have been handed down and three of those indicted have been acquitted.[47] A number of cases have now been handed over to the Rwandan Prosecutor-General, to be tried within the national court system and the ICTR is planning to complete its mandate at first instance by 2009, and all its work including appeals by 2010.[48]

By conducting fair trials, listening to the parties, establishing the facts and applying the law in an impartial manner, the ICTR is providing a broad picture of the 1994 events and the period preceding them. Guilty pleas, combined with expressions of remorse, are believed to represent a core element in the process of reconciliation in Rwanda.[49] The location of the ICTR outside the country where the genocide was committed has allowed the Tribunal to benefit from more adequate operational facilities and has helped to protect its security and independence. However, its distance has not facilitated interaction with the local population, its accessibility to the victims and its proximity to evidence and witnesses. Furthermore, the location of the ICTR in Arusha, Tanzania, prevented the Tribunal from increasing the capacity of Rwandan national lawyers and from allowing the national justice system to benefit subsequently from its physical infrastructure.

In Sierra Leone, where the post-war domestic judiciary was described as weak and partisan,[50] lessons learnt from the ICTR led to the establishment of a mixed tribunal that was mandated to try those who bore the greatest responsibility for crimes against humanity, war crimes and other serious violations of international law that were committed during the 1991–1999 conflict, although only for crimes that were committed from 1996 onwards.[51]

As two retributive justice institutions driven by the international community, the Rwanda and the Sierra Leone tribunals have been criticised both for their limited reach and their limited capacity to have an impact on the domestic judicial system due to technical and political constraints such as victim and witness fears to testify; insufficient time to carry out investigations; the lack of public support; and inadequate funding.[52]

More generally, international criminal mechanisms on the continent have paid minimal attention to African accountability mechanisms and in doing so have paved the way for their limited acceptance and ownership by local populations. In response, some countries in Africa have adopted their own models of accountability. For example, traditional *gacaca* courts have been set up in post-genocide Rwanda to hear cases from various categories of perpetrator and apportion punishment appropriately.[53] In Northern Uganda, even though victims of the twenty-year armed conflict do not see justice and peace as mutually exclusive, the existence of endogenous accountability mechanisms has led leaders from the communities most affected by the conflict to question the timing of the indictment of Lord's Resistance Army (LRA) commanders by the ICC, notwithstanding a 2000 Amnesty Act which was considered as an incentive for rebels to disarm.[54]

Many African governments unfortunately only pay lip service to supporting the principles of rule of law and democracy and continue to resist accountability processes. Despite the proclamation of such principles in nearly every constitutional framework on the continent, democracy and the rule of law remain in contradiction with the actual human rights and governance records of most AU member states. For political transitions to succeed in ensuring democratisation in post-conflict countries or former authoritarian states, lessons should be learned from the transitional processes that have so far been implemented in Africa. In addition, greater consideration should be given to more home-grown and

Afrocentric peacebuilding and accountability mechanisms that could augment the standards and principles adopted by the AU.

THE AFRICAN UNION AS THE ENGINE

Established in 1963, the former Organisation of African Unity (OAU) was principally aimed at eradicating the remaining vestiges of colonisation and apartheid on the continent, co-ordinating and intensifying co-operation for development, and safeguarding the sovereignty and territorial integrity of member states. With the transformation of the OAU into the AU in 2002, African governments have emphasised the need to promote peace, security and stability on the continent. Advancing democracy, popular participation and good governance, as well as human and people's rights have also been recognised as specific objectives. To achieve these objectives, the AU recognises the right of the continental organisation to intervene in a member state pursuant to a decision of the AU in respect of circumstances such as genocide, war crimes and crimes against humanity. Other principles governing the functioning of the AU include gender equality, respect for democratic principles, human rights, the rule of law and good governance, the promotion of social justice, and the condemnation and rejection of unconstitutional changes of government. All these objectives and principles, together with the corresponding institutions established under the AU, can be used to inform transitional justice processes in Africa.[55]

Efforts to restore democracy and the rule of law in post-conflict African countries have succeeded in diverse ways. In South Africa, the model of the TRC and the constitution-making process was crucial for ensuring a peaceful transition from the apartheid regime to a democratically functioning system. In Ghana the NRC[56] reconciled Ghanaians through the establishment of an accurate and complete historical record of massive human rights abuses that were committed between March 1957 and January 1993[57] (see Chapter 9 in this volume). Made public in April 2005, the report of the NRC contained important recommendations, including the provision of meaningful reparations to the victims, as well as a range of institutional reforms in the security services, the judiciary and other sectors.

However, clear-cut democratic rules and practices, as well as effective justice resulting from the various transitional mechanisms implemented on the continent, still need to be observed and sustained. Amnesties and limited criminal prosecutions under transitional justice processes both in South Africa and in

Ghana did not receive unconditional approval from human rights activists. In Chad, a commission of inquiry into the crimes committed by the regime of Hissène Habré was established to investigate the illegal imprisonments, detentions, assassinations, disappearances, torture and other human rights violations that were committed between 1982 and 1990. The commission gathered evidence that pointed to the responsibility of the Habré government for an estimated 40 000 political killings and documented an unspecified number of cases of torture and arbitrary detention. Nevertheless, no criminal proceedings were conducted.[58] In 2006, following years of attempts to have former president Habré charged, the AU eventually convinced the Republic of Senegal to try Habré for abuses of human rights committed during his tenure.[59] Though Senegal initially announced that the trial would not start until at least the three years needed to organise the judicial process had passed,[60] the AU has appeared as a renewed body that can assist with revitalising democratisation processes and the rule of law on the continent.[61]

Principles of popular participation in the activities of the AU through its Constitutive Act and its Economic, Social and Cultural Council (ECOSOCC), as well as the promotion of gender equality, can bring about change from the top down in countries which remain reluctant to accept and observe such principles. By establishing a platform through which civil society can engage governments on issues concerning their daily lives and take part in regional policy-making and decision-making processes, the ECOSOCC presents an opportunity to widen continental support for policies and programmes aimed, *inter alia*, at promoting peace, security and stability in Africa, defending a culture of good governance, democracy, social justice, human rights, popular participation, as well as advocating a culture of gender equality.

Furthermore, the Conference on Security, Stability, Development and Co-operation in Africa (CSSDCA),[62] as well as the New Partnership for Africa's Development (NEPAD) and its related African Peer Review Mechanism (APRM),[63] all have the potential for monitoring whether countries shifting from conflict and authoritarian rule effectively adopt and abide by universal principles of democracy and the rule of law. Aimed at consolidating the work of the AU in the areas of peace, security, stability, development and co-operation, the CSSDCA process provides a forum for elaborating and advancing common values, including respect for democracy and the rule of law, within the main policy organs of the AU. One of NEPAD's focus themes – democracy and good political governance – also engages African countries to promote democracy, good governance, peace and security by ensuring that their national Constitutions reflect democratic principles and provide for visibly accountable governance. In November 2007, 25 countries signed the Memorandum of Understanding in which they agreed to participate in the self-monitoring APRM.[64]

Adopted in 2007, the AU Charter on Democracy, Elections and Governance has complemented the continental framework for establishing democracy and the rule of law in Africa. Among its objectives, the Charter engages African governments to promote and defend democracy and respect for human rights, enhance their commitment to the rule of law, consolidate good governance, encourage citizen participation and accountability in the management of public affairs, and promote gender balance and equality in governance and development processes. The monitoring of the Charter rests principally with the AU Commission, which serves as the central co-ordinating structure for its implementation. Besides the Charter on Democracy, Elections and Governance, the African Charter on Human and People's Rights[65] and subsequent instruments such as the African Union Protocol on the Rights of Women in Africa[66] are existing standards that adequately serve as yardsticks that can be used to measure the compliance of African states to the principles of human rights and the rule of law.

The 1981 Human and People's Rights Charter provides for the rights and fundamental freedoms that individuals and groups can claim in order to establish and sustain democratic governance and the rule of law, including in post-conflict situations. By acknowledging that women play a crucial role in developing and strengthening democracy African states have also developed norms which advocate the 'full and active participation of women in the decision-making processes and structures at all levels as a fundamental element in the promotion and exercise of a democratic culture'.[67] The AU Women's Protocol and the 2004 Solemn Declaration on Gender Equality in Africa[68] further engage AU member states to 'ensure the full and effective participation and representation of women in peace processes including the prevention, resolution, management of conflicts', and in all aspects of planning, formulation and implementation of post-conflict reconstruction and rehabilitation.

The African Charter on Human and People's Rights and its Protocol on the Rights of Women in Africa are implemented by state parties under the scrutiny of regional mechanisms, such as the African Commission and, shortly, the African Court on Human and People's Rights.[69] Inaugurated in 1987, the Human Rights

Commission has the mandate to promote and protect human and people's rights across the continent. By examining state parties' reports, considering communications or complaints, and by advocating and monitoring human rights situations on the continent through its special procedures, the commission serves as the guarantee needed to hold African countries accountable to principles to which they have voluntarily subscribed.

Recommendations formulated by the commission have covered issues such as legal and institutional reform,[70] reparations to be provided to victims of human rights abuses,[71] including abuses of social, economic and cultural rights,[72] and, more recently, gender issues.[73] Enhanced by the legally binding nature of decisions that are pronounced by the African Court on Human and People's Rights, the African human rights system has the potential to assess whether transitional justice processes implemented on the continent effectively result in restoring democracy and the rule of law in post-conflict countries and post-authoritarian regimes.

In tandem with the regional human rights framework, the emerging peace and security architecture of the AU provides another opportunity to develop regional integration towards the promotion of peace and justice in Africa.[74] Having recognised the link that exists between developing strong democratic institutions, observing human rights and the rule of law, implementing post-conflict recovery programmes and sustainable development policies and promoting collective security, sustainable peace and stability, AU member states have established the Peace and Security Council (PSC), supported by, among other institutions, a Panel of the Wise. The PSC features an operational structure mandated, *inter alia*, to:

> [F]ollow-up, within the framework of its conflict prevention responsibil-ities, the progress towards the promotion of democratic practices, good governance, the rule of law, protection of human rights and fundamental freedoms, respect for the sanctity of human life and international humanitarian law by Member States.[75]

By adopting norms and establishing institutions that have the potential to prevent conflicts, ensure peace and enhance democracy and the rule of law on the continent, the AU has developed a significant system that can be adequately used to monitor and assess transitional processes that are implemented in African countries emerging from conflict or authoritarian rule. The question remains, however, as to how effective such norms and mechanisms are in achieving their ideals.

CONCLUSION

Transitional processes that have been implemented in African post-conflict countries and post-repressive regimes have structurally aligned themselves with previous mechanisms that were aimed at building democracy and restoring the rule of law in societies that suffered under protracted violent conflict or authoritarian rule. However, a brief study of their establishment process, their resulting product and their effective impact[76] demonstrates that transitional justice mechanisms implemented in Africa have had only limited success in re-establishing democracy and the rule of law. These shortcomings have been explained by a context in which the state is considered 'a deliberately and instrumentally informalised entity in which an entrenchment of the rule of law may not often correspond with the logic of politics'.[77]

Most African countries that have implemented transitional justice have established truth-seeking mechanisms in the form of truth and reconciliation commissions or inquiry organs. For truth commissions to fulfil the requirements of democracy and the rule of law they must have credible commissioner selection criteria and processes and should enjoy meaningful independence. Moreover, they must be seen as moral, just, representative, consultative and open to public scrutiny in various aspects of their work and at all stages, namely their establishment, functioning and handing over of the final report.

Besides truth-seeking commissions, African countries have used criminal prosecutions to bring perpetrators of human rights abuses to account. In the cases of Rwanda and Sierra Leone prosecutions were coupled with some form of restorative justice in order to address the legacies of the genocide and of the violent ten-year war. In other countries, such as Uganda, criminal prosecutions that were undertaken by the international community did not receive the full support of the local population, including victims of the protracted conflict in the northern part of the country. Building democracy and restoring the rule of law in post-conflict settings therefore requires integrated approaches that should take into account the context of their implementation. Community support and ownership of the process by the public are key elements and consideration should be given to local mechanisms for ensuring accountability and achieving reconciliation in post-conflict communities. Furthermore, when combining non-prosecutorial mechanisms and criminal actions, it is essential that transitional justice processes include co-existence principles that clarify their collaboration in order to avoid the tensions that arose as a result of the co-existence of the TRC and the SCSL in Sierra Leone (see Chapter Seven in this volume).

An African conception of transitional justice which simultaneously embraces the universal principles of accountability and due reparation and maintains and revives traditional African accountability processes should be developed. This regionalised transitional justice will take into account recent trends, developed at the international level, towards fighting impunity while ensuring that criminal proceedings initiated against the perpetrators of international crimes are understood and endorsed by local populations, including their victims. Achieving reconciliation and setting up participatory societies that comply with the rule of law further calls for effective reparations and due screening processes to be implemented. Harmonised norms and principles that take into account the reality on the ground should therefore be developed and effectively implemented by and within the AU and sub-regional organisations.

For the AU to serve capably as the legitimate umbrella organisation for the establishment and restoration of democracy and the rule of law on the continent, the set of rules adopted by its member states should be completely ratified and effectively implemented. Democratisation in post-conflict countries and following post-authoritarian regimes is a long-term process that cannot be achieved during the period of temporary transitional measures. Assessment and monitoring of transitional processes under the AU should therefore ensure that perpetrators of grave human rights abuses are effectively held accountable for their deeds and serve their sanctions, that measures recommended by truth-seeking commissions are implemented and that institutions are established which both reinstate democracy and the rule of law and function efficiently. Broad and sustained interventions at local, national and regional levels should, ultimately, ensure that international assistance is used to strengthen reconciliation and accountability, thereby enhancing sustainable peace and justice across the continent.

NOTES AND REFERENCES

1. 'International Criminal Court Judges embody "our collective conscience", says Secretary-General to inaugural meeting in the Hague'. Press release, UN Doc SG/SM/8628, L/3027 (11 March 2003), Amnesty International (June 2006), *Liberia truth, justice and reparation: Memorandum on the Truth and Reconciliation Commission Act*.

2. Y. Sooka, 'Dealing with the past and transitional justice: Building peace through accountability', *International Review of the Red Cross* 88(862), 2006: 311–325.

3. See M.M. Kaminski, M. Nalepa and B. O'Neill, 'Normative and strategic aspects of transitional justice', *Journal of Conflict Resolution* 50(3), 2006: 295–302.

4. R.G. Teitel, 'Transitional justice genealogy', *Harvard Human Rights Journal* 16, 2003: 69–94.

5. P. van Zyl, UN Security Council debate, 'Justice and the rule of law: The role of the United Nations', statement made at 'Arria Formula' Meeting, International Centre for Transitional Justice, 30 September 2004, www.globalpolicy.org/security/mtgsetc/040930ictj.pdf (accessed 20 March 2007).

6. See L.M. Olson, 'Provoking the dragon on the patio: Matters of transitional justice: penal repression vs amnesties', *International Review of the Red Cross* 88(862), 2006: 275–294.

7. N.J. Kritz, 'The dilemmas of transitional justice', in N.J. Kritz (ed.), *Transitional justice: How emerging democracies reckon with former regimes, vol. I: General considerations* (Washington, DC: United States Institute of Peace Press, 1995), pp. xii–xiii.

8. National conferences were organised in Benin, Gabon, Congo-Brazzaville, Niger, Mali, Togo, former Zaire and Chad that led to mixed successes. See D. Bangoura, 'Une conférence nationale, seul moyen de sortir de la crise', *Géopolitique Africaine*, 2004, www.african-geopolitics.org/show.aspx?ArticleId=3819 (accessed 16 April 2007).

9. M. Parlevliet, 'Bridging the divide, exploring the relationship between human rights and conflict management', Occasional Paper, Centre for Conflict Resolution (CCR), University of Cape Town, 11(1), 2002: *Track Two*, p. 26.

10. Read *Post-conflict recovery in Africa: An agenda for the Africa region*. World Bank, Africa Region Working Paper Series (30 April 2002), www.worldbank.org/afr/wps/wp30.pdf (accessed 9 November 2007).

11. G.B. Helman and S.R. Ratner, 'Saving failed states', *Foreign Policy* 89, 1993: 3–20, in G. Baechler, 'Conflict transformation through state reform', Berghof Research Centre for Constructive Conflict Management, 1993 (edited version August 2004), www.berghof-handbook.net (accessed 20 April 2007).

12. Report of the Secretary-General, 'The causes of conflict and the promotion of durable peace and sustainable development in Africa', UN General Assembly Security Council, A/52/871–S/1998/318 (13 April 1998), www.un.org/africa/osaa/reports/A_52_871_Causes%20of%20Confict%201998.pdf (accessed 9 November 2007).

13. Post-conflict reconstruction. A joint project of the Centre for Strategic and International Studies (CSIS) and the Association of the United States Army (AUSA), Task Framework (May 2002), www.strategicleader.us/ExperientalLearningPapers/PostConflictReconstruction.pdf (accessed 20 April 2007).

14. Sooka, 'Dealing with the past and transitional justice'.

15. Political History of Ghana, www.ghanaweb.com/GhanaHomePage/republic/polit_hist.php (accessed 9 November 2007).

16. L.K. Bosire, 'Overpromised, underdelivered: Transitional justice in sub-Saharan Africa', *SUR, International Journal on Human Rights* 5, 2005, www.surjournal.org/eng/index.php (accessed 20 April 2007).

17. T.D. Sisk, 'Democratization and peacebuilding: Perils and promises', in C.A. Croker, F.O. Hampson and P. Aall (eds.), *Turbulent peace: The challenges of managing international conflict* (Washington, DC: United States Institute of Peace Press, 2001), pp. 785–800.

18. Sisk, 'Democratization and peacebuilding'.
19. Sooka, 'Dealing with the past and transitional justice'.
20. Bosire, 'Overpromised, underdelivered'.
21. Report of the UN Secretary-General, First report of the Secretary-General on the United Nations Integrated Office in Burundi, S/2007/287 (17 May 2007), daccessdds.un.org/doc/UNDOC/GEN/N07/341/80/PDF/N0734180.pdf?OpenElement (accessed 22 May 2007).
22. B.K. Dougherty, 'Searching for answers: Sierra Leone's Truth and Reconciliation Commission', *African Studies Quarterly* 8(1), 2004, www.africa.ufl.edu/asq/v8/v8i1a3.htm (accessed 13 November 2007).
23. Benetech Human Rights Data Analysis Group, *Statistical appendix to the Report of the Truth and Reconciliation Commission of Sierra Leone*, report to the Truth and Reconciliation Commission (5 October 2004), www.trcsierraleone.org/pdf/APPENDICES/Appendix%201%20-%20Statistical%20Report.pdf (accessed 13 November 2007).
24. Baechler, 'Conflict transformation through state reform'.
25. Comments made by participants at a policy seminar organised by the CCR, 'Peace versus Justice? Truth and Reconciliation Commissions and War Crimes Tribunals in Africa', 17–18 May 2007, Cape Town, South Africa.
26. D.A. Crocker, 'Truth commissions, transitional justice and civil society', in R.I. Rotberg and D. Thompson (eds.), *Truth v justice: The morality of truth commissions* (Princeton, NJ: Princeton University Press, 2000), www.publicpolicy.umd.edu/faculty/crocker/RotbergPaper.PDF (accessed 16 April 2007).
27. Report of the UN Secretary-General, 'The rule of law and transitional justice in conflict and post-conflict societies', UN Security Council, S/2004/616 (23 August 2004), daccessdds.un.org/doc/UNDOC/GEN/N04/395/29/PDF/N0439529.pdf?OpenElement (accessed 11 January 2007).
28. Kritz, 'The dilemmas of transitional justice'.
29. P. Hazan, 'Morocco: Betting on a Truth and Reconciliation Commission', United States Institute of Peace, Special Report 165 (July 2006), www.usip.org/pubs/specialreports/sr165.pdf (accessed 20 April 2007).
30. Hazan, 'Morocco'.
31. R. Mani, 'Promoting the rule of law in post-conflict societies', in L. Wohlgemuth, S. Gibson, S. Klasen and E. Rothchild (eds.), *Common security and civil society in Africa* (Uppsala: Nordiska Afrikainstitutet, 1999), pp. 145–162, 148. The author also gives a minimalist conception of the rule of law, presented as a minimum of clear and widely known rules that are objectively applied, and of a functioning judiciary and justice system which guarantees individuals a certain degree of freedom if they know and obey the rules.
32. Report of the UN Secretary-General, 'The rule of law and transitional justice in conflict and post-conflict societies'.
33. Report of the UN Secretary-General, 'The rule of law and transitional justice in conflict and post-conflict societies'. Also read R.K. Belton, 'Competing definitions of the rule of law: Implications for practitioners', *Rule of Law Series*, Carnegie Papers 55 (January 2005), www.carnegieendowment.org/files/CP55.Belton.FINAL.pdf (accessed 12 January 2007).

34. CCR/UNIFEM, 'Women in post-conflict societies in Africa', seminar report, November 2006, ccrweb.ccr.uct.ac.za (accessed 7 January 2008).

35. J.M. Mba, 'Strategies for increasing women's participation in government: Case study of Rwanda', Expert Group Meeting on Democratic Governance in Africa, 6–8 December 2005, Nairobi, Kenya, in *Women's rights in post-conflict countries in Africa: Implementing the African Union Protocol to the African Charter on Human and People's Rights on the Rights of Women in Africa in emerging post-conflict countries*, www.un.org/africa/osaa/reports/Democratic%20Governance%20Case%20study%20RWANDA.pdf (accessed 19 November 2007).

36. US Council on Foreign Relations (6 March 2003), 'The role of women in peacebuilding and reconstruction: Lessons from Rwanda, East Timor, and Afghanistan', www.cfr.org/publication/5729/role_of_women_in_peacebuilding_and_reconstruction.html (accessed 22 January 2007).

37. Report of the UN Secretary-General, Fourth report of the Secretary-General on the United Nations Integrated Office in Sierra Leone, UN Security Council, S/2007/257 (7 May 2007), news.sl/drwebsite/publish/article_20055491.shtml (accessed 21 May 2007).

38. Belton, 'Competing definitions of the rule of law'.

39. See E. Ebrahim, 'The management of and debate about the democratization process', www.issafrica.org/AF/profiles/SouthAfrica/satpaxcdrom/files/Ebrahim.pdf (accessed 10 May 2007).

40. Report of the UN Secretary-General, Fourth report of the Secretary-General on the United Nations Integrated Office in Sierra Leone.

41. Mani, 'Promoting the rule of law in post-conflict societies'.

42. Report of the UN Secretary-General, Fourth report of the Secretary-General on the United Nations Integrated Office in Sierra Leone.

43. Report of the UN Secretary-General, Fourth report of the Secretary-General on the United Nations Integrated Office in Sierra Leone. Also see *International Criminal Tribunal for Rwanda, The Prosecutor versus Jean-Paul Akayesu*, Case No ICTR-96-4-T (decision of 2 September 1998), 69.94.11.53/default.htm (accessed 22 May 2007).

44. See E. Zorbas, 'Reconciliation in post-genocide Rwanda', *African Journal of Legal Studies* 1(1), 2004: 29–52.

45. Justice in Perspective: Ethiopia, www.justiceinperspective.org.za/countries/ethiopia.htm (accessed 20 April 2007).

46. UN Security Council Resolution 955 (adopted 8 November 1994), daccessdds.un.org/doc/UNDOC/GEN/N95/140/97/PDF/N9514097.pdf?OpenElement (accessed 19 November 2007).

47. Achievements of the ICTR, 69.94.11.53/default.htm (accessed 20 April 2007).

48. UN Security Council Resolution 1503 (adopted 28 August 2003), daccessdds.un.org/doc/UNDOC/GEN/N03/481/70/PDF/N0348170.pdf?OpenElement (accessed 13 November 2007).

49. E. Mose, 'ICTR: Fighting impunity, ensuring accountability, allowing reconciliation', *Journal of International Criminal Justice* 3, 2005: 920–943.

50. Amnesty International (2000), *Sierra Leone: Ending impunity – an opportunity not to be missed*, web.amnesty.org/library/Index/ENGAFR510642000?open&of=ENG-SLE (accessed 22 May 2007).

51. The Special Court for Sierra Leone, www.sc-sl.org/ (accessed 16 May 2007).

52. Bosire, 'Overpromised, underdelivered'.

53. See Zorbas, 'Reconciliation in post-genocide Rwanda'.

54. Refugee Law Project, *Whose justice? Perceptions of Uganda's Amnesty Act 2000: The potential for conflict resolution and long-term reconciliation.* Working Paper 15 (February 2005).

55. Articles 3 and 4, Constitutive Act of the African Union (adopted in Lomé, Togo, July 2001 and entered into force May 2001), www.africa-union.org/root/au/AboutAU/Constitutive_Act_en. htm (accessed 9 January 2008).

56. International Centre for Transitional Justice: Ghana, www.ictj.org/en/where/region1/647.html (accessed 20 April 2007).

57. The National Reconciliation Commission Act 611 of 2002 (entered into force 11 January 2002). The National Reconciliation Process in Ghana.

58. Rapport de la Commission, Report of the Commission, reprinted in N.J. Kritz (ed.), *Transitional justice: How emerging democracies reckon with former regimes, vol. III* (Washington, DC: United States Institute of Peace Press, 1995).

59. AU Assembly, Decision on the *Hissène Habré* case and the African Union, Assembly/AU/ Dec.127(VII), Assembly of the African Union, 7th Ordinary Session, Banjul, The Gambia (1–2 July 2006), www.africa-union.org/root/au/Conferences/Past/2006/July/summit/doc/ Decisions_and_Declarations/Assembly-AU-Dec.pdf (accessed 14 November 2007).

60. K. Barber, 'Trial of former Chad leader Hissène Habré to be delayed 3 years', *Voice of America*, 31 January 2007, www.voanews.com/english/archive/2007-01/2007-01-31-voa37.cfm?CFID= 126526820&CFTOKEN=93251893 (accessed 25 April 2007).

61. J. Cilliers, 'Commentary: Towards the African Union', *African Security Review* 10(2), 2001, www.iss.co.za/pubs/ASR/10No2/Cilliers.html (accessed 13 November 2007). Also see C. Mutasa, 'The Africa Union–civil society contract: An act of democracy?', www.un-ngls.org/ cso/cso5/AfricaUnion.pdf (accessed 13 November 2007).

62. Solemn Declaration AHG/Decl.4 (XXXVI) on the Conference on Security, Stability, Development and Co-operation in Africa (CSSDCA), adopted by the 36th Ordinary Session of the Assembly of Heads of State and Government of the OAU, held in Lomé, Togo, 10–12 July 2000.

63. Declaration AHG/Decl.1 (XXXVII) on the New Partnership for Africa's Development (NEPAD), adopted by the 37th Ordinary Session of the AHSG of the OAU, held in Lusaka, Zambia, 9–11 July 2001.

64. These are Algeria, Angola, Cameroon, Republic of Congo (Brazzaville), Egypt, Ethiopia, Gabon, Benin, Burkina Faso, Mali, Mauritius, Senegal, Tanzania, Lesotho, Sierra Leone, Malawi, Ghana, Kenya, Mozambique, Nigeria, Rwanda, South Africa, Sudan, Uganda and Zambia, www.nepad.org/aprm/ (accessed 23 May 2007).

65. Adopted by the 18th AHSG, Nairobi, Kenya, June 1981, www.achpr.org/english/_info/ charter_en.html (accessed 21 May 2007).

66. Protocol to the African Charter on Human and People's Rights on the Rights of Women in Africa, adopted by the 2nd Ordinary Session of the AU, Maputo, 11 July 2003, www.achpr.org/english/_info/women_en.html (accessed 21 May 2007).

67. Article 29, African Charter on Democracy, Elections and Governance, adopted by the 8th Ordinary Session of the AU, Addis Ababa, Ethiopia, 30 January 2007, www.africa-union.org/root/au/Documents/Treaties/text/Charter%20on%20Democracy.pdf (accessed 19 November 2007).

68. Assembly of the AU, 3rd Ordinary Session, Addis Ababa, Ethiopia, 6–8 July 2004, www.africa-union.org/AU%20summit%202004/gender/decl.pdf (accessed 22 May 2007).

69. Protocol to the African Charter on Human and People's Rights on the Establishment of an African Court on Human and People's Rights, Ouagadougou, Burkina Faso, 10 June 1998, www.africa-union.org/root/au/Documents/Treaties/treaties.htm (accessed 22 May 2007).

70. Communications 54/91, 61/91, 98/93, 164–196/97 and 210/98, *Malawi African Association and others v Mauritania*, decided at the 27th Ordinary Session (May 2000), 13th Annual Activity Report (2000) 149 *African Human Rights Law Report*, www.chr.up.ac.za/centre_publications/ahrlr/ahrlr-text.pdf (accessed 26 May 2007).

71. Communication 249/2002, *Institute for Human Rights and Development in Africa (on behalf of Sierra Leonean refugees in Guinea) v Guinea*, decided at the 36th Ordinary Session (December 2004), 20th Activity Report (2004) 57 *African Human Rights Law Report*, www.chr.up.ac.za/centre_publications/ahrlr/2004-text-final.pdf (accessed 26 May 2007).

72. Communication 155/96, *Social and Economic Rights Action Centre and the Centre for Economic and Social Rights v Nigeria*, decided at the 30th Ordinary Session (October 2001), 15th Annual Activity Report (2001) 60 *African Human Rights Law Report*, www.chr.up.ac.za/centre_publications/ahrlr/ahrlr-2001-text.pdf (accessed 26 May 2007).

73. Communication 227/99, *Democratic Republic of the Congo v Burundi, Rwanda and Uganda*, decided at the 33rd Ordinary Session (May 2003), 20th Annual Activity Report (2004) 19 *African Human Rights Law Report*, www.chr.up.ac.za/centre_publications/ahrlr/2004-text-final.pdf (accessed 26 May 2007).

74. Protocol relating to the Establishment of the Peace and Security Council of the AU, adopted by the 1st Ordinary Session of the Assembly of the AU, Durban, 9 July 2002, www.africa-union.org/root/au/Documents/Treaties/Text/Protocol_peace%20and%20security.pdf (accessed 22 May 2007).

75. Article 7(*m*), Protocol Relating to the Establishment of the Peace and Security Council of the African Union.

76. P. Hayner, *Unspeakable truths: Facing the challenge of truth commissions* (New York: Routledge, 2001), p. 252.

77. P. Chabal and J.P. Daloz, 'Africa works: Disorder as political instrument', in L. Bosire (ed.), *Overpromised, underdelivered: Transitional justice in sub-Saharan Africa* (Bloomington, IN: Indiana University Press, 1999).

PART II

Truth and Reconciliation Processes

6

South Africa's Truth and Reconciliation Commission from a Global Perspective

Alex Boraine

INTRODUCTION

Following 45 years of apartheid rule and decades of armed struggle against the apartheid state, South Africa's Truth and Reconciliation Commission (TRC) was conceived in 1994[1] to help guide the country's transition to democracy.[2] The commission was premised on the belief that the country could move forward only by honestly confronting its painful past of killings, torture, disappearances, imprisonment and officially sanctioned racial discrimination. In undertaking this challenging process of national reconciliation by uncovering and documenting the truth, South Africa's TRC brought international attention to the truth commission model that has proliferated over the past decade.

This chapter examines the impact of South Africa's TRC from a global perspective.[3] In order to ground this analysis, the chapter briefly outlines the history of the TRC and then discusses three subsequent truth commissions in Sierra Leone, Timor-Leste and Peru, which were built, in part, upon South Africa's legacy.[4] The experiences in these countries raise numerous questions worthy of further consideration: How effectively has the South African model been implemented in other post-conflict societies? How has the model been reconceived and modified to fit into the relevant national context? How have subsequent truth commissions altered or improved upon the South African model, and what have been their successes and shortcomings?

SOUTH AFRICA'S TRUTH AND RECONCILIATION COMMISSION

South Africa's TRC, although preceded by other commissions in South and Central America, brought the truth commission model into the international spotlight.

This was due partly to the major personalities involved, including Archbishop Desmond Tutu, partly to the selected format of public hearings in which both victims and perpetrators detailed the gruesome realities of apartheid, and partly to the controversial decision to grant individualised amnesties to those who testified truthfully about their crimes.

Serious discussions concerning the establishment of a truth commission for South Africa began following Nelson Mandela's election as president in 1994. The more democratic approach to the TRC's formation distinguished it from previous truth commissions that had often been shaped by decree rather than a participatory process. By contrast, in South Africa, public debate about the mandate, goals and procedures of the commission was encouraged. After considerable dialogue with civil society, in mid-1995, the South African parliament passed the Promotion of National Unity and Reconciliation Act 34 of 1995. In the interests of transparency, seventeen commissioners, all South African, were then appointed from nominees who had been proposed by non-governmental organisations (NGOs), churches and political parties. Candidates were publicly interviewed by a selection panel before being appointed by the president.[5]

The commission's detailed empowering Act gave the TRC the power to grant individualised amnesties, search premises and seize evidence, subpoena witnesses and even run a witness-protection programme. Its mandate, however, focused exclusively on 'gross violations of human rights', with the additional caveat that these abuses had to have been committed with a political motive.[6] The time period that was subject to investigation was limited to that from 1 May 1960 through to the elections in May 1994. With a staff of approximately 300, housed in four offices throughout the country, and an annual budget of approximately US$18 million for two-and-a-half years, South Africa's TRC represented a major departure in both scale and ambition from prior truth commissions.

During its existence, the commission took testimony from more than 21 000 victims and witnesses, of whom approximately 2 000 testified publicly. In addition to hearings that focused on crimes against individuals, the commission also convened special sessions that were devoted to key institutions and their contributions to the apartheid structure. These hearings addressed the religious community, the legal community, business and labour, the health sector, the media, prisons and the armed forces. Media coverage of the commission's work was intense, with daily reporting in newspapers and on television, four hours of hearings broadcast live daily over national radio and a weekly special television report on the TRC that became the most-watched news programme in South Africa.

By far the most controversial of the TRC's powers, as well as its greatest departure from prior truth commissions, was its ability to grant individual amnesty to those who fully confessed to politically motivated crimes. The commission received over 7 000 applications for such amnesty. For gross violations of human rights an applicant was required to appear publicly to answer questions from the commission, the legal counsel representing the victims and their families and directly from the victims themselves.

It is regrettable, in my view, that no other commission has included or is including any opportunity to grant conditional amnesty to perpetrators. There can be no doubt that this is a very controversial issue but there is a distinct difference between *blanket* amnesty and *conditional* amnesty. It is also true that South Africa gained more information and more knowledge of what happened during the apartheid era from the perpetrators' evidence than it did from witnesses' stories. Most transitions take place under abnormal circumstances and inevitably some form of amnesty is offered. Introducing an amnesty clause into the truth commission helps to prevent collective amnesia and also introduces the possibility of the reintegration of perpetrators into society. Although the TRC amnesty was conditional and not general, there is nevertheless the important concern that this could encourage perpetrator impunity. It is noteworthy that no other state has provided for amnesty in its truth commission legislation.

The commission's final five-volume report was released in October 1998. When the report was formally considered in parliament several months later, Deputy President Thabo Mbeki, speaking in his capacity as president of the African National Congress (ANC), stated that the party had 'serious reservations' about the Truth Commission's process and report because it de-legitimised or criticised the ANC's liberation struggle.[7] As a result, the government made no commitment to implementing the commission's recommendations, which included the significant suggestion that victims identified by the TRC receive reparations from the government. Although urgent interim reparations were paid to some victims in a relatively timely manner, the final reparations eventually received by approximately 19 000 identified victims were substantially lower than the amounts that had been suggested by the TRC. Moreover, while some symbolic reparations measures have been implemented, meaningful community and institutional reparations, such as improved housing, medical care and psychological services, remain limited. This failure to execute a timely and adequate reparations policy has renewed political tensions and threatens to undermine some of the successes of the TRC's work.

SIERRA LEONE

Sierra Leone is still emerging from a decade-long conflict. The war began in March 1991 when the rebel Revolutionary United Front (RUF) launched attacks that were purportedly aimed at removing a corrupt and oppressive government from power. The ensuing civil war left the country in physical and economic ruin. Tens of thousands of civilians were killed and many more were raped, mutilated, tortured, abducted or forcibly conscripted.

In July 1999, the government of Sierra Leone and the RUF leadership signed a peace agreement in Lomé, Togo. The Lomé Peace Accord included a comprehensive amnesty provision, strongly criticised by local and international human rights groups, which granted 'absolute and free pardon and reprieve to all combatants and collaborators in respect of anything done by them in pursuit of their objectives, up to the time of the signing of the present Agreement'.[8] The government and RUF also agreed to establish a TRC that would be mandated to 'create an impartial historical record of violations and abuses of human rights and international humanitarian law related to the armed conflict in Sierra Leone' as well as 'to address impunity, to respond to the needs of victims, to promote healing and reconciliation, and to prevent a repetition of the violations and abuses suffered'.[9] The creation of a TRC received strong support from civil society groups that hoped for some measure of accountability despite a peace agreement that was viewed as unduly sympathetic to former combatants.

Although the TRC's enabling Act passed into law in February 2000, a resumption of hostilities in Freetown in May 2000 delayed the beginning of its work until July 2002.[10] Once operational, the TRC's tasks mirrored, to a large extent, those of South Africa's commission: the power to conduct investigations of both specific violations and the surrounding context, to record statements and testimony, to hold public hearings, to ensure constructive interchanges between victims and perpetrators and to present a final report, including recommendations, to the government. The commission was also granted the discretion to decide whether or not to name perpetrators.[11] Unlike South Africa's TRC, the commissioners in Sierra Leone were a mixture of nationals and internationals. This was intended to ensure a requisite balance of impartiality and local legitimacy.[12] Provision was also made for the specific involvement of traditional leaders in the commission's work at the community level.[13] Moreover, although the commission had a temporal mandate that extended from the outbreak of conflict in 1991 to the signing of the Lomé Peace Accord in 1999, it was granted the additional flexibility to examine 'to the fullest degree possible, including their antecedents, the context in which the violations and abuses occurred'.[14] Finally, the Sierra Leone TRC, unlike other commissions, approached its work in defined phases, allotting four months for statement taking, four months for public hearings and four months for report writing.

At its peak, the commission's core staff numbered approximately 40, and its total operating budget was approximately US$4.5 million. During its existence, the TRC engaged in numerous outreach and public awareness-raising activities, including town hall meetings in each of Sierra Leone's twelve provinces. It also gathered approximately 8 000 statements during a private process, followed by a period of public hearings in which approximately 350 people testified in the capital as well as the provinces. The public hearings covered representative cases as well as particular events, including the 1992 and 1997 coups, the attack on Freetown in 1999 and the taking of peacekeepers as hostages in 2000. The public process also included thematic hearings on good governance, the role of civil society, management of mineral resources and corruption, women and girls, and children and youth, as well as institutional hearings that addressed the role of the armed forces, police, media and political parties. Following the example of South Africa, the Sierra Leone TRC held closed hearings specifically designated to listen to women's experiences, particularly those related to sexual abuse, and such hearings were conducted exclusively by female commissioners with only female staff present.

The TRC submitted its final report to the Sierra Leonean government in October 2004.[15] This document detailed causes of the conflict, provided an account of the abuses committed during the civil war and recommended how best to address past events and move forward. However, the report was not easily available to the general public due to the limited number of copies printed and the fact that an electronic version was not easily accessible. This serious deficiency created the impression that the report was intended for foreign elites rather than the average Sierra Leonean and this led to widespread disillusionment.[16]

Although Sierra Leone's TRC enjoyed some success with its statement-taking process and provincial hearings, it did not make a widespread impression on the national public debate like that which occurred with the South African TRC. This failure can be linked to many factors, including a lack of general public engagement with the TRC's work. Although attendance at hearings was higher in the provinces than in the capital, the public seemed generally uninvolved in the process. This apathy might be attributable to the gap between Sierra Leone's largely illiterate and rural population and the policymakers in Freetown, to the lack of adequate information about the TRC and attendant confusion between the TRC and the Special Court, or to the fact that the TRC's methods for truth-telling were not consonant with local customary practices for addressing past crimes. In addition, because the disarmament, demobilisation and reintegration (DDR) of former combatants was largely completed by the time the TRC began its work, there was little incentive for former combatants to engage with the commission. Potential witnesses, not understanding the relationship between the TRC and the Special Court, might have feared that their testimony would prove self-incriminating before the Special Court. As a result, some perpetrators have returned to their communities without any accountability for past crimes. Furthermore, the relationship between the TRC and the government was strained. Although publicly supportive of the TRC process, the government was largely unresponsive to requests for information from the TRC and demonstrated a lack of serious engagement with the TRC's findings and recommendations. For example, although the government released a White Paper in July 2005 responding to the TRC's recommendations, it did so without consulting civil society or committing itself to a strategy or timeline for implementing the recommendations. These problems were compounded by the public view that the commission lacked political independence. The national commissioners were widely perceived as being sympathetic to the ruling Sierra Leone People's Party (SLPP) and this view was reinforced when, contrary to the TRC's recommendation that the president apologise to the population for the government's actions and inactions since 1961, the TRC's chairman supported the president's refusal to apologise. Finally, public confusion about the respective roles of the TRC and the Special Court, as well as competition and even hostility between advocates of the two institutions, led to a strained relationship between the TRC and the Special Court.[17]

Since the TRC completed its work, a Human Rights Commission has subsequently been tasked with implementing the TRC's recommendations. The Act creating the TRC specifically envisioned such follow-up procedures and committed the government to fulfilling the TRC's recommendations.[18] The Human

Rights Commission is therefore charged with submitting quarterly reports on the status of the implementation of the TRC's recommendations, and the government itself is required to submit quarterly reports, which will be made public, about its own efforts to fulfil the recommendations.[19]

TIMOR-LESTE

East Timor, a former Portuguese colony, was forcibly annexed by Indonesia in 1975. For the ensuing 24 years, East Timor suffered the effects of violent counter-insurgency tactics used against nationalist guerrillas, including widespread human rights abuses. In 1999, after the fall of the authoritarian regime led by General Suharto, Indonesia reluctantly accepted that the Timorese population would hold a referendum on the territory's future. On 30 August 1999, nearly 80 per cent of the East Timorese population voted for independence.

That vote was preceded by an extensive campaign of intimidation that turned to violent reprisals after election results confirmed overwhelming popular support for independence. Pro-Indonesian militias killed an estimated 1 400 East Timorese civilians and destroyed most of the territory's infrastructure. Violence included murder, assault, rape and torture as well as widespread looting and arson. More than 200 000 individuals fled or were forced into Indonesian West Timor. The violence ended only with the intervention of United Nations (UN)-authorised troops and the establishment of the UN Transitional Administration in East Timor (UNTAET). In May 2002, East Timor finally became an independent state, the Democratic Republic of Timor-Leste.

In early 2002, UNTAET established a Commission for Reception, Truth and Reconciliation (CAVR) to:

- investigate the facts and establish the truth about human rights violations committed in East Timor between 1974 and 1999;
- foster reconciliation; restore the human dignity of victims and help reintegrate perpetrators of less serious offences into their communities; and
- recommend to the government measures to prevent future abuses.[20]

This commission thus mirrors the South African TRC in many of its stated objectives and functions. As in South Africa, it was tasked with the ambitious goals of both establishing the truth about past violations by reporting on their nature and contributing factors and making recommendations regarding reforms and initiatives to prevent their recurrence.[21]

However, the CAVR can be distinguished in several important ways from its South African and Sierra Leonean predecessors. Firstly, the CAVR was unique in its creation. While the UN had previously supported the launch of other truth commissions, as in Sierra Leone where it helped to negotiate the peace agreement through which the commission was established, the CAVR was created by a legal Act of the UN at a time when the territory of East Timor was under transitional UN administration.

Secondly, the CAVR prioritised the goals of conflict management and reintegration of lesser perpetrators. The CAVR model 'is less an amnesty solution designed to re-establish a democratic system in a transitional state than a model for conflict management permitting perpetrators who have been involved in the commission of lower-level crimes to return to their homes'.[22] To this end, CAVR included a Community Reconciliation Process that permitted perpetrators of lower-level crimes to gain immunity from criminal and civil prosecution upon both taking responsibility for their crimes and carrying out some form of community service that would benefit the local population. This approach did, however, exhibit some parallels to South Africa. In both countries, preference was given to individualised amnesties and the processes required an individualised statement that outlined the acts for which reconciliation was sought, as well as an explanation of the relationship between the act and the political context.[23] However, the CAVR went beyond the South African TRC in addressing not only the issue of amnesty but in attempting to deal with the reintegration of perpetrators receiving amnesty.

Moreover, unlike its South African equivalent, the Timorese model limited immunities to the least serious offences and predicated amnesty upon the performance of a visible act of remorse that would directly serve the interests of those affected by the original offence.[24] Thus, the reconciliation process was intended 'both as a stabilizing function through the use of the act of reconciliation as a special form of public apology to alleviate the anger and tension persisting at a local level, and as a limitation on individual criminal responsibility though the extension of immunity for less serious crimes'.[25] Under the limited-amnesty approach adopted by the CAVR, no immunity was available to those who had committed a 'serious criminal offence', and this included genocide, crimes against humanity and war crimes as defined in the Rome Statute of the International Criminal Court (ICC), as well as torture, murder and sexual offences as defined in the Indonesian Criminal Code.[26] These serious offences were reserved for prosecution before special panels; only lower-level crimes could be subjected to a reconciliation procedure and the granting of immunity.

Finally, following the South African example, the CAVR adopted many procedures that were largely judicial in character. In practice, it was designed to operate as part of the broader judicial system. The commission exercised legal decision-making powers in, for example, determining whether acts disclosed through a reconciliation process were to be quantified as serious or less serious crimes, and in conducting the reconciliation procedure.[27] In addition, certain fair-trial guarantees common in criminal proceedings governed public hearings conducted by the commission, such as the protection against self-incrimination and the right to be represented by legal counsel.[28]

Throughout its three-year lifespan, CAVR held a number of successful and emotional public hearings and took more than 7 000 statements from victims throughout the country. As in Sierra Leone, it also undertook a range of outreach efforts that included disseminating videos in rural communities about its work, publishing materials to raise awareness, and convening discussion forums. Its final report, which concluded that Indonesian security forces had committed massive, widespread and systematic human rights abuses that amounted to crimes against humanity and war crimes against the Timorese population, was presented to President Xanana Gusmão in October 2005. He then distributed the report to the Timorese parliament and prime minister in late November 2005 but chose not to release it publicly. The commission found that at least 102 800 Timorese people had died as a direct result of the 24-year Indonesian occupation. This slaughter equals approximately 10 per cent of Timor-Leste's present population. The CAVR also determined that Indonesian forces had used starvation as a weapon of war, committed arbitrary executions and had routinely inflicted horrific torture, including organised sexual enslavement and sexual torture of Timorese women, on any individuals suspected of sympathising with pro-independence forces.

In its final report, the CAVR made a series of recommendations for achieving justice, including:

- that the UN renew the mandates and funding of the Serious Crimes Unit and Special Panels established to prosecute those responsible for serious violations;
- that the international community apply principles of universal jurisdiction to bring cases against Indonesian perpetrators;
- that the government of Timor-Leste implement a national reparations programme, including both economic and symbolic compensation, for

the victims of human rights violations, with the cost born primarily by
Indonesia;

- that additional truth-seeking measures be undertaken with the aim of
strengthening prospects for criminal justice; and
- that the final report be widely disseminated.

Although the transitional justice situation in Timor-Leste remains particularly
complex because it involves two countries, the work of the CAVR is widely thought
to have been a success. Indeed, the new prime minister of Timor-Leste, José
Ramos-Horta, expressed an interest in implementing the commission's
recommendations during his swearing-in ceremony in 2007.

PERU

Peru's internal conflict, which lasted from 1980–2000, began when Sendero
Luminoso (Shining Path or SL), the national Communist Party, launched an armed
struggle to impose a new political, social and economic order. In Peru, in contrast
to other internal conflicts in Latin America, SL, rather than the state, was the
primary perpetrator of violence that included selective executions and
assassinations, massacres and the destruction of property, mainly in rural and
impoverished areas of the country. The violence only increased in 1984 with the
emergence of a second insurgent group, the Movimiento Revolucionario Tupac
Amaru (MRTA), which also committed murders, kidnappings and hostage-takings,
although on a lesser scale. The Peruvian government, unable to contain the
insurgency, acknowledged the militarisation of the conflict and increasingly foisted
responsibility for the struggle onto the armed forces, which, in their effort to
fight terrorism, in turn employed strategies of systematic repression and civil
and human rights violations against dissenting civilians. In November 2000, the
public exposure of an extensive network of corruption and authoritarianism at
the highest levels of government and the ensuing outcry from civil society led to
President Alberto Fujimori's self-imposed exile in Japan. An interim government
was put in place and in late July 2001 newly elected President Alejandro Toledo
was sworn into office.

The fall of the Fujimori regime led to judicial and congressional investigations
of both corruption and human rights abuses. The nascent transition to a new
democratic order prompted the local human rights community to propose the
creation of a truth commission. A working group comprised of representatives

from the ministries of Defence, Justice, Home Affairs, Women's Advancement and the Catholic and Protestant churches drafted a decree that was submitted to the president and enacted in June 2001, formally establishing the commission. President Toledo subsequently expanded the originally envisioned commission to a twelve-member body and pledged to implement its recommendations. The selection of commissioners was similar to the process adopted in South Africa: the cabinet selected seven people from a list of names proposed by a committee of government officials and civil society representatives, although President Toledo then added a few members of his own choosing.

The Comisión de la Verdad y Reconciliación (CVR) was charged to investigate and 'clarify the process, facts, and responsibilities related to the terrorist violence and human rights violations that [had] occurred between May 1980 and November 2000, which were perpetrated both by terrorist organizations and by State agents, as well as to propose initiatives aimed at consolidating peace and harmony among Peruvians'.[29] This mandate is temporally expansive, covering the regimes of former presidents Belaúnde, García and Fujimori, and encompassing the actions of both the SL and the MRTA guerrilla groups. The mandate is also broad in terms of its subject matter, addressing disappearances, massacres, extrajudicial executions, torture, prison conditions and prosecution under anti-terrorism legislation. However, the commission explicitly lacked jurisdictional powers and its work was not meant to be a substitute for trials. In fact, it was charged to identify, when appropriate, presumptive responsibilities in order to assist judicial efforts to investigate and prosecute. The CVR was further expected to foster 'national reconciliation, the rule of law and the strengthening of the constitutional democratic system'.[30] Finally, the commission was tasked with preparing proposals for reparations to repay and dignify victims and their families.[31]

As in South Africa, and unlike prior Latin American truth commissions, the CVR opted to hear testimony publicly from victims and their relatives. These public hearings, which were widely publicised and occurred in different cities around the country, were also broadcast on national public television and received extensive press coverage. In addition to hearing individual stories, the CVR convened thematic hearings on topics such as innocents in prison, the applicability of international humanitarian law and anti-terrorism legislation. Finally, the CVR undertook its own public education campaign, collaborating with NGOs and the media to produce materials in a variety of formats and to maximise the dissemination of information about its work.

The CVR's original nineteen-month mandate, which was to end in February 2003, was extended by six months and the commission presented its final report to the government on 28 August 2003. The report, based on almost 17 000 testimonies and fourteen public hearings, comprises nine volumes that analyse the causes and consequences of the conflict and outline the magnitude of the serious human rights violations that occurred. The CVR found that insurgent violence and counter-insurgency tactics had caused an estimated 69 000 deaths and disappearances between 1980 and 2000, mostly in indigenous communities.[32] In terms of apportioning responsibility for these crimes, the CVR determined that SL had been responsible for 54 per cent of the deaths and disappearances, and the armed forces for 37 per cent.[33] In its proposal for preventing the recurrence of such violence, the CVR recommended not just prosecutions and institutional reforms but a Comprehensive Reparations Plan comprising symbolic and economic, as well as individual and collective, reparations.

In early 2004 the president created a High-Level Multi-Sector Commission to design, co-ordinate and supervise state policies regarding peace, reparations and national reconciliation.[34] This body, made up of seven ministerial and four civil society representatives, is widely recognised as the commission tasked with following up on the CVR's recommendations. It has proposed a Policy Framework for Actions by the State Related to Peace, Reparation, and National Reconciliation, and a subsequent Comprehensive Reparations Plan, under which the state would focus on restoring citizens' rights, providing education and health-related reparations and facilitating a solution to the housing crisis.[35] In August 2006, the Council of Ministers approved the payment of 15 million soles (about US$5 million) for reparations promised during the Toledo government and designated another 30 million soles (about US$10 million) for reparations from voluntary contributions by the mining industry. However, the commission's impact has been limited due to a lack of funding and its functional subordination to the Council of Ministers. As a result, actual implementation of the reparations measures outlined by the commission has not yet begun. Accordingly, there is a high level of disappointment, disillusionment and distrust among victim-survivors, especially those under the mistaken impression that testifying before the CVR would result in compensation for their suffering.[36]

Moreover, although Peru did not offer political amnesties, as South Africa did, its judicial system remains unable to prosecute perpetrators in a timely or credible manner. In a 2001 decision by the Inter-American Court of Human

Rights, the Court ruled that Peru should repeal a blanket amnesty law from 1995 that prevented the investigation and prosecution of all human rights abuses committed by the security forces during the internal conflict.[37] Accordingly, following its first public hearings in April 2002, the CVR decided to establish a Special Investigations Unit to prepare and organise legal cases against individual perpetrators and present such cases to the attorney-general for criminal prosecution. Upon terminating its work, the CVR transferred 43 representative cases of strongly documented human rights abuses to the Minister of the Interior for further investigation. Although the judiciary is attempting to reassert itself as a protector of human rights – for example, by creating a special prosecutor's office to investigate human rights violations – the majority of these cases are still pending; over half have not yet been opened for investigation and only one, which resulted in an acquittal, has gone to trial.[38]

CONCLUSION

The South African model is believed to have influenced many subsequent truth commissions, but these commissions have learnt as much from the mistakes or failures of the South African model as they have from its successes. The fact that most truth commissions follow the South African model by holding hearings in public rather than behind closed doors was one of the more important contributions of the South African experience. Other unique features, such as widespread consultation, the powers of subpoena and search and seizure, the access of the media to the work of the commission and the introduction of institutional hearings as well as hearings for individuals, have all informed subsequent truth commissions.

The South African model failed in some important respects, however. Firstly, the commission was unable to persuade the overwhelming majority of whites that its work had a very specific impact on their role during the apartheid years. All whites, irrespective of their views about apartheid, were beneficiaries and the commission tried very hard to encourage these beneficiaries to attend the public hearings, but with limited success. Thus, while the commission reached out across the country through radio, television and the print media, it certainly did not pierce the hard shell of white complicity. Secondly, the TRC did not recover all of the truth. This is particularly true of the involvement of the military in the governing of South Africa in the 1980s. The generals were evasive and smart and the not-guilty verdict in the trial of the former Minister of Defence made it much easier for the top brass in the military to eschew the commission. Thirdly, the TRC did not succeed in securing even a minimal amount of justice in relation to those who actually drew up the policies that resulted in death squads, torture, imprisonment and assassinations. There was no paper trail that linked senior politicians, generals and those who served as colonels, captains and foot soldiers. Fourthly, the commission did not succeed in persuading the government to grant swift and adequate reparations to the victims. Finally, the commission made a strong recommendation that those who applied for but were denied amnesty and those who failed to apply for amnesty but should have applied, should be prosecuted. This did not happen.

Despite these shortcomings, no new commission can ignore the South African model in its own deliberations. It is not so much that the South African experience should be duplicated but rather that, because the commission broke new ground and had the most ambitious programme of any commission before or since, there are many insights to be gleaned from its experience. Perhaps one of the greatest lessons emerging from the TRC that has influenced truth commissions and can influence future commissions is the fact that in its recommendations it has urged the government and all the people of South Africa to consolidate democracy, build a human rights culture and focus on economic justice, thereby making sustainable peace and political stability a possibility.

NOTES AND REFERENCES

1. Even before the first democratic election in April 1994, I left the Institute for a Democratic Alternative in South Africa (IDASA) to start a new NGO called Justice in Transition. I hoped that this would be a vehicle for exploring the possibilities of a truth commission in South Africa. Flowing from two major conferences, 'Dealing with the past' and 'The healing of a nation?', I was asked by the then Minister of Justice, Dullah Omar, to work with him on draft legislation for the proposed commission. Together with many others, we prepared a draft, solicited comments from organisations throughout South Africa, and the amended draft was finally placed before parliament. Nelson Mandela appointed me as vice-chairperson of the Truth and Reconciliation Commission and I served in that capacity for the period of the commission's life. For further details, refer to A. Boraine, *A country unmasked: Inside South Africa's Truth and Reconciliation Commission* (Oxford and New York: Oxford University Press, 2000).

2. According to a report of the former UN Secretary-General, truth commissions are 'official, temporary, non-judicial fact-finding bodies that investigate a pattern of abuses of human rights or humanitarian law committed over a number of years. These bodies take a victim-centered approach and conclude their work with a final report of findings of fact and recommendations.'

See Report of the Secretary-General on The Rule of Law and Transitional Justice in Conflict and Post-Conflict Societies, UN Doc S/2004/616 (2004), para. 50, p. xiv.

3. I wish to recognise the considerable assistance I have received from Susan Farbstein, an intern at the International Centre for Transitional Justice, Cape Town.

4. There are also several other commissions, namely those of Morocco, Ghana and Liberia, which were strongly influenced by the South African model, but in this chapter there is only space to focus on Sierra Leone, Timor-Leste and Peru.

5. Boraine, *A country unmasked*, pp. 71–72.

6. Promotion of National Unity and Reconciliation Act 34 of 1995, Chap. 4, sec. 18.1.

7. P. Hayner, *Unspeakable truths: Confronting state terror and atrocity* (New York and London: Routledge, 2001), pp. 44–45.

8. Lomé Peace Accord, signed between the government of Sierra Leone and the RUF (7 July 1999), art. 9.

9. Sierra Leone Truth and Reconciliation Commission Act 2000, sec. 6(1).

10. During that interim period the government asked the UN to help it establish a Special Court. In August 2000, the UN Security Council passed Resolution 1315 mandating the creation of a Special Court to prosecute those bearing the greatest responsibility for violations of international humanitarian law. The SCSL was established by an agreement between the UN and the government of Sierra Leone in January 2002.

11. Sierra Leone Truth and Reconciliation Commission Act, sec. 6(2)(*a*)(1).

12. The panel included four commissioners from each of Sierra Leone's four regions, as well as one commissioner each from South Africa, The Gambia and Ireland.

13. Sierra Leone Truth and Reconciliation Commission Act, sec. 7(2).

14. Sierra Leone Truth and Reconciliation Commission Act, sec. 6(2)(*a*)(1).]

15. The *Final Report of the Truth and Reconciliation Commission of Sierra Leone*, www.sierra-leone.org/trc-documents.html (accessed 18 October 2007).

16. Subsequently, the commission produced both a children's version and a video version of the *Final Report*, in collaboration with UNICEF and WITNESS. These versions were more broadly available although release of the multi-volume written report was delayed.

17. Much of the debate over the relationship between the TRC and the Special Court focused on whether the TRC should be required to disclose information gathered in confidence to the Special Court and, if so, under what circumstances. Supporters of the TRC feared this would undermine attempts at reconciliation, while supporters of the Special Court focused on its legal status and the supremacy of international over domestic law. In reality, this conflict was defused by a commitment from the prosecutor of the Special Court not to seek information from the TRC, although no formal agreement was ever reached.

18. 'The Government shall faithfully and timeously implement the recommendations of the report that are directed to state bodies and encourage or facilitate the implementation of any recommendations that may be directed to others.' Sierra Leone Truth and Reconciliation Commission Act, art. 17.

19. Sierra Leone Truth and Reconciliation Commission Act, art. 18.

20. On the Establishment of a Commission for Reception, Truth and Reconciliation in East Timor, UNTAET REG/2001/10 (13 July 2001), www.un.org/peace/etimor/untaetR/Reg10e.pdf (accessed 17 October 2007).

21. East Timor Truth and Reconciliation Commission Act, secs. 3.1, 13.1.

22. C. Stahn, 'Accommodating individual criminal responsibility and national reconciliation: The UN Truth Commission for East Timor', *American Journal of International Law* 95, 2001: 957.

23. Compare UNTAET Regulation 2001/10, sec. 23.1 and the South African Truth and Reconciliation Act, sec. 20.

24. This approach drew more closely upon the community-based mechanisms employed in Sierra Leone, where the TRC could 'seek assistance from traditional and religious leaders to facilitate its public sessions and in resolving local conflicts arising from past violations or abuses or in support of healing and reconciliation'. See Sierra Leone Truth and Reconciliation Commission Act of 2000, sec. 7(2). Nevertheless, the commissions differed in important respects: in Sierra Leone the TRC was vested only with investigative powers, while in East Timor the CAVR could additionally utilise a comprehensive reconciliation mechanism, the Community Reconciliation Process.

25. See Sierra Leone Truth and Reconciliation Commission Act of 2000, sec. 7(2).

26. UNTAET REG/2001/10, sec. 31.1.

27. See Sierra Leone Truth and Reconciliation Commission Act of 2000, secs. 24.1, 27.5.

28. See Sierra Leone Truth and Reconciliation Commission Act of 2000, secs. 17.1, 18.1, 18.3.

29. Presidential Decree 065-2001-PCM (4 June 2001), art. 1.

30. Presidential Decree 065-2001-PCM (4 June 2001), art. 1.

31. Presidential Decree 065-2001-PCM (4 June 2001), art. 2(*c*).

32. *Comisión de Verdad y Reconciliatión, Final Report* (2003), General Conclusions, para. 2.

33. *Comisión de Verdad*, para. 13.

34. Presidential Decree 003-2004-JUS (6 February 2004).

35. Presidential Decree 062-2004-PCM (27 August 2004).

36. L.J. Laplante and K. Theidon, 'Truth with consequences: Justice and reparations in post-Truth Commission Peru', *Human Rights Quarterly* 29, 2007: 241.

37. *Barrios Altos*, Inter-American Court of Human Rights (Ser C) 75 (2001). The case involved a massacre committed by a death squad linked to the army. The Court held that the state had an obligation to investigate and prosecute criminal suspects and that amnesty laws with the effect of impeding investigations of crimes against humanity were void as contrary to the American Convention on Human Rights.

38. Laplante and Theidon, 'Truth with consequences', p. 244.

7

Reflecting on the Sierra Leone Truth and Reconciliation Commission
A Peacebuilding Perspective

Thelma Ekiyor

INTRODUCTION

The Sierra Leone Truth and Reconciliation Commission (SLTRC) released its final report to the public in 2005, ending a process that had involved receiving and analysing 8 000 statements and holding countrywide victim and thematic hearings. The report raised high expectations that the injustices and scars of the country's decade-long civil war would finally be addressed. However, to date, the country continues to struggle with implementing the recommendations of the report, drawing criticisms that the lengthy and costly process did not ultimately achieve a great deal. This chapter reflects on the TRC process in Sierra Leone as one-half of an experimental transitional justice mechanism implemented alongside a Special Court – The Special Court for Sierra Leone (SCSL) is analysed in a later chapter (see Chapter 11 in this volume) – and focuses on the different stages of the TRC, the roles played by various actors, its interactions with the SCSL and the impact of the entire process on consolidating peace in the country.

BACKGROUND

Sierra Leone emerged from a decade-long, brutal civil war in 2000. The complex conflict between the government of Sierra Leone and the Revolutionary United Front (RUF) resulted in thousands of deaths. Millions of people were displaced, thousands suffered some form of amputation and tens of thousands of women and children were raped, many of whom were forced into rebel factions as child soldiers and 'bush wives'.

The journey to restore some semblance of peace to the country was a tumultuous one. Several attempts to convene warring factions resulted in short-lived agreements. The Abidjan Peace Accord in 1996 and the Conakry Peace Plan in 1997 had truncated lifespans as both sides in the conflict reneged on the terms of the agreements. Intensive fighting reached a crescendo on 6 January 1999 with the RUF attack on Freetown, which resulted in an estimated 6 000 people being injured, maimed or raped. This level of destruction in one day brought the realisation to all sides that the only credible strategy for ending the violence was to embark on a negotiated political process. Through the interventions of a number of actors such as the Sierra Leone Inter-Religious Council, human rights groups, and the British-led International Contact Group on Sierra Leone, support for peace talks grew and the Lomé peace talks were organised. A key development in the talks was the invitation to the negotiations of all sides in the conflict and their involvement in these negotiations.[1] However, this situation meant that new challenges had to be faced, as it was apparent from the outset that compromise was inevitable in any attempt to accommodate divergent and contentious interests and demands.

The most controversial demand was the RUF's request for blanket amnesty. This request ushered in the recurring debate of peace versus justice. Whether or not to include amnesty clauses in the final agreement was controversial both locally in Sierra Leone and internationally. Human rights proponents believed that the amnesty clause would lead to impunity and a lack of accountability for the atrocities committed during the war. However, the amnesty provision had been previously approved by a large number of civil society actors at a national conference that had been organised to gain consensus on the terms of a peace agreement. The inclusion of the amnesty clause was seen as a peacebuilding[2] strategy aimed at ensuring that the RUF sign the agreement. Subsequently, in an attempt to balance the need for peace against the need to safeguard justice, the agreement allowed for the establishment of a TRC. Learning from the South African experience, human rights activists, the main proponents for the TRC, hoped it would serve as a safety net to ensure that the atrocities committed during the war were accounted for.

As a peacebuilding instrument the Lomé Peace Accord did not end the war in Sierra Leone. However, by addressing issues of disarmament, demobilisation and reintegration (DDR) as well as the touchy topics of justice, reconciliation and forgiveness, it provided the first real avenue for the country to commence post-conflict peacebuilding. The mandate of the TRC within the agreement was for the commission to address impunity, break the cycle of violence, provide a forum for both victims and perpetrators of violations to tell their story and form a clear picture of the past in order to facilitate genuine healing and reconciliation.[3]

Truth commissions have been defined as bodies which are set up to investigate a past history of violations of human rights in a particular country, which can include violations exercised by the military, other governments or armed opposition forces.[4] Investigating the past and healing wounds is a tall order for any TRC but particularly so for one set up to heal the deep wounds and scars left behind by Sierra Leone's brutal and often inhumane war. The task of addressing the past and providing a forum for victims to tell their stories required the establishment of an effective and functional commission. Priscilla Hayner delineates four main characteristics of truth commissions:

- They focus on the past. The events may have occurred in the recent past, but a truth commission is not an ongoing body akin to a human rights commission.
- Truth commissions investigate a pattern of abuse over a set period of time rather than a specific event.
- A truth commission is a temporary body, usually operating over a period of six months to two years and completing its work by submitting a report.
- Truth commissions are officially sanctioned, authorised or empowered by the state.[5]

On paper the SLTRC met all four criteria. The commission was expected to function for one year (in 2000) and was enacted into law through an Act of parliament. In practice, however, the commission encountered a number of challenges that hampered its ability to meet its mandate and lengthened the stipulated timeframe.

A DIFFICULT START

As a symbol of peace in the country it was imperative that the TRC got things right from the start. However, the task of operationalising the commission was a fraught one. The first real challenge the commission faced was setting up an interim secretariat. A key characteristic of the secretariat was for it to appoint commissioners through impartial processes. The TRC Act called for an equitable and transparent process for selecting commissioners. It also stressed that the 'members of the commission should be persons of integrity and credibility who would be impartial in the performance of their functions . . . and would enjoy the confidence generally of the people of Sierra Leone'.[6] The Act outlined the process for nomination. The formula was for the United Nations High Commissioner for Human Rights (UNHCR) to recommend three international commissioners, while the selection co-ordinator, the Special Representative of the Secretary-General in Sierra Leone, co-ordinated the selection of four national members in collaboration with an advisory committee and a selection panel. The president was responsible for making the final appointments once statutory procedures had been followed. The expectation that a country polarised by violent civil war would be able to embark convincingly on an impartial process for appointing staff to a maiden restorative justice institution was ambitious. Memories of and wounds from the conflict were still very fresh and deep divisions structured around political affiliations were rife. Consequently, it was no surprise that the appointment of the interim executive secretary was seen as politically driven[7] and lacking transparency, immediately calling into question the independence of the commission. All sides in the conflict wanted reassurances that the commission would not be used as a tool to scapegoat and blame opponents for atrocities committed during the war. These initial institutional challenges delayed the work of the commission. Recruitment processes dragged on, and when staff were finally hired there were criticisms that they were unqualified for the task or lacked experience in transitional processes. A further critic called the secretariat staff 'unqualified and redundant'.[8]

With its credibility already at stake at this early stage, the focus of the commission shifted from trying to achieve its mandate to an attempt to get its house in order. The situation was compounded by a resurgence of violence that further delayed the commencement of work. These teething problems worsened as international donors got cold feet and funding was not forthcoming. Unlike other TRC processes, which were mainly supported by national governments, the Sierra Leonean system depended mainly on international funding sources. This dependence meant that Sierra Leoneans were not in control of the commission's pace of work. The process ground to a halt in 2000, when the United Kingdom, the main donor, froze its contributions to the UN Office of the High Commissioner for Human Rights (OHCHR).

Linked to the funding challenges were issues of ownership and independence. Though all stakeholders called for the process to be owned by Sierra Leoneans, early on there were questions and doubts about ownership and where decision-making powers on the TRC resided. Specifically, questions were asked about the role and responsibilities of the UN Human Rights offices. The TRC Act called for the commission to be fully independent but the commission was implemented as a project of the OHCHR in Geneva, which partnered with the UN Development Programme (UNDP) office in Freetown to provide administrative support. This resulted in bureaucratic delays and disagreements over the priorities of the commission. The overlap between these two offices diminished the commission's independence and led to the criticism that outsiders were manipulating the process.[9]

A DIVIDED PROCESS

After a turbulent start the TRC began engaging the Sierra Leonean public in July 2002. The process was implemented through public education initiatives and media relations. Public education involved raising awareness of the commission's mandate, its role, the implementation plan and the differences between the TRC and the SCSL.

Other phases in the process included the Barray (Town Hall) phase, the statement-taking phase, the hearings, and the report-writing phase. The Barray phase involved week-long, awareness-raising initiatives in all twelve districts by TRC commissioners and staff. The commission's personnel explained its mandate, methodology and procedures to diverse groups. This phase provided a unique opportunity for the commission to address any concerns raised by communities. It was also during this phase that the TRC identified certain key themes on which to focus during its research and investigation. The Barray phase yielded varied results: participation by communities varied as some district officers sensitised their communities about the TRC and the arrival of the commissioners while others did not, resulting in a low turnout in many places. Overall, the visits were not well organised. Too many visits were planned over too a short period of time and the phase had a limited impact.

The statement-taking phase commenced in December 2002 and lasted four months. By the end of this period 7 706 statements had been collected. The statement-taking exercise targeted victims, witnesses, perpetrators and those who wished to give a statement on behalf of someone else. In collaboration with civil society, the commission implemented a rigorous sensitisation campaign to get people to give statements. The magnitude of the violations committed made it impossible for the commission to investigate all cases. However, the statement-takers managed to record statements from most chiefdoms. Out of 149 chiefdoms 9 were not covered due to difficult terrains and inadequate means of transportation. Nevertheless, the statement-taking exercise can be described as a relative success as it provided a general sampling of the violations committed and people's experiences.

The hearings phase of the commission's work also lasted four months. Commissioners and staff conducted week-long hearing sessions in each of the twelve districts. The public hearings provided an opportunity for victims and perpetrators to share their experiences with the nation. Victims, witnesses and perpetrators came forward to give testimony about their experiences or roles in the conflict and to answer questions from the commission. This was a significant moment as it was the first time many Sierra Leoneans had talked publicly about the war and its impact on their lives. The commission's sensitivity to the needs of victims was central to the hearing process. Each district hearing consisted of one day of closed sessions organised for victims of sexual abuse, children, ex-combatants and perpetrators who were ambivalent about speaking in public. Though attendance was not high in all areas, the hearings, similar to the statement-taking phase, provided a general picture of the common experiences of Sierra Leoneans.

Through the Barray, statement-taking and hearing phases, the commission strove to carry out its mandate as outlined in the TRC by attempting to:

> [C]reate an impartial historical record of the violations and abuses of human rights and international humanitarian law related to the armed conflict in Sierra Leone, from the beginning of the conflict in 1991 to the signing of the Lomé Peace Agreement.[10] The Commission also had to investigate the cause, nature and extent of violations committed during the war, the context within which those violations occurred and whether those violations were as a result of the deliberate planning, policy or authorization of any government, group or individual.[11] The Act also called on the Commission to work towards restoring human dignity of victims and promoting reconciliation by providing a platform for victims and perpetrators to relate their experiences.[12]

Central to the commission's performance of these functions was the participation of the Sierra Leonean population during the different phases. Sierra Leoneans were urged to tell the truth about the past and be willing to be reconciled. The SLTRC used the South African model as a reference point in the truth-seeking process. Four different types of truth were addressed:

- *Factual or forensic truth*, which involves capturing an accepted version of events once all the facts have been examined and can be supported by evidence.
- *Personal and narrative truth*, which consists of a witness's personal truth told through statements or at hearings.
- *Social truth*, which is the truth established after interaction and dialogue that will be accepted by all after the myths and the lies have been discredited and disproven.
- *Healing and restorative truth*, which is necessary for the nation to cope with its pain. It is the truth of what happened and involves an acknowledgement of people's pain and suffering by the nation.[13]

These types of truth are important components of reconciliation processes but questions remained as to whether all Sierra Leoneans were ready to tell the truth and recount the past, and concerning whose truth would be told. The country had different perspectives of the roles played by key actors in the conflict. For example, many Sierra Leoneans believed that the Civil Defence Force (CDF) protected communities from RUF attacks. Conversely, some Sierra Leoneans believed that the CDF was as culpable as the RUF for atrocities committed.[14]

Furthermore, Sierra Leoneans were divided on the issue of whether truth-telling and recounting the past were necessary for reconciliation. Support for the TRC was high among religious leaders, non-governmental organisations (NGOs) and educated Sierra Leoneans. However, many in local communities favoured a more culturally accepted approach of 'forgive and forget'. Thus, the commission had to raise awareness on the necessity for Sierra Leoneans to participate in the process. There were mixed feelings about the sensitisation process. Some Sierra Leoneans believed that the sensitisation exercise during the preparatory phase was deficient,[15] and that the commission made the wrong assumption that radio messages would be sufficient to alert Sierra Leoneans to the existence of the TRC. Though the sensitisation process improved in the operational phase of the commission's work, many Sierra Leoneans still had to be convinced to participate in the process, raising criticisms that the process was not locally owned and driven. Critics assert that the TRC process should have complemented traditional

amputées

and local reconciliation processes but that in many instances the TRC had interrupted ongoing private and indigenous processes of social recovery that had commenced without its assistance. To these communities the focus on public truth-telling and reliving the past was a distraction.[16]

Widespread misconceptions of what was involved in testifying or giving statements further complicated the process. Many Sierra Leoneans believed that they would be remunerated for testifying, in the same way that ex-combatants had received money during the country's DDR process. It was difficult to convince some sectors of society to testify and give statements without being able to offer incentives. For example, the War Affected Amputee Association of the Aberdeen Road Camp refused to participate in the process until the government had met the needs of the community as stipulated in the Lomé Peace Accord. The War Affected Amputees were a visual reminder of the gravity of the violence. They were an important victim group and their testimonies were crucial to the commission's work. To get beyond this impasse the commission had to embark on a series of dialogue sessions with the amputees in order to clarify the roles and responsibilities of the commission and the government. These dialogue sessions culminated in an agreement between the commission and the amputees whereby some amputees were trained to be statement-takers within the amputee camps, with the result that some amputees in different districts participated in the process and gave statements to the commission.

The commission's ability to adapt to the needs of the population during the hearing and statement-taking phases, and its willingness to address the concerns of communities, was an unheralded part of its work. It was apparent that as the hearings progressed more Sierra Leoneans understood the purpose of the commission and wanted to participate in the hearings. However, the hearings' one-week duration in each district did not accommodate them and caused frustration for both the staff of the commission and the communities.[17]

CIVIL SOCIETY AND THE TRC

Civil society plays a key role in post-conflict recovery. It has the potential and capacity to promote reconciliation, enhance local ownership of peacebuilding initiatives and contribute towards democratisation processes. Without civil society countries that are emerging from wars are unable to establish effective truth commissions.[18] There is no doubt that civil society in Sierra Leone played an invaluable role during the TRC process. The involvement of civil society in the conceptualisation of the TRC, both prior to and during the Lomé peace talks and in subsequent stages of the process, is viewed as one of the key achievements of the Sierra Leone experience.[19]

Civil society was instrumental in keeping the momentum of the TRC alive during the commission's two-year hiatus between 2000 and 2002. It was during this period that key civil society organisations (CSOs) kick-started the process of analysing both the causes of the conflict and potential entry points for the TRC's work. Local human rights and pro-democracy NGOs such as the Campaign for Good Governance and the National Forum for Human Rights conducted conflict-mapping exercises and carried out studies on the role of indigenous practices and institutions in Sierra Leone. They considered how these could interface with the commission. Reports of the outcomes of these initiatives were submitted to the TRC to assist with its work.

Truth commissions are implemented in the public domain and the success of the commission's work hinges on public awareness, participation and acceptance. Inadequate human and financial resources meant that the SLTRC had to rely heavily on civil society to raise awareness of its mandate and operations whilst generating participation in the process. For example, leading human rights organisations such as the National Forum for Human Rights and the International Center for Transitional Justice (ICTJ) developed a citizen's handbook that explained in simple language the structure and operations of the commission and the SCSL.[20]

Accountability and monitoring are two of the major roles civil society plays in any social order. Civil society actors in Sierra Leone remained vigilant during the process, monitoring the pace and effectiveness of the commission's work. During the awareness-raising phases many were frustrated at the pace of the commission's work as well as its inability to embark on early awareness-raising programmes aimed at educating ordinary Sierra Leoneans about the process.[21] In some instances civil society filled this gap by organising various workshops and informal sessions about the TRC.

International CSOs also played important capacity-building and awareness-raising roles during the TRC process. However, there have been criticisms of the role of some international NGOs in the process. An assessment of the TRC process carried out by the Working Group on Truth and Reconciliation, and the Network Movement for Justice and Development (NMJD) found that in some cases international NGOs had a conflict of interest as a result of the multiple roles they had assumed. For example, some international NGOs simultaneously provided expert services to the TRC, the SCSL and civil society. This undermined their role of supporting effective independent monitoring or advocacy by local civil society of either the TRC process or the SCSL.[22] The Sierra Leone experience raises the issue of the nature of collaboration between international NGOs and local actors during transitional justice processes. Generally, because international NGOs have better access to funding and are more organised as a result, they tend to eclipse the voices and visibility of local groups. When this occurs, it becomes problematic to galvanise local ownership of the process and its outcomes. As seen in the Sierra Leonean case, the overshadowing presence of international NGOs also allowed local actors to be less accountable for any failures in the process.

A positive outcome of the TRC process and post-conflict peacebuilding in Sierra Leone has been the exponential increase in civil society's local, national and regional organisation. Among civil society and other actors there is heightened consciousness of the importance of building peace. Groups such as the Mano River Women's Peace Network (MARWOPNET) and the Network for Collaborative Peacebuilding in Sierra Leone (NCP-SL) have been playing central roles in conflict prevention, management and resolution. Lessons that were learnt with regard to the spill-over effects of conflicts in the region to neighbouring countries have led to partnerships with regional networks such as the West African Civil Society Forum (WACSOF).

WOMEN, CHILDREN AND THE TRC

The war in Sierra Leone affected all sectors of the population though it is widely acknowledged that women and children were the most affected. The TRC Act urged the commission to pay special attention to the experiences of women and children.

Women account for 51 per cent of the Sierra Leonean population. In pre-war Sierra Leone, women had been marginalised from key decision-making positions. This marginalisation extended to both cultural and traditional practices, which discriminated against women. During the war all sides in the conflict systematically targeted women and girls. From the start of the war in 1991 atrocities committed against thousands of women ranged from rape, sexual slavery and forced marriages to abductions and imprisonment.[23]

Any attempt by the TRC to reflect on the past and the crimes committed during the war therefore had to focus on the impact of the war on women and girls. The TRC Act of 2000 asked the commission to give special attention to sexual abuse. The implementation of the TRC process also coincided with the adoption of international instruments calling for the inclusion of women in peace processes. Notably, UN Security Council resolution 1325 calls for the consideration of women's and girls' special needs in post-conflict reconstruction and for the involvement of women in the implementation of mechanisms of peace agreements.[24] This instrument strengthened the argument for the TRC process to be gendered. Some TRC commissioners had previous experience with gendered truth and reconciliation processes that proved critical for the Sierra Leone process. However, not all commission staff understood the importance of gender sensitivity. Earlier attempts to interview victims revealed that staff needed to learn sensitivity. Victims were asked questions such as 'What were you wearing when it happened?' and 'What were you doing out alone?'[25] In response to this, the UN Development Fund for Women (UNIFEM) and other women's organisations set up training sessions for commission staff, covering topics such as gender and violence against women as well as practicalities, such as how to interview rape victims and how to support and protect female witnesses.

The public hearings brought national attention to the plight of women during the war and provided an opportunity for women in Sierra Leone to show solidarity against sexual violence. Large numbers of women attended the hearings in Freetown and provided emotional support to victims who gave testimonies.

The TRC process revealed that sexual violence had remained Sierra Leone's silent war crime.[26] Though large numbers of women came forward to speak of their experiences, it is believed that many more remained silent. This could be attributed to fear of reprisal attacks from perpetrators and the cultural stigmatisation and shame associated with rape and other sexual crimes. It has to be noted that though the TRC brought attention to the impact of the conflict on women, it did not stem the occurrences of violence against women in Sierra Leone. Domestic violence is still very common and the structures needed for redress for violations against women are still lacking.

The war adversely affected children too. Many suffered forced conscriptions, disengagement from families, rape, torture and psychological abuse. The process therefore also paid special attention to the experiences of children during the war. The Lomé Peace Accord specified that the commission examine the role of child soldiers during the war. In collaboration with the UN Children's Fund (UNICEF), the commission conducted sessions with children in ways that it hoped would not exacerbate the psychological impact of the conflict. Though most

Sierra Leoneans were aware of the roles children had played as perpetrators, many wanted to forget the past and move on. In many communities indigenous healing and reconciliation processes were used to reintegrate children into the community. Contrary to the 'tell-all' approach of the TRC, children who underwent indigenous processes were required not to speak about their experiences and were taken through cleansing processes that would make them new individuals.

STRANGE BEDFELLOWS: THE SLTRC AND THE SCSL

Justice is an important component of post-conflict peacebuilding.[27] Restoring peace to societies fractured by violent conflicts often requires that perpetrators are held accountable for the violations they have committed. Nevertheless, the need for justice has to be complemented with the broader need in society to rebuild relationships and assist individuals with psychosocial healing. This is where reconciliation becomes relevant although tensions inevitably surface when attempting to promote both justice and reconciliation in transitional justice processes. This tension was evident in the relationship between the SLTRC and the SCSL.

A plethora of commentators have written about the relationship between the SLTRC and the SCSL.[28] The simultaneous establishment of these two institutions in Sierra Leone was unprecedented in transitional justice processes. Some scholars saw the concurrent establishment of both institutions as a unique opportunity to advance complementary processes for accountability.[29] Initially it was believed that the institutions would complement each other but in practice the relationship became strained. For the Sierra Leonean public the side-by-side existence of a commission that urged them to 'tell the truth' and a court that possibly waited to prosecute was confusing. This confusion deterred many ex-combatants from testifying despite reassurances that the Court would prosecute only 'those who bear the greatest responsibility' for atrocities committed and that information in testimonies to the commission would not be handed over to the Court. The Court also had an impact on the commission's mandate to record an impartial historical record of the war. An infamous example of this was the request by the commission that Chief Sam 'Hinga' Norman, an indictee of the Court, testify at the commission. Chief Norman had played a prominent role in the conflict as the leader of the CDF and his testimony was seen as crucial if a complete story of the conflict were to be told. The refusal of this request by prosecutors and judges at the SCSL resulted in an inter-institutional dispute that was decided only by a legal ruling which stated that the right to a public and fair trial superseded societal needs – for example, the need to compile an impartial historical record. The fallout from this incident undermined the TRC, which was seen as an inferior institution to the SCSL. This perception was compounded by the fact that in comparison to the TRC the Court was better funded, operated more efficiently and seemed to have the trust and goodwill of the international donor community.

The main losers in this turf conflict between the commission and the Court were the Sierra Leonean people. Many felt that the power struggle had little to do with bringing peace to Sierra Leone and more to do with satisfying international agendas. With the TRC's work now complete and the SCSL's mandate soon to be completed it is important that local and international stakeholders collectively reflect on the 'Sierra Leone experiment', why it failed and its impact on the country's restorative justice process.

TRC REPORT

A truth commission's report is described as its legacy. TRC reports contribute towards validating the experiences of victims and make proposals on how reparations can be made for the harm they have suffered.[30] The SLTRC submitted its long-awaited report to the government in 2004 and to the public in 2005. The comprehensive and well-written report provides an outline of the commission's mandate, its institutional structures, its procedures and how it implemented its mandate.

The report contains key recommendations that will be important to long-term peacebuilding in Sierra Leone. For instance, it provides a conceptual framework for how it addressed the issue of reconciliation and its implementation in Sierra Leone. It stresses that reconciliation is a process not an event and that it has many components: national reconciliation, community reconciliation, and reconciliation between individuals, such as that between victims and perpetrators. It emphasises that national reconciliation is important as it provides a context in which community and individual reconciliation can occur. The report also highlights the importance of indigenous reconciliation and healing mechanisms to peacebuilding, and the importance of including traditional and religious leaders at all levels of the reconciliation.[31]

Abiding by the legislative mandate of the commission, the report makes recommendations of reforms and measures to be taken to prevent a repetition of the violations and abuses suffered, to address impunity, to respond to the needs of victims and to promote healing and reconciliation. The recommendations are divided into three categories: 'imperative', 'work towards', and 'seriously consider'. Imperative recommendations are those covered by the TRC Act. 'Work towards' recommendations are those that require the planning and marshalling of resources in order for them to be implemented. 'Seriously consider' recommendations are those which the government is under no obligation to implement but which nevertheless require its thorough evaluation.

Amidst other issues,[32] the TRC report makes recommendations for the implementation of a reparations programme. These recommendations call for measures to address the needs of victims on issues of health, pensions, education, skills training and micro-credit. Specifically, the commission recommends free lifetime healthcare for categories of victims, for example, amputees, the war-wounded and victims of sexual violence. Monthly pensions are also recommended for all adult amputees. Free education until senior secondary school level is recommended for children who are amputees or who had been abducted or conscripted and for those who are orphans of war.

These recommendations are laudable and demonstrate that the commission gained an accurate understanding of the needs of the population. Traditionally, however, implementing TRC recommendations is a challenging exercise. Governments' priorities do not necessarily coincide with the commissions' recommendations. Nevertheless, the Sierra Leone government is required by the TRC Act to implement the recommendations of the commission, despite their implementation being very expensive for Sierra Leone. The country's dire economic situation means that it might once again have to look to international funding sources or other external parties for the resources that will be needed to implement the recommendations.

The newly established UN Peacebuilding Commission's (PBC's) focus on Sierra Leone provides one such possibility. The task of the PBC is to assist Sierra Leone in post-conflict peacebuilding. Four priority focus areas have been identified by the PBC: youth employment and empowerment, capacity-building of government institutions to deliver essential services, judicial and security sector development, and reinforcing democracy and governance.[33] Several consultative processes and the country-specific meetings on Sierra Leone that have been organised by the PBC have called on the government to implement the TRC recommendations in these priority areas.

To date, the main development emanating from the TRC recommendations is the establishment of the Sierra Leone Human Rights Commission. The TRC report calls for a Follow-up Committee to be established which should be part of the Human Rights Commission (HRC). The enabling Act to establish the HRC was passed in 2004[34] but commissioners were only appointed in 2006. Early indications are that the commission will endure similar institutional challenges to those faced by the TRC; human rights commissioners already complain about the lack of human and financial resources required to implement their mandate.[35] Ensuring that the HRC has the capacity to fulfil its mandate should be a priority if the commission is to monitor the implementation of the TRC recommendations efficiently.

CONCLUSION

Five years after the war in Sierra Leone ended and two years after the TRC released its report, Sierra Leone enjoys relative but fragile peace. Many of the structural problems that existed in 1991 persist. Post-conflict peacebuilding continues to be important. While the TRC process did not bring either peace or reconciliation it provided a platform for Sierra Leoneans to reflect collectively on the past and map out strategies for long-term peacebuilding.

In retrospect the TRC had an impossible task that was exacerbated by the credibility issues it faced and which were rooted in its preparatory phases. Those initial problems clouded many of its later achievements. An analysis of the successes and failures of the commission should focus on the extent to which it fulfilled the mandate stipulated in the TRC Act. From a peacebuilding perspective, the TRC succeeded on two fronts: it brought national attention to the atrocities and violations committed during the war and it provided a chronological understanding of the causes of the war. It also provided a forum in which victims and perpetrators could share their experiences. Though not all Sierra Leoneans participated in the process, the involvement of a significant number of the population is an achievement, especially given the commission's funding challenges and the pressure of working within a limited timeframe.

Despite these achievements the TRC was ineffective in ensuring that Sierra Leoneans owned the process. Though local civil society played a pivotal role in raising awareness of the commission, assisting with capacity-building and local peacebuilding initiatives, the dominant roles played by different international actors ranging from the Geneva-based OHCHR and international donors to international civil society diluted local ownership of the process. Furthermore, the TRC's activities should have prioritised support for indigenous reconciliation activities by using bottom-up approaches instead of a prescriptive top-down approach.

The Sierra Leonean experience highlighted the importance of recognising contextual realities when establishing TRCs. While it is important to share experiences and learn lessons from different transitional justice processes, it is more important that each process is conceptualised with due attention to the culture, needs and behaviour of people in that country. The SLTRC was largely structured with the South African TRC in mind. Proponents of the SLTRC were keen to implement a South African-styled TRC in Sierra Leone and attempted to do so without addressing the fundamental contextual differences between the two.

Each country's post-conflict peacebuilding needs are distinct. Transitional justice mechanisms such as TRCs should respond to each conflict's specific set of circumstances by being unique in their composition, prioritisation, timing and sequencing of phases in the process. The Sierra Leone conflict was a civil war that lacked the ideological dimension that was present in the South African liberation struggle. Some scholars have accurately posited that, unlike South Africa, Sierra Leone lacked unifying figures around whom they could rally, such as Nelson Mandela and Desmond Tutu, and this made reconciliation in the Sierra Leonean context more challenging. These differences called for a methodical conflict analysis of the typology of the Sierra Leonean conflict, which would have helped with the decision as to what type of commission would have best suited the context.

The SLTRC process also revealed the need for more reflection on the effectiveness of concurrently implementing retributive and restorative justice processes in post-war African societies. The TRC and SCSL experiment in Sierra Leone highlighted the complexities of overlapping these two processes. Critical lessons should be learned from this experience before attempting it elsewhere.

Finally, it is important that the TRC report is not seen as an end to a process but rather as the launch pad for a more critical process of long-term transformation and peacebuilding. The report has publicised all of the key issues that relate to the Sierra Leonean conflict and the areas on which future peacebuilding should focus. Efforts should be made by all those involved to act on and implement the recommendations of the commission as set out in the report. A commitment to doing so will perhaps convince Sierra Leoneans that the process was ultimately worth it.

NOTES AND REFERENCES

1. D. Francis, *Torturous path to peace: Lomé Peace Accord and post-war peace building in Sierra Leone, security dialogue* (London: Sage Publications, 2000).

2. Peacebuilding is the process of restoring normal relations between people. It requires the reconciliation of differences, apology, forgiveness of past harm and the establishment of a co-operative relationship between groups, replacing the adversarial or competitive relationship that previously existed (a definition by Conflict Research Consortium, University of Colorado, United States).

3. Article XXVI (1) of the Lomé Peace Accord, signed 7 July 1999.

4. P. Hayner, 'Fifteen truth commissions, 1974–1994: A comparative study', in N.J. Kritz (ed.), *Transitional justice: How emerging democracies reckon with former regimes, vol. I: General considerations* (Washington, DC: United States Institute of Peace Press, 1995), pp. 3–31.

5. P. Hayner, *Unspeakable truths: Confronting state terror and atrocity* (New York and London: Routledge, 2001), p. 40.

6. The Truth and Reconciliation Act, 2000, art. 3(2)(*b*), Part II.

7. International Crisis Group (2002), *Sierra Leone's Truth and Reconciliation Commission: A fresh start.* Report of the International Crisis Group: Africa Briefing.

8. B. Dougherty, 'Searching for answers: Sierra Leone's Truth and Reconciliation Commission', *African Studies Quarterly* 8(1), 2004, www.africa.ufl.edu/asq/v8/v8i1a3.pdf (accessed 28 January 2008).

9. Article 19 Forum of Conscience, *Contextualising the Truth and Reconciliation Commission*, August 2000, www.article19.org (accessed 29 January 2008).

10. The Truth and Reconciliation Act, 2000, art. 6(1).

11. The Truth and Reconciliation Act, 2000, art. 6(2)(*a*).

12. The Truth and Reconciliation Act, 2000, art. 6(2)(*b*).

13. The *Final Report of the Truth and Reconciliation Commission of Sierra Leone*, vol. 1, chap. 3, www.trcsierraleone.org (accessed 10 April 2007).

14. Y. Sooka, 'Dealing with the past and transitional justice: Building peace through accountability', *International Review of the Red Cross* 88862, 2006: 311–325.

15. Sierra Leone Working Group on Truth and Reconciliation, 'Searching for truth and reconciliation in Sierra Leone', 2006, http://www.pambazuka.org/en/category/rights/32427.

16. R. Shaw, 'Rethinking Truth and Reconciliation Commissions: Lessons from Sierra Leone', United States Institute for Peace, Special Report 130, February 2005, www.usip.org (accessed 15 April 2007).

17. Dougherty, 'Searching for answers'.

18. D.A. Crocker, 'Truth commissions, transitional justice and civil society', in R.I. Rotberg and D. Thompson (eds.), *Truth v justice: The morality of truth commissions* (Princeton, NJ: Princeton University Press, 2000), p. 117.

19. Dougherty, 'Searching for answers'.

20. P.J. Allen, S.B.S. Lahai and J. O'Connell, *Sierra Leone's Truth and Reconciliation Commission and Special Court: A citizen's handbook*, National Forum for Human Rights and International Centre for Transitional Justice (ICTJ), 2003, www.ictj.org (accessed 12 April 2007).

21. International Crisis Group, *Sierra Leone's Truth and Reconciliation Commission: A fresh start*.

22. Seirra Leone Working Group on Truth and Reconciliation, 'Searching for truth and reconciliation'.

23. B. Nowrojee, 'Making the invisible war crime visible: Post-conflict justice for Sierra Leone's rape victims', *Harvard Human Rights Journal* 18 (Spring), 2005, www.law.harvard.edu/students/orgs/hrj/iss18/nowrojee.shtml (accessed 11 April 2007).

24. UN Security Council Resolution 1325, S/RES/1325 (2000).

25. See World Bank, 'Gender, justice and truth commissions', World Bank Report, June 2006, www.worldbank.org (accessed 11 April 2007).

26. 'Sierra Leone – "we'll kill you if you cry": Sexual violence in the Sierra Leone conflict', *Human Rights Watch Report* 15(1A), 2003, www.hrw.org.

27. W. Lambourne, 'Post-conflict peacebuilding: Meeting human needs for justice and reconciliation', *Peace, Conflict and Development* 4 (April), 2004: 1–24.

28. See, for example, A. Tejan-Cole, 'The complementary and conflicting relationship between the Special Court for Sierra Leone and the Truth and Reconciliation Commission', *Yale Human Rights and Development Law Journal* (January), 2003: 139–159.

29. See M. Wierda, P. Hayner and P. van Zyl, *Exploring the relationship between the Special Court and the Truth and Reconciliation Commission of Sierra Leone* (New York: The International Centre for Transitional Justice, 2002); see Tejan-Cole, 'The complementary and conflicting relationship between the Special Court for Sierra Leone and the Truth and Reconciliation Commission'.

30. World Bank, 'Gender, justice, and truth commissions'.

31. The *Final Report of the Truth and Reconciliation Commission of Sierra Leone*, vol. 3b, chap. 7: 'Reconciliation', trcsierraleone.org (accessed 10 April 2007).

32. The SLTRC's *Final Report* recommendations cover the following areas and themes: protection of human rights, establishing the rule of law, the security services, promoting good governance, fighting corruption, youth, women, children, external actors, mineral resources, the commission and the special court, reparations, reconciliation, a national vision for Sierra Leone, archiving, dissemination of the report, and the follow-up committee.

33. Sierra Leone Priority Plan document for the UN Peacebuilding Fund (PBF) shared during the National Consultation on the Peacebuilding Commission, organised by the Centre for Conflict Resolution (CCR) in Freetown, Sierra Leone, December 2006.

34. The Human Rights Commission of Sierra Leone Act, 2004.

35. Newly appointed human rights commissioners outlined the commission's institutional challenges during the commission's visit to the CCR in Cape Town May 2007.

8

Peace versus Justice?

A View from Nigeria

Matthew Kukah

INTRODUCTION

After the collapse of the Berlin Wall in 1989 and with what the experts came to refer to as the 'end of history', most African countries seemed unsure how best to commence the process of their individual or collective integration into the so-called new world order.[1] The late 1980s and early 1990s witnessed the emergence of Sovereign National Conferences (SNCs) across the African continent, beginning in Benin.[2] Initially, the excitement created by SNCs gave the impression that Africans had found a new strategy for laying the foundation for transitions from authoritarianism to democracy. From Algeria to Benin, Togo to Zaire, the foundations of the old order were subjected to intense pressure as civil society organisations (CSOs) stormed the bastions of their authoritarian states. In some cases the foundations of the old states collapsed while in others the old order was merely undermined. Either way, in less than five years it seemed clear that hopes for a new order in Africa had been laid on a rather weak foundation.[3]

It was in South Africa that the rays of hope began to emerge. Nelson Mandela's 'long walk' out of prison, the subsequent end of apartheid and the transformation of the largest and most experienced mass movement, the African National Congress (ANC), into a political party, all gave an impetus to the struggle for democracy on the African continent. Mandela's subsequent victory at the polls, and the emergence of the Government of National Unity in 1994 under the shadow of a 'rainbow coalition' gave further hope to Africa that, indeed, democracy had the potential to rekindle the hopes of national cohesion and integration among its peoples. Many were fixated on the success story that South Africa had come to symbolise.

When that country subsequently announced the setting up of its Truth and Reconciliation Commission (TRC), many of the citizens of the continent sat up in curious excitement. It was then that most of us heard of the idea of the TRC for the first time. Led by forceful personalities such as President Mandela and Archbishop Desmond Tutu, the world watched a drama that set the good, the bad and the ugly side by side. By the time the TRC finished its work, many observers in Africa had begun to savour the prospect that this was the way forward for post-authoritarian regimes if they wanted to lay a solid foundation for national cohesion.

Consequently, when Nigerians woke up to the news that the new government headed by retired General Olusegun Obasanjo had set up a Human Rights Violations Investigation Commission (HRVIC), many were curious as to what the commission was all about. The doubts and cynicism seemed to give way to hope when Nigerians were told that the commission was more or less a Nigerian variant of the South African TRC.[4] Its implementation so early in the days of the administration gave Nigerians the impression that, indeed, building a human rights culture would be a key component of the Obasanjo administration.

This chapter attempts to situate the Nigerian HRVIC against the wider backdrop of Africa's struggle for peace and justice using the instruments of TRCs and war tribunals. The first section outlines the nature of the legal and political instruments that were employed and attempts to explain the circumstances leading to the setting up of the HRVIC. The second section considers the methodology that the commission employed to carry out its assignment. The key themes that emerged from the work of the commission are examined and highlighted in the third section and, finally, the major issues are reviewed and attention drawn to the impediments and hopes inherent to the initiative.

BACKGROUND

CSOs and the media especially were quick to break into a song and dance as they celebrated the end of military rule in Nigeria. Amid this excitement, some cautioned that it was too early to celebrate and that we could be dancing on a wet grave.[5] I constantly warned that, despite our excitement, we needed to remain cognisant of the fact that, unlike apartheid, military rule in Nigeria did not end as a result of international revulsion or from a combination of international and national civil society pressures but from a combination of circumstances, the realities and intentions of which are still the stuff of cloak-and-dagger conspiracy theories.[6] I also argued that a measure of whether military rule had really ended in Nigeria could be seen in the light of the fact that we had ended up with a retired general as president. It was also rather curious that this so-called end of military rule had saddled us with a wide spectrum of retired generals who surfaced as some of the most powerful ministers, security advisers, governors and senators. The presence of the military in almost every facet of the nation's life, from agriculture, banking and industry to traditional institutions was evidence of the fact that in Nigeria's case, the old order had merely changed jerseys and repositioned itself. It had not surrendered. This fact, in my view, will shape (and continue to shape) every facet of our national life for a long time. And, as I will show, it had an effect on the work of the commission and its subsequent outcome.

The circumstances that led to the setting up of the HRVIC remain more or less a mystery to the members of the commission itself and almost all Nigerians. All of us who served on the commission have different stories to tell as to how we were contacted regarding our participation in the work of the commission. Yet they are all tales of how we were caught unawares and had very little input in our participation.[7] The commission was made up of a chairperson and six members. From a gender perspective, it had five males and two females, all drawn from diverse backgrounds.[8] The apparent secrecy in the composition of the membership of the commission became a major factor early on. The diverse backgrounds of the members and their lack of experience in civil society work meant that the commission had some initial difficulties finding its way. The presidency seemed confused even in terms of how to delineate authority and what procedures should be adopted for reporting the commission's work and progress.[9]

The commission was set up using the Tribunals of Inquiry Act, a somewhat controversial piece of legislation that had been abused by the military and used as an instrument of selective justice.[10] Using this instrument, the commission was, among other things given, the mandate to:

- Ascertain or establish the causes, nature and extent of human rights violations or abuses with particular reference to all known or suspected cases of mysterious deaths and assassinations or attempted assassinations committed between 1 January 1994 and 29 May 1999.

- Identify the person or persons, authorities or institutions or organisations which may be accountable for such mysterious deaths and assassinations or violations or abuses, the victims and the circumstances thereof and the effect on such victims or the society generally of the atrocities.
- Determine whether such abuses or violations were the product of deliberate state policy or the policy of any of its organs or institutions, or whether the abuses by state officials of their office or whether they were the acts of any political organisations, liberation movements, or other groups or individuals.
- Recommend measures which may be taken, whether judicial, administrative, legislative, or institutional, to redress the injustices of the past and to prevent or forestall such future violations or abuses of human rights.
- Make any recommendations which are, in the opinion of the panel, in the public interest and necessitated by the evidence.[11]

The commission had three months within which to submit its report.[12]

GETTING STARTED

Whatever the limitations may have been, many Nigerians were too excited to bother about the deeper questions concerning how the commission and its membership had been conceived. Despite their feelings of revulsion towards the military, ordinary Nigerians had voted overwhelmingly for Obasanjo, the retired military general who had governed the country and then willingly surrendered power to a civilian administration nearly twenty years earlier. The establishment of the commission was greeted with much joy and its initiation so early in the life of the administration was taken by CSOs as evidence of the government's commitment to issues of justice, peace and reconciliation. Nigerians were also delighted at the presence of certain persons in the commission. The chairperson of the commission, retired Justice Chukwudifu Oputa, considered one of the nation's most respected and brightest Supreme Court judges, had impeccable moral credentials. He had a track record of concern over issues of human rights, the rule of law, justice and equity. He had also sat on at least six tribunals of inquiry during the course of his career. Despite being in his eighties, he still possessed a very sharp and critical mind. Many people considered his presence alone to be key to the success of the commission.

There was also Elizabeth Pam, a no-nonsense widow who was already in her seventies. Her husband had been one of the victims of the first military coup of 15 January 1966. She had a lot of experience with the bureaucracy and had worked very closely with both Generals Gowon and Obasanjo. She had a track record that revealed a high moral character and had served as a state chairperson of an electoral body during one of the nation's transitions to civil rule programmes.

As for myself, I had served as secretary-general of the Catholic Bishops' Conference and had been active in the politics of advocacy, especially under the military.

This combination of people was enough for many to be hopeful about the work of the commission. Without wishing to take anything away from the other members of the commission, none of the remaining four members had been in the public domain before.[13]

The commission set to work immediately by calling for memoranda from the Nigerian public. An advertisement was placed in all the major national newspapers, on radio and on television. It spelt out the terms of reference of the commission. We adopted no format for writing a petition so as to avoid either complications or intimidating ordinary citizens. Citizens were told that all they needed to do was to write out their complaints in a manner in which they were comfortable. Experienced CSOs such as the Civil Liberties Organisation (CLO) offered to write briefs free of charge for prospective petitioners.[14]

Initially, many citizens were confused as to what constituted human rights violations. There was also a high level of cynicism based on the fact that ordinary citizens had learnt to expect very little in terms of accountability from their governments. There were those who simply thought that nothing would come out of the initiative and others who believed that either no one would bother about their cases or that they themselves would merely reconcile themselves to their fate. More importantly, at that time, no one, including the members of the commission, was clear as to what format the work of the commission would take. However, well into the third week in August 1999, many memoranda began to pour in with the Ogonis submitting a consolidated set of 8 000 memoranda.

As public interest increased, we decided to leave the doors open for the collection and collation of memoranda. The office of the attorney-general assigned two senior legal officers to the commission. We also hired about ten other lawyers to work with them. For more than three months these legal officers went through all the memoranda and summarised the petitions and the prayers of the various petitioners. In the course of its work the secretariat painstakingly categorised all the memoranda into the following groupings:

- Physical and Mental Torture;
- Unlawful Arrest and Detention;
- Murder/Assassination;
- Assault/Battery;
- Intimidation/Harassment;
- Communal Violence; and
- Disappearances.[15]

Beyond the work of the secretariat, the commission adopted other strategies for enriching its work. Given that there had been no debate within CSOs and the national assembly about the commission's work, we were a bit unsure as to how to progress with the work. However, we decided to use our initiative to reach out to CSOs and others within the society whose contributions we considered to be important to our work.

Firstly, we decided to design a mechanism that could feel the pulse of the nation and also that would set the tone for the work. We chose several sub-themes and decided to organise interactive sessions and lectures throughout the country. The main sub-themes were: human rights violations, women, corporate life, military rule and media. We invited experts in the fields in question and through lectures and interactive sessions were able to enrich the database of the work of the commission. Secondly, we decided to organise an international conference on truth commissions around the world. We invited people from across the globe to share their stories with us so we could gain insight from their experiences. Thirdly, we decided to visit the TRC secretariat in South Africa in order to understand the nature of its experience and discover what we could learn for our own assignment. There was a general feeling that South Africa's TRC had hastened that nation's sense of national cohesion and helped to make the elections relatively peaceful. Unfortunately, when we contacted the commission, we realised that it had already completed its work. We were, however, informed that the Reparation Sub-committee was still working and we could visit it and still see its processes at work in Cape Town. The four-day visit was enriching for us.

Fourthly, we decided to assemble a broad spectrum of scholars who would be drawn from the academia and research institutes in the country. We commissioned these individuals and institutions to do extensive research into the extent of human rights violations in the six geopolitical zones across the country. In each zone we identified the best of those individuals who were already engaged in the area of human rights work.[16] These initiatives enabled us to take on neglected themes such as gender, domestic violence, economic justice and so on.[17] Once these initiatives had been implemented we felt ready to move to the next phase.

We finally decided to adopt a public hearings mechanism as a strategy for dealing with the petitions. It was here that the petitioners were able to confront the alleged perpetrators. We decided to arrange our sittings and public hearings according to the six geopolitical zones.[18] In doing this we took cognisance of two realities. Firstly, we wanted to make things easier for petitioners. We were aware that some petitions could go on for over two or more days and therefore thought it would be better to ensure that petitioners were not frustrated by logistical difficulties, especially given the fact that we had not prepared a budget to move and accommodate petitioners or witnesses. Secondly, we also believed that once it got under way, the general public would be interested in the work of the commission and that many people would simply like to walk in and out to witness the conduct of the public hearings. We believed that such an interactive atmosphere would enrich the work of the commission and engender public participation.

What we had not been prepared for was the reaction of the general public to the work of the commission once the public hearings began. In the first few months the commission's media team recorded and then edited the proceedings of the day, which were then broadcast on the National Television Authority (NTA). Gradually, as the hearings progressed, some private television stations began to air the proceedings too. Suddenly almost an entire nation became caught up with watching Oputa Panel. The transmissions usually went on into the early hours of the morning. Owing to public demand, the NTA began a live transmission of the proceedings. Soon other private channels followed suit.

Once the commission had settled the issue of public hearings, the next issue was how best to conduct its proceedings without creating an adversarial environment. We finally decided that the best way forward was first of all to ensure that victims had an opportunity to tell their stories in the most dignified atmosphere. We were also anxious to make sure that those alleged perpetrators who had been demonised by a series of accusations, especially towards the end of military rule, were given a chance to clear their names. Unlike South Africa, we did not have an amnesty clause[19] so, although the proceedings ended up looking like an adversarial trial – with victims making accusations against perpetrators – the maturity and experience of the chairperson ensured that each side was, on balance, given a fair chance to express itself.

The commission assured all petitioners that the lawyers employed by the commission were at their disposal. However, some wealthy petitioners opted to come to the commission with their own lawyers and wealthy perpetrators hired some of the best lawyers in the country. Indeed, it was said that the period of the commission's work was extremely lucrative for the men in silk.[20]

KEY THEMES

With each of these initiatives, each county has usually had a period, an administration or a phase during which human rights violations were at a peak. There is therefore the tendency to focus either on an administration or on the role of certain individuals whose misdeeds would automatically have become part of the public memory. To that extent people will tend to judge the success of the initiative according to whether these individuals or regimes were dealt with or whether they escaped justice and were not held to account. Such periods easily become the focus of the work of the commission. In Nigeria, although many people seem to focus on the period in which General Sani Abacha served as the nation's head of state, the fact is that the foundation for the tragedy that climaxed at that period had been laid many years previously as part of the baggage of military rule. Despite the fact that the commission's work was supposed to have focused on human rights violations, the instrument that set up the commission did not specify what really constituted human rights violations. We were flexible in allowing individuals to determine what in their view constituted human rights violations. Revealing their stories was part of the healing process.

The military institution

Even before the setting up of the commission Nigerians who had lived under military rule had come to despise and ridicule that institution. The military had become associated with violence, corruption and a threat to democracy. The renowned musician, the late Fela Anikulapo Kuti, who had suffered at the hands of the military, had come to refer to them as 'Zombie' and had held them responsible for reducing democracy to a *dem-all-crazy*.[21] During cross-examination in cases that involved the military, the military as an institution came under very serious scrutiny and in most cases public ridicule. For example, during cross-examination at the public hearings, Nigerians marvelled at how low things had sunk during military rule when senior military officers admitted to begging their very junior officers who held public office for pecuniary favours and reprieve from torture.[22] Through the commission the Nigerian public learnt in detail how coups and counter-coups were conceived, and of the unbridled greed that drove soldiers to undermine their country through these coups. It became clear to citizens that an accumulation of all this had led to the collapse of a culture of *esprit de corps* within the military. All in all, Nigerians came to realise that, indeed, the military had been the first casualty of its own misrule.

Impunity and the generals

As a corollary to the issues of military rule, the question concerning the appearances of some of the generals who had been heads of state before the commission also took centre stage. It will be recalled that the commission's secretariat had requested all petitioners to provide their full residential and postal addresses to the commission in their petitions. Thus, when the secretariat concluded its summary of the petitions it issued letters to both the petitioners and their alleged perpetrators. In the letters both parties were informed of the dates for the hearings of their cases and were requested to appear before the commission either to state or defend their allegations. Similar letters were sent to Generals Ibrahim Babangida, Abdusalam Abubakar and Major General Muhammadu Buhari, against whom there were petitions. When their cases came up some people in the northern media began to question why these particular generals had been selected. Accusations of regional and religious bias were made against the commission, but it was simple to refute these arguments: they were the perpetrators against whom the commission had received petitions.

For more than three months the commission was locked in a tussle with the military officers and their lawyers. In the end they resorted to seeking redress in the courts as a means of avoiding appearing before the commission. Unlike the case of South Africa, in which it was the TRC that went to court against former President P.W. Botha, in Nigeria it was the perpetrators who went to court in an attempt to stop the work of the commission.[23] Eventually the commission decided to issue a ruling concerning the generals. In this ruling the commission informed the public and the generals that although it had legal powers to compel the generals to appear, it did not believe that witnesses could be forced to testify under duress. Rather than resorting to legalism the commission opted for the path of moral persuasion in deference to the status of the men in question. This was a rather controversial decision by the commission and many Nigerians felt that it should have gone further in order to compel the generals to appear.

The police and the state security services

Like the military, the police force and other security agencies had also become notorious in the minds of ordinary Nigerian citizens. They were infamous for their brutality, corruption and inefficiency. The military had tended to take on aspects of law enforcement and had eroded the authority of the police. The police had frequently taken their frustrations out on the civilian population. During the commission's hearings we heard stories of illegal detention and unnecessary torture of civilians during interrogations, extortion and deaths in detention. There were stories of the complicity of the police force in hindering citizens' quest for justice and accounts of the disappearance of witnesses, summary executions and other forms of impunity by the police authorities.[24] We also heard the tales of ordinary citizens who had suffered at the hands of the security agencies. There were allegations that security centres had become synonymous with torture and disappearances. Civilians complained of being detained in military facilities. Prior to the commission these stories had been the subject of speculation but now ordinary citizens were able to confront their tormentors and put a face to all these dark forces for the first time.

Muzzling the messenger

One of the most trenchant critics of the military dictatorship and its attendant consequences on Nigeria was the mass media, especially the printed media. This phase of the history of the Nigerian media has already been well told. It is a period marked by what has come to be known as 'guerrilla journalism'.[25] Indeed, it was through the media that early anti-colonial struggles began in opposition to British colonialism. This media continued with this role well into the struggle against apartheid. The media gained confidence in these struggles and, when the need arose, it turned its attention to exposing the injustices of military rule. The military reacted by jailing and torturing media men and women. The commission offered the media an opportunity to draw public attention to its historical and contextual role in the struggle against gross human rights violations that were committed against both the media and society at large. The most celebrated case remains that of Dele Giwa, the nation's most colourful journalist, who was killed by a letter bomb on 19 November 1986. His case was presented to the commission.[26]

The collapse of the rule of law

At the heart of the work of the commission was the failure of law enforcement, which created the conditions for human rights violations. However, a critical issue in appreciating the context of military rule is the extent to which that system of governance makes the rule of law the first casualty. This is why I have argued elsewhere that military rule and civil society cannot co-exist since the survival of one is the defeat of the other.[27]

The military governs by decree. This suspension of the Constitution usually appears in the first paragraphs of the speech of every military regime in order to clear the way for its contrived legitimacy. It can be taken for granted, therefore, that any government that has no constitutional basis for governance automatically denies its citizens any opportunity to have access to justice. The commission offered many citizens a chance to contest issues that, under the military regime, they had not been allowed to table before a court of law precisely because the judges were prone to taking refuge beneath claims that 'their hands were tied' by the ouster clauses in the various decrees. Many other issues were highlighted but we have mentioned these merely to draw attention to the very positive role that the commission played as a means of catharsis for those who had encountered injustice under the old order. To that extent we can argue that the commission fulfilled one of the key roles of TRCs.

By way of summary and conclusion, the final section explores the lessons learnt and the place of the HRVIC in the struggle to end impunity and human rights violations in Nigeria.

CONCLUSION

In assessing the work of TRCs, especially in Africa, critics tend to focus on the *failures* of these commissions. Most of the failures have been based on claims that these commissions did not deliver on justice, truth or reconciliation. Most of the literature on TRCs has been written by insiders or by outsiders-looking-on-the-inside (academics and journalists). The victims have hardly told their stories themselves. As with other political bodies, TRCs soon became an industry, hiring consultants from around the world to proffer solutions for post-conflict African nations. We have therefore gone in circles and with a sense of guilt are left asking whether, as the Hausas say: *'Kwaliya ta biya ladan sabulu'*.[28] Sadly we have not had the confidence to ask whether these were the proper tools for addressing the problems of conflict in Africa. The jury is still out on that issue.

For better or worse, TRCs serve a particular purpose and I would argue that perhaps there is no such thing as a 'good' or 'bad' TRC. We must appreciate the fact that, as a heuristic device, TRCs have helped many nations to pause for a moment and get what athletes refer to as a 'second wind'.[29] In assessing the Nigerian initiative I have been amazed at how those who were so removed from the events, whether by emotions, cynicism, space or time, have surfaced as critics of the commission. Unfortunately, its critics focus with such narrow lenses that they lack the capacity to see, even if in metaphorical terms, the range of possibilities that the commission's work engendered. Critics have told me: 'You guys did a great job and look how the president messed you people up. Where is the report now? And why did those generals not appear?'

I believe that the inability of the presidency to work assiduously towards releasing the report to the public was a disservice and I have no doubt that it diminished public appreciation of the work of the commission. In addition, the non-appearance of the generals was unfortunate in the work of the commission. While we must leave the rest to history, there is a point to be made about how civil society and the Nigerian community approached issues of advocacy in a post-conflict situation. The approaches of civil society to engaging in post-conflict situations have tended to be ambivalent. If we see the struggle for justice as a work in progress then the success of the HRVIC lay in the volumes of material that it brought into the public domain. To that extent, it offered Nigerian advocates for justice material with which to confront the state at various political levels.

It is undeniable that the commission suffered from many problems. However, I believe that several of these problems were more symptoms than the disease itself. They were symptomatic of the environment in which we were operating, an environment in which the old order had not yet surrendered. It is clear that retired General Obasanjo, who in 1979 had willingly handed over power and engaged the state so vigorously, was a different Obasanjo from the man who became president in 1999. General Obasanjo the head of state did not need a national assembly to pass a budget or make a decree; he did not need the consent of Nigerians to rule over them and he had no opposition to contain. President

Obasanjo the politician seemed concerned only with pulling the threads of power into his hands and staying in power for much longer than the democratic order was willing to allow. I would therefore argue that with hindsight it seems that the setting up of the commission was meant to provide an arsenal for the president to use in the same manner he had used the material that had been provided by the Kolade Panel, which he set up barely one week into office.[30]

When people ask whether the commission was effective the answer must surely be, 'Yes, it was as effective as it could be under the circumstances'. It is important to note that mere appearances, symbolic as they may be, do not necessarily bring us closer to the truth or reconciliation. Indeed, one of our petitioners prefixed her appearance by saying that she had come to 'find the truth and not seek reconciliation'.[31]

The lack of a vibrant debate within civil society, together with the rather lackadaisical attitude of the national assembly with which it was mired in its first two years, amidst allegations of corruption among its members, did not help matters. The National Assembly did not possess the moral authority to take up the issue of the establishment of a constitutional basis for governance.[32]

The constraints imposed on the polity (the lack of a legally negotiated or even contested transition), the ubiquity of the military classes and the preponderance of their business allies who had resurfaced as recycled politicians and contractors took its toll on the state's capacity for introspection. I can only conclude that the real success of the commission lay in the fact that it took place at all. To ask whether this or any of the commissions were able to deliver on the themes of justice, truth or reconciliation is, to my mind, the wrong way to frame the question. I believe that the answer to those issues can be found only in a democratic environment. Thus, the presence of democratic space around which TRCs take place is the victory song of TRCs. The issues of peace, justice, truth and reconciliation are works in progress and not ends in themselves; TRCs could therefore never have offered them. Indeed, the inconclusiveness of TRCs should help us to appreciate the fact that they are not meant to solve the problems of the nations that set them up. Rather, they are meant to provide both a rear-view mirror and a good set of headlights to shed light on the future. For those in Nigeria, the fact that the commission at least exposed the underbelly of the military in terms of its incipient corruption and bankruptcy went a long way towards helping Nigerians say with a loud voice, 'Never again' to military rule. We cannot find a more solid rock on which to lay the foundations of democracy.

We must remind ourselves that most of the victims who came to us went away happy not because perpetrators were convicted or because they themselves had received compensation but rather because they had seen and confronted the demi-god of the past and 'told the whole world their story'.[33] For them that was justice enough. If the victims of yesterday's injustice believe they got justice from telling their stories to the whole world can we as spectators cry more than the bereaved?

NOTES AND REFERENCES

1. For the better part of the first ten or so years after the collapse of communism two rather controversial theses advanced by both Francis Fukuyama and Samuel Huntington dominated debates around the future of the world after communism. See F. Fukuyama, *The end of history and the last man* (New York: The Free Press, 1992); and S. Huntington, *The clash of civilisations and the remaking of the new world order* (New York: Simon and Schuster, 1996).

2. P. Robinson, 'The national conference phenomenon in Francophone Africa', *Comparative Studies in Society and History* 36(3), 1994: 575–610.

3. In Algeria, the local elite, in collaboration with the French ruling classes, ensured that the old order did not surrender; in Benin, Mathieu Kerekou quickly declared a conference that later disempowered him and ushered in the processes that brought Neciphore Soglo, a World Bank economist, to the helm of affairs. Soglo was unable to win the next elections and Kerekou returned to power, wearing the toga of a born-again Christian. In Zaire, Mobutu held on beyond the pressures of the SNC until other forces overcame him.

4. In Nigeria and abroad, members of the commission, trying to explain their assignment, tended to hang their legitimacy on the fact that the HRVIC was like the TRC in South Africa. Very often, and for effect, the chairperson was compared to Archbishop Tutu.

5. M. Kukah, *Democracy and civil society in Nigeria* (Ibadan: Spectrum Books, 1998).

6. There are still court cases in the United States alleging that Chief M.K.O. Abiola, the winner of the 1993 elections that were cancelled, did not die a natural death. Many Nigerians speculate that the choreographed nature of the deaths, exactly one month apart, of both General Abacha (8 June 1998) and Chief Abiola (8 July 1998) were more than happenstance.

7. Details are in my forthcoming book on the commission.

8. Composition of the commission: chairperson: Chukwudifu Oputa; members: Father Matthew Hassan Kukah, Barrister Bala Ngilari, Elizabeth Pam, Mrs Modupe Areola, Mallam Bamali and Tunji Abayomi.

9. For example, the offices of the Secretary of the Government of the Federation and the attorney-general seemed both to claim that the commission was answerable to them alone. The commission often found itself caught between the president, attorney-general and the office of the Secretary of the Government, depending on the issues that needed to be attended to.

10. Tribunals of Inquiry Act, Chapter 447, Laws of the Federation of Nigeria, 1990, Volume XXIII, www.nigeria-law.org/Tribunals%20of%20Inquiry%20Act.htm (accessed 12 February 2009).

11. Tribunals of Inquiry Act, sec. 6.

12. It turned out that the three-month period was a format designed by the government for all the commissions or committees it set up before and after the commission. This was the first sign that the government itself was not very clear as to what it wanted to achieve.

13. Modupe Areola was the wife of a retired navy officer and had worked with the state security services. Bala Ngilari was a fine lawyer but had no record of civil society involvement. Tunji Abayomi, a prominent civil society activist and one of the lawyers to the president, was a member but had to be dropped by the president. A seasoned lawyer, Dr Mudiaga Odje, replaced him but unfortunately he was too old and sick to participate fully in the work of the commission. He finally dropped out of the commission due to ill health and died in 2005.

14. The Civil Liberties Organisation (CLO) founded and headed in the mid-1980s by Olisa Agbakoba, a much-respected lawyer, did a lot of great work, especially under the military. The CLO laid the foundation for human rights activities in Nigeria.

15. This categorisation was broad but it did not cover all the petitions. As time went on and the work of the commission became the subject of television, more petitions poured in, some covering flippant domestic and personal quarrels.

16. Dr Bala Usman, Omafume Onoge, Professor Aaron Gana and Aisha Imam, among others.

17. For example, we commissioned Baobab, the leading women's research outfit and also the Centre for Democracy and Development (CDD) specifically to look at the issues of human rights violations as they related to women.

18. Abuja, Enugu, Kano, Lagos, Port Harcourt. We had very few petitions from both Northeast zones and so we combined the two zones and sat in Kano. We also sat twice in Abuja to take on cases that had not been concluded in the different zones.

19. The lack of debate around the setting up of the commission also accounted for this.

20. Almost all alleged perpetrators, from the retired generals to the family of the late General Sani Abacha, retained the services of Senior Advocates of Nigeria (SAN). There were unconfirmed rumours that SANs were charging a minimum of N5 million for appearances at the commission.

21. 'Zombie' became a hit track on an album by that title and was popular even among the military.

22. Retired and serving military officers who were not holding political offices were often vulnerable to the vagaries of economic life. The military had decided that only lieutenant-colonels and colonels could be governors. As such, these governors were well placed to give out contracts and donate lands and cash to their seniors, who were known as 'Desk Generals'. The word for this in military circles is 'welfare'.

23. All three generals went to court seeking various protections, which ranged from attempts to stop the commission from summoning them to seeking the disbandment of the commission and the non-release of its report. See 'Generals evade Nigeria rights panel', BBC news, 1 November 2001, news.bbc.co.uk/2/hi/africa/1632714.stm (accessed 12 February 2009). Ironically, this is the platform the federal government used for its refusal to release the final report.

24. For a most comprehensive account, see I. Chukwuma, *Above the law: An account of extra-judicial killings in Nigeria* (Lagos: Civil Liberties Organisation Publications, 1996).

25. This concept was coined to describe the underground tactics that the print media resorted to as a means of surviving under General Abacha's rule. For a summary of the issues, see A. Olutokun and D. Seteolu, 'The media and democratic rule in Nigeria', *Development Management Policy Network Bulletin* 3, September 2001.

26. See evidence of the police commissioner who investigated this case in A. Tsav, 'The evidence of Abubakar Tsav to the Human Rights Violations Investigation Commission', personal paper, 3 July 2001.

27. Kukah, *Democracy and civil society in Nigeria*.

28. Literally translated: 'Has the cleanliness of the cloth justified the amount spent on the washing powder?'

29. I am told that a 'second wind' is the new energy that long-distance runners get when they refuse to succumb to exhaustion.

30. The panel set up by the president, known as the Kolade Panel, was asked to investigate contracts that had been hurriedly awarded in the dying days of the Abdusalam administration. There were rumours that the panel's report was later to become a tool for blackmailing opponents who had made a fortune by way of contracts in 1998–1999. Dr Kolade has been Nigeria's high commissioner in the United Kingdom since 1999.

31. Testimony of Mrs Rewane at the public hearings of the commission in Lagos, November 2000.

32. Part of this irony was seen in the senate having three senate presidents in the first four years of its life, three national chairpersons of the party throughout the commission process, and two speakers in the first two months.

33. This expression came through when many ordinary citizens left the venue of the public hearings. They believed that since their testimonies had been broadcast live and such Nigerian television outlets had international reception, they could take consolation in the fact that the whole world had heard their stories.

9

A Path to Peace and Justice

Ghana's National Reconciliation Commission in Retrospect

Kenneth Agyemang Attafuah

INTRODUCTION

The National Reconciliation Commission (NRC) of Ghana was created in May 2002. Its objective was to seek and promote reconciliation in a country whose people had been deeply fractured by a long period of egregious human rights violations and abuses that had been perpetrated by public officers, particularly during the many periods of military rule that had punctuated Ghana's political development since independence on 6 March 1957 and prior to the nation's return to civilian constitutional rule on 3 January 1993. The goal of reconciliation was to be achieved through the excavation of the nation's history of human rights violations, the establishment of a complete and accurate historical record of the violations and the provision of appropriate recommendations to redress victims' grievances and to prevent the recurrence of such violations in future.[1] I write this chapter from the vantage point of an insider with intimate knowledge of the reconciliation process in Ghana, having served as executive secretary of the NRC from its inception to its conclusion in December 2004.[2]

A truth and reconciliation commission (TRC) is an institutional mechanism that is available to societies that are in the process of transition from sustained conflict and antagonism to peacebuilding and democracy. Usually such a body allows politically troubled societies to uncover and preserve the truth about past human rights violations, ensure justice, foster healing, promote reconciliation, combat impunity and prevent the recurrence of such violations and the conditions that produced them. In the interests of justice and in an effort to undermine impunity, prosecutions, either national or international, are a fashionable outcome or expectation of many truth commissions. In the case of Ghana, it is my contention that prosecutions, either national or international, of the perpetrators of egregious human rights violations would have been most inappropriate.

This chapter reviews the purposes and mandate of the NRC, offers a profile of the witnesses who appeared before it, considers the extent to which it addressed gender-based violence committed during the mandate period, reviews the role of civil society in the national reconciliation process and addresses briefly the suitability or otherwise of a war-crimes tribunal for Ghana. In addition, it discusses the extent to which the work of the NRC was politicised and the underpinnings of that politicisation. Finally, the chapter assesses the key achievements and failings of the NRC.

REASONS FOR THE ESTABLISHMENT OF THE NRC

In its post-independence history Ghana experienced four major *coups d'état* – in February 1966, January 1972, June 1979 and December 1981. The military governments to which these coups gave birth occasioned and supervised horrendous and large-scale human rights violations and abuses. Such violations severely fractured the country along political, ethnic and civil versus military lines. Countless attempted *coups d'état* also brought in their wake widespread and systematic human rights violations and abuses that destabilised the nation politically and economically, driving thousands of Ghanaians into exile. Paradoxically, Ghanaians did not escape serious violations of their fundamental human rights during periods of constitutional rule either.

Although various commissions of inquiry were set up by successive regimes to investigate some of the violations, the many antecedents, contexts, causes, circumstances and ramifications of the conflicts that gave birth to the coups, as well as the violations they occasioned, had never been examined. Four key justifications underpinned the creation of the NRC:

- the compelling need to break the cycle of vengeance and vendetta that had characterised politics in post-independent Ghana in order to free up the energies of Ghanaians to facilitate national development;
- the Ghanaian public's need for the truth;
- the quest for 'justice' by victims of human rights violations; and
- the effects of special transitional provisions in the Ghanaian Constitution (1992) that had barred all access to judicial redress for those violations.

MANDATE OF THE NRC IN RELATION TO THE TRANSITIONAL PROVISIONS

Many acts of gross human rights violations had not been addressed because of the double effects of the fear and intimidation the violations had induced on the one hand and the legal effects of transitional provisions that were entrenched in the Ghanaian Constitution of 1992 on the other.[3] The provisions prevented the judiciary or any other tribunal from questioning any action taken, or claimed to have been taken, in the name of any of the unconstitutional governments or their operatives. These provisions also made it illegal for the judiciary or any tribunal to provide redress for any person claiming to have been wronged by any such action. Thus public officers who had committed human rights violations under the authority of the government during unconstitutional regimes were indemnified or granted amnesty from prosecution. While probe after probe chronicled and made public the misdeeds of both the civilian and the two military regimes, the crimes of the Armed Forces Revolutionary Council (AFRC) and the Provisional National Defence Council (PNDC) remained unexamined. In addition, until the birth of the NRC, the pain of the victims remained unacknowledged.

The creation of the NRC had been promised in the 2000 manifesto of the ruling National Patriotic Party. President John Agyekum Kufour reiterated this promise in his first inaugural speech as president on 7 January 2001. He observed that Ghana had gone through turbulent times, that the country's greatest enemy was poverty and that the fight against this would start with reconciling Ghanaians and forging ahead in unity, appeasement and forgiveness. In his maiden State of the Nation address to parliament on 15 February 2001, the president further assured Ghanaians that a national forum would be provided in which victims could 'air their grievances in order to promote the goal of national reconciliation' and which would signal that Ghana did not endorse 'a culture of impunity'. Thereafter, in December 2001, the Ghanaian parliament passed the National Reconciliation Commission Act 611 of 2002, establishing the NRC.[4] The mandate of the NRC was to investigate human rights violations and abuses relating to killings, abductions, disappearances, detentions, torture, ill-treatment and the seizure of properties suffered at the hands of a public institution, public office-holder or someone who claimed to act on behalf of the state during periods of unconstitutional government, that is, the military regimes that had reigned from 24 February 1966 to 21 August 1969, 13 January 1972 to 23 September 1979, and 31 December 1981 to 6 January 1993. The NRC was also given the discretionary power to investigate and, where necessary, make appropriate recommendations in respect of any petition alleging similar human rights violations, but which allegedly took place during periods of constitutional rule between 6 March 1957 and 6 January 1993.

In addition, the NRC had the mandate to investigate the context as well as 'the causes and circumstances under which the violations and abuses occurred'. In order to strike at impunity the NRC was given the power to name names – to 'identify the individuals, public institutions, bodies, organisations, public office holders or persons purporting to have acted on behalf of any public body responsible for or involved in the violations and abuses'. Victims were to be specifically identified and appropriate recommendations made to ensure redress for them. The NRC was also charged with the responsibility of determining whether the violations had been deliberately planned and executed. It had the flexibility to conduct any 'investigations relevant to its work' and to 'investigate any other matters' necessary for achieving national reconciliation. Finally, the NRC was required to educate the public and give sufficient publicity to its work so as to encourage broad public participation in the reconciliation process.

The commission was equipped with the traditional powers of the police in its investigations and the judicial powers of a High Court in its hearings. The latter included the power to compel people to testify before it. Despite this feature the NRC was not a court but an investigative body.

Modelled after the South African TRC, which has been described as 'the recognized gold standard' of truth commissions,[5] the NRC comprised nine distinguished Ghanaians appointed by the president in consultation with the council of state – a non-partisan constitutional body of eminent Ghanaians that advises the president. It was to be chaired by a retired Supreme Court judge, Justice K.E. Amua-Sekyi.

Operations

The NRC was inaugurated on 6 May 2002 and opened its doors to the public on 3 September 2002 to take and receive statements concerning violations that had allegedly occurred between 6 March 1957 and 6 January 1993. The statement-taking exercise closed on 13 January 2004. A total of 4 240 petitions had been received and these covered all the political regimes in the country's history. Public hearings commenced on 14 January 2003 throughout the country and ended on 13 July 2004. A total of 1 866 petitioners testified as 'victims', while 79 respondents, including former president Jerry John Rawlings and his national security adviser of many years, Captain Kojo Tsikata, appeared before the NRC to assist it in its work.[6] Victims came from all backgrounds and professions whilst perpetrators were mostly from the military, the police, the prisons service and other government departments.

To further facilitate its work the NRC established six special committees to examine the role of several key state institutions and civil society organisations (CSOs) in human rights violations, as well as their potential role in preventing such violations and abuses in the future. The committees covered the activities of the media; student, youth and labour movements; security services; the legal profession (including the judiciary); other professional bodies; religious bodies; and the chieftaincy institution.

Civil society was a critical partner in the national reconciliation process. The NRC could not have succeeded in executing its mandate without the active support of several CSOs, especially the Centre for Democratic Development (CDD-Ghana), which saw the reconciliation process as critical to the stabilisation and consolidation of democracy and good governance in Ghana. In order to make a principled, focused, broad-based and non-partisan contribution to this process, CDD-Ghana, in conjunction with a number of other CSOs, established the CDD-Civil Society Coalition on National Reconciliation, which gave the NRC tremendous support in most areas of its work.

On 12 October 2004 the NRC submitted its report to the president of Ghana – a day before its mandatory submission date.[7] The report chronicled the experiences and accounts of more than 4 200 petitioners who claimed to have been victims of various forms of human rights violations that had been perpetrated by public office-holders or persons purporting to have held public office. The violations that were investigated by the commission spanned the entire mandate period. In a White Paper issued in 2005, the government accepted all the findings and recommendations contained in the NRC report.[8]

Challenges

The NRC itself was questioned on several grounds, including the very purpose of its establishment. Some critics contended that the scale of human rights violations perpetrated in Ghana did not warrant the establishment of a truth commission as they in no way approximated the systematic atrocities that had enveloped South Africa, consumed Sierra Leone and ravaged Liberia – countries in which the establishment of a TRC is seen as readily justifiable. Critics argued that Ghana had not undergone a widespread and divisive conflict that had pitted different groups against one another.[9]

It is my opinion that such a view reflects a narrow appreciation of the historical contexts in which TRCs, as an important mechanism for reconciliation, have been adopted and applied to good use, not to mention their broad, elastic and expanding purposes. As Martingai Sirleaf aptly observes: '[T]he choice of transitional justice mechanism is individualized for each country and must depend on the post-transition context: the nature of the peace settlement, the type of transition, the international context, culture, financial considerations, and the legacy of the past'.[10] The history of truth commissions worldwide shows a dynamic plurality of models, mandates and methods; no two truth commissions are alike, no matter the degree of congruence in their objectives or the confluence in their methods. There is no predetermined scale of conflict that must be considered necessary in order to trigger the establishment of a TRC.

The fundamental question about a truth commission is not, 'What is the scale of the atrocities to be investigated by a truth commission?' but rather, 'Why is a truth commission established?' Indeed, what reasons underpin their creation? For the answer it is helpful consider the benefits of a TRC identified by the National Executive Committee of the African National Congress (ANC) of South Africa, when it responded to the Motsuenyane Commission's report in 1993, which recommended the establishment of a TRC for South Africa. It observed, drawing upon the experiences of Chile, Argentina and El Salvador, that the process of getting at the truth was also a cleansing experience.

For Ghana, even though the word 'truth' is not to be found in the name of its 'transitional' justice institution, the foremost reason for the establishment of the commission is to reconcile the people of Ghana by establishing an accurate and complete historical record of human rights violations that occurred, to use the truth as a basis for providing redress and healing for victims and for preventing such atrocities from ever happening again. For the 4 240 aggrieved persons who made statements to the NRC the mechanism was an instrument of 'justice' that could overcome the barriers that had been imposed on them by the Transitional Provisions in the Constitution of 1992.

A second controversy that dogged the work of the NRC was the so-called window versus-door debate. The claim was persistently made in sections of the Ghanaian media that the NRC gave only a 'window of opportunity' to persons who wished to complain about human rights violations and abuses during constitutional regimes, while it opened a 'door' for those who wished to complain about similar events during periods of constitutional rule. Section 3(2) of the NRC's enabling statute accommodated the concerns of many Ghanaians, strongly articulated by the leadership of the opposition National Democratic Congress (NDC), who felt that human rights violations and abuses were not the exclusive province of military dictatorships and that civilian constitutional governments had also revealed a penchant for such conduct throughout Ghana's history.

In practice, the NRC interpreted this discretionary power in a positive way and exercised it in a manner that made no distinctions between petitions alleging human rights violations during periods of either constitutional or unconstitutional rule. Accordingly it did not require persons wishing to petition about violations during periods of constitutional rule to make application to that effect; it simply received and processed all petitions regardless of the constitutional or unconstitutional nature of the government in power at the time of the alleged violation or abuse.

Throughout the NRC's lifespan and despite evidence to the contrary, which the NRC made public regularly and consistently through the appropriate media, this idea persisted in certain political circles. The view was simultaneously expressed that the NRC was a manoeuvre designed to shore up the democratic credentials of the political antecedents of the ruling New Patriotic Party (NPP), while raking up public disaffection against the NDC that had been founded and led by former President Rawlings, whose two military governments had executed eight former military officers, including three former Ghanaian heads of state, and had supervised a number of state-sponsored disappearances, tortures, detentions, malicious confiscation of property and other egregious human rights violations.

The 'window versus door' argument is forcefully reiterated by Robert Ameh,[11] when he correctly contends that its intent was discriminatory against unconstitutional regimes in Ghana. Although he concedes that in practice the NRC gave such a liberal interpretation to its general mandate that no one who wished to petition against any regime was denied the opportunity to do so, Ameh argues that the perception remained one of the reconciliation process being a political witch hunt.

In practice, no such exclusion occurred. On the contrary, the NRC encouraged, received, investigated and heard petitions against all regimes. Among the first cases heard by the NRC were those alleging human rights violations during periods of constitutional rule. The NRC's outreach and educational public campaigns emphasised the right of persons to petition against violations suffered under any regime in Ghanaian history.

The following events and controversies also generated considerable political and social tension in Ghanaian society and elicited outright denunciation from some opposition political parties, particularly the NDC and the People's National Congress (PNC):

- The death of a London-based Ghanaian barrister, Kwadwo Ampah, on 5 June 2005 within three minutes of starting his testimony before the NRC in Accra. He collapsed from the witness seat as he uttered the name of former President Rawlings and was rushed to the nearby Ridge Hospital, where he was pronounced dead on arrival. Some private newspapers accused the NRC of 'killing Mr Ampah', who died of massive cardiac failure. His death prompted the immediate establishment of an Emergency Medical Response Unit that provided screening and appropriate medical services and advice to each witness prior to testifying.

- The inadvertent live broadcast to television viewers and radio listeners of the chairperson's infamous whispered comment on 5 March 2003 to another NRC member that retired Commissioner of Police David Walenkaki, who testified before the commission, had 'made a fool of himself'. The opposition NDC, in whose administration Walenkaki had served, demanded the chairperson's immediate resignation or, failing that, his dismissal by the president. Even the leadership of several respected pro-NRC CSOs joined the strident calls for the chairperson to apologise and resign. He stood his ground and the tempest passed.

- The granting by the NRC of a *limited safe passage* to Chris Asher, a fugitive from justice residing in the United Kingdom to enable him to testify before it in respect of documentary evidence he claimed to possess on the question of who bore the ultimate responsibility for the abduction and cold-blooded murder of three High Court judges and a retired army officer on 30 June 1982. His testimony and subsequent cross-examination by former Attorney-General Dr Obed Asamoah were some of the most dramatic moments in the work of the NRC.

- The issuance of subpoenas against former President Rawlings, his long-serving national security adviser, Captain Kojo Tsikata, and his long-time friend, lawyer Tsastu Tsikata, to compel their appearance before the NRC, and the regular application of the commission's normal rules of procedure to regulate their testimonies. The propriety of issuing subpoenas against the three, including the circumstances under which subpoenas might be issued, became matters of fierce public commentary and debate in the media.

Achievements

One of the NRC's major tasks was to explore concrete and viable measures that might redress the wrongs of the past. The NRC promoted forgiveness as an important precondition to healing and reconciliation and encouraged interpersonal reconciliation wherever possible. The most dramatic instance of these public displays of forgiveness and reconciliation took place at one of the earliest sittings of the NRC when a torture victim, Rexford Ohemeng, and the powerful former Director of Prisons Benson T. Baba, who allegedly ordered the tortures, hugged each other after the latter had openly apologised for his actions. 'We were young and could have done a few things out of exuberance. Forgive me,' Baba pleaded. When Ohemeng walked over to Baba and embraced him the commission's auditorium reverberated with thunderous applause.

The commission also kept within its allotted timeframe, making it the first TRC in Africa to have done so. It submitted a comprehensive five-volume report detailing its work and recommendations to the president.[12] This was a substantial accomplishment.

Significantly, the work of the NRC underscored the importance of the rule of law, a concept that had been severely undermined through decades of abuse of authority. The NRC accorded preferential treatment to no one, although it was solicitous to the needs of witnesses who warranted commiseration. Unlike the experiences in South Africa and Nigeria, where 'the generals' snubbed the commission and got away with it, no Ghanaians could eschew the NRC, regardless of their attitude towards it, their position in society or their connections to power (see Chapters 6 and 8 in this volume).

The commission's work also highlighted the importance of restorative justice, of the healing of wounds for victims and of the need for victims to reclaim their lost dignity, even if only partially. Indeed, a July 2006 CDD-Ghana survey of opinions from the Greater Accra, Volta and Western Regions of Ghana on victims' experiences with the NRC showed that such experiences were 'largely positive' and the majority expressed the belief that the NRC had helped to reconcile the country and to facilitate healing on an individual level.[13] Most respondents were also positive in their assessment of the NRC as an institution, as well as of the performance of the officials and commissioners.[14]

Another major achievement of the NRC was the extent to which it integrated gender perspectives in all spheres of its work – from staff recruitment through training, posting, work assignment, supervision, coaching, monitoring, and remuneration to retrenchment. The NRC took steps to ensure the equal and effective participation of women in its workforce such that, at the start of its public hearings, most of the departments and units were headed by women. The NRC also created and maintained a gender-sensitive and supportive work environment that was grounded in the triple principles of gender equality, gender equity and employment equity. It also developed and utilised gender-sensitive training manuals for its staff.

Through its investigations and hearings the NRC uncovered considerable evidence validating the long-held suspicion that women had been deliberately targeted, especially by soldiers, to whom corruption had an unmistakable feminine face. Patterns of gender-targeting in the victimisation process were particularly evident in the two periods of military rule headed by former President Rawlings in 1979 and 1982–1993.

Approximately 79 per cent of all victims who made statements to the TRC were males, while 19 per cent were females.[15] Women were victims of sexual and gender-based violations in 42.9 per cent of cases.[16] While such women victims were raped their male counterparts, who preponderate in the statistics, were frequently forced to simulate sexual activity with a hole in the ground, sometimes to the point of bleeding, or had electric shocks administered to their penises. A majority of the petitions filed with the NRC by women concerned subjection to economic violence and physical and sexual brutalities.

The NRC made a number of gender-specific recommendations, particularly on the rehabilitation of women victims of human rights abuses. Some of the key recommendations were that the president should make a formal apology to Ghanaian women for the violations and abuses perpetrated against them by holders of public office during the mandate period, and that a monument in honour of Ghanaian women be built. [17]

Failings

A major criticism of the NRC is that it failed to address adequately the question of the continued retention of the transitional provisions in the Ghanaian

Constitution. These are entrenched provisions, however, and the commission could only recommend their removal in accordance with the lawful procedures established in the Constitution.

It is probable that, as a result of its initial financial difficulties, the commission's decision to establish zonal instead of regional offices affected its ability to reach deeply into the remote areas of the country to take statements. CDD-Ghana yielded more than 120 additional statements even as the NRC began to wind down the statement-taking process, which suggests clear gaps in the efficacy of the exercise. Similarly, the commission's counselling services for witnesses, especially victims, could also not cover all those who needed it.

A key limitation of the NRC was its inability to maintain media interest in its proceedings throughout its lifespan. NRC hearings became a form of public theatre and the anticipated drama as well as the stature of the dramatists strongly influenced the type of media coverage the hearings received. Against the backdrop of a politically polarised society, media interest in the work of the NRC ebbed and flowed with the appearance of 'big shots' and so-called 'star witnesses', such as current and past associates of former President Rawlings. The farther away the commission moved from Accra the less print media interest, although the more than 100 private and community radio stations that were spread across the country helped to sustain local public interest.

WAR CRIMES TRIBUNAL AND THE GHANAIAN CONTEXT

The International Criminal Court (ICC) based in The Hague, The Netherlands, is one of the foremost mechanisms of accountability for violations of human rights and international humanitarian law and for ending impunity. War crimes, genocide and crimes against humanity constitute the three most serious crimes of international concern falling within the jurisdiction of the ICC. War crimes are violations of the laws of war that incur individual and criminal responsibility.[18] They are crimes committed during war that exceed the 'normal' parameters of acceptable conduct during war and are punishable under international law. There is no immunity from prosecution for war crimes and there is no statute of limitation for such crimes. A claim of compliance with a 'superior order' is not a legitimate defence to a charge of a war crime.

Depending on the circumstances under which they were committed, the following acts may constitute war crimes: murder, torture, inhumane treatment, hostage-taking, passing of sentences without due process, the recruitment of children under fifteen years of age, rape and other forms of sexual violence, and attacks against 'innocent' persons and facilities, civilians, humanitarian personnel and protected buildings, for example, schools,[19] hospitals and places of worship. Moreover, depending on whether they were committed *in the course of* an international or non-international armed conflict, the following acts may also constitute war crimes: use of certain types of weapon and use of means or methods of warfare that cause unnecessary suffering.

For Ghana a war crimes tribunal was not an option for several reasons. To constitute a war crime an act must have been committed in the *context of* or in *association with* an armed conflict. The impugned acts must also have been carried out against persons who are protected under the Geneva Conventions, namely non-combatants, civilians, and medical and religious personnel not actively involved in the hostilities.

While many types of conduct falling within the jurisdiction of a war crimes court were perpetrated in Ghana during the period 1957–1993, those acts did not occur 'in the context of and in association with an armed conflict', nor were they perpetrated against persons protected under the Geneva Conventions during such conflicts or hostilities. On the contrary, although all the military coups in Ghana occasioned egregious human rights violations, they were perpetrated by public officials during peace time.

In addition, none of the alternative mechanisms of accountability, other than a truth and reconciliation commission, was an option for Ghana. As a nation that had not undergone prolonged armed conflicts of the scale experienced in Sierra Leone or Liberia the use of a Special Court was also out of the question. It would have been a most inappropriate response to the challenge of combating impunity and redressing the human rights atrocities of the past. Similarly, the pursuit of justice in the traditional sense of criminal justice via the law courts of Ghana was also not available to Ghanaians as a result of the Transitional Provisions in the Constitution which prohibit judicial scrutiny of any official conduct of public officers under unconstitutional regimes.

Furthermore, had Rawlings or any of his close associates been put on trial before a war crimes tribunal, the polarised political atmosphere in Ghana, coupled with the strong personality cult built around the populist and charismatic former president, would probably have combined to create an explosive situation that could have severely destabilised the nation. Indeed, demands for a war crimes tribunal came largely from minority elements on the political right in Ghana and such a tribunal was not a serious option for even the most strident advocates of 'justice'.

It was therefore deemed unnecessary, beyond individualising guilt to the extent possible, to pursue justice in the traditional sense of prosecuting the perpetrators found by the NRC to have committed or facilitated gross human rights violations. This position derived from an appreciation of the imminent dangers in exposing the country's fragile peace and security to criminal trials against former leaders and individuals against whom evidence of heinous crimes had been established through the NRC process. Undoubtedly, some of the leaders had a powerful, organised personal following and public appeal that could have been easily mobilised and this, in turn, could have triggered full-scale national instability.

The NRC therefore decided not to recommend criminal prosecutions even where it was persuaded that there was a reasonable basis in the evidence for doing so. Even before he had read the Executive Summary of the NRC report and the other four volumes accompanying it, President Kufour declared that his government would not prosecute anyone for past human rights violations and atrocities but 'would leave them to their consciences'. That position was consistent with the NRC's stance, which considered it sufficient to establish 'an accurate, complete and historical record of violations and abuses of human rights', and to individualise the guilt for those violations and abuses by establishing the identities of the perpetrators without prosecuting them.

For Ghana, the price of lasting peace was the liberty of the criminals who had visited untold suffering on the populace. It was hoped, however, that the establishment of an accurate historical record (even if aspects of it were contested) that clarified the past and individualised the guilt would help to consolidate human rights and democracy and prevent the recurrence of such crimes.

Although not every Ghanaian is fully satisfied with the outcome of the reconciliation process, especially the lack of criminal justice, Ghanaian society remains firmly intact, even if partisan political rhetoric continues to highlight ethnic divisions in the country. Ultimately, by adopting the less dramatic approach of not mounting criminal prosecutions against past perpetrators of egregious human rights violations and abuses, the peace of the country was maintained, human rights were promoted and impunity was undermined.

CONCLUSION

One distinguishing feature of Ghana's NRC is that, unlike most of its counterparts elsewhere, it was not established as an integral component of the country's transitional arrangements from the long period of unconstitutional military rule to constitutional, civilian and democratic governance. On the contrary, it was created nine years after the restoration of civilian democratic governance. The post-transitional creation of the NRC distinguishes it, along with Morocco's Equity and Reconciliation Commission (ERC), and to some extent the Truth and Community Reconciliation Project (TCRP) of the American city of Greensboro, North Carolina, as a new genre of truth and reconciliation institution with mandates that transcend the traditional objectives of such commissions worldwide. Emerging long after the transitional phases in these places were technically over, these bodies, by being created, represent an expansion of the contexts in which truth commissions may be set up as well as a widening of the uses to which they may be put. They may fulfil most of the traditional goals of TRCs, such as documenting and memorialising an ignoble national past, striking at impunity, promoting justice and fostering reconciliation through forgiveness, healing and reparations. They may also venture into broader political purposes, such as the stabilisation and consolidation of an established democratic dispensation.

This development has important implications for theorising about the emergence, nature, purposes and impact of truth commissions, as well as for expanding the possibilities that, in different social formations and contexts, truth commissions may be employed for such varied and legitimate ends as *furthering* democratic stabilisation and consolidation, healing the body politic, and invigorating and renewing broad consensus in societies on the virtues of national unity. Truth commissions are flexible instruments for grappling with a nation's troubled past; they may be *temporally* distant from the transitional phase of the past they investigate and they often have direct political consequences for regime consolidation and the stabilisation of a country's peace process.

NOTES AND REFERENCES

1. Specifically, the goal of the NRC, as expressed in the long title to Act 611, was to 'seek and promote national reconciliation among the people of this country by recommending appropriate redress for persons who have suffered any injury, hurt, damage or grievance or who have in any other manner been adversely affected by violations and abuses of their human rights arising from activities or inactivities of public institutions and persons holding public office'.
2. I had been involved in earlier public discussions on the potential virtues of a truth commission for Ghana and subsequently had the privilege of serving as the rapporteur to the National Consultation Forum held in October 2001 to review the Draft Bill on National Reconciliation.

The forum was sponsored by the Ghana Centre for Democratic Development (CDD-Ghana), a leading CSO, whose activities were indispensable to, and remain vital in, the promotion of national reconciliation in Ghana.

3. *Constitution of the Republic of Ghana* (Accra: Government Printer, Assembly Press, 1992), pp. 199–202.

4. The law came into force on 9 January 2002, when it received presidential assent.

5. E. Cose, *Bone to pick: Of forgiveness, reconciliation, reparation, and revenge* (New York: Atria Books, 2004), p. 184.

6. President Rawlings was subpoenaed to produce an audio recording of the alleged confessions of Joachim Amartey Kwei, a close confidant of Rawlings who had been tied to the post in readiness for his execution for his role in the abduction and gruesome murder of three High Court judges and a retired army officer on 30 June 1982. He was also to produce the video recording of the extrajudicial killing of several 'dissidents' arrested on suspicion of having participated in the 19 June 1983 coup attempt to topple the Provisional National Defence Council (PNDC) government. Captain Tsikata was also subpoenaed to answer questions on the murder of the judges and the officer.

7. To my knowledge, Ghana's NRC became the first transitional justice institution to submit its final report within the allotted timeframe.

8. In September 2006, nearly two years after receiving the NRC report, the government commenced the long and arduous process of implementing the recommendations contained in the report, particularly the payment to the victims of token sums of money as some compensation for the violations and abuses they suffered.

9. See M. Wain, 'Ghana's National Reconciliation Commission', *Peace Magazine*, April–June 2003: 4, www.peacemagazine.org/archive/v19n2p18.htm (accessed 30 January 2008).

10. M. Sirleaf, 'National reconciliation and transitional justice processes in West Africa: A comparative study of Sierra Leone and Ghana', unpublished MA dissertation, University of Ghana, Legon, 2005.

11. R.K. Ameh, 'Uncovering truth: Ghana's National Reconciliation Commission excavation of past human rights abuses', *Contemporary Justice Review* 9(4), 2006: 352–355.

12. Scholarly works on human rights in Ghana proliferate but the NRC report provides the best excavation and analyses to date of the history of human rights violations and abuses in the country. In addition, the report provides a blueprint for charting a more reconciled society – cohesive, humane, tolerant and peaceful.

13. CDD-Ghana, *Opinions of victims of past human rights abuse in Ghana after the national reconciliation Commission's public hearings, Accra*, July 2006, p. v. http://www.cddghana.org/ (accessed 23 February 2009).

14. CDD-Ghana, *Opinions of victims of past human rights abuse in Ghana*, p. 1.

15. The sex of 2 per cent of victims was not captured in the database.

16. *The National Reconciliation Commission Report*, Executive Summary. Accra, 12 October 2004, p. 164, www.ghana.gov.gh/ghana/national_reconciliation_commission_report.jsp_0 (accessed 11 February 2008).

17. See *National Reconciliation Commission Report*, vol. 1 chap. 8, p. 183.

18. Rome Statute of the International Criminal Court, 1998, art. 7.

19. Rome Statute, art. 8.

10

Peace and Justice

Mozambique and Sierra Leone Compared

John L. Hirsch

INTRODUCTION

This chapter seeks to compare and contrast the experiences of Mozambique and Sierra Leone in dealing with the aftermath of protracted civil wars.[1] In Mozambique, where traditional rituals, local community practices, the churches and civil society replaced Western models of justice, a decade-and-a-half later there is a broad consensus that a significant measure of reconciliation was achieved. There was a conscious political choice not to 'look back' or to assign formal responsibility for harm to individual persons but rather to look ahead to rebuilding the country's infrastructure and establishing democratic governance. In contrast, in Sierra Leone the overlapping processes of the Special Court for Sierra Leone (SCSL) established by the United Nations (UN) Security Council and the Truth and Reconciliation Commission (TRC) established under the Lomé Peace Accord have been largely marginal to post-conflict reconciliation. Although eight mid-level leaders have been convicted by the SCSL and Charles Taylor is on trial in The Hague, most Sierra Leoneans attach relatively little importance to these formal processes and seem more concerned with rebuilding their country than the fate of these individuals. My hypothesis, based upon these two examples, is that decisions about whether to grant amnesty or invoke 'the duty to prosecute' in the wake of protracted conflict are context-dependent and thus in many cases are more successful when generated out of domestically based processes rather than exclusively through the Security Council or other international instruments.

The two wars in Mozambique – first the liberation struggle against Portuguese colonialism and then the civil war between the Liberation Front of Mozambique (FRELIMO) and the Mozambican National Resistance (RENAMO) – lasted more than 26 years, from 1966–1992. An estimated 900 000 to 1 million people died and 1.7 million became refugees in Zimbabwe, Malawi and South Africa.[2] The Sierra Leone civil war between successive military and civilian governments, on the one hand, and the Revolutionary United Front (RUF), on the other, lasted eleven years, from 1991–2002 (although the Lomé Peace Accord was signed in 1999). More than 50 000 people were killed, thousands were the victims of brutal mutilations at the hands of child soldiers and at least 200 000 people became refugees in Guinea and Liberia.

External as well as internal factors played a part in both wars. Mozambique was a major player in the liberation struggle of the Front Line States against apartheid South Africa, and this in turn mobilised white Rhodesian and South African special forces and proxy Mozambican forces of RENAMO against the ruling FRELIMO government. Similarly, the Sierra Leone conflict drew opposing camps in the Economic Community of West African States (ECOWAS) into the two sides of the civil war. From 1996 onwards Nigerian and Ghanaian forces defended the democratically elected government of Ahmed Tejan Kabbah while RUF attacks on the civilian population were supported and abetted by the leaders of Libya, Burkina Faso and the National Patriotic Front of Liberia (NPFL) under the command of Charles Taylor. Following Taylor's election as president in August 1997 the Liberian government actively supported the RUF insurgency, including the attacks on Freetown in January 1999. In both cases UN Peace Operations were instrumental in finally ending these conflicts. The UN Mission in Mozambique (ONUMOZ) facilitated the process of democratic transition, the establishment of an integrated army and the conversion of RENAMO from a guerrilla force into an established political party. After a shaky start the UN Mission in Sierra Leone (UNAMSIL) forced the final capitulation of the RUF, initiated the process of demobilisation and disarmament and facilitated the successful conduct of the 2002 elections.[3]

CONTRASTING APPROACHES

Mozambique and Sierra Leone, however, adopted strikingly different approaches to the issues of post-conflict peace and justice. In Mozambique, FRELIMO provided a legislative amnesty to all combatants even before the start of the

Rome negotiations under the aegis of the Community of Sant' Egidio which led to the Mozambican General Peace Agreement (*Acordo Geral de Paz*, AGP) of 4 October 1992. During those negotiations there was no discussion of any transitional justice institutions and neither a TRC nor any tribunal was established. A joint decision by FRELIMO and RENAMO to look to the future and put the past aside prevailed. In contrast, in Sierra Leone the Lomé Peace Accord of 8 July 1999 provided for the establishment of a TRC. UN Envoy Francis Okelo appended a caveat to the agreement stating that the amnesty provisions did not apply to war crimes and crimes against humanity under international law, opening the way for subsequent indictments of RUF leaders. At the request of President Kabbah a hybrid Special Court was mandated through UN Security Council Resolution 1335 of 14 August 2000 to try those 'most responsible for crimes against humanity and war crimes'. For the past fifteen years Mozambique has made no effort to render accountability for the massacres and crimes of the war years, while in Sierra Leone the human rights violations which occurred have been the object of intense legal scrutiny in an ongoing process. The capture and subsequent trial of Charles Taylor in The Hague, which may well go on for longer, will have an impact on other dictators in Africa and elsewhere. It is also cited as an example of a broken promise, as Taylor went into exile in Nigeria on a promise of impunity only to be later turned over to the Court in Freetown.

WAR AND PEACE IN MOZAMBIQUE
An historical overview

Mozambique was one of the proxy theatres of the Cold War. From its inception FRELIMO relied on and received military and financial support from the Soviet Union. In the United States conservative forces wanted the Reagan administration to extend support to RENAMO.[4] With the end of the Cold War both FRELIMO and RENAMO lost the support of their external backers for continued military operations. Instead, the United States and the Russian Federation, in the new spirit of co-operation in the UN Security Council, worked closely with Aldo Ajello, the Secretary-General's Special Representative, to assure implementation of the AGP.

The 26 years of war in Mozambique need to be divided into two phases: the ten years of struggle for independence from Portugal (1966–1976), viewed as part of the liberation struggle against colonial rule that swept through Africa in the post-Second World War era, and the subsequent sixteen-year war (1976–1992) between the FRELIMO government and the Mozambique National Resistance, later called RENAMO. The former war is understandably regarded by Mozambicans as noble and heroic, the latter as a 'dirty war' against 'armed bandits' serving as proxies first for the Rhodesian regime of Ian Smith and then for the white apartheid regime in South Africa. Many Mozambicans avoid calling this a civil war, viewing RENAMO primarily as an externally motivated and funded guerrilla movement that sought to destabilise and bring down the fledgling FRELIMO government.[5] FRELIMO itself was a leading member of the Front Line States that sought to bring an end to apartheid rule in South Africa. Maputo was the home in exile of notable African National Congress (ANC) members, including Ruth First, Albie Sachs and Joe Slovo.[6]

South Africa and Mozambique had a complex and ambivalent relationship during the years of civil war. By the early 1980s Samora Machel, Mozambique's charismatic first president, had made a pragmatic decision to put the survival of his fragile government ahead of overt support for the South African liberation struggle. In 1984 the two countries signed the Nkomati Accords in which the South African government pledged to cease the destabilisation of Mozambique while the latter pledged to prevent Mozambican territory from being used by the ANC against the Vorster government. The South Africans quickly broke the agreement and South African Special Forces continued to supply RENAMO with arms and supplies. There are still widespread suspicions that South African intelligence was responsible for the mysterious aircraft crash in April 1986 that killed Machel and senior members of his government.[7]

The war in Mozambique claimed an estimated 600 000 to 1 million lives. According to Human Rights Watch/Africa Watch, there were widespread incidents of mutilation and other physical violence against civilians, forced relocation, sexual slavery, forced recruitment and the creation of famine. Under the direct supervision of older RENAMO commanders, teenage males perpetrated many acts of mutilation. In addition to all this violence most of Mozambique's infrastructure was destroyed or rendered inoperable, hundreds of thousands of people were internally displaced or forced to become refugees in neighbouring countries and virtually the entire country became dependent on international aid.[8]

The General Peace Agreement

Why did the war end in 1992 and not continue, as it did in Angola, for another decade? By 1992 the population was exhausted and close to starvation. It had been a long, drawn-out and debilitating conflict and most Mozambicans lived on the brink of survival. Most importantly, the international and political situation had changed. With the fall of the Berlin Wall, the demise of the Soviet Union and the end of Communist party rule in Moscow, FRELIMO no longer had an external political supporter or supplier of weapons. RENAMO, too, had lost the patronage of its friends in the United States. The South African government, now led by F.W. de Klerk, sought to save the National Party's image and its control of the reins of government. Moreover, unlike Angola, there were no diamonds or oil over which to continue fighting. The population was clearly keen for a respite from the protracted war and its manifold displacements.

Already by 1989 President Joaquin Chissano, Machel's successor, had made a controversial but ultimately wise decision to negotiate a peace settlement with RENAMO rather than continue to press on for an uncertain victory. In turn, RENAMO's leader, Alfonso Dhlakama, agreed to negotiate once the possibility of a continuing political role and the transformation of RENAMO from a guerrilla movement to a political party became a viable option. The international circumstances noted above, the engagement of the lay Catholic order Sant' Egidio as a reliable, friendly mediator, with Rome as a neutral venue, and the willingness of a newly energised UN Security Council to provide peacekeeping forces to monitor the demobilisation and disarmament provisions of the AGP and to conduct the 1994 elections, all contributed to the success of the transition.[9]

The three key components of the AGP were a retrospective blanket amnesty for all individuals, including those formerly identified as armed criminals (*bandidos armados*), a pledge by both sides to participate in a fair democratic process and to resolve their remaining differences peacefully rather than through violence, and a commitment to engage in a process of disarmament, demobilisation and reintegration (DDR) of former combatants. The amnesty was the easiest part; the FRELIMO government without controversy introduced legislation in parliament providing for a blanket amnesty.[10] There was no discussion in Rome of a TRC or any other quasi-judicial instrument.[11]

The amnesty and its consequences

How was the amnesty accepted by the population and was it a wise decision? The young and courageous Mozambican scholar, Victor Igreja, argues that the

amnesia + impunity

peace agreement was built on 'unjust foundations, that is, amnesia and impunity' and that this type of peace agreement is 'morally apopleptic because silence is an unacceptable offence' (see Chapter 14 in this volume). Yet in my interviews in Maputo with a wide range of actors both inside and outside of FRELIMO and RENAMO, I encountered a very different perspective. First of all, I was told that people had not forgotten about the past; there was no amnesia. The parties had made a conscious decision to look ahead to rebuilding the nation rather than deal with the atrocities of the past. There was, of course, the self-interest of the political parties. But – as best can be judged from across the distance of time – there was not a great thirst for vengeance. As Bishop Denis Sengulane told me, had there been such a strong desire for revenge there would have been many murders. This, however, had not happened.[12] According to Fernando Lima, then an editor of the Mozambique News Agency, AIM, there were very few letters to the press calling for revenge or prosecutions.[13] In a country with massive illiteracy there was almost no knowledge of the specific terms of the AGP; it was the awareness that peace had been achieved that counted. Moreover, the AGP was entered into two years before the establishment of the South African TRC, itself the outcome of a very different political process. So in any case there was no template for a Mozambican TRC.

ALTERNATIVES TO POST-CONFLICT JUSTICE MECHANISMS

In Mozambique, traditional healing rituals and the role of the churches provided avenues for achieving reconciliation or at least for enabling people to move on with their lives. These mechanisms stand in sharp contrast to the formal legal roles of the TRC and SCSL that have figured so prominently in Sierra Leone. For most Mozambicans the end of the war was itself perceived as a positive event. In a totally impoverished country there was no expectation that the government could or should provide reparations. In an important insight Helena Cobban has written that Mozambique's underdevelopment paradoxically meant that 'age-old cultural resources had not been destroyed by "the march of modernization" ... these traditional sets of understandings and their associated practices did a lot to help Mozambicans withstand the tragedies and existential disruptions of the war era'.[14] Several anthropologists have described the community rituals which enabled child soldiers to be reintegrated into their communities. These often involved a ceremony in which the child soldier is re-accepted in the community after all his clothes have been burned, his weapons have been destroyed and he has undergone a cleansing ritual performed by a traditional practitioner.[15] In Gorongosa province in central Mozambique women who had been traumatised by sexual violence were healed by *magamba* spirits, a form of healing in which a traditional practitioner, in the presence of the community, enables a woman to make overt and manifest the brutal experience she has suffered.[16] Although there are no firm statistics it would appear that these community instruments for reintegrating child soldiers and for assisting women to recover from the most brutal wartime experiences were quite widespread in the rural areas.

The Catholic and Protestant churches, and especially the Christian Council of Mozambique, played an important role in preparing the population for peace, providing opportunities for personal confession and for directing people's energies to creative forms of healing. Even before the AGP was signed church leaders were holding meetings advising their parishioners that the war would soon be over and soliciting their concerns. These revolved mostly around the proliferation of weapons and land requisitions. The churches organised a major 'swords into plowshares' project by which an estimated 600 000 weapons were handed over at various collection points in exchange for 'instruments of production' – that is, farm implements.[17] Local artisans were encouraged to create works of art from disassembled weapons, such as a marvellous 'Tree of Life', whereby they utilised pieces of weapons to make the trunk and branches as a metaphor for renewal and hope. The completion of the 'Tree of Life' was marked by a formal ceremony in Maputo prior to its shipment to London, where, with an accompanying video, it is on permanent display in the British Museum's Africa galleries.

The post-war political process itself has proven remarkably resilient and effective. Three national elections, as well as several rounds of local elections, have clearly established FRELIMO's dominance as the ruling party. At the same time RENAMO has become a genuine political party with significant, albeit declining, representation in the parliament. The financial assistance the UN provided to RENAMO to facilitate its transition from guerrilla movement to political party may be regarded by some as an unnecessary 'reward' for brutal behaviour. In practice, UN Special Representative Aldo Ajello's decision to facilitate RENAMO's entry into the political arena has proven to be wise. In the 1994 elections RENAMO won 36 per cent of the popular vote, demonstrating that it had a significant domestic base primarily in the central region. It offered an alternative market-based political agenda with strong appeal, especially to the rural population that had been adversely affected by forced relocations onto collective farms. As FRELIMO has moved away from its Marxist–Leninist roots to a more pragmatic social and economic approach it has undercut much of RENAMO's initial appeal. In 2004, RENAMO was the only other party to meet the 5 per cent threshold for parliamentary representation; even if weakened by Dhlakama's faltering leadership and numerous defections, it remains a legitimate political force.

WAR AND PEACE IN SIERRA LEONE
The Lomé Peace Accord

Sierra Leone approached the issues of post-war justice in two separate phases: the Lomé Peace Accord of 8 July 1999 provided for a TRC while the UN Security Council authorised the hybrid Special Court on 14 August 2000. The conflict's domestic and regional origins, the corrupt practices of successive undemocratic governments after 1967, the connections between Foday Sankoh and Charles Taylor established in Libya in the late 1980s, the civil war launched from Liberia into eastern Sierra Leone in March 1991, and the cross-border connections between the RUF and the Taylor government after 1997 have been described in extensive detail elsewhere.[18] It is the different trajectory of the war's conclusion that allows for such a stark contrast with the outcome of the war in Mozambique. In Sierra Leone the war also left a ruined landscape, a bankrupt economy and an exhausted population. More than three decades of corrupt governance had already ravaged the economy, destroyed the civil service and led to the collapse of public services and the education system. The army was a shambles, made all the worse by the National Provisional Ruling Council's recruitment of released criminals and unemployed youth, while the police had been thoroughly demoralised both by the lack of the most rudimentary law-enforcement equipment and abysmally low salaries.

It is, however, the circumstances in which the Lomé Peace Accord took place that need to be recalled. The details of Sierra Leone's peace agreement had been determined in Abuja twelve months earlier. The Kabbah government, in exile in Conakry, Guinea, since the Armed Forces Revolutionary Council (AFRC)/RUF coup of 25 May 1997, was completely dependent on the willingness of the regional peacekeeping force, the Economic Community of West African States Military Observer Group (ECOMOG), and above all its Nigerian troops, to remain in the field. The former UN Development Programme (UNDP) official Ahmed Tejan Kabbah, who had returned to an unrecognisable Sierra Leone after 30 years as an international civil servant to become the country's first democratically elected president, had made common cause with General Sani Abacha, arguably one of Africa's worst military dictators. When Abacha suddenly died on the night of 8 June 1998 in the company of two Indian prostitutes, the political equation changed. His interim successor, General Abdulsalam Abubakr, made clear his intention to conduct elections within a year. By early 1999 former General Olusegun Obasanjo, soon to become head of state, and the newly empowered Nigerian parliament made clear that they were not prepared to keep Nigerian troops in Sierra Leone indefinitely. The Lomé agreement was thus a forced compromise. While under pressure from President Bill Clinton's envoy Jesse Jackson to resume negotiations with Foday Sankoh (who had just been released from a death sentence in Freetown), Kabbah had no choice but to accede to RUF demands for an amnesty and a power-sharing arrangement.

The amnesty provision was the *sine qua non* of the agreement; the RUF would not have signed without these guarantees. Moreover, the amnesty provision had been approved by a large number of civil society actors at a national conference in Freetown that had been organised in advance to obtain public support for the peace agreement.[19] The amnesty provisions were subsequently severely criticised by the human rights community and members of Kabbah's government but it is also worth recalling that a similar provision of the Abidjan Peace Agreement of 30 November 1996 had evoked no outcry (see Chapter 11 in this volume[20]). To UN Envoy Okelo's caveat limiting the applicability of the amnesty to crimes under Sierra Leonean law, which had been appended to the agreement in handwriting at the last minute, the RUF, having its demands for power-sharing met, paid little heed.[21] According to Eldred Collins, who led the RUF negotiating team, Sankoh was primarily concerned with obtaining the vice-presidency and control of the nation's strategic resources.[22]

The Truth and Reconciliation Commission[23]
The TRC had a difficult start. The UN Development Programme (UNDP) and a number of international donors questioned the impartiality of the Interim Secretariat and raised serious questions about its credibility and effectiveness. This led to severe funding constraints that in turn created problems with organising public information and sensitisation campaigns. After four months of hearings, which started in December 2002 in Freetown and in the districts, the six international and national commissioners were only able to work together

intermittently. The final report was edited in South Africa, where a number of the international commissioners convened in January 2005. The four-volume report was presented to President Kabbah and UN Secretary-General Kofi Annan on 5 August 2005 after considerable technical difficulties with its publication in Ghana.[24]

Despite the limited dissemination of the TRC's final report (see below), that body has arguably played an important role in the process of national reconciliation. Firstly, the hearings brought national attention to the atrocities and violations committed during the war and provided an opportunity for women and children who were the primary victims to be heard and their memories recorded and preserved. Secondly, the report rendered a detailed and impartial analysis of the causes of the war, holding the country's political leaders responsible for the collapse of institutions and norms. It was unsparing in its criticism of the ruling political elites in the Sierra Leone People's Party (SLPP) and the All People's Congress (APC), whose corrupt, undemocratic practices were found to have been responsible for the breakdown of governance.[25] Thirdly, the report concluded with important recommendations for the future, calling for significant resources to be allocated to address the needs of victims, including the provision of pensions, educational opportunities, skills training and micro-credit. It called for reparations as well as free lifetime healthcare for amputees, war wounded and victims of sexual violence.

The overlap between the TRC and the SCSL created an unprecedented situation. Many Sierra Leoneans did not understand the distinction between their separate objectives and mandates. Despite prosecutor David Crane's assurances that testimony presented to the TRC would not be used in the Court's proceedings, a number of RUF members were reluctant to testify at the TRC hearings. The Court blocked the TRC's request for the head of the Civil Defence Forces (CDF), Chief Sam 'Hinga' Norman, to testify, even though the commissioners of the TRC felt that, as an important player in the conflict, Norman's testimony was central to the historical record. In its final report the TRC criticised the constraints imposed on it by the SCSL. A major failing throughout was the absence of a consultative process between the TRC and the Court.[26] Moreover, the glaring disparity between the TRC's meagre US$4.6 million budget (even if it could have requested further funding) and the estimated US$150 million budget for the Court through to the end of 2007 has underscored the public's perception of the TRC's inferior position.

Print and CD versions of the TRC report in English and Krio, including abridged texts for primary and secondary schoolchildren, have been produced, though only a small number of the 1 000 copies of the report have been disseminated. In the rural areas where there is widespread illiteracy the lack of radio transmissions has further limited outreach efforts. Of equal significance, the government had at best an ambivalent attitude towards the TRC's recommendations. The White Paper – which received more local publicity than the report itself – expressed major reservations about key TRC recommendations, including the abolition of the death penalty and the provision of reparations for amputees and other war victims.[27] The government has repeatedly underscored its severe resource constraints. In addition, a number of observers have criticised the excessive regard accorded to President Kabbah, whose testimony was seen as self-serving and politically motivated. In various interviews the government was alleged to have been 'lukewarm' towards or to have 'abandoned' or 'shelved' the report.[28]

The Special Court: What is justice?

Under the terms of reference established by the UN Security Council, the SCSL was to prosecute those 'who bear the greatest responsibility for serious violations of international humanitarian law and Sierra Leonean law committed within Sierra Leone since 1996' (see Chapter 11 in this volume). This definition, ostensibly a pragmatic compromise, limited both its subject matter and temporal jurisdiction. A number of important leaders will never be prosecuted, especially Muammar Qaddafi of Libya and Blaise Camporé of Burkina Faso. From the late 1980s Qaddafi had bankrolled and supported the RUF and the NPFL; Camporé had facilitated the covert shipment of arms and ammunition from the Ukraine through Ouagadougou Airport to Taylor's forces in Monrovia; these arms were then given to the RUF and used in the ferocious attack on Freetown in January 1999.[29]

The Court's proceedings have focused mainly on atrocities committed in the aftermath of the May 1997 coup, including attacks and seizures of UNAMSIL hostages after the signing of the Lomé Peace Accord. Of the thirteen original indictees, four are now dead or missing. RUF head Foday Sankoh died in Pademba Road prison in 2003. His second-in-command, Sam 'Mosquito' Bockarie, was killed in Liberia in the same year, presumably by Taylor's forces. AFRC head Johnny Paul Koroma is presumed to have been killed in Liberia, although his body has not been recovered. Sam 'Hinga' Norman, head of the CDF, died in a Senegalese hospital in February 2007. Thus, aside from Liberian President Charles Taylor who is currently on trial in The Hague, the eight remaining indictees, five of whom have now been convicted, are all mid- or lower-level members.

The UN Office of Legal Affairs initially sought to find someone from a Commonwealth country, preferably an African, to serve as the prosecutor. When no suitable candidate could be identified the United States proposed David Crane, a lawyer from the Department of Defense who did not have a strong human rights background. Crane brought a number of former United States ex-military personnel as well as others to serve as his investigators, giving his office an American flavour. Crane played the key role in determining who would be prosecuted. From the outset he decided that it would be important to demonstrate impartiality and to concentrate on specific acts rather than on political context. Hence he decided to prosecute the leaders of the three primary parties to the conflict, the leaders of the RUF and AFRC who had worked to topple the democratically elected government, and those of the Civil Defence Forces (also known as the Kamajors), who were fighting to save that government.

On 10 March 2003, the Sierra Leone police, on Crane's instructions, arrested Norman, then Minister of the Interior and former Deputy Minister of Defence. He was ignominiously handcuffed in his office and taken for four months, along with RUF and AFRC indictees, to Bonthe Island, where he was held in a squalid, makeshift prison without access to his family until the new detention facilities for the Court in Freetown were completed. For the next three years Norman was – until the arrest of Charles Taylor in 2006 – the highest-ranking official in the Court's custody. Norman was charged with responsibility for atrocities committed by the CDF while the Kabbah government was in exile in Conakry. Repeated delays held up the trial. Norman and Issa Sesay, the ranking RUF leader in custody, were taken to a military hospital in Dakar, where Norman died on 22 February 2007 in post-operative care after hip surgery. Norman's death has left a bitter aftertaste for his many supporters. The controversial circumstances of his death and protracted incarceration leave many questions unanswered as to whether justice has been served. With his death Norman's responsibility for the CDF's acts will never be legally established. The huge crowds that viewed his body at Victoria Park in Freetown and at his burial in Mongere, his home village near Bo, attest to the esteem in which he was (and is) held by many Sierra Leoneans.[30]

Overall, the SCSL has had some important achievements, creating a significant precedent for an international criminal tribunal having its legal basis in an agreement between the UN and a member state. The conviction on 20 June 2007 of three members of the AFRC for their role in the destruction of Freetown in January 1999 includes the first conviction in history of the unlawful recruitment of children under the age of fifteen into an armed force.[31] On 2 August 2007 the Court convicted the two CDF defendants for a wide range of offences, including unlawful killings, terrorising the civilian population and the use of child soldiers.[32] The Court has carried out an extensive outreach campaign throughout the country; there is a widespread awareness that those who committed these crimes have received severe sentences.[33] President Kabbah, just before the 11 August elections, described the sentences of 45–50 years for the three AFRC defendants as 'most timely' and expressed the hope that they would serve as a deterrent to anyone contemplating renewed violence.[34]

The Court has not lived up to its initial conception as a hybrid court, however. All cases have been tried under international rather than Sierra Leonean law. The current prosecutor, Stephen Rapp, is again an American and his deputy prosecutor, Christopher Staker, is an Australian. While Court President Gelaga King and Justice Bankole Thompson are Sierra Leoneans, generally nationals have had relatively little input to the Court's proceedings and decisions.[35] There had been an expectation that the Court would contribute to strengthening the moribund Sierra Leonean judicial system but to date very little has happened and the Court's legacy remains problematic. The facility itself is too expensive for the government to maintain once the Court concludes its work. One suggestion would be to turn the venue over to a West African Court of Human Rights. Other proposals include strengthening the witness-protection and witness-support programme, involving more Sierra Leonean lawyers in the defence teams, and developing an intern programme for law school students but at present there is no organised effort to determine and implement a legacy. By the time it concludes its deliberations the SCSL will have cost an estimated US$200 million – an enormous expenditure for a country desperately in need of resources for development (see Chapter 11 in this volume[36]).

The major outstanding matter is the prosecution of former Liberian President Charles Taylor in The Hague. Taylor's trial is a significant step in the effort to deny impunity to one of Africa's worst dictators who wrought great violence on the citizens of a neighbouring country. In my view this outweighs the controversy over both Crane's role in unsealing the indictment while Taylor was attending an ECOWAS summit in Accra and the circumstances of his apprehension in Nigeria. The prosecution must still prove Taylor's responsibility for atrocities committed in Sierra Leone, both as NPFL warlord and later as president of Liberia. After extensive delays – caused, in part, by Taylor again dismissing his lawyer and the new defence team requesting further time to review the voluminous documentation – the trial resumed on 7 January 2008, almost two years after his arrest.[37] Taylor's conviction, if it eventually happens, will go a long way towards redeeming the Court's standing

CONCLUSION

What conclusions can we draw from these two strikingly different experiences? I would suggest that the decision whether to grant amnesty or invoke 'the duty to prosecute' is context-specific and in many cases may be best taken by the citizens of the country rather than by the international community through the UN Security Council or another instrument. Mozambique, where traditional rituals, local community practices, the churches and civil society replaced Western models of justice, has achieved a measure of reconciliation. There was a conscious political choice not to 'look back' and not to assign formal responsibility for harm to individual persons during the 26 years of war. The broader population appears to have acceded to this choice without rancour or misgivings. The judgement held by a number of researchers who have closely studied the Mozambique story derives from a 'consequentialist' outcome-based analysis – that is, from the opinions of Mozambicans themselves over the past fifteen years. As Helena Cobban has noted, this is a bold conclusion which challenges the 'mainstream' view of the international human rights movement that all perpetrators of human rights abuses need to be prosecuted.[38] Mozambique demonstrates that this is not necessarily the case.

In Sierra Leone, it is perhaps too soon to reach a definitive judgement. However, I would contend that justice has not been well served by the overlapping timeframes of the Special Court and the TRC or by the lack of co-ordination between them. This has been, at best, a flawed process. Many Sierra Leoneans were confused as to their relationship, viewing the TRC as a subsidiary body of the SCSL. The TRC lacked the resources and staff to disseminate its findings to the Sierra Leonean population. The government has been unable and unwilling to implement its primary recommendations for reparations and compensation.

Moreover, the absence of any structure charged with monitoring and pressing for its implementation has largely vitiated the value of its work. As for the SCSL, its significant achievements were marred with the controversial prosecution of Chief Norman, which ignored the political context of the conflict. Norman's protracted incarceration and death in a Senegalese hospital hardly suggests justice. With the AFRC and CDF convictions, the SCSL in Freetown is left to wrap up the trials of the remaining RUF mid-level defendants and the appeals process.

It is evident from these two examples that there is no 'one size fits all' template for post-conflict justice in Africa. An important variable is whether post-conflict justice decisions are internally decided, as in Mozambique, or whether they are internationally driven – as with the SCSL or earlier by UN Security Council resolutions establishing the International Criminal Tribunals for the former Yugoslavia and Rwanda. Even if a country 'gets it wrong', it is at least its own decision. In Mozambique the emphasis is on improving governance and economic performance as well as strengthening institutions – arguably more important than re-visiting the violence of the past. In Sierra Leone the Court's verdicts may serve as a deterrent to the recurrence of violent conflict but the important issues of ending corruption, developing a culture of integrity and good governance and transcending the culture of dependency remain major challenges. From my interviews it would appear that most Sierra Leoneans are prepared to reconcile with those who harmed them less because of the TRC and the SCSL than because of their own traditions and the raw necessity of getting on with their lives.

Finally, I would ask what, with the passage of time, will be remembered as a result of these different approaches? Who will control the historical record and what will it say? I have not dealt with this complex issue directly but one of the ostensible purposes of international tribunals and TRCs is to inform the current and future generations. Yet the reality of what one generation may remember or receive from its predecessor is far more complex than what can be recorded in these formal proceedings.

In Mozambique there are no public memorials to those killed in the conflict nor is any remembrance day dedicated to their memory. Several war cemeteries in remote locations are virtually inaccessible. This leaves remembrance to the artisans of the Tree of Life and other sculptures, and to Mozambican writers such as Mia Couto in his marvellous novel *Under the frangipani*[39] or journalists such as Paul Fauvet and Marcelo Mosse in their important account of the work and death of the journalist Carlos Cardoso.[40] In Sierra Leone the battle over the meaning of the conflict remains politicised. The 2007 election in which the ruling SLPP has ceded both the presidency and the parliament to the APC suggests that the historical record may again be rewritten. Sierra Leonean writers such as Syl Cheney Coker or Ishmael Beah's powerful memoir of his experience as a child soldier[41] have reached an international audience but have little readership at home. The new Human Rights Commission is charged with seeking to develop new respect for human rights. It will need all the help it can get. With low levels of literacy, short lifespans and pressing contemporary challenges, the preservation of memory will inevitably remain fragile and difficult.

NOTES AND REFERENCES

1. This chapter is based on my experience as United States Ambassador to Sierra Leone (1995–1998), my research work at the International Peace Academy from 2001–2005 and my visits to Maputo and Freetown on 20–24 May and 23–30 July 2007 respectively. I am deeply grateful to Ulrich Golaszinski of the Friedrich Ebert Foundation and Ambassador Thomas Hull and the United States Embassy staff in Freetown, who arranged interviews with a wide range of governmental and UN officials, journalists and civil society and religious leaders. My appreciation goes also to Ambassador Peter Chaveas, who offered useful comments.

2. See H. Cobban, *Amnesty after atrocity? Healing nations after genocide and war crimes* (Boulder, CO: Paradigm, 2007), pp. 136–182; P. Hayner, *Unspeakable truths: Confronting state terror and atrocity* (New York and London: Routledge, 2001), pp. 183–205 for two incisive accounts of how Mozambicans dealt with the aftermath of the civil war.

3. See F. Olonisakin, *Peacekeeping in Sierra Leone: The story of UNAMSIL* (Boulder, CO: Lynne Rienner, 2008) for an excellent overview of how UNAMSIL changed from a nearly failed to a successful peacemaking and peacebuilding mission.

4. In 1986–1987 Senator Jesse Helms, Chairperson of the Senate Foreign Relations Committee, delayed confirmation of career diplomat Melissa Wells as the United States ambassador for over a year in an unsuccessful effort to pressurise the Reagan administration to give RENAMO formal recognition and assistance.

5. Cobban, *Amnesty after atrocity?*, p. 148.

6. Ruth First was killed by a letter bomb and Albie Sachs lost his right arm in a car bomb explosion. Joe Slovo went on to become Minister of Housing in Nelson Mandela's first cabinet.

7. See P. Fauvet and M. Mosse, *Carlos Cardoso: Telling the truth in Mozambique* (Cape Town: Double Storey, 2003), pp. 155–165.

8. Human Rights Watch, 'Africa watch', in *Conspicuous destruction: War, famine and the reform process in Mozambique* (New York: Human Rights Watch, 1992).

9. See A. Ajello, 'Mozambique: Implementation of the 1992 peace agreement', in C.A. Crocker, F.O. Hampson and P. Aall (eds.), *Herding cats: Multiparty mediation in a complex world* (Washington,

DC: United States Institute of Peace Press, 1999), pp. 615–642; C. Hume, *Ending Mozambique's war: The role of mediation and good offices* (Washington, DC: United States Institute of Peace Press, 1994).

10. Cobban, *Amnesty after atrocity?*, pp. 150–155.

11. Interviews with Teodato Hungwana, FRELIMO negotiator, and Raul Domingues, principal RENAMO negotiator, 22–23 May 2007. Hungwana and Domingues gave the same account.

12. Interview with Anglican Bishop Denis Sengulane, Maputo, 23 May 2007.

13. Interview with Fernando Lima, 22 May 2007.

14. Cobban, *Amnesty after atrocity?*, p. 157, also citing C. Nordstrom, *A different kind of war story* (Philadelphia: University of Pennsylvania Press, 1997), pp. 142–143.

15. See A. Honwana, 'Children of war: Understanding war and war cleansing in Mozambique and Angola', in S. Chesterman (ed.), *Civilians in war* (A project of the International Peace Academy) (Boulder, CO: Lynne Rienner, 2001), pp. 123–144.

16. Victor Igreja describes in considerable detail the role of *magamba* spirits not only in facilitating healing for the individual victim but in giving the community a vehicle for coming to terms with the violence and injustice of the past (see Chapter 14 in this volume).

17. Interview with Bishop Denis Sengulane, 23 May 2007.

18. J.L. Hirsch, *Sierra Leone: Diamonds and the struggle for democracy* (International Peace Academy Occasional Paper Series) (Boulder, CO: Lynne Rienner, 2001); J.L. Hirsch, 'Sierra Leone', in D.M. Malone (ed.), *The UN Security Council: From the Cold War to the 21st century* (Boulder, CO: Lynne Rienner, 2004), pp. 521–536; also P. Richards, *Fighting for the rainforest: War, youth and resources in Sierra Leone* (Oxford and New Hampshire: James Currey and Heinemann, 1996); Y. Bangura, 'Understanding the political and cultural dynamics of the Sierra Leone war: A critique of Paul Richard's *Fighting for the Rainforest*', *African Development* 22(2–3), 1997: 134; A. Adebajo, *Building peace in West Africa: Liberia, Sierra Leone and Guinea-Bissau* (International Peace Academy Occasional Paper Series) (Boulder, CO: Lynne Rienner, 2002).

19. Thelma Ekiyor provides a detailed account of the TRC's proceedings and problems (see Chapter 7 in this volume).

20. In Chapter 11 of this volume Abdul Tejan-Cole argues that the amnesty was a manifest breach of Sierra Leone's Constitution and international law.

21. Olonisakin, *Peacekeeping in Sierra Leone*, p. 40.

22. Interview with Eldred Collins, 30 July 2007.

23. The Truth and Reconciliation Act 2000; see International Crisis Group, 'Sierra Leone's Truth and Reconciliation Commission: A fresh start', December 2002.

24. Interview with Commissioner Yasmin Sooka, Johannesburg, South Africa, 25 May 2007.

25. The *Final Report of the Truth and Reconciliation Commission of Sierra Leone*, vol. 3B: chapter 7: 'Reconciliation', trcsierraleone.org (accessed 10 September 2007).

26. Interview with Registrar Herman von Hebel and Deputy Registrar Binta Mansaray, 24 July 2007.

27. See the White Paper on the Truth and Reconciliation Report, 29 June 2005. http://www.mnadvocates.org/sites/608a3887-dd53-4796-8904-997a0131ca54/uploads/White_paper.pdf (accessed 12 February 2009).

Mia Couto

28. Interviews with Christiana Thorpe, National Electoral Commission Chairperson, I.B. Kargbo, and Mohamed Suma, Director of Sierra Leone Court Monitoring Programme, *New Citizen,* 25–26 July 2007.

29. See Olonisakin, *Peacekeeping in Sierra Leone*, pp. 32–33, 37–38; also *Gunrunners*, Frontline/World, May 2002 (PBS) contained footage of covert arms shipments to Monrovia and their use in the RUF attack on Freetown.

30. Interview with former United Kingdom High Commissioner Peter Penfold, London, 1 June 2007.

31. The three AFRC members were convicted of eleven of fourteen counts, SLSC, 20 June 2007. Alex Tamba Brima and Santigie Borbor Kanu were sentenced to 50 years in prison; Brima Bazzy Kamara was sentenced to 45 years.

32. CDF Moinina Fofana was found guilty on four of eight counts, including unlawful killings, physical violence and mental suffering, looting and burning, and terrorising the civilian population and collective punishments; Allieu Kondewa was also found guilty for the use of child soldiers, 2 August 2007.

33. Interviews with Deputy Registrar Binta Mansaray and student political leaders, 24–27 July 2007.

34. Interview with President Kabbah, 26 July 2007.

35. Justice Bankole Thompson acquitted both CDF defendants on the eight counts of which they were accused.

36. In Chapter 11 of this volume Abdul Tejan-Cole provides a further analysis of the Court's limited impact on the Sierra Leonean judicial system.

37. M. Simons, 'Liberian ex-leader's war crimes trial is stalled', *The New York Times*, 27 August 2007.

38. Cobban, *Amnesty after atrocity?*, p. 195.

39. M. Couto, *Under the frangipani* (Cape Town: Double Storey, 2001).

40. Fauvet and Mosse, *Carlos Cardoso*.

41. I. Beah, *A long way gone: Memoir of a boy soldier* (New York: Farrar, Straus and Giroux, 2007).

PART III

War Crimes Tribunals

11

Sierra Leone's 'not-so' Special Court

Abdul Tejan-Cole

INTRODUCTION

On 23 March 1991, a motley collection of bandits calling themselves the Revolutionary United Front (RUF)[1] entered Sierra Leone from Liberia. The attack was initially dismissed as an isolated act of banditry that had spilt over from the Liberian war.[2] In retrospect, it marked the commencement of a brutal war that would rage on until January 2002.[3] The war was characterised by vicious atrocities committed against the civilian population. Around 100 000 people were killed. An estimated 2 million were displaced or forced to seek refuge abroad. An unquantifiable number of women and girls were raped, forcibly 'married' or taken into sexual servitude.[4] Over 10 000 children were conscripted.[5] Several thousands had their arms or limbs amputated.[6]

Between 1996 and 1999 several attempts were made to resolve the conflict. In May 1999, following a devastating attack on Freetown, a ceasefire agreement was signed by the government and the RUF under the auspices of the Economic Community of West African States (ECOWAS). Two months later RUF leader Foday Sankoh was released from prison in Nigeria to attend negotiations with President Ahmad Tejan Kabbah. A peace agreement, the Lomé Peace Accord, was signed in Lomé, Togo, on 7 July 1999.[7] It provided a complete and unconditional blanket amnesty for all crimes committed by the combatants since 1991.[8] The RUF was to transform itself from a rebel movement into a political party and join a broad-based Government of National Unity. Under the Lomé Peace Accord, rebel leader Foday Sankoh was appointed chairperson of the Board of the Commission for the Management of Strategic Resources, National Reconstruction and Development and elevated to the status of vice-president of Sierra Leone. Several rebel leaders were appointed to key government positions.[9]

The only justice component in the Accord was the provision for the establishment of a Truth and Reconciliation Commission (TRC) to address impunity, break the cycle of violence and provide a forum for victims and perpetrators of human rights violations to tell their stories, better understand the past and facilitate genuine reconciliation and healing. At the time of the signing of the Accord, the United Nations (UN) Secretary-General's Special Representative, Francis Okello, entered a caveat at the eleventh hour that stated that the amnesty provisions of the Lomé Peace Accord would not be applicable to genocide, crimes against humanity, war crimes or other serious violations of international humanitarian law.[10] At present, the amnesty provision remains binding on crimes committed under domestic law, prohibiting the government of Sierra Leone from prosecuting crimes committed from 1991–1999 under Sierra Leonean law.[11]

The Lomé Peace Accord embodied the triumph of peace over justice. Proponents of the Lomé amnesty argued that the blanket amnesty was necessary to end the hostilities and bring peace to Sierra Leone. They assumed that the RUF would not sign any peace deal without an amnesty and therefore offered a pre-emptive amnesty to the rebels even before they requested it. As a result of brutal force the democratically elected government had been coerced into granting an unconditional amnesty and sharing power with a ruthless rebel movement.[12] The government was faced with Hobson's choice. Although it would have preferred to punish the rebels rather than negotiate with them, it granted them an amnesty out of political necessity and expediency and as a result of pressure from international negotiators. It lacked the muscle to defeat the rebels on the battleground; it therefore capitulated to the demands of the rebels and the negotiators, fearing that failure to reach a deal would inevitably result in prolonged conflict and the eventual overthrow of the government. The government had been deposed once before in 1997 and it did not want to risk the same fate again. It contended that in opting for amnesty it was neutralising violent conflict, opening the political process to serve a public good and bringing the earliest possible end to the violence.

The Lomé amnesty was a manifest breach of Sierra Leone's Constitution and a violation of international law. The Constitution does not give the president of Sierra Leone the power to grant amnesties and it guarantees the rights of citizens to seek redress before the courts. Awarding amnesty in advance of any prosecutions or convictions clearly exceeded the powers of the president as enumerated in the Constitution of Sierra Leone and is thus unconstitutional.[13] Under Sierra Leone's criminal laws individuals who commit criminal acts such as murder, wounding or treason have to be prosecuted before the issue of pardon can arise.

The impact of Lomé: Renewed violence

Pursuant to the Lomé Peace Accord, in October 1999 the UN Security Council established the UN Mission in Sierra Leone (UNAMSIL) to assist in implementing its provisions. Although disarmament began and peacekeeping troops were present in Sierra Leone, the peace was tenuous. Hostilities did not cease and the atrocities continued.[14] The peace was short-lived. Despite the best efforts of the government of Sierra Leone, the UN and Economic Community of West African States Military Observer Group (ECOMOG), problems soon emerged and Sierra Leone slipped back into another cycle of violence. In November 1999, barely four months after the Accord was signed, the RUF resumed its armed attacks. The UN troops were inhibited by their mandate and could not intervene. They had very little access to most parts of the country. Following the taking of UN peacekeepers as hostages and the killing of civilians by the RUF during a demonstration organised by civil society groups, in May 2000 the government of Sierra Leone reassessed its stance on the blanket amnesty.

The government's gamble backfired; its strategic choice to opt for what was politically expedient over what was legal did not yield the desired result. The RUF breached the provisions of the Lomé Peace Accord by attacking civilians and UN personnel. The government learnt that the absence of justice would not lead to peace in Sierra Leone. As in the past, the rebels, soldiers and other armed militia who had terrified the people of Sierra Leone had been rewarded. It was now time to bring an end to this vicious cycle. Prosecuting the perpetrators was now viewed as the only mechanism that could bring an end to the ongoing cycle of violence. The government made a dramatic volte-face; at the urging of the same international diplomats who had lobbied for the Accord President Kabbah wrote to the UN Secretary-General requesting the establishment of a tribunal to address the violations committed during the war. Following months of negotiation,[15] in July 2001 the Security Council endorsed the establishment of a Special Court and, on 16 January 2002, the agreement establishing the Special Court for Sierra Leone (SCSL) was signed.[16]

The subsequent decision by the government to prosecute persons who bore the greatest responsibility for the atrocities in Sierra Leone was not in conflict with the Lomé Peace Accord. As the SCSL Appellate Chambers subsequently maintained, no reasonable tribunal would hold that the government of Sierra Leone had reneged on its undertaking by agreeing to article 10 of the Statute which is consistent with the developing norm of international law and with the declaration of the representative of the UN Secretary-General on the execution of the Lomé Peace Accord.[17]

Prosecution was necessary in Sierra Leone. The Lomé Peace Accord forced victims to live under the rule of war criminals who were allowed to go unpunished for the mass atrocities they had committed. This type of peace raised vital questions about governance and developmental challenges faced by war-torn states. The logic supporting a blanket amnesty assumes that perpetrators of war crimes will refrain from committing such atrocities once they are absolved of their crimes. It presupposes that rebels, once sanctioned with state authority, can become democrats. The blanket amnesty for rebels also sets a negative precedent as it sends a dangerous message to likely insurrectionists that violence can be a legitimate means of effecting change and gaining political power. From the Sierra Leone case it was clear that without justice, democratic institutions and the rule of law the peace itself could not last. The failure of the Lomé amnesty was the failure of 'peace' and it hammered home the need for justice, even if it was only for the few.

THE SPECIAL COURT FOR SIERRA LEONE

Following the government's decision to opt for some form of justice instead of a blanket amnesty, negotiations commenced between the government of Sierra Leone and the UN regarding the form of prosecutions. There were three broad options: an ad hoc tribunal similar to those established for Rwanda and the former Yugoslavia, domestic prosecutions in the national courts of Sierra Leone, or a hybrid tribunal.

The option of an international tribunal was considered and discounted because of the failures of the two above-mentioned tribunals. The runaway costs, management flaws and communication failures of the ad hoc tribunals for Rwanda and the former Yugoslavia had generated fatal donor fatigue and called into question the efficacy of international criminal justice.[18] Consequently, the UN Secretary-General decided against another ad hoc tribunal.

The option of domestic trials was also dismissed because of the huge problems with the national judiciary, which had been seriously decimated by the conflict. The novel structure of the SCSL was a direct response to the successes and failures of previous tribunals such as the International Criminal Tribunal for the Former Yugoslavia (ICTY) and the International Criminal Tribunal for Rwanda (ICTR).[19] The creation of the SCSL represented an innovative attempt by the UN to establish a more efficient and effective international criminal tribunal.[20]

Whereas the UN was criticised for situating the ICTR and ICTY outside of Rwanda and Yugoslavia, the SCSL sits in Freetown, the capital of Sierra Leone. One of the initial objectives of the Court was to help Sierra Leone rebuild a strong national judicial system; locating the Court in Freetown was meant to facilitate this objective. The judicial process was to have been both visible and accessible to the people of Sierra Leone. The plan was that the SCSL would give the important message that international and domestic trials are complementary parts of an integrated approach to justice.

MAIN FEATURES OF THE SPECIAL COURT
Personal jurisdiction

Initially the secretary-general proposed that the personal jurisdiction of the SCSL be extended to cover 'persons most responsible' for the commission of crimes under the jurisdiction of the court.[21] This would have meant that accused persons would have included not only political or military leaders but also others in authority further down the chain of command, depending upon the severity of the crime.

The UN Security Council rejected the Secretary-General's proposal and agreed on the language of prosecuting persons 'who bear the greatest responsibility for the commission of crimes'. The SCSL is empowered to prosecute 'those who bear the greatest responsibility for serious violations of international humanitarian law and Sierra Leone law committed within Sierra Leone since 1996'.[22] The Court's focus was on prosecuting persons who played 'leadership roles' in the Sierra Leone conflict. As a result, its personal jurisdiction reached only a very small number of the many people responsible for the atrocities committed in Sierra Leone. The ICTY and ICTR statutes were wider in scope in so far as they were empowered to prosecute 'persons responsible' rather than 'persons who bear the greatest responsibility'.[23]

The prosecutor has indicted thirteen individuals associated with every faction on various charges of war crimes, crimes against humanity and other serious violations of international humanitarian law.[24] Eight indictees from the government-backed Civil Defence Forces (CDF) and the rebel forces, the RUF and the Armed Forces Revolutionary Council (AFRC) are currently in the custody of the Court. Of the indictees not in custody three are dead, one is believed to be dead, and one, former Liberian President Charles Taylor, is on trial in The Hague. Three trials commenced in 2004 and two were concluded by the end of 2007. The Taylor trial started in January 2008.

Unlike the ICTR, which is empowered to prosecute offences committed by Rwandans in both Rwanda and neighbouring states, the SCSL, like the ICTY, is empowered to prosecute only those offences committed within the territory of Sierra Leone. And unlike the ICTR, which is located in a neutral state, Tanzania, the seat of the Court is in Sierra Leone.[25]

Subject-matter jurisdiction

The subject-matter jurisdiction of the SCSL comprises crimes under international humanitarian law and Sierra Leonean law. These include practices of murder, extermination, enslavement, deportation, imprisonment, torture, rape, sexual slavery, enforced prostitution, forced pregnancy and any other form of sexual violence, persecution on political, racial, ethnic or religious grounds, and other inhumane acts. The Court also has subject-matter jurisdiction over violations of common article 3 of the Geneva Conventions and the Additional Protocol II thereto. With Sierra Leone being party to the Geneva Conventions, the SCSL has subject-matter jurisdiction over violations of international humanitarian law that occurred during the ongoing conflict. These crimes included intentionally directing attacks against the civilian population or against individual civilians not taking direct part in hostilities, intentionally directing attacks against personnel, installations, material units or vehicles involved in humanitarian assistance or peacekeeping missions in accordance with the UN Charter, as they are entitled to the protection given to civilians or civilian objects under the international law of armed conflict, as well as the abduction and forced recruitment of children under the age of fifteen years into armed forces or groups for the purpose of using them to participate actively in hostilities.[26]

With reference to the above, customary international law prohibits attacks on the civilian population, as well as attacks on peacekeepers. The SCSL also has subject-matter jurisdiction for crimes under Sierra Leonean law. These include crimes under the 1926 Prevention of Cruelty to Children's Act and crimes of arson under the 1861 Malicious Damage Act.

Article 2 of the Statute is akin to article 3 of the ICTR Statute but unlike the SCSL, the ICTR requires a discriminatory *animus* for crimes against humanity. Article 3 of the Statute of the ICTR defines crimes against humanity as 'the following crimes when committed as part of a widespread or systematic attack against any civilian population on national, political, ethnic, racial or religious grounds'. Unlike the SCSL, the subject-matter jurisdiction of the ICTR includes the crime of genocide. As there was no evidence of genocide in Sierra Leone's war, this crime was omitted in its Statute. The ICTY, by contrast, has subject-matter jurisdiction to prosecute persons committing or ordering the commission of grave breaches of the 1949 Geneva Conventions, violation of the laws or customs of war, genocide and other crimes against humanity.

Temporal jurisdiction

Sierra Leone's civil war dates back to 23 March 1991. In determining a beginning date for the temporal jurisdiction of the SCSL, the UN Secretary-General was guided by three main considerations:

- the period should be reasonably limited in time so that the prosecutor would not be overburdened and the Court overloaded;
- the beginning date should correspond to an event or to a new phase in the conflict without necessarily having any political connotations; and
- it should encompass the most serious crimes committed by persons of all political and military groups and in all geographical areas of the country.

In the light of the above, three alternative dates were considered:

- 30 November 1996, which was the date of the conclusion of the Abidjan Peace Agreement between the government of Sierra Leone and the RUF;
- 25 May 1997, the date of the AFRC *coup d'état* against the Sierra Leone People's Party (SLPP) government that had come to power in 1996; and
- 6 January 1999, the date on which the AFRC and RUF launched a second rebellion and took control of the capital, Freetown.

The date of 30 November 1996 was determined to be most appropriate. There is no end date to the temporal jurisdiction of the SCSL but the Court is due to conclude operations on 1 December 2009.

The decision to include in the Court's temporal jurisdiction only events from late 1996 may have been a practical decision related to the internal administration of the SCSL. However, in the context of Sierra Leone's war, the limited temporal jurisdiction was arbitrary. The temporal jurisdiction of the Court is unjust because it focuses on atrocities committed in and around Freetown and against UN troops. The start of the Court's temporal jurisdiction, November 1996, corresponds precisely to the time when Freetown first came under attack, while most of the conflict prior to November 1996 took place outside Freetown. The result has been that those responsible for the most heinous crimes before 1996 will not be held accountable for their actions. For instance, the bulk of the evidence of atrocities committed by Foday Sankoh can be found for acts committed prior to November 1996. Rather than ensuring that the prosecutor is not overburdened, limiting temporal jurisdiction has made his job even more arduous.

THE SPECIAL COURT, PEACEBUILDING AND RECONCILIATION

The SCSL was one of several bodies created to assist Sierra Leone in recovering from the war. The national judiciary had been devastated by the war and an interim measure was needed to help prosecute those who bore the greatest responsibility, to help the process of healing and reconciliation and to rebuild the justice sector in Sierra Leone.[27] Well past halfway through its lifespan the key question is: How well has the Court discharged its mandate?

The 'successes' of justice

The SCSL has made significant strides in the development of international criminal law. As a result of the nature and the process of its creation, it is a unique and innovative institution in the field of international criminal justice. It is the first international criminal tribunal to have as its legal basis an agreement between the UN and a member state. It is also the first established tribunal with both an international and a national component. In addition, the tribunal has made significant contributions to the development of substantive international criminal law, particularly in the law relating to the recruitment of child soldiers and gender-based crimes.

One of the most notable features of the Sierra Leonean conflict was, in fact, the widespread use of child soldiers. In May 2004 the SCSL issued a landmark decision that ruled that an individual could be held criminally responsible for the offence of recruiting child soldiers into armed conflict. The Court held that the offence under article 4(*c*) of its Statute does not violate the international legal prohibition on retroactive criminal liability (*nullum crimen sine lege*).[28] The Court found that the prohibition against recruiting child soldiers had crystallised into a crime under customary international law before November 1996 and that, accordingly, individuals may be prosecuted for this offence at any time under the temporal jurisdiction of the SCSL.[29]

As from 1991, when the war began, thousands of Sierra Leonean women and girls were raped, gang-raped, held in sexual slavery or raped with objects, including weapons, wood and umbrellas. All sides of the conflict subjected females of all ages and ethnic groups to sexual violence of extraordinary brutality. Many women and girls suffered irreparable vaginal tearing; some bled to death as a result of the extreme violence with which they were raped.[30] To contextualise the issue, the UN Special Rapporteur on the Elimination of Violence Against Women, Radhika Coomaraswamy, estimated that 72 per cent of Sierra Leonean women and girls had experienced human rights abuses during the war and that more than 50 per cent were victims of sexual violence.[31] The rapes were primarily committed by rebel forces and, to a lesser extent, by government soldiers throughout the country. The prosecutor paid particular attention to gender-based crimes and from the outset ensured that they were thoroughly investigated, charged and prosecuted. The prosecution made a concerted effort to deliver justice to Sierra Leonean victims of sexual violence. The work of the SCSL has repeatedly demonstrated that, even with extreme constraints, the political will of the prosecutor and his senior staff can shift the balance towards justice for victims of sexual crimes.[32]

The listing of sexual slavery as a crime against humanity in the Statute of the SCSL provided important recognition of this specific form of slavery.[33] While the Rome Statute produced the first acknowledgement of sexual slavery as a violation of international humanitarian law, the inclusion of this crime in the Statute for the SCSL solidified the concept and helped to advance the international norm prohibiting sexual slavery. In addition, it is likely that the Court will be the first of the two institutions to prosecute an individual for the crime of sexual slavery, given the number of extant indictments charging this crime and the short timeline for the work of the Court.

The Court also reached a landmark decision on gender-based offences. During the Sierra Leone war it was a widespread practice for combatants to abduct women as 'wives', forcing them to have sex and bear children. In May 2004 the Trial

Chamber of the SCSL approved the addition of 'forced marriage' to the counts contained in an indictment against six defendants accused of heading the former rebel AFRC and RUF. The Trial Chamber's decision marks the first time that an international court will have recognised 'forced marriage' as a possible category of 'other inhumane acts' within the legal category of crimes against humanity.[34]

Arguably, to date, the SCSL's most legally significant accomplishment was the unanimous ruling, handed down on 31 May 2004 by its Appeals Chamber, that former Liberian President Charles Taylor did not enjoy immunity from prosecution before the Court despite the contention by his counsel that he was the incumbent head of a sovereign state at the time the criminal proceedings against him were initiated. The Court ruled expansively that 'the principle of state immunity derives from the equality of sovereign states and therefore has no relevance to international criminal tribunals which are not organs of a state but which derive their mandate from the international community'. The Court also concluded that the principle now seems established that the sovereign equality of states does not prevent a head of state from being prosecuted before an international criminal tribunal. The decision reaffirms the idea that the long arm of international criminal law could extend to reach the most powerful state official, in so far as that person commits crimes that shock the conscience of the international community.[35] Finally, the SCSL could certainly claim some credit for removing Charles Taylor from office in Liberia. The indictment issued by the Court was clearly one of the key factors that forced Taylor to accept asylum in Calabar, Nigeria. Despite these notable advances, however, the court has also suffered from significant shortcomings.

THE SHORTCOMINGS OF JUSTICE
Ad hoc development and underfunding
Many of the SCSL's problems stemmed not from a flawed institutional design but rather from ad hoc development and underfunding in challenging circumstances. The Court's funding primarily came from voluntary contributions from UN member states.[36] Consequently, several of the Court's senior officials spent a considerable amount of time worrying about funding rather than concentrating on strategic planning. Many plans had to be abandoned, delayed or commenced with at very short notice. International donors' reluctance to provide the requisite funding plagued the Court's work and forced it to dilute its brand of international justice and work less effectively, in particular slashing the outreach efforts necessary to

affect the local culture of justice. Not even the best strategic plan can overcome donor indifference.[37]

Sierra Leonean input was secondary

The SCSL was intended to be a mixed court in every sense: to be mixed in jurisdiction and composition. However, in practice the reality has been different. While the Statute made provision for jurisdiction over both international and national crimes, the prosecutor decided from the outset that no charges would be laid for any of the crimes under Sierra Leonean law that were included in the Statute. Although no official reason was given for this decision, it was suggested that it was based on the perceived difficulty of prosecuting crimes under Sierra Leonean law. It was also feared that the amnesty would be raised as an issue with respect to national crimes. However, international crimes for which charges were proffered are no easier to prove than the crimes under Sierra Leonean law. In order to bring charges for crimes against humanity under the Statute the prosecutor has to prove that the crimes form part of a widespread or systematic attack against a civilian population. No crime under Sierra Leonean law has a similar element to prove.

Furthermore, amnesty was raised as an issue with respect to the international crimes and dealt with by the Appellate Chamber. Had it been raised in respect of the national offences it would have been dealt with by the same Chamber and set a precedent, which would have been of persuasive authority for the courts of Sierra Leone. It may seem that the crimes under Sierra Leonean law were added to the Statute as some form of tokenism rather than as a serious attempt to prosecute people for these crimes. Many of the benefits that may have been derived from the prosecution of Sierra Leonean offences in national courts, such as precedents that would have carried persuasive authority, were lost. At present, until the law is changed and the draft Rome Statute Implementation Act is enacted in national laws, very few of the precedents set by the SCSL will be of any use or relevance to the national courts.

The Statute provides that the Appellate Chamber is to comprise five judges: two shall be judges appointed by the government of Sierra Leone and three shall be appointed by the UN Secretary-General.[38] In the Trial Chamber one shall be a judge appointed by the government of Sierra Leone and two shall be appointed by the UN Secretary-General.[39] The first draft of the agreement between the government of Sierra Leone and the UN provided that the two judges in the

Appellate Court and the one in the Trial Chamber were to be Sierra Leonean. This was amended at the request of the Sierra Leone government, which requested that they be 'nominees of the Sierra Leone Government' rather than Sierra Leoneans. In the end, only one active Sierra Leonean judge, George Gelega-King, was appointed to sit in Chambers.[40] A former Sierra Leonean judge, Justice R. Bankole-Thompson, who had left Sierra Leone in the 1980s to lecture in the United States, was appointed to the Trial Chamber.

The government of Sierra Leone nominated a well-known Australian lawyer, Geoffrey Robertson, as its second nominee for the Appellate Chamber. When the second Trial Chamber was established the government appointed Justice Richard Lussick from Samoa as its nominee. This decision alienated the SCSL from the Sierra Leone judiciary and the benefit that would have been gained from having active members of the Sierra Leonean bench serve in the court was never realised.[41] In addition, the huge salaries paid to the SCSL judges compared to the paltry sums paid to their Sierra Leonean colleagues were another source of discontent. One SCSL official did not help the situation by reminding Sierra Leoneans that a security guard at the Court was better paid than some domestic judges.

The scenario was the same in terms of the position of the deputy prosecutor of the Court. The original draft document provided that the deputy prosecutor should be a Sierra Leonean. This was subsequently changed at the request of the government of Sierra Leone. A Sri Lankan-born British Queen's Counsel, Sir Desmond de Silva, who was called to the Sierra Leone bar in 1969 and practised law in the country (defending the former attorney-general in what was Sierra Leone's first treason trial), was appointed deputy prosecutor. His appointment meant that there was no Sierra Leonean, and for that matter no African, in any senior position in the Court. Senior management of the Court therefore made decisions with little or no input from nationals – in a court that was supposed to be a hybrid.

The government's argument that it could not find qualified Sierra Leoneans to fill the position was untenable. Some Sierra Leonean lawyers who were initially suspicious of the Court were further alienated by these decisions and became openly opposed to the Court. As a result, many members of the legal community who could have helped to bridge the gap between the national court and the SCSL became indifferent or opposed to the Court and whatever benefits were expected to accrue to the judiciary simply did not materialise. Ultimately, the benefits that the domestic legal system ought to have gained from the tribunal being a hybrid, were not realised.

Nationals versus internationals

A primary rationale behind the creation of the SCSL was to combine the best of the national and international justice systems. Ideally, the Court's value was to lie in its flexibility and ability to adapt to local culture, language and law while maintaining core values of international criminal law.[42] The national staff within the Court could have helped to ease the tension between the Court and the local community. However, within the Tribunal there were clear tensions between nationals and internationals at every level. Although the Court had some excellent international and national staff it also had some very pedestrian staff with little or no experience in prosecution at either the national or the international level. For instance, a Sierra Leonean lawyer who had more than twenty years of prosecution experience in the national court, was given the same status and rank as a foreigner who had just passed his bar exams. This, in addition to the fact that nationals felt that their voice was not being heard, made many of the national staff disgruntled and caused them to leave the Court. Even in areas where it was clear that national staff members were better suited to play a role, they found themselves sidelined.

Compared to the Office of the Prosecutor, the Defence Office was more cosmopolitan. Many of those accused chose mixed teams of internationals and Sierra Leoneans to represent them. Whilst there were still tensions between the nationals and the internationals, here they were less obvious, perhaps because many of the international lawyers were frequently out of the country. In court it always seemed as if they were pitted against one another: a predominantly international prosecution team versus a predominantly national defence team.

Restricted interpretation of the mandate of the Court

Even before it became operational, questions were raised about what the SCSL's legacy would be. It was hoped that it would help to rebuild the justice system. Some staff within the Court, including myself, called for the appointment of a legacy officer but this request was rejected on the grounds that there was no funding. A few staff members within the Court took ad hoc and disparate initiatives in an attempt to leave a lasting legacy but these were unco-ordinated and too few. The Court as an institution failed to throw its entire weight behind such a measure.

It was evident from some of the statements of the first prosecutor of the Court that his only priority was prosecution, prosecution and yet more prosecution. On a number of occasions he stated that his job was to bring to justice those who had committed the carnage in Sierra Leone. While I agree that the primary role of the Court was to bring to justice those who bore the greatest responsibility, it is my view that the Court had other equally important tasks to perform and far greater challenges with which to deal. In a country in transition the Court had additional functions, including but not limited to, promoting healing and reconciliation and rebuilding the local justice system. Simply imprisoning a few perpetrators would not suffice, not least because of the huge amount of money that had been spent on the Tribunal in comparison to that committed to the local judiciary.[43] Not too long after the commencement of the operations of the Court, at meetings I attended and on radio discussions, many Sierra Leoneans began asking questions as to whether it was worth spending so much money on prosecuting a few people. These questions may not have been raised had the Court also been assisting in rebuilding the local judiciary or helping to reform laws in Sierra Leone.[44]

Legacy: A missed opportunity

After more than a decade of war the Sierra Leonean judiciary had neither the human capacity nor the physical infrastructure to host a war crimes tribunal, a vast, complex and expensive undertaking. The judiciary was badly decimated by the war and at the time of the establishment of the SCSL could barely function outside Freetown.[45] The national bench and bar anticipated that the creation of the SCSL would help to diffuse legal knowledge from international experts to local judicial officials and thus would assist in rebuilding the judicial system.[46] The Court was expected to be an instrument for transforming the local judiciary. Its focus should have been not only on immediate post-judgment compliance but also on the enduring influence of the Tribunal as an example for the local judiciary. The long-term improvement of the national justice system would have helped to create a culture of justice and accountability and ensured that the legacy of the Special Court would not vanish once it had fulfilled its mandate. Given the time and money expended on post-conflict mechanisms, the failure to catalyse meaningful long-term change detracts from their credibility and value. When establishing the SCSL even the UN Security Council recognised the need to adopt a model that could leave a strong 'legacy' in Sierra Leone, one that would include improved infrastructure, respect for the rule of law and trust in public institutions, as well as improved professional standards. The Security Council referred specifically to the pressing need for international co-operation to assist in strengthening the judicial system of Sierra Leone.[47]

Sadly, at the time of writing, the impact of the Court on the local judiciary has been minimal. There is no direct relationship between the SCSL and the judicial system either in theory or in practice. The SCSL was created as a separate and distinct entity from the local judiciary and it always maintained its distance. The provision in the Statute that stated that the SCSL has supremacy over national courts was never explained and consequently was misinterpreted; this greatly angered national judges.

The situation was the same with the bar. I was once asked by the attorney-general and minister of justice of Sierra Leone to provide him with a copy of the judgment of the Court in relation to the Lomé Peace Accord. Court officials assumed that by putting the judgments online they were accessible to all. At the time, the attorney-general's office did not have Internet facilities and, even if it had, downloading such files was usually a slow and laborious process. Some Sierra Leoneans within the Court felt that the focus of the Court was to provide materials to the international community and that it paid very little attention to addressing the needs of the local community.

Although it is still not clear what will happen to the SCSL's massive building and materials there has been some suggestion that this will be inherited by the national judiciary. If this was the plan from the outset, the national judiciary or the ministry of justice ought, at the very least, to have been consulted or have been involved in the design and construction of the building. They were not. The building and facilities of the Court did not take into consideration local conditions and circumstances. The judiciary, which is grossly underfunded, does not have the resources to maintain the SCSL facilities. In a country where power supply is anything but regular, generators are required to run the air conditioners for the prefabricated structures. On its current budget this is a bill that the judiciary surely cannot be expected to foot.

Clashes between the Court and the Truth and Reconciliation Commission

Those who designed the SCSL and the TRC undoubtedly did not intend for them to be at odds with one another. At Lomé, only a TRC was proposed and there was no plan for a tribunal. Owing to the government's refusal to act, continuing hostilities and funding issues, the TRC was not launched until 2 July 2002. It commenced statement-taking on 4 December 2002 and hearings on 14 April 2003. The final report of the TRC was published in October 2004. Consequently, Sierra Leone was in the unique position of having a TRC and a tribunal functioning at more or less the same time. In many countries TRCs are viewed as an alternative to prosecution and therefore they can result in the suspension of prosecution or obviate the latter. Not so in Sierra Leone. This unprecedented situation created tensions and misunderstandings in the minds of many.

From an examination of the mandate and jurisdiction of both institutions, it is clear that their work overlaps. Both have related functions and the same common goals: ensuring accountability in Sierra Leone, bringing sustainable peace to the country and building a culture of respect for human rights. Without a clearly defined relationship, the danger exists that the institutions may duplicate one another's work, thereby wasting their limited resources. In the absence of a well-defined relationship between the two institutions, Sierra Leoneans were confused about the roles of each. In addition to clarifying perceptions on the ground, clearly defining this relationship could have helped to reduce the tension and rivalry that emerged between the two institutions. Both institutions lost credibility because they were seen to be in conflict.

The primary tension between the SCSL and the commission was over the testimony of witnesses. Many witnesses worried that evidence given to the commission could be used against them in the SCSL. It is impossible to assess to what extent this had an impact on the work of the commission but it was clear that many perpetrators did not come before the TRC to testify. This was also due to the fact that they had already been granted amnesty.

Both institutions also competed for the same resources and personnel. Although both were supported by the UN, each had limited funds and relied on the voluntary contributions of UN members. Lobbying for funds to address shortfalls also created tensions between the institutions. Many international non-governmental organisations (NGOs) were openly more supportive of one institution over the other and their local partners followed suit. The average Sierra Leonean never understood the distinction between the two institutions and was left confused as a result of their constant fighting.

THE TAYLOR INDICTMENT

The first case filed and the first indictment issued by the Court was against then Liberian President Charles Taylor. On 7 March 2003, Taylor's indictment was the first approved by the bench. The prosecutor, however, applied to the Court that the indictment be sealed and kept confidential. Almost at the same time that the indictment was approved diplomatic efforts to avert another catastrophe in Liberia also intensified. With various rebel movements trying to depose Taylor, the African Union (AU) and ECOWAS sought to avert more carnage in the capital, Monrovia, by negotiating Taylor's removal from office. Taylor, however, continued to demonstrate a keen ability to survive through a tight grip on political power, sanctions-busting and a series of convenient alliances.

Although both the legal and the diplomatic processes continued separately, they soon came into conflict. On 4 June 2003, Charles Taylor attended peace talks in Ghana that were intended to end the civil war in Liberia. On that day the prosecutor, without the leave of the SCSL, unsealed the indictment and appealed to Ghanaian authorities to recognise that their guest was indicted for war crimes and arrest and extradite him to Sierra Leone.[48]

The prosecutor claimed to have unsealed the indictment at the first auspicious opportunity for actually securing custody of Taylor. He believed that the June peace talks in Accra presented that opportunity. When it was clear that Taylor was travelling to Accra the Court's registrar stated in a 4 June press release that 'copies of all the relevant documents were served this morning personally on the Ghanaian High Commissioner in Freetown. In addition, copies of those documents were electronically transmitted to the Ghanaian Ministry of Foreign Affairs and acknowledgement of receipt of those documents has been received by telephone from a senior official in that ministry.'[49] It later emerged that the High Commission had not transmitted the documents to Ghana nor had the electronic documents been forwarded to the top echelons of the Ghanaian government before the SCSL made it public.

The timing and means by which the prosecutor publicly announced the unsealing of the indictment led to severe condemnation of his decision. That same day a Ghanaian Foreign Ministry official denied receiving any documents relating to the arrest warrant. The SCSL said it did not notify Ghana earlier because it could not be certain that officials would not warn Taylor. The Ghanaians brusquely refused to arrest Taylor and gave Taylor a presidential plane to return quickly to Liberia. The Ghanaian government complained that it had been blind-sided and embarrassed by the 'surprise' request to send Taylor to the Court. In an interview in *New African* magazine, Ghanaian President John Kufuor commented:

[I] felt betrayed by the international community . . . Five African presidents were meeting in Accra to find ways of kick-starting the Liberian peace process, and Mr Taylor had been invited as president of Liberia. We were not even aware that a warrant had been issued for his arrest. Incidentally, the African leadership had taken the initiative to convince Mr Taylor to resign and allow all the factions in Liberia to negotiate. It was when the presidents were leaving my office for the Conference Centre where Mr. Taylor was expected to make a statement that word came in that a warrant had been issued for his arrest. I really felt betrayed by the international community [and] I informed the United States of the embarrassment that the announcement caused.[50]

Criticisms of the way the Court handled this announcement are severe. Many accused Crane of thinking more about the interests of the United States than Sierra Leone and the sub-region. Some argued that the Court might have secured Taylor had it consulted with the Ghanaians prior to the announcement. African and American officials sponsoring the talks in Accra, angry that their efforts had been thwarted, complained that the 'overzealous' prosecutor was jeopardising their peace initiative. The prosecutor continued to assert that the parties at the peace talks needed to know that they were trying to negotiate with an indicted war criminal who, in the Court's opinion, could never be trusted. Many African leaders interpreted the prosecutor's action as contemptuous and the incident left an indelible and negative impression of the Tribunal's work.[51]

THE NORMAN TRIAL

The indictment of Charles Taylor received international attention, while Samuel 'Hinga' Norman's indictment made national headlines. Norman was the deputy defence minister and head of the CDF militia. He was accused of various crimes against humanity and violations of the laws of war in connection with his leadership of the CDF.

The Norman case created further divisions amongst Sierra Leoneans and his indictment was viewed with mixed feelings. Many were grateful to him for the sacrifice he had made in leading the CDF that had defended the public during the RUF onslaught and when the national army had abandoned them. They considered him to be a hero who should have been commended. He commanded a great deal of support, particularly in the southern and eastern regions of the country and is still viewed by many as a war hero who protected civilians from attacks by RUF and AFRC rebels. A small minority view Norman as a man with a controversial past who had committed atrocities and had condoned the atrocities of others in the CDF, but even among this group serious questions were raised as to whether he bore the greatest responsibility for the serious violations of international humanitarian law that were committed in Sierra Leone. Many questioned the rationale behind the prosecutor's decision to try him and to use one of the RUF's key masterminds, Gibril Massaquoi, as a witness.

Aggravating the situation was the belief that Norman's arrest was not based on the evidence but was influenced by key political figures who were using the Sierra Leone police force. Many suspected that the Norman indictment was part of a plot to eliminate him from the political scene. A spokesperson for the opposition party described Mr Norman 'as a sacrificial lamb' who was offered to the SCSL as a way of eliminating him from the presidential race.[52]

If his indictment was justified, the manner of his arrest and detention left many disappointed. At the time of his arrest Norman was a sitting minister of interior whose portfolio included control of the police. He was considered a war hero by many and posed little or no flight risk and yet he was arrested, handcuffed and, in the view of some, humiliated by the police. He was then taken to the remote island of Bonthe for incarceration. The treatment meted out to Norman and his incarceration with the 'bad guys' further alienated the Court from some of the local population. Indeed, their discontented voices were the most vocal in the country and in the diaspora.

Norman's case further amplified the tensions between the TRC and the SCSL. The TRC submitted a request to the Court to hold a public hearing to secure Norman's testimony. The SCSL only allowed the application in part. It gave the TRC access to Norman but denied the possibility of a public hearing. Norman refused to testify under such circumstances and the commission was unable to hear evidence from one of the key players in the conflict.[53]

Further grievances arose as a result of the manner of his death in Senegal. The Court had taken Norman out of Sierra Leone to a military hospital in Senegal for medical treatment. Prior to his departure for Dakar he was quoted by a national newspaper as saying 'I won't come back alive' and 'I am very much afraid for my life as it is put in the hands of people I do not trust to administer any form of medical treatment'.[54] Norman's family complained that he was gravely ill and was not receiving the medical care he required. They blamed the Court for failing to take his health concerns seriously, for taking him to a place in Senegal that was 'very much unsatisfactory and not conducive to human living' and, ultimately, for his death.[55] These allegations are at this stage entirely speculative and have not been substantiated by any concrete evidence of misconduct on the part of the SCSL.

Following his death, the local press hailed Norman as a hero. The *Concord Times* stated that Norman 'is today considered to be a hero by a majority of his countrymen'. *The Exclusive*, in an article headlined 'The death of a hero', refers to him as 'the great son of Sierra Leone' who will 'always be remembered by patriotic Sierra Leoneans'.[56] The local media also speculated that Norman's death was linked to his active political role even whilst he was behind bars. *The African Champion* reported that many of Mr Norman's supporters believe that sitting Vice-President Solomon Berewa was implicated in Mr Norman's death because the SLPP wanted to 'see that Chief Norman dies in jail because he is popular among the people'.[57]

Norman's death not only angered many and further alienated the Court from the populace but it provoked questions about the Court's relevance. For the SCSL, his death was a further disaster. It marked the loss of one of the few senior officials in any of the factions. With Foday Sankoh and Sam Bockarie already dead and Johnny Paul Koroma missing, Norman and Sankoh's successor, Issa Sesay, had been the only leaders of any of the factions in detention. As Lans Gberie points out: '[W]ith the death of Norman . . . most of the others in detention are virtually unknown and their fate is of little concern to the wider public in Sierra Leone. The idea that their trial would have any valence with respect to impunity, therefore, is totally moot, indeed highly unlikely.'[58]

CONCLUSION

The SCSL has been affected by a host of other problems, leading to questions about its efficacy. Some of its critics will cite the Court's failure in order to argue that we should have settled for the amnesty under the Lomé Peace Accord and moved on, or perhaps to argue that justice ought not to have prevailed over the blanket amnesty. Such arguments are flawed. The shortcomings of the SCSL are more properly attributed to poor implementation rather than to problems with pursuing justice per se. Proper implementation and sufficient funding could have addressed many of the shortcomings of the 'justice option' and would have better fostered a more lasting peace.

Sierra Leone, like all states, has an obligation enshrined in international law that requires accountability for international crimes. Prosecutions give peace processes an added impetus but they must not be pursued simply for the sake of locking up a few bad guys; they must contribute to reconciliation and nation-building and build a legacy of justice and the rule of law.

The example of the SCSL clearly throws into relief the important and legitimate questions raised by the debate concerning peace versus justice and shows that they are too important to be left in the hands of mediators and lawyers. Trade-offs between peace and justice must involve society as a whole and must be locally owned and accepted. On the one hand, advocates for justice can no longer fail to appreciate the importance of ending the war and preventing ongoing violations. On the other hand, peacebuilders cannot afford to disregard the contributions of various forms of justice and accountability to achieving a sustainable peace. At most times, the relationship between peace and justice will be complementary; at some times there will be tensions and dilemmas. These will have to be dealt with on a case-by-case basis rather than drawing sweeping conclusions about the incompatibility of peace and justice.

It is also important to note that punitive or retributive justice is not the only form of justice.[59] In situations where gross human rights violations have occurred even the most effective criminal justice systems cannot prosecute all of those responsible. Transitional justice approaches include and go beyond simply prosecuting perpetrators. They also include conditional amnesties, reparations, truth seeking and reforming institutions such as the judiciary. The processes of building sustainable peace and dealing with human rights abuse will take many years and may involve a range of initiatives that include justice throughout and after the peace negotiations.

NOTES AND REFERENCES

The views expressed in this chapter are those of the author in his personal capacity and do not necessarily represent those of any organisation he works for or represents.

1. The RUF is a loosely organised guerrilla group that started the war in 1991 seeking to topple the government of Sierra Leone and to retain control of the lucrative diamond-producing regions of the country. It was headed by Foday Sankoh, a former corporal in the Sierra Leone army.
2. See S. Ellis, 'War in West Africa', *The Fletcher Forum of World Affairs* 25(2), 2001: 33–39.

3. See P. Richards, *Fighting for the rainforest: War, youth and resources in Sierra Leone* (Oxford and New Hampshire: James Currey and Heinemann, 1996).

4. See 'Violence against women rife during Sierra Leonean war', *Agence France-Presse*, 20 March 2002.

5. I. Zarifis, 'Sierra Leone's search for justice and accountability of child soldiers', *Human Rights Brief* 9(3), 2002: 9.

6. For a detailed account of the atrocities in Sierra Leone see A. Tejan-Cole, 'Human rights under the Armed Forces Revolutionary Council: A catalogue of abuses', *African Journal of International and Comparative Law* October 1998: 481.

7. The Lomé Peace Accord, www.sierra-leone.org/lomeaccord.html (accessed 19 June 2007).

8. The UN, one of the moral guarantors to the Accord stated a proviso that the amnesty and pardon provisions would not apply to violations of the international crimes of genocide, crimes against humanity, war crimes and other serious violations of international humanitarian law.

9. Johnny Paul Koroma, the leader of a coup in 1997, was appointed as the chairperson of the Commission for the Consolidation of Peace.

10. The statement by the special representative of the secretary-general does not appear in the text of the agreement published by the UN (UN Doc S/1999/777). The TRC was shown an official copy of the Lomé Peace Accord to which the statement was appended in handwriting.

11. K. Gallagher, 'Note, no justice, no peace: The legalities and realities of amnesty in Sierra Leone', *Thomas Jefferson Law Revue* 149(155), 2000: 23.

12. A. Tejan-Cole, 'Amnesty under the Lomé Peace Accord in Sierra Leone', *African Journal of International and Comparative Law* 9(2), 2000: 481.

13. A. Tejan-Cole, 'Painful peace: Amnesty under the Lomé Peace Accord in Sierra Leone', *Law, Development and Democracy* 2, 1999: 239.

14. For a detailed account see Human Rights Watch, 'Sierra Leone: Getting away with murder, mutilation, rape: New testimony from Sierra Leone', July 1999, www.hrw.org/hrw/reports/1999/sierra/ (accessed 23 February 2009); A. Tejan-Cole, 'The Special Court for Sierra Leone: Conceptual concerns and alternatives', *African Human Rights Law Journal* 1, 2001: 107. See also sierra-leone.org/slnews0500.html (accessed 18 December 2007); J. Rupert and D. Farah, 'Liberian leader urges Sierra Leone rebels to free hostages', *Washington Post Foreign Service*, 20 May 2000, p. A20.

15. The Security Council passed a resolution mandating the secretary-general to negotiate an agreement with the government of Sierra Leone to create an independent Special Court. See Resolution 1315 (2000) of 14 August 2000. The Report of the Secretary-General on the Establishment of a Special Court for Sierra Leone (SCSL), UN SCOR, UN Doc S/2000/915 (2000). On 4 October 2000 the Secretary-General submitted his report to the Security Council, annexing the draft agreement between the UN and the government of Sierra Leone and the draft Statute for the establishment of the Court. Several letters between the president of the Security Council and the Secretary-General from December 2000 to July 2001 made revisions to the Statute.

16. Hans Correll for the UN, and Solomon Berewa for the government of Sierra Leone, signed the agreement.

17. *Prosecutor v Kallon*, Case No SCSL-2003-07-PT, Preliminary Motion based on lack of jurisdiction/abuse of process: Amnesty provided by the Lomé Accord (16 June 2003).

18. E. Higonnet, 'Restructuring hybrid courts: Local empowerment and national criminal justice reform', *Arizona Journal of International and Comparative Law* 23(2), 2006: 347.

19. N. Fritz and A. Smith, 'Current apathy for coming anarchy: Building the Special Court for Sierra Leone', *Fordham International Law Journal* 25(391), 2001: 391.

20. For a general discussion of the Special Court see M. Frulli, 'The Special Court for Sierra Leone: Some preliminary comments', *European Journal of International Law* 11, 2000: 857; G. Bosco, 'The Special Court for Sierra Leone and the Extraordinary Chambers for Cambodia', *Rivista della Cooperazione Giuridica Internazionale* 15, 2003; R. Cryer, 'A "special court" for Sierra Leone?', *International and Comparative Law Quarterly* 50, 2001: 435; S. Linton, 'Cambodia, East Timor and Sierra Leone: Experiments in international justice', *Criminal Law Forum* 12, 2001: 185; A. McDonald, 'Sierra Leone's shoestring Special Court', *International Review of the Red Cross* 84, 2002: 121; S. Beresford and A.S. Muller, 'The Special Court for Sierra Leone: An initial comment', *Leiden Journal of International Law* 14, 2001: 635; C. Schocken, 'The Special Court for Sierra Leone: Overview and recommendations', *Berkeley Journal of International Law* 20, 2002: 436; A. Tejan-Cole, 'The Special Court for Sierra Leone', *Interights Bulletin* 14, 2002: 37; J. Cerone, 'The Special Court for Sierra Leone: Establishing a new approach to international criminal justice', *ILSA Journal of International and Comparative Law* 8, 2002: 379; Fritz and Smith, 'Current apathy for coming anarchy', p. 391; M. Miraldi, 'Overcoming obstacles of justice: The Special Court of Sierra Leone', *New York Law School Journal of Human Rights* 19, 2003: 849.

21. A. Tejan-Cole, 'The Special Court for Sierra Leone: Conceptual concerns and alternatives', *African Human Rights Law Journal* 1(1), 2000: 107.

22. Rome Statute for the International Criminal Court (17 July 1998), Article 1.1, www.icc-cpi.int/library/about/officialjournal/Rome_Statute_120704-EN.pdf (accessed 11 March 2007).

23. The expression 'persons responsible' designates named individuals who alone may be considered to have criminal responsibility under international law.

24. It is highly unlikely that anyone else will be indicted as the Court has started winding up its operations.

25. This not withstanding, provision is made in the Statute for the Court to sit outside Sierra Leone.

26. B. Amnrinade, 'International humanitarian law and the conflict in Sierra Leone', *Notre Dame Journal of Law, Ethics and Public Policy* 15(391), 2001: 393.

27. 'The promises of international prosecution', *Harvard Law Review* 114, 2001: 1957. See, for example, P. Akhavan, 'Beyond impunity: Can international criminal justice prevent future atrocities?' *American Journal of International Law* 95(7), 2001: 30–31; G.K. Young, 'Amnesty and accountability', *UC Davis Law Review* 35(427), 2002: 433–441.

28. Conscripting or enlisting children under the age of fifteen years into armed forces or groups using them to participate actively in hostilities.

29. D.M. Amann, 'Calling children to account: The proposal for a Juvenile Chamber in the Special Court for Sierra Leone', *Pepperdine Law Review* 29, 2002: 167.

30. D. Farah, 'A war against women: Sierra Leone rebels practised systematic sexual terror', *Washington Post*, 11 February 2000.

31. 'Violence against women rife during Sierra Leonean War'.

32. S. Eaton, 'Sierra Leone: The proving ground for prosecuting rape as a war crime', *Georgetown Journal of International Law* 35, 2004: 873.

33. Article 2(g) of the Statute of the Special Court for Sierra Leone, Composition of the Chambers, www.sierra-leone.org/specialcourtstatute.html (accessed 18 December 2007).

34. See *Prosecutor v Brima, Kamara & Kanu*, Case No SCSL-04-16-PT, Decision on prosecution request for leave to amend the indictment, 6 May 2004.

35. *Prosecutor v Charles Ghankay Taylor*, SCSL-2003-01-I, Decision on immunity from Jurisdiction Appeals Chamber, 31 May 2004, www.sc-sl.org/Documents/SCSL-03-01-I-059.pdf (accessed 18 December 2007).

36. See A. McDonald, 'Sierra Leone's shoestring Special Court', *International Revue of the Red Cross* 84(845), 2002: 124.

37. C. Schocken, 'Notes and comments, the Special Court for Sierra Leone: Overview and recommendations', *Berkeley Journal of International Law* 20(436), 2002: 437–438.

38. Article 12(1)(*b*) of the Statute of the Special Court for Sierra Leone.

39. Article 12(1)(*a*) of the Statute of the Special Court for Sierra Leone.

40. Even then he subsequently resigned from the Sierra Leonean judiciary in the course of the proceedings.

41. This conclusion arose in discussion with some members of the judiciary and was expressed at two Bar Association conferences.

42. E. Higonnet, 'Restructuring hybrid courts: Local empowerment and national criminal justice reform', *Arizona Journal of International and Comparative Law* 23, 2005: 347.

43. L. Gberie, *A dirty war in West Africa: The RUF and the destruction of Sierra Leone* (Bloomington, IN: Indiana University Press, 2005), p. 212, points out that the SCSL's huge budget, estimated at more than US$80 million, has come in for a lot of criticism when compared to the underresourced Sierra Leonean judiciary.

44. There were some great opportunities in which the Court could have helped to promote law reform. While I was working at the Court, the then attorney-general and minister of justice of Sierra Leone wrote a letter to the Court requesting a position paper on the death penalty. The paper was provided but much more could have been done to lobby for the abolition of the death penalty. A lot more could also have been done to reform Sierra Leone's rape and other sexual offences Statute. It seemed much easier to prove rape and some of the other sexual offences stated in the Statute than to prove similar offences under Sierra Leone's anachronistic laws.

45. For the effect of the war on the Sierra Leone judiciary see, *In pursuit of justice: A report on the judiciary in Sierra Leone*, Report by the Commonwealth Human Rights Initiative, www.humanrightsinitiative.org/publications/Sierra%20Leone%20Report.pdf (accessed 30th March 2007).

46. Opening address by the then Chief Justice Timbo at the Annual Conference of the Bar Association in Sierra Leone.

47. V.O. Nmehielle and C.C. Jalloh, 'The legacy of the Special Court for Sierra Leone', *The Fletcher Forum of World Affairs* 30, 2006: 107.

48. As the prosecutor of the Special Court had applied to the Court to seal Taylor's indictment, it could be argued that he was required to seek the leave of the Court to unseal the same. The rules are silent on this issue and the defence never raised it as an issue so the point is moot.

49. International Crisis Group, 'The Special Court for Sierra Leone: Promises and Pitfalls of a "New Model"', *Africa Briefing* 16 (4 August 2003): 8.

50. *New African*, May 2006, pp. 10–17.

51. See C. Taylor, 'Why me?', *New African*, May 2006, pp. 10–17. See also 'The Special Court for Sierra Leone: Promises and pitfalls of a "new model"', *ICG Africa Briefing* 16, 2003, www.crisisgroup.org/home/index.cfm?id=1803&l=1 (accessed 22 February 2007).

52. 'The death of a hero!', *The Exclusive*, 23 February 2007.

53. *Prosecutor v Norman*, Case No SCSL-03-08-PT-122, Decision on appeal by TRC and accused against the decision of His Lordship Justice Bankole Thompson to deny the TRC request to hold a public hearing with Chief Norman, 28 November 2003.

54. 'I won't come back alive', *Concord Times*, 23 February 2007, socrates.berkeley.edu/~warcrime/SL-Reports/SamuelHingaNorman_SpecialReport.html (accessed 18 December 2007).

55. '"Hinga" Norman bled to death', *Awareness Times*, 23 February 2007.

56. '"Hinga" Norman bled to death'.

57. '"Hinga" Norman's death is disaster for SLPP', *The African Champion*, 23 February 2007. See also 'He is dead!', *The Spark*, 23 February 2007; 'Chief Norman died a martyr, a hero?', *Concord Times*, 23 February 2007.

58. 'Sierra Leone: What use the Special Court?', *New African*, April 2007, p. 21.

59. N.J. Kritz, 'Coming to terms with atrocities: A review of accountability mechanisms for mass violations of human rights', *Law and Contemporary Problems* 59(4), 1996: 132.

12

Charles Taylor, the Special Court for Sierra Leone and International Politics

Abdul Rahman Lamin

INTRODUCTION

The arrest of former Liberian President Charles Taylor in Nigeria in March 2006 and his subsequent transfer to the Special Court for Sierra Leone (SCSL) to face war crimes charges has once again brought to the fore the debates surrounding this 'hybrid' international criminal tribunal, which was established to prosecute 'individuals who bear the greatest responsibility for war crimes and crimes against humanity' that had been perpetrated during Sierra Leone's decade-long conflict. The SCSL has, since its inception in 2002, been caught up in a number of controversies and sceptics have repeatedly raised questions concerning its long-term relevance and its contribution to peacebuilding in Sierra Leone. Whether it is the controversial decision by the prosecution to indict leaders of the Civil Defence Forces (CDF) or the strategically poor manner in which Taylor's indictment was unsealed – on the day West African leaders converged in the Ghanaian capital, Accra, in their attempt to broker a peace agreement for Liberia – or even the decision to move Taylor's trial to The Hague as opposed to keeping it in Sierra Leone, it is indeed timely to raise questions concerning the Court's purpose and, more importantly, to assess its impact on peace in Sierra Leone.

Although it has finally succeeded in securing convictions against two groups of indictees,[1] five years after the SCSL was set up, Taylor's trial arguably puts the Court back into the spotlight in terms of its long-term impact on consolidating Sierra Leone's peace. It is legitimate to examine the political and legal significance of the Court and assess its impact on curbing impunity. Taylor's transfer from Freetown to The Hague – without much consultation in the sub-region – to face trial at the premises of the International Criminal Court (ICC), while legally grounded in its Agreement,[2] raises fundamental questions about whether the importance of ensuring that 'justice is not only done, but is seen to be done' was a serious consideration when making that decision. It is also fair to ask whether the idea of prosecuting 'individuals who bear the greatest responsibility for war crimes and crimes against humanity', as noble as it sounds, did not play second fiddle to other political agendas.[3]

In light of the above, this chapter raises questions that are intended to provoke debate about the continued relevance of the SCSL. To be clear, suggesting that the Court's relevance should be rethought must not be confused with support for impunity in Sierra Leone – or anywhere else for that matter. On the contrary, I have called elsewhere for accountability for atrocities committed in Sierra Leone.[4] The two issues should therefore remain completely separate. Rather, by calling for a re-evaluation of the SCSL's relevance, in light of all the controversies surrounding it, this chapter merely suggests that the SCSL, while originally well-intentioned, unfortunately may have become so overly politicised and perhaps even polarised that its credibility as an independent and impartial body will remain contested for some time to come.

To justify this call for a rethinking of the relevance of the SCSL, three arguments are advanced here. Firstly, I argue that while the original intention to prosecute war crimes violations in Sierra Leone may have been well-founded and justified, operationalising this concept of judicial accountability has raised doubts about its usefulness to long-term peace. Secondly, the overpoliticisation of the Court has meant that not much has been done to effect redress for the victims in whose name the Court was initially established. David Crane, the chief prosecutor of the SCSL from its inception in 2002 until 2005, pronounced upon his appointment that the trial of all individuals indicted by the Court must take place 'at the crime scene', in Sierra Leone.[5] This pronouncement, however, seems to have been reneged upon with Taylor's transfer to The Hague, where his trial will be accessible to a largely European audience rather than to the victims in Sierra Leone. Finally, it is unclear why the Sierra Leone government, which negotiated the Special Court Agreement, failed to push for the inclusion of an exclusionary clause (in the Agreement) that would have limited the prosecution's power to indict individuals from all factions, particularly leaders of the CDF. While acknowledging the controversy surrounding that argument, it is nonetheless my contention that insisting on 'prosecuting all and sundry' without any deference to the context and political environment within which the conflict occurred, has led to the resentment and alienation of many victims who credit their survival to the sacrifice made by the CDF in fighting off rebels of the Revolutionary United Front (RUF) and its allies.

TROUBLES IN THE MANO RIVER UNION IN THE 1990s

For much of the 1990s Charles Taylor gained notoriety as the mastermind behind brutal armed conflicts in West Africa, beginning with the assault by the National Patriotic Front of Liberia (NPFL) on his native Liberia in 1989. After more than a decade of destruction and plunder that saw the war in Liberia spread into Sierra Leone, Taylor finally met his 'Waterloo' in 2003 when he accepted an offer by the Nigerian government to take up asylum in the south-eastern city of Calabar. Taylor's final departure from the Liberian political scene was preceded by a seventeen-count indictment for war crimes and crimes against humanity that had been unsealed while he was in Accra, Ghana, for peace talks designed to end the Liberian civil war. Although he was not apprehended immediately after the indictment was unsealed in June 2003, it must be acknowledged that this bold action by the prosecution, even if controversial, accelerated Taylor's departure from power in Liberia.

Taylor's invasion of Liberia, designed to unseat the dictatorial regime of President Samuel Doe, quickly degenerated into ethnic conflict, with the Gio and Mano on the one hand fighting against the Krahn and Mandingo on the other.[6] The early months of the war saw the NPFL occupying more than 70 per cent of Liberian territory. This rapid military success by rebel forces had two immediate consequences for Liberia and West Africa as a whole. In Liberia itself, it increased pressure on Doe to negotiate a peaceful settlement with his adversaries. The defeat of Liberian forces by NPFL fighters led to the departure of senior government officials from the country, which further isolated Doe and put pressure on his regime to negotiate.[7]

Sub-regional response to the situation in Liberia was swift and decisive. Less than a year after the conflict started leaders of the Economic Community of West African States (ECOWAS) deployed a multi-national peacekeeping force to the war-ravaged country. The Economic Community of West African States Monitoring Group (ECOMOG) was mandated to enforce a ceasefire that had been agreed upon earlier between a break-away rebel group that controlled parts of Monrovia and the beleaguered Doe regime. The peacekeepers were also mandated to protect innocent civilians from further massacre. The significance of this collective sub-regional response to the Liberian conflict cannot be downplayed, as Liberia became one of the first test cases in the post-Cold War era in which Africans could demonstrate their commitment and capacity in solving their own problems.[8] That ECOWAS was willing to deploy troops to one of its member states, to enforce a ceasefire and protect civilians, without prior United Nations (UN) Security Council authorisation, marked a new chapter in post-Cold War peacekeeping in Africa. This intervention model was later replicated in Sierra Leone and other theatres of conflict on the continent, albeit with significant modifications.

The NPFL's vehement opposition to regional intervention in Liberia made ECOMOG's mission problematic from the outset. In an interview with the British Broadcasting Corporation (BBC) shortly after ECOMOG troops entered Monrovia, Taylor promised to ensure that Sierra Leone tasted 'the bitterness of war' for hosting ECOMOG while it deployed troops into Liberia.[9] The NPFL's opposition to ECOMOG's intervention was vividly demonstrated by its attack on the first contingent of peacekeepers that arrived at the port of Monrovia in August 1990. Taylor's threat against Sierra Leone and the subsequent attack on ECOMOG forces by fighters loyal to him reinforced long-held beliefs that he was indeed directly involved in fomenting trouble in Sierra Leone. That NPFL combatants played a visible role in the early incursions into Sierra Leone in 1991 was neither a surprise nor an accident. Taylor's calculations were always clear: destabilise Sierra Leone and consequently undercut ECOMOG's effectiveness in Liberia, which would in turn strengthen the NPFL and allow it to seize power via the military.

On 23 March 1991, fighters loyal to the RUF attacked Sierra Leone from across the border in Liberia, seeking to overthrow the All People's Congress (APC) government of President Joseph Saidu Momoh. RUF leader Foday Sankoh and Taylor had developed a close relationship that dated back to the 1980s when both men were in military training camps in Libya.[10] In the 1980s Tripoli had become the convergence point for dissidents and future warlords like Taylor and Sankoh who wished to reinforce their ambitions and hone their 'revolutionary skills' in preparation for taking power in their respective countries. Thus, in 1989, when Taylor launched an attack against the repressive Liberian regime of Doe, Sankoh and other Sierra Leonean dissidents who had trained alongside him in Libya joined the NPFL.[11] Similarly, in 1991, when the RUF launched an attack against the corrupt and unpopular Momoh regime in Sierra Leone, they received tremendous help from their NPFL brethren in Liberia. That the conflict in Sierra Leone originated from the rebellion in Liberia is hardly in dispute. It is therefore inevitable that any serious analysis of Sierra Leone's political turmoil, particularly in the 1990s, be located in the context of events in neighbouring Liberia, of which Charles Taylor was at the centre.

THE GENESIS OF THE SPECIAL COURT FOR SIERRA LEONE

The legal foundation for the SCSL is enshrined in the Agreement signed in Freetown, on 16 January 2002, by Sierra Leone's former Attorney-General Solomon Berewa, and the UN's former Chief of Legal Affairs Hans Correl. The idea of setting up a court to prosecute individuals for war crimes resulting from the armed conflict in Sierra Leone came in the aftermath of the near collapse of the 1999 Lomé Peace Accord. Although prior to 1999 a number of Sierra Leonean and international human rights campaigners had been lobbying for the establishment of an independent body to investigate human rights violations in the conflict,[12] the Lomé Peace Accord had stopped short of doing that. The Accord instead established a Truth and Reconciliation Commission (TRC), mandating it to provide both victims and perpetrators with an opportunity to tell their stories and thus help to promote reconciliation.[13] Given its mandate, the TRC had little power and was not designed to mete out punishment against individuals, even those who clearly confessed to taking active part in perpetrating human rights abuses during the conflict. Its role was limited to facilitating a process of 'truth-telling' in the hope that, through this cathartic process, the healing of past wounds would be enhanced.

Interestingly, even though the UN special representative present at the Lomé talks clearly indicated his organisation's discomfort with the amnesty provision of the Accord and issued a disclaimer distancing the UN from it, no immediate step was taken to establish a body with a mandate different from that of the TRC, to hold individuals criminally accountable for their acts during the conflict. Indeed, the Sierra Leone government – and other external actors for that matter – only began to consider seriously the idea of setting up a Special Court to investigate and prosecute war crimes violations after the Lomé Peace Accord threatened to collapse in May 2000. Specifically, the abduction of about 500 UN peacekeepers by RUF fighters and the subsequent capture of Sankoh led the government to examine the need to establish a court that would prosecute 'spoilers' of the peace process. It was this new dynamic in the conflict that precipitated a request from President Kabbah, who wrote to the Security Council in August

2000, seeking UN assistance in setting up a tribunal specifically to prosecute the RUF and its allies for undermining the Lomé Peace Accord.[14] The Security Council subsequently mandated then Secretary-General Kofi Annan to enter into negotiations with the Sierra Leonean authorities on how best the UN could assist in the establishment of such a court.

However, although Kabbah's letter to the Security Council was very specific in its request, namely, UN assistance in establishing a court to 'prosecute the RUF and its allies' for widespread atrocities, the eventual agreement reached between the two parties instead created a court with a prosecutor given wide powers to 'prosecute individuals' without exception, who 'bear the greatest responsibility' for violations of international humanitarian and human-rights law in Sierra Leone, dating back to 30 November 1996. As a result of these wide powers vested in the prosecutor, leaders of all armed groups, including the CDF, a well-known ally of the Sierra Leone government, became the subject of criminal investigation and subsequent prosecution. By indicting even the allies of the government the SCSL succeeded in creating a sense of 'moral equivalency' between the real perpetrators of atrocities and those who were merely defending their respective communities.[15] Of course proponents of the Court have argued that by indicting even CDF leaders the prosecution succeeded in demonstrating its independence and impartiality. While it is generally true that international tribunals are often expected to prosecute 'perpetrators' from all sides in a conflict, it is also becoming increasingly clear that unless these tribunals pay heed to the context and political environment in which those violations occurred and, more importantly, the long-term impact of their prosecutorial decisions on peace, they risk creating a backlash, as the Norman and CDF indictments have illustrated in the case of Sierra Leone.

If the prosecutor's judgement in indicting Norman and other CDF leaders along with the RUF leader, Sankoh, is questionable, it is the Court's handling of the Taylor case and its strategically unsophisticated management of the politics surrounding the matter that has opened it to harsher criticism, and consequently undermined its credibility in the sub-region and beyond. Interestingly, the Court has, in an ironic way, succeeded in transforming Taylor into a symbol of African resistance to an evolving international criminal justice regime that is increasingly perceived on the continent as a system designed to tame 'lawless' Africans but one that is reluctant to get anywhere close to other similarly gruesome theatres of human rights abuses around the world.

THE SPECIAL COURT AND RECONCILIATION IN SIERRA LEONE

Can a criminal tribunal, whether domestic or international, help to promote reconciliation in a post-conflict society? Is the concept of justice, in the sense of retribution, compatible with the notion of reconciliation in the same post-conflict society? These questions are not only central to understanding the controversy surrounding the SCSL but they also broadly form part of the puzzle that transitional societies must solve when they are confronted with the choice between what scholars have theorised as 'retributive' and 'restorative' approaches to justice.[16] Needless to say, consensus on how to resolve this dilemma is hard to come by. Both approaches possess their own unique advantages[17] and transitional societies across the globe, particularly since the early 1990s, have tended to either adopt one or the other but have rarely utilised both simultaneously. However, in Sierra Leone, unlike other preceding transitional experiences, a TRC began operating alongside a Special Court in 2002, although as noted earlier the two institutions had separate mandates. The logic of simultaneously adopting both approaches was that they would complement each other. Proponents had hoped that it would be possible for both institutions to help promote national reconciliation while at the same time seek justice through criminal prosecutions.

Contrary to the prosecutor's repeated argument that the Court's mandate was not fundamentally in opposition to that of the TRC, it was clear from the outset that the institutions were bound to clash. Crane's assurances that the prosecution of key perpetrators of human rights violations would nicely complement the work of the TRC, which was tasked with unravelling 'the truth' about the conflict and which in the process would contribute to healing past wounds, did very little to ease tensions between the two bodies. There are obviously a variety of reasons why this was the case though we shall focus only on two here.

The first problem clearly had to do with the interpretation of the Special Court Statute. Specifically, article 8(2) of the Statute gives the Court 'primacy' over the 'national courts of Sierra Leone'. Although no specific mention is made of the TRC in the Statute it became clear as both institutions evolved that the SCSL would seek to interpret this as broadly as it could to include the TRC. In effect, while the expectation, particularly within the TRC, was that it would be 'co-equal' to the SCSL, the latter's broad interpretation of its statute prevented that from being the case.

A dramatic illustration of this tension and the legal tussle between the two bodies occurred at the height of the TRC hearings, when the Court refused to grant the TRC access to the indictees, including Norman and other CDF leaders, who the TRC wished to have testify publicly about their respective roles in the conflict. In an unprecedented move, the prosecution filed an application before the Trial Chamber, opposing the TRC's request to have the indictees appear before it. By upholding the prosecution's application not to allow Norman and other indictees to testify publicly before the TRC, the Chamber essentially deprived Sierra Leoneans of the opportunity to hear directly from some of the principal actors about their role in the conflict. The overall effect of this is that, comprehensive as the TRC report turned out to be, it has to be acknowledged that it is still to some extent incomplete.

In addition to the controversy regarding primacy, the prosecutor's failure and inability to take into account fully the political context and dynamics of the conflict led to his own questionable decision to bring indictments against CDF leaders alongside RUF leaders.[18] While it would have been controversial for the prosecution to bring indictments only against RUF leaders, especially given its broad mandate, one would have imagined that a clear understanding of the political dynamics of the conflict might have dissuaded it from bringing charges against the CDF leaders in particular, given the resentment that action caused. Indeed, while some would argue that there were no 'clean perpetrators' in the conflict and hence the Court would have been constrained if it had limited itself to indicting only RUF leaders, the fact that Norman's role in the conflict continues to be celebrated by many in Sierra Leone, even after his unfortunate death,[19] suggests that the 'victims' on whose behalf the prosecution claimed to be working did not share the same enthusiasm about categorising the CDF and RUF as 'two sides of the same coin'.

The Norman indictment still remains a polarising issue, to the point that it was partly responsible for the defeat of the ruling Sierra Leone People's Party (SLPP) in the recently concluded presidential and parliamentary elections. The ruling party suffered a major setback at the polls, particularly in its historic strongholds of the southern and eastern provinces. This was largely because many voters in those regions blamed the former government for 'sacrificing' Norman and other CDF leaders in the interest of political expediency. Many voters in the southern and eastern regions of Sierra Leone simply heeded the call of the break-away third party, the People's Movement for Democratic Change (PMDC), to vote the SLPP government out of office, for its complicity in the 'Norman affair'. As a result, the leading opposition party, the APC, benefited politically, winning both the presidential and parliamentary election. In essence then, rather than complementing the reconciliation process, the Court actually succeeded in further polarising Sierra Leonean society.

REGIONAL AND INTERNATIONAL INTERESTS

Although the indictment of Charles Taylor by the SCSL did not come as a surprise to many observers, the poor management by the Court of the politics surrounding that case has, to a large extent, seriously undermined its credibility. Given the prosecutor's mandate 'to prosecute individuals who bear the greatest responsibility' for grave human rights violations in Sierra Leone, it was clear from the outset that a literal interpretation of that mandate meant that no one was exempt from the 'long arm' of the law. That Taylor helped to fund the RUF during its decade-long bitter conflict in Sierra Leone is hardly in doubt. The fact that diamonds were used to fuel the war in Sierra Leone and Taylor's role in facilitating that enterprise cannot be easily disputed. A number of studies over the years have established the connection between the RUF and Taylor, particularly with respect to their collaboration in illegally smuggling diamonds from Sierra Leone in exchange for weapons to fight the war.[20] It would therefore have been naive for anyone, including Taylor himself, not to have anticipated the action subsequently taken against him by the SCSL prosecutor. In fact, as suggested earlier, the Court's decision expedited his exit from power, even if the timing in unsealing the indictment against Taylor may not have been very strategic.

It is the manner in which his indictment was unsealed to the public that has drawn the sharpest criticism. To be clear, though the decision to indict Taylor had been approved by the Court's Trial Chamber as far back as March 2003, the prosecution only chose to make the indictment public when the deposed former president flew into Accra, in June 2003, to attend peace talks hosted by ECOWAS and African Union (AU) leaders. The Court's failure to brief regional leaders properly about Taylor's pending indictment illustrates insensitivity and a lack of respect for any peacemaking efforts that were already underway. It therefore came as no surprise that the then ECOWAS chairperson, Ghana's President John Kufuor, along with his colleagues, refused to honour the Court's warrant of arrest against Taylor but instead facilitated Taylor's swift return to Monrovia. At the very least, the prosecutor's over-reliance on the letter of his mandate blinded him to the importance of seeking political and diplomatic support among regional actors when he legitimately sought to enforce that mandate.

Upon his arrest in Nigeria and subsequent transfer to the SCSL in March 2006, concerns were immediately raised about the potential repercussions of holding Taylor's trial in Sierra Leone. The new Liberian government of President Ellen Johnson-Sirleaf was understandably concerned that putting Taylor on trial anywhere close to Liberia had the potential to threaten the fragile peace in that country. In a very ironic way, the Office of the Prosecutor, which had never previously raised concerns about the security threats that its presence might have in the sub-region, suddenly became a forceful advocate for moving the trial out of Sierra Leone and essentially rehashed the same argument that Johnson-Sirleaf had made. In a matter of days the prosecution was transformed into an advocate for political stability in West Africa. Strangely, the Sierra Leone government, a known party to the Special Court Agreement, remained largely silent on the issue, only supporting the decision to transfer Taylor to The Hague after others had pronounced themselves on the matter.

Opinion within civil society in both Liberia and Sierra Leone was divided between those who felt that Taylor's presence in the sub-region might spark another rebellion by his supporters and those who believed that his trial in Sierra Leone, which Prosecutor Crane had originally referred to as 'the crime scene', would serve a useful purpose, because 'justice will not only be done, but will be seen to be done'. My view on that question is quite clear: the transfer of Taylor to The Hague on the grounds that his trial might create a security threat to the sub-region is problematic. While it cannot be disputed that Taylor still commands some influence among his supporters in the sub-region, the impact that his trial would have had on reversing the gains made in the various peacebuilding processes in both Sierra Leone and Liberia was, in my view, grossly overstated. If anything, the trial of Norman and other CDF leaders who, unlike Taylor, remain heroes to many in Sierra Leone, was more likely to have created an immediate security backlash, though perhaps that is yet to happen.

It is important to place in context the drama that surrounded Taylor's arrest to help us understand further the interests involved in that matter. By early 2006 it had been widely reported in the Liberian and international press that Liberian President Johnson-Sirleaf had formally requested Taylor's extradition from Nigeria to face charges before the SCSL. Equally dominating the news were reports suggesting that Nigerian President Olusegun Obasanjo was already consulting several of his peers, including South African President Thabo Mbeki, on how to handle the Taylor affair.[21]

The critical questions raised then and which remain relevant even today are, firstly, why did the Liberian government suddenly request Taylor's extradition when only a few months earlier Johnson-Sirleaf had indicated that the issue was not among her government's top priorities?[22] Secondly, why did Obasanjo find it necessary to consult Mbeki and other African leaders on how to deal with this matter? Clearly, it could be argued that Johnson-Sirleaf's request to Nigeria to end Taylor's exile and hand him over for trial suggests that she was under enormous pressure to do so. I would note that Johnson-Sirleaf's request to Nigeria was made shortly before her first official visit to the United States as president of Liberia, notwithstanding denials of this by the Liberian government.[23] I speculate that she anticipated pressure would be brought to bear on her by human rights groups as well as from United States law-makers, many of whom had long called for Taylor's extradition from Nigeria. Given Liberia's pressing economic and developmental needs following years of devastating war, it is not far-fetched to suggest that Johnson-Sirleaf knew well ahead of her visit that United States' assistance to her government would be somehow tied to her willingness to deal directly with the Taylor issue, 'once and for all'. While there was enough goodwill in the United States towards her government, she also understood that sooner or later she would have to address the Taylor issue decisively or risk losing some of the support of the United States, a price that would be costly for her administration.

Obasanjo's own consultation with other African leaders on how to handle the Taylor issue was somehow consistent with Nigeria's pronouncements, in 2004, that it would consider sending Taylor back to Liberia if an elected government in that country made the proper request.[24] Clearly, that pronouncement was designed to leave the door open for Nigeria to save face politically in the event that it finally extradited Taylor. It was politically safer for Obasanjo to send Taylor to the SCSL in Freetown, via Monrovia, than if he had been flown directly from Abuja. That Obasanjo consulted with Mbeki and other African leaders is consistent with the consultative process that had evolved among these leaders since the inception of the AU. In this regard, it should be noted that when Taylor left Liberia for exile in Nigeria, in 2003, he was escorted out of the country by Presidents Obasanjo of Nigeria, Mbeki of South Africa, Kufuor of Ghana and Chissano of Mozambique. The presence of these leaders in Monrovia on the day of Taylor's departure was an indication of their endorsement of his asylum agreement with Nigeria. Thus when Obasanjo ultimately took the decision to hand Taylor back to the Liberian authorities that decision was presented as one that had the blessing of his peers.[25] This inevitably insulated him politically from criticisms of capitulation to external pressure.

CONCLUSION

From the above analysis it can be seen how the Taylor case and, for that matter, the CDF indictments by the SCSL have been rife with tensions and controversies in which various interests have collided. For instance, while Liberia may not necessarily have seen the need to focus on the Taylor matter in the immediate aftermath of Johnson-Sirleaf's election, when it badly needed the support of the United States the government had little or no choice but to succumb to pressures to request Taylor's extradition from Nigeria. Similarly, while Nigeria may have in the past resisted pressure to hand Taylor over, it is interesting that Obasanjo finally yielded to this pressure at a time when he was also contemplating seeking a 'third term' in office, a move that was roundly defeated in the Nigerian national assembly.

One of the unique features of the SCSL is that, unlike other ad hoc international criminal tribunals established since the end of the Cold War, it came into being as a result of an agreement between the Sierra Leone government and the UN. In the strict sense of the word therefore, unlike its predecessors, namely the International Criminal Tribunal for the Former Yugoslavia (ICTY) and the International Criminal Tribunal for Rwanda (ICTR), the SCSL is not a UN body. As a party to the agreement that established the Court, it is fair to question the role of the government in creating this problem that it currently faces. Although it is justifiable to criticise the Court it is equally important to call into question the government's failure to negotiate the inclusion of some exclusionary clauses into the agreement, something that, though controversial, in hindsight might have averted many of the criticisms currently levelled against that body.

In summary, this chapter has tried to illustrate that throughout its operation the SCSL has engendered numerous controversies that encourage a rethinking of its relevance, particularly if this 'hybrid' model of ad hoc international tribunal were ever to be considered for use in other transitional societies. I have argued that though the initiative was a good one and was at the outset supported by a wide range of people, including myself, it has unfortunately turned out to be an instrument for promoting interests that probably have nothing to do with seeking justice for the victims of Sierra Leone's war. In overly politicising the process and openly prioritising those interests, the Court may have inadvertently raised doubts in the minds of many, myself included, about its long-term impact on peace in Sierra Leone.

NOTES AND REFERENCES

1. In June 2007, indictees of the Armed Forces Ruling Council (AFRC) were convicted and sentencing was handed down in July 2007. The CDF indictees were convicted in August and sentenced in October 2007.
2. Article 10 of the Special Court Agreement states that the seat of the court shall be in Sierra Leone but then goes on to say that it 'may be relocated outside Sierra Leone if circumstances so require'.
3. See B. Bender, 'Liberia's Taylor gave aid to Qaeda', *Boston Globe*, 2 August 2004; C. Ragavan, 'African most wanted: Charles Taylor is an accused war criminal: A UN-backed court wants him, Washington is dithering', *US News and World Report*, 8 May 2005.
4. A.R. Lamin, 'Building peace through accountability in Sierra Leone: The Special Court and the Truth and Reconciliation Commission', *Journal of Asian and African Studies* 38(2–3), 2003: 295–320.
5. Prosecutor's meeting with US-based Sierra Leonean lawyers and professional staff at the embassy of Sierra Leone in Washington, DC, June 2002.
6. Even though Charles Taylor is a Kongo of Americo-Liberian descent, the bulk of NPFL fighters were drawn from the Gio and Mano ethnic groups, with the Krahn and Mandingos largely supporting the Doe regime.
7. For domestic reactions to conflict resolution efforts in Liberia, see D. Elwood Dunn, 'Liberia's internal responses to ECOMOG's interventionist efforts', in K.P. Magyar and E. Conteh-Morgan (eds.), *Peacekeeping in Africa: ECOMOG in Liberia* (New York: St Martin's Press, 1998), p. 84.
8. For an analysis of the imperatives for sub-regional intervention in Liberia, see A. Adebajo, *Building peace in West Africa: Liberia, Sierra Leone and Guinea Bissau* (International Peace Academy Occasional Paper Series) (Boulder, CO: Lynne Rienner, 2002).
9. BBC *Focus on Africa* radio interview, August 1990.
10. I. Abdullah, 'Bush path to destruction: The origin and character of the Revolutionary United Front', *African Development* XXII (3 & 4), 1997: 203–235.
11. Abdullah, 'Bush path to destruction'.
12. See, for instance, Human Rights Watch, *Getting away with murder, mutilation, rape: New testimony from Sierra Leone* (New York: Human Rights Watch, 1999).
13. Article 26(1) of the Lomé Peace Accord provides for the establishment of a Truth and Reconciliation Commission.
14. UN Security Council (2000), Letter dated 9 August 2000 from the permanent representative of Sierra Leone to the United Nations addressed to the president of the Security Council, S/2000/786, August 2000.
15. A.R. Lamin, 'The politics of reconciliation in the Mano River Union: Challenges and prospects for peacebuilding', *IGD Occasional Paper* No. 45, July 2004.
16. P. Hayner, *Unspeakable truths: Confronting state terror and atrocity* (New York: Routledge, 2001); N.J. Kritz (ed.), *Transitional justice: How emerging democracies reckon with former regimes* (Washington, DC: United States Institute of Peace Press, 1995).

17. See, for instance, K. Moghalu, *Global justice: The politics of war crimes trials* (London: Praeger, 2006); K. Moghalu, 'Reconciling fractured societies: An African perspective on the role of judicial prosecutions', in R. Thakur and P. Malcontent (eds.), *From sovereign impunity to international accountability: The search for justice in a world of states* (Tokyo: United Nations University Press, 2004), pp. 217–218.

18. Lamin, 'The politics of reconciliation in the Mano River Union'.

19. Norman died in Dakar, Senegal, earlier in 2007, following hip surgery that was reported to have been successful.

20. J.L. Hirsch, *Sierra Leone: Diamonds and the struggle for democracy* (Boulder, CO: Lynne Rienner, 2001); I. Smillie, L. Gberie and R. Hazleton, *The heart of the matter: Diamonds and the struggle for power in Sierra Leone* (Ontario, Canada: Partnership Africa Canada, 2000); D. Farah, *Blood from stones: The secret financial network of terror* (New York: Broadway Books, 2004).

21. A.R. Lamin, 'Getting its own back', *Mail & Guardian*, 20 March 2006.

22. BBC news online, 'Nigeria to give up Charles Taylor', 25 March 2006. http://news.bbc.co.uk/1/hi/world/africa/4845088.stm (accessed 23 February 2009).

23. Lamin, 'Getting its own back'.

24. A.W. Dukulé, 'Nigeria Obasanjo hijacks Liberian elections', *The Perspective*, 8 August 2005.

25. C. Duodo, 'Charles Taylor: Will Liberia get him back?', *The Guardian*, 17 March 2006.

13

The International Criminal Tribunal for Rwanda

Reconciling the Acquitted

Wambui Mwangi

INTRODUCTION

After a conflict that has resulted in the extermination of a tenth of the population, such as the genocide in Rwanda in 1994, the concept of rebuilding a nation and implementing a proactive policy of national reconciliation demands more than simply bringing those who have committed crimes to justice. The choice between the pursuit of truth through a judicial process or reconstructing peace necessitates a delicate balancing act. While it is evident that criminal justice systems play an important role in efforts to regulate past injustices and restore the rule of law, an essential step towards social reconciliation through a criminal justice process is that of ownership. This stems from a perception that the society that has risen from the ashes of the conflict has a degree of ownership in the process that is intended to restore national reconciliation and peaceful co-existence. It is often the case that victims can make peace with their perpetrators only if their suffering is both publicly acknowledged and justice is seen to have been done.

In the past 50 years the international community has experimented with varying models of transitional justice that range from international ad hoc tribunals, hybrid courts, truth and reconciliation commissions (TRCs), and grass-roots systems of justice to 'official amnesia'. All of these systems have been created as part of the international peacebuilding effort that comes in the wake of conflict. As the African continent strives to find models for both the prosecution of perpetrators and the broader role these prosecutions could play in the national reconciliation of countries emerging from post-conflict environments, examining the effect of acquittals on these processes could play a crucial role. The question discussed in this chapter is whether, when examined in relation to acquitted individuals, truth, justice and peace can co-exist in the process of reconciliation.

The first section of the chapter critically reviews the establishment of the International Criminal Tribunal for Rwanda (ICTR), questioning the 'ownership' of the process by both the government and the people of Rwanda. The chapter then outlines some general considerations in relation to acquitted persons and concludes with a discussion of one issue that will prove crucial in future debates: whether the success of the ICTR in delivering justice, if it is unable to implement its judgments of acquittal fully, should also be measured according to its ability to contribute to national reconciliation in Rwanda. It is not my intention to discuss the arguments of restorative versus retributive justice; however, particular aspects of both play an important role when examining the questions raised here.

THE PERCEPTION OF OWNERSHIP

In the search for the most appropriate balance when prosecuting atrocities such as those witnessed in Rwanda both the international community and civil society have been equally divided. In recognition of the complexity of the issues raised there is also a need to acknowledge the fragile tension that prevails when attempting to find a suitable mechanism that both pursues justice and works towards repairing the human psyches, relationships and societies in post-conflict situations such as Rwanda. In that society the competing interests of truth, justice and peace played a unique role in relation to the overall perception of ownership, particularly with respect to the prosecution of members of the former interim government.

In what was a revealing statement in January 2007, the permanent representative of Rwanda to the United Nations (UN) stressed the need for Rwanda to regain full national ownership of the process of the administration of justice for crimes committed during the genocide.[1] This would seem a somewhat odd statement to be made eighteen years after the establishment of the ICTR. Albeit in the context of the transfer of the ICTR's cases to national jurisdictions, the statement raised the question of ownership as it relates to the pursuit of international justice. However, to gain some insight into such a comment it needs to be examined in the context of the establishment of the ICTR and the debates that ensued during its creation.

The Rwandan government was afforded ample opportunity to take control of the national reconciliation process during the 1994 genocide and in its aftermath. Up to the very day before the shooting down of President Juvénal Habyarimana's aircraft in April 1994, certain members of the UN Security Council were still hailing the Arusha Peace Agreement as the blueprint for national reconciliation.[2] Although it would be misleading to come to the immediate conclusion that the Rwandan government or its people were deprived of a chance to retain a degree of ownership in the process, it is also the case that the circumstances in which the ICTR was created were fraught with political complications, both in the Great Lakes Region and in the UN Security Council, of which Rwanda was a member in 1994.

In early 1994 the Security Council expressed its intention for the parties in the Rwandan conflict to avail themselves of the Arusha Peace Agreement as an important aspect in the process of national reconciliation. From the records of Security Council meetings at the time it is apparent that strong messages were sent to the relevant actors that they should take control of the situation and utilise the existing mechanism of the Arusha Peace Accords to achieve this goal. The Security Council, primarily between 21 April and 10 August 1994, appeared insistent that the Arusha Peace Agreement was the only 'viable' and the most 'appropriate framework' for the resolution of the conflict and the basis for the promotion of national reconciliation in Rwanda.[3] Even four months after the genocide the Security Council was still urging the government of Rwanda to maintain an open dialogue with all political interest groups in the country in an effort to achieve genuine reconciliation between all elements of Rwandan society within the frame of reference of the Arusha Peace Agreement.[4] However, by mid-October 1994, when it became apparent that no visible agreement was in sight, the Security Council established the ICTR. This was not viewed as an integral part of the reconciliation process but, in addition to the prosecution of those most responsible for the genocide,[5] as a contribution to this process.

The cracks in the previously unified position of the international community in creating the ICTR began to show a month later. By November 1994 the UN Security Council had decided on the establishment of the ICTR but the tensions between the international community and the government of Rwanda, which occupied one of the rotating seats of the Security Council, were clearly evident. The Security Council and the government of Rwanda had widely diverging views of the role of the ICTR and the concepts of ownership, justice and reconciliation.

While some members envisaged the ICTR playing a valuable role in the process of reconciliation, they could not agree on the degree of its involvement. It was clear that even if the ICTR were to be an 'instrument of national reconciliation', to ensure that those responsible for the crimes committed were punished would be the 'major' but not the sole task of the ICTR.[6]

Of the statements made that November one comment by the Czech Republic was unique in its simple encapsulation of the mandate of the ICTR. The representative noted that justice and reconciliation were opposites and that while the '[T]ribunal might become a vehicle of justice . . . it is hardly designed as a vehicle of reconciliation'. This statement succinctly defined the creature that was later created – a vehicle for justice, not an instrument of national reconciliation.

Ownership raises important and yet exceedingly complex questions, both here and for future tribunals, woven as it is in an intricate web of both judicial and political interests. Rwanda was the strongest advocate of the establishment of the ICTR in 1994; President Pasteur Bizimungu had appeared before the UN General Assembly in October 1994 and told the international community that 'it is absolutely urgent that this international Tribunal be established'.[7] However, of the fifteen members of the UN Security Council, only one country voted against the creation of the ICTR in November 1994: Rwanda.[8]

Since 1994 the government of Rwanda has criticised the ICTR on a myriad of issues, including, but not limited to, the costs involved, the slow pace of the trials, the transfer of cases to other jurisdictions and the possibility of Rwandan Patriotic Front (RPF) indictments. However, it is arguable that the common thread in its critique, irrespective of whether it is justified or not, stems from its sense of a loss of control and ownership in the process of setting up the ICTR. At the UN Security Council meeting in November 1994 Rwanda gave several reasons to explain its sole dissenting voice against the creation of the ICTR.[9] Rwanda's 'no' vote was an early indication of the relationship that would then ensue between the government and the ICTR. To date, the relationship between the ICTR and Rwandan authorities is still not known for its co-operation or mutual respect.

In 1994 Rwanda argued that the genocide witnessed in April of that year was the result of a long period of planning – several massacres had occurred as early as 1990. For this reason Rwanda sought to have the temporal jurisdiction of the ICTR account for crimes committed before 1994. However, Rwanda was unable to influence the temporal jurisdiction of the ICTR as determined by the UN Security Council. The limitation that was set automatically excluded crimes committed prior to 1 January 1994 and limited the jurisdiction of the ICTR to an end date of 31 December 1994.

Rwanda also had no control over the composition and structure of the ICTR. At the time it requested that more trial judges be appointed and that a separate Appellate Chamber and prosecutor be created. Ironically, apart from the Appellate Chamber, these same requests were to be granted seven years later. On 14 August 2002, in accordance with UN Security Council resolution 1431 (2002), the Security Council, in the light of the looming completion strategy deadline, established a pool of *ad litem* judges to assist in the work of the ICTR and expedite proceedings. On 28 August 2003, pursuant to UN Security Council resolution 1503 (2003), the Security Council was convinced that the ICTR would meet its responsibilities more 'effectively and efficiently' if it had its own prosecutor. In addition, Rwanda expressed its unease at being unable to influence the election and composition of judges who could have been nationals of certain member states that Rwanda believed had taken 'an active part in the civil war'.

Rwanda also felt removed from the consultation process that determined the crimes the ICTR would prosecute. The permanent representative for Rwanda expressed concern that genocide might be 'relegate[ed] to a secondary level' as neither the draft resolution nor the statute 'indicat[ed] the order of priority for crimes considered by the Tribunal'.

Furthermore, Rwanda felt that the decision to enforce the sentences of those convicted by the ICTR outside the territory that the crimes occurred in was difficult to accept, especially as those third states would 'reach decision about the detainees'. The permanent representative of Rwanda stressed that this should be a decision for 'the international Tribunal or at least for the Rwandese people to decide'. In 2007, Rwanda repeated this request, arguing that 'it [was] vital' that those convicted at the Tribunal should serve their sentences in the country where they had committed their crimes.[10]

On the related issue of fugitives, Rwanda expressed concern at the demise of a draft resolution that would have recommended and authorised 'State Members of the United Nations that [were] harbouring known Rwandese criminals to arrest them and to place them in preventative detention'. The issue of fugitives was again addressed in the UN Security Council meeting on 18 June 2007, where the prosecutor-general of Rwanda, Martin Ngoga, appealed to the international community to 'take urgent measures to ensure that those indictees did not evade justice'.[11]

At the time, the Rwanda Penal Code provided for the imposition of the death penalty for those who 'devised, planned and organized the genocide'. Rwanda stressed that, by excluding the possibility of capital punishment as a sentence, this would create a disparity in sentences between the ICTR and the domestic prosecutions and would not be 'conducive to national reconciliation in Rwanda'. Accordingly, in July 2007, Rwanda enacted legislation abolishing the death penalty in that country.[12]

In 1994 the Rwandan permanent representative, regretting that the seat of the ICTR would not be in Rwanda, hoped that it would take Rwandan realities into account.[13] At the time and in light of the extreme physical and structural devastation in the country, including the capital of Kigali, it seemed sensible to establish the ICTR in a country other than Rwanda. However, lack of proximity to the ICTR left Rwandans extremely limited in their ability to observe and participate in the trials. Except for those testifying before the ICTR or those with the means to travel to Tanzania, Rwandans have remained otherwise detached from the ICTR's proceedings. It was, therefore, whether justified or not, very clear from the beginning that Rwandan communities felt removed from the ownership of the very Tribunal that had been created to try those most responsible for the violations of international humanitarian law that had been committed in their country.

The question of ownership comes in tandem with that of national reconciliation and the role of the justice process. In this case, the UN Security Council envisaged the use of an international justice system to salve the wounds of the Rwandan nation so that the country could begin the arduous task of moving on. However, in the context of establishing this Tribunal, the relevant stakeholders viewed the definition of 'reconciliation' quite differently. Upon examination of the official records of the Security Council it would appear that the Tribunal was created for two specific purposes: firstly, as a 'vehicle of justice' to prosecute those responsible for serious violations of international humanitarian law in the territory of Rwanda and, secondly, to ensure that the international community took account of the events that had occurred in Rwanda. This was a measure taken to *contribute* to the process of national reconciliation in Rwanda and to the maintenance of peace in the region.

The ICTR and the government of Rwanda have always maintained tense relations, with the government criticising a court it claims has had no impact on Rwanda. In spite of the more recent auxiliary efforts of the ICTR to reach out to the Rwandan people through its Outreach Programme and the undeniable contribution the ICTR has made to the development of international humanitarian law, its impact on the restoration of relationships between, or reconciliation among, the people of Rwanda has been anything but remarkable. In a notable survey conducted by the Human Rights Centre at the University of California, Berkeley, it was found that of the 2 091 persons interviewed, 87.2 per cent claimed either not to be well informed or informed at all about the ICTR.[14] According to this survey, many felt that they could not express an opinion about the Tribunal due to a lack of information. However, despite the lack of information, there was a generally positive attitude to the work of the ICTR. Of those who felt sufficiently informed (22.8 per cent), more than 50 per cent were of the opinion that the Tribunal functioned well. The conclusion of the survey was that a negative opinion of the Tribunal remained a minority one – in stark contrast to the overwhelmingly negative rhetoric of the Rwandan government. This view does not translate into accessibility on the part of the ICTR to the local Rwandan, however. The survey showed that 55 per cent of those interviewed were of the opinion that the Tribunal had promoted reconciliation in Rwanda but only 29.5 per cent of respondents felt that it had contributed or significantly contributed to this process. Most of the respondents (79.1 per cent) felt that it was the domestic genocide trials held in Rwanda that had either contributed or significantly contributed to reconciliation.[15] Tangible successes are, however, imperative to building support and enthusiasm for initiatives such as the ICTR. Judging from this survey, the Tribunal had a limited impact on the Rwandan people in terms of ownership, accessibility and information.

These issues, which have caused the government of Rwanda much dissatisfaction with respect to the ICTR, its work and its structure, have only intensified. The current contentious issues relate to ownership of the Tribunal's work upon closure, the transfer of pending cases, the legacy of the Tribunal and the location of the archives. Rwanda insists that it should play a bigger role in the completion strategy of the Tribunal and take over the functions of future prosecutions and the preservation of its legacy.[16] As the ICTR approaches the final stretch of its mandate it is apparent that Rwanda has played a minimal role in the discussions concerning the legacy and residual mechanisms that will succeed the Tribunal after December 2010.

One thing is clear: there is no magic formula and no clear or easy answers. In a nation so evidently torn apart and still grappling with the fact that a tenth of its population has been exterminated, the business of seeking justice *and* reconciliation whilst ensuring that the communities most affected retain a sense of ownership in the process is a decidedly tricky and messy one.

RECONCILING THE ACQUITTED

In light of the above, what impact do acquittals have on the concepts of ownership, reconciliation and the competing interests of truth, justice and peace? When an international tribunal such as this one is established to 'contribute' to a national healing process, justice as seen and done is not limited to victims and witnesses but to those accused and, in this case, those acquitted.

Since 2001, the ICTR has acquitted five persons: Ignace Bagilishema (former mayor of Mabanza commune), Andre Ntagerura (former minister of transport), Emmanuel Bagambiki (former *prefet* of the Cyangugu), Jean Mpambara (former mayor of Rukara commune), and Andre Rwamakuba (former minister of primary and secondary education). Of these, Bagilishema, Bagambiki and Mpambara have been successfully relocated to states where their immediate families reside. Ntagerura and Rwamakuba remain in Arusha, with no prospect of a state to which they can relocate.

In certain circumstances acquittals may not only call into question the credibility of the institution involved but may also result in consequences that, although arguably necessary, may not be entirely fair. The situation of Hans Fritzsche uniquely demonstrates this scenario and the effect an acquittal may have upon a society going through a reconciliation process. In October 1946, the International Military Tribunal in Nuremberg acquitted Hans Fritzsche, a senior official in Goebbels's ministry of popular enlightenment and propaganda as well as head of the ministry's Radio Division from 1942 onwards.[17] Fritzsche had been charged with conspiracy to commit crimes against peace, war crimes and crimes against humanity as well as for using propaganda as an instrument of aggression, 'an important and essential factor in the success of the conducting of an aggressive war'.[18] However, shortly after his acquittal, in what today would probably be considered a case of double jeopardy, Fritzsche was re-arrested and prosecuted before a German court in Nuremberg, the *Spruchkammer I*, in connection with the de-Nazification trials that were conducted in Germany after the Second World War. The court decided that Fritzsche belonged in a category of Nazi criminals comprising those most guilty and sentenced him to nine years of forced labour for his participation as a 'major offender' in the criminal Nazi regime.[19]

In a similar context, of the five men acquitted by the ICTR, two were government ministers, two were mayors and one was a *prefet*. All men had significant power, were influential in their own right and were charged with the most serious crimes, including genocide.

In June 2001, the acquittal of Ignace Bagilishema was not well received by the non-governmental organisation (NGO), Ibuka. Although it accepted the verdict, Ibuka stated that 'it would profoundly regret if such people were to be acquitted because of inadequacies, incompetence or negligence on the part of prosecutors or Tribunals'.[20] This highlights the perception that the acquittals by the Tribunal were not testament to the innocence of those accused but rather to a lack of due diligence by the ICTR. More recently, in March 2006, the government of Rwanda announced its intention to prosecute Bagambiki for rape and sexual violence as a crime against humanity, a charge not previously brought before the Tribunal.[21] Just over eighteen months later Bagambiki was tried and convicted in Rwanda of these crimes *in absentia*. While there is no question that rape and sexual violence played an integral role in the 1994 genocide, it is debatable whether it would be legally appropriate for Rwanda to try Bagambiki on those charges, given that the ICTR, both at the trial and at his appeal, found that he could not be held responsible for the massacres either directly or through command responsibility. It would therefore follow that he also could not be held responsible for the sexual violence that accompanied those massacres. Rwanda has since called for the extradition of Bagambiki so he may stand trial for these crimes in Rwanda.

The charging and re-arrest of acquitted persons upon a judgment of acquittal on different or similar charges is not an inconsistent pattern with acquittals related to the Rwandan genocide. The government of Rwanda in June 2007 stated that '[w]ith regard to those who have been acquitted by the Tribunal, it is the policy of our country to welcome home every Rwandan who happened to be abroad for any reason. The doors remain open to those who have been acquitted by the Tribunal.'[22] Since 2002, Human Rights Watch has voiced concern about several cases in Rwanda where those tried, acquitted and released were re-arrested following public protests. According to its report:

[E]ight detainees acquitted in Butare in December 2000 were never released and were to be tried a second time on 'new facts'. Magistrates involved in their acquittals have been transferred to other posts with the result that no judgements in genocide cases were issued in that jurisdiction in the first quarter of 2001. Three judges arrested in 2000 on charges of genocide remained in jail; two had served on panels that had acquitted accused persons in well-publicised cases prior to their own arrests.[23]

Notably, after the acquittal of both Ntagerura and Bagambiki in February 2004, the cities of Kigali and Cyangugu in Rwanda saw thousands of protestors take to the streets.[24] At the time, civil society leaders and genocide survivors denounced both the ICTR and the acquitted men and the ministry of justice sent out a communiqué 'categorically denouncing' the acquittals.[25] Acquittals at the ICTR have in general caused public protest and civil disquiet in the regions most affected by the decisions. As was the case with Hans Fritzsche, it appears that Rwanda may not be ready to reconcile itself to acquittals for those it considers to have played an influential role in the genocide of 1994.

As discussed earlier, the ICTR was a measure established, *inter alia*, to contribute to the national reconciliation of Rwanda in the aftermath of the genocide. While it is correct to aver that one aspect of this task would be the enforcement of sentences of those convicted by the Tribunal, surely a related side of the same coin would be to ensure that acquittals are seen as a necessary function of dispensing justice and a visible part of the reconciliation process?

This raises serious difficulties for the ICTR. Although acquittals are a natural consequence of fair trials, in the event that a person is acquitted, the ICTR has no mechanisms to implement this final aspect of justice. Irrespective of the assurances given by the government of Rwanda, the political climate in that country does not appear to make repatriation to Rwanda an attractive prospect for persons acquitted by the ICTR. However, the efforts made by the Tribunal to relocate the acquitted persons to third-party states raise questions such as whether:

- addressing the needs of the acquitted persons contributes to the reconciliation process in Rwanda;
- the dispensing of justice in such cases would serve to threaten peace in the country; and
- the relocation of acquitted persons as a means of fostering peace and ensuring justice should be taken into account by those who establish tribunals and other criminal justice mechanisms that are intended to address such atrocities.

As noted in the survey referred to earlier, the Rwandan population is not fully and adequately informed about the work of the ICTR.[26] More importantly, the survey's significance is in its illustration of the local communities' perception of the ICTR: its lack of contribution to the reconciliation process and the limited impact in terms of ownership, accessibility and information. The underlying reasons behind the demonstrative public outcry in the face of acquittals are therefore neither complicated nor unexpected.

CONCLUSION

The current situation at the ICTR is highly unsatisfactory. The measures the Tribunal has been forced to adopt may hold the pieces together in the short term but this 'Band-Aid' approach only masks the obvious conflict between the concepts of justice and peace as part of a reconciliation process. Justice demands that the acquitted persons are released, permitted to join their families and reintegrated back into society without fear of reprisal. The fragile peace that currently holds Rwanda together requires that they remain hidden and under the control of the ICTR, for concern that their visibility could cause them harm or re-arrest or could create instability in the territory to which they relocate. In order to maintain peace, silence has prevailed.

The specific example of acquitted persons at the ICTR demonstrates how the value of such trials can be severely undermined by other factors brought about by a lack of meaningful participation in the process by those most affected by the crime.[27] The record of the Tribunal in fulfilling its mandate to contribute to the reconciliation process in Rwanda is notably poor. Nevertheless, it would be unacceptable to conclude that Africa is not ready for the co-existence of peace and justice in the aftermath of events such as those in Rwanda in 1994. Furthermore, it would be inconceivable that, in an era that has catapulted international criminal systems into the twenty-first century, national healing should demand convictions and be incapable of tolerating acquittals, however fair the determination may be.

It remains questionable in this case whether a sense of justice can ever develop in the wake of acquittals, if the majority of those communities affected remain not only passive in, but removed from, such a system's proceedings. Notwithstanding that acquittals are a testimony to justice at work, justice on its own, while undoubtedly a necessary dimension of any reconciliation process and sustainable peace, is incapable of rebuilding a society that enjoys restored relationships, trust and co-operation.[28] It seems that in the aftermath of a mass atrocity, the pursuit of the fragile and necessary balance between peace and justice can be achieved only where restorative efforts and reconciliatory initiatives go hand in hand and are not seen as alternatives to each other. As Africa considers the different options available to it in the future, one significant lesson that emerges from the circumstances of the acquitted persons at the ICTR is that a model that draws upon both the restorative and the retributive theories of justice will not only result in a prevailing sense of justice but will also serve to balance what at first may appear to be insurmountable competing interests.

NOTES AND REFERENCES

The views expressed in this chapter are those of the author, a legal officer at the UN, and do not necessarily reflect the views of the UN.

1. S. Nieuwoudt, 'Rwanda tribunal under pressure to wind up', Institute of War and Peace Reporting, 22 January 2007, www.iwpr.net/?p=acr&s=f&o=328694&apc_state=heniacr6636bfa152948a 9e9efa6f2d15aa424e (accessed 12 September 2007).
2. Official Records of the Security Council, UN Doc S/PV.3358 (5 April 1994), p. 6.
3. Official Records of the Security Council, UN Doc S/PV.3368 (21 April 1994); UN Doc S/PV.3371 (30 April 1994), p. 3; UN Doc S/PV.3377 (16 May 1994), pp. 9, 12, 15; UN Doc S/PV.3388 (8 June 1994), pp. 11, 12; UN Doc S/PV.3392 (22 June 1994), p. 9; UN Doc S/PV.3402 (11 July 1994), p. 4; UN Doc S/PV.3405 (14 July 1994), p. 2; UN Doc S/PV.3414 (10 August 1994), p. 3.
4. Official Records of the Security Council, UN Doc S/PV.3436 (14 October 1994), p. 3.
5. Official Records of the Security Council, UN Doc S/PV.3326 (6 January 1994), p. 9.
6. Official Records of the Security Council, UN Doc S/PV.3453 (8 November 1994).
7. Official Records of the General Assembly, UN Doc A/49/PV.21 (6 October 1994), p. 5.
8. China was the only member of the UN Security Council to abstain.
9. Official Records of the Security Council, UN Doc S/PV.3453 (8 November 1994), pp. 13–16.
10. Official Records of the Security Council, UN Doc S/PV.5697 (18 June 2007), p. 33.
11. Official Records of the Security Council, UN Doc S/PV.5697 (18 June 2007), p. 32.
12. Official Records of the Security Council, UN Doc S/PV.5697 (18 June 2007), p. 33.
13. Official Records of the Security Council, UN Doc S/PV.3453 (8 November 1994), p. 16.
14. T. Longman, P. Pham, and H. Weinstein, 'Connecting justice to human experience: Attitudes towards accountability and reconciliation in Rwanda', in E. Stover and H. Weinstein (eds.), *My neighbor, my enemy: Justice and community in the aftermath of mass atrocity* (Cambridge: Cambridge University Press, 2004), pp. 206–225.
15. Longman et al., 'Connecting justice to human experience'.
16. Longman et al., 'Connecting justice to human experience'.
17. R. Gellately (ed.), *The Nuremberg interviews conducted by Leon Goldensohn* (New York: Alfred A Knopf, 2004), p. 47; T. Taylor, *The anatomy of the Nuremberg trials* (Toronto: Little, Brown and Company, 1992), pp. 460–462.

18. H. Goring, *The trial of German major war criminals: Proceedings of the International Military Tribunal sitting at Nuremberg, Germany, 20th November 1945 to 1st October 1946* (London: HM Stationery Office, 1946–1951), p. 526.

19. *Hans Fritzsche Judgment*, Aktenzeichen I/2398, Spruchkammer I, Stadtkreis Nürnberg, 31 January 1947, Staatsarchiv München, SpKa Karton 475, pp. 1, 3–4, 8–9, 15.

20. 'Belgian justice', Hirondelle News Agency (Lausanne), 11 June 2001, www.hirondelle.org/ hirondelle.nsf/caefd9edd48f5826c12564cf004f793d/655dbe9da551e5fec1256a69004272e7? opendocument (accessed 6 May 2007).

21. 'Rwanda intends to prosecute ex-Governor Emmanuel Bagambiki for rape', Hirondelle News Agency (Lausanne), 8 March 2006, www.publicinternationallaw.org/warcrimeswatch/archives/ wcpw_vol01issue03.html#rw2 (accessed 6 May 2007).

22. Official Records of the Security Council, UN Doc S/PV.5697 (19 June 2007), p. 33.

23. Human Rights Watch, 'World Report 2002: Rwanda', hrw.org/wr2k2/africa9.html (accessed 11 May 2007).

24. S. Nieuwoudt, 'Rwandan compensation award sets precedent', Institute of War and Peace Reporting, 2 April 2007, www.globalpolicy.org/intljustice/tribunals/rwanda/2007/ 0402compensation.htm (accessed 11 May 2007).

25. Global Policy Forum, 'Thousands demonstrate against the UN tribunal', 29 February 2004, www.globalpolicy.org/intljustice/tribunals/rwanda/2004/0229against.htm (accessed 11 May 2007).

26. Longman et al., 'Connecting justice to human experience'.

27. W. Lambourne, 'The pursuit of justice and reconciliation: Responding to genocide in Cambodia and Rwanda', International Studies Association, 40th Annual Convention, Washington, DC, 16–20 February 1999; I. Amadiume and A.N. Abdullahi, 'Facing truth: Voicing justice', in I. Amadiume and A.N. Abdullahi (eds.), *The politics of memory: Truth, healing and social justice* (London: Zed Books, 2000), pp. 1–19.

28. A. Rigby, *Justice and reconciliation: After the violence* (Boulder, CO: Lynne Rienner, 2001), pp. 175–188.

PART IV

Indigenous Justice

14

The Politics of Peace, Justice and Healing in Post-war Mozambique

'Practices of Rupture' by *Magamba* Spirits and Healers in Gorongosa

Victor Igreja

INTRODUCTION

This chapter addresses the politics of peace, healing and justice in the aftermath of the civil war in Mozambique. Specifically, it examines 'practices of rupture' implemented by war survivors in post-civil war Gorongosa (central Mozambique) in order to keep peace, create healing and attain justice. 'Practices of rupture' refer to a set of socio-cultural mechanisms and strategies involving spiritual agents that induce war survivors in Gorongosa to break the silence imposed by the national political elites over the civil war abuses and crimes. These 'practices of rupture', which are bodily and discursively enacted, are culturally rooted in many societies in sub-Saharan Africa. A key feature of these practices is that spiritual agents play different roles in order to help living people make sense of violent wartime experiences. These practices illustrate a local form of post-war justice in which war survivors are called upon to assume their own individual and collective responsibilities over some of the events of the civil war.

The Mozambican civil war terminated without one military faction vanquishing the other. Both historically and recently, in cases of military victory, the victorious faction has been able to shape, without much commotion, the course of the transitional justice processes.[1] Whether or not transitional justice following due processes[2] or revolutionary justice is placed *en démarche*, the victorious faction is free to use its own laws and political strategies to reckon with the past without major political impact.

The fact that the Mozambican transition from civil war to peace and from a totalitarian dictatorship to a liberal democracy was continuously under the control of the FRELIMO-led government, coupled with the fact that the transition was enacted through a negotiated process and that the parties in conflict had been involved in the perpetration of serious abuses and war crimes, may have shaped the choice of the model of transitional justice that was followed. Consequently, peace was forged through silence, amnesties and impunity. Samuel Huntington notes that 'virtually every authoritarian regime that initiated its transformation to democracy also decreed an amnesty as a part of that process' since they 'obviously did not wish to be prosecuted for crimes they may have committed'.[3] Clearly criminal justice is not the only mechanism available to deal with past abuses and crimes in periods of transition. That is, 'consolidating democracies have a wide range of options with regard to justice and accountability: they can pursue selective prosecutions, purges and even commissions of enquiry that lay bare the legacy of the past'.[4] Despite this array of alternatives, which could have lent more legitimacy to the Mozambican transitional process, very little was done to reconcile the country to the horrors of the civil war.

The parties to the Mozambican General Peace Agreement (*Acordo Geral de Paz*, AGP), the Liberation Front of Mozambique (FRELIMO) and the Mozambican National Resistance (RENAMO), deliberately precluded any possibility for the enactment of a mechanism for justice that could reckon with the grave abuses and war crimes. Justice was considered inimical to the peace-building process and was therefore replaced with a discourse of reconciliation that was expressed through oblivion and silence. Within this context of political and legal impunity and attempts to forge silence and amnesia, this chapter sets out to explore the 'practices of rupture' that have been used as an alternative to the formal political processes and community-based strategies normally employed to deal with the intricate legacies of a civil war. It has been demonstrated that through these 'practices of rupture', unleashed at community level, it is possible to achieve a balance between peace and justice. Specifically, this chapter examines the role played by a war-related spirit called *gamba* (*magamba* in the plural) which creates serious afflictions and post-war healing as well as establishes the opportunity for war survivors to foster a durable peace, experience healing and find justice in Gorongosa, a district located in Sofala Province in central Mozambique. This former war zone was chosen because of the high degree of violence there during the civil war. The majority of civilians remained within the war zones; they continuously and dangerously shifted from being under the control of the governmental forces to being under that of the rebels and vice versa. At the end of the war the former perpetrators, victims, bystanders and cowards all had to live in precisely the same places where the violence had taken place. This type of post-war circumstance, coupled with the official silence and impunity, is generally considered to be prone to the eruption of new cycles of violence. The post-war Gorongosa context offers an opportunity to check the cross-cultural validity of these assumptions and also to demonstrate, following Clifford Geertz, that law and justice are indeed 'crafts of place: they work by the light of local knowledge'.[5] In order to grasp the local dimensions of attaining justice, Geertz suggests the need to focus on how different legal institutions 'translate between [the] language of imagination and one of decision and form thereby a determinate sense of justice'.[6]

This chapter is divided into three sections. The following section describes some aspects of the civil war and the way in which the peace negotiations were conducted. This includes two sub-sections that demonstrate how the parties to the Mozambican peace agreement seemed obsessed with the future, as if there had been no terrible past for which they were responsible and as if the millions of victims waiting for words of recognition and acknowledgement did not exist. The second section presents the central theme of this chapter: the 'practices of rupture' enacted by *magamba* spirits that have allowed many survivors from the former epicentres of the civil war to create healing and justice. This general description is complemented by a case study of someone suffering under the influence of a *gamba* spirit, to more vividly illustrate the values of truth, justice, authority and healing that are embodied by these war-related spirits. The final section presents the main conclusions of the chapter and suggests the need for further research into community-based practices that attempt to deal with the multiple dimensions of the legacies of civil war.

THE CIVIL WAR AND THE POLITICS OF PEACEBUILDING

For nearly 30 years Mozambicans, particularly those from rural areas, have lived under overwhelming cycles of violent instability. There have been ten years of an armed struggle for independence (1964–1974), direct foreign aggression perpetrated by the Ian Smith regime from former Rhodesia, a decade of Marxist–

Leninist dictatorship under FRELIMO party rule, and a post-colonial civil war that lasted for sixteen years (1976–1992). The most overwhelming experiences took place in the wake of the civil war that set the military forces of the FRELIMO-led government against the rebel movement, RENAMO. It was a protracted and very bloody war that resulted in incredible tragedies.[7] In the rural areas, in particular, villages and properties were destroyed, people and their villages suffered aerial bombardment, men accused of supporting the rebel movement were subjected to extrajudicial torture and killing, women were raped and young girls were forced to marry soldiers. There were also betrayals by neighbours and family members, food deprivation and fatal famine. Civilian people living in the war zones were divided between RENAMO-controlled areas and the government-controlled communal villages. They shifted continually from one controlled area to another in search of safety. This search was in vain, as neither area provided safety from the extreme insecurity and continual traumatic experiences of the war.

In the mid-1980s the civil war spread across the entire country, engendering a staggering spectrum of destruction and death. At approximately the same time a contingent of the Zimbabwean army joined the war in Mozambique in support of the FRELIMO-led government but even the involvement of these external forces in the direct military combat did not make it possible for either side to achieve a military victory. The military rhetoric and propaganda of 'enemy defeat' could no longer be sustained and the civil war was characterised by brutal violence that was perpetrated by all the sides, a fact that clearly indicated that there could be no military solution to the situation. Towards the end of the 1980s, Christian religious groups that were in close consultation with the FRELIMO-led government initiated attempts at peace negotiations between FRELIMO and RENAMO. After various failed attempts, the most serious peace talks were initiated in Rome in 1990, involving a team of national and international mediators – both religious and non-religious – as well as diplomatic efforts aimed at brokering the peace talks.[8]

The politics of peacemaking precluded the possibility of pursuing this goal in parallel with transitional justice measures such as retributive and restorative justice. Reconciliation was used as the main tool for peacemaking and took a particular form, based as it was on two interrelated principles. The first was, 'together we stand, divided we fall', and in order for Mozambicans to stand together, a second principle was applied: focus on what unites and rule out what divides. The Catholic Archbishop of Beira (Sofala Province), Don Jaime

Gonçalves, one of the Mozambican mediators in the peace process, stated that without these two principles it could have proved very difficult to reach a peace settlement. The implementation of justice was perceived to be a highly incendiary process and was therefore never brought to the negotiation table.[9]

Reconciliation through the adoption of a policy of silence about the extreme violent episodes of the past and through embracing new attitudes was regarded as the necessary precondition for the ceasefire. Because neither the peace nor the rules that would govern the new democratic society was militarily imposed, 'sweeping the dust under the carpet' seemed to be the pragmatic strategy to adopt in reaching a peace settlement that would prove conducive to terminating the war. Nevertheless, the AGP does not contain a specific clause or protocol that mandates the opponents to forgive one another and to forget what happened. The past was hushed up through a gentlemen's agreement.

Impunity within the political context of incredible human rights violations and crimes raises serious questions regarding responsibility for the plight of the victims – those ordinary men, women and children who were killed by acts that far exceeded the bounds of the ordinary laws of war. Whose responsibility is the predicament of those individuals who were severely tortured or murdered simply on suspicion of being a FRELIMO or RENAMO member? There are also a number of civilians that the Zimbabwean troops assassinated, mainly in the centre of Mozambique.

The civil war fostered hatred and deep divisions among families and community members at the grassroots level. Many soldiers from FRELIMO and RENAMO committed unlawful acts of sexual intercourse: the rape of young and virgin girls, the rape of married and older women. Moreover, under the command of the late President Samora Machel, the FRELIMO-led army was responsible for dropping heavy bombs intended 'to transform the centre of Mozambique into the grave of the armed bandits',[10] which instead killed thousands of civilians. Under these circumstances it is appropriate to doubt the validity of the official adoption of silence and impunity about these abuses and war crimes. In contexts of emergent plural democracies there is a need to pose critical questions about the future of formal state-building processes that preclude measures of legal accountability for war crimes and neglect the plight of countless victims.

The peace agreement and the serious neglect of the victims

The conclusion of the Mozambican peace agreement was regarded as a reconciliation event.[11] However, during this event the authorities erased all mention of the war victims from their speeches as though they had never existed. They seemed uniquely obsessed with the future, insisting on 'multi-party elections'. None of the authorities used this momentum for reconciliation to assume their share of responsibility and remorse for the plight and suffering of the living and dead victims, or even to demonstrate compassion for and understanding of their predicament.

For instance, Joaquim Alberto Chissano, the former FRELIMO party president and Mozambique's president from 1986–2004, pursued the strategy of amnesia by affirming that the peace agreement meant: 'A victory of the Mozambican people where there was no place for losers or for winners.'[12] It remains unclear to which people Chissano was referring – FRELIMO members or the large majority of non-partisans, the living or the dead, or rural versus urban. Chissano avoided the issue by stating: 'The national reconciliation is the responsibility of all Mozambicans; we all together must engage in healing the wounds, to replace the hatred with understanding and solidarity, vengeance with forgiveness and tolerance, the distrust with fraternity and friendship.' He did not seek to address directly the demands and suffering of the victims but focused instead on the need for reconciliation.

Afonso Dhlakama, RENAMO's president, attempted to address the issue a little more openly when he stated at the beginning of his speech:

> We want to address some words for those who fell in this event. We remember in the first place, our dead brothers, all the Mozambicans, combatants and non-combatants, from one or the other side, fallen in this fratricidal struggle: their blood was not shed in vain and above their sacrifice a renewed and reconciled nation will rise up . . . Let's start anew, let's work together to rebuild the country.[13]

Dhlakama's statement was a positive starting point in that it suggested adopting the politics of acknowledgement, that is, an official and public recognition of people's suffering as a result of one's own actions or the wrongdoings of the group one represents. However, Dhlakama did not give any explicit indication that he regretted that so many people had been dehumanised and brutally killed during the conflict and that he and his army had been one of the parties responsible for this. He did not propose any tangible efforts or ideas on how to start anew or on exactly how the renewed and reconciled nation would rise up from its shattered past.

Various experts in the field of transitional justice have defended the idea that in the aftermath of gross human rights violations and crimes truth must prevail over denial and oblivion, and justice over impunity.[14] In the various arguments defending the necessity of some measure of accountability as part of the transitional justice process, one underlying preoccupation is that of keeping faith with the victims in terms of their honour and dignity. For instance, Alex Boraine, a key figure on the South African Truth and Reconciliation Commission (TRC), emphasised the centrality of the victims and of justice in itself to justify the struggle against impunity in that country (see Chapter 6 in this volume). He stated: 'For the sake of justice, for stability and restoration of dignity to victims, there must be accountability for the past.'[15] In this context, silence is an unacceptable offence, 'a shocking implication that the perpetrators in fact succeeded [and] inaction by legal institutions means that the perpetrators prevailed in paralysing the instruments of justice'.[16]

In Mozambique, the authorities involved in the peace negotiations generally failed to restore the dignity of the war victims. Mozambican survivors, as with survivors in many other war-affected countries, were considered by the state to be unimportant, isolated peoples living in remote areas.[17] Instead, the Mozambican authorities adopted what Bruce Ackerman calls a forward-looking approach through constitutional change, and so the establishment of institutions for the development of democracy was given priority status.[18]

Perhaps the responsibility for the failure to engage in any formal process of transitional justice in Mozambique and to develop measures to restore the dignity of victims cannot be attributed solely to the principal political actors, FRELIMO and RENAMO. Other agents of transitional justice, particularly victims, helpers, resisters, neutrals, promoters, judges and prosecutors,[19] should have played an active role in promoting a fairer resolution of the course of the transition in Mozambique. However, they did not organise themselves as civil society groups in order to pressurise the political elites into developing specific policies to deal with the gruesome past.[20]

Post-war politics and issues of timing, amnesties, revenge and forgiveness

From a careful analysis of the AGP and the speeches made during the official ceremony at which the peace agreements were signed it could be argued that the issue of post-war justice was omitted only because it had not been explicitly ruled out of post-war politics. It is obvious that at a later date, in a period of democratic consolidation, a new scenario may emerge in which the necessity for justice could prevail. It is known that 'what is feasible varies not simply with the particular context of each country, but with the "period" of transition the country is in'.[21]

In Mozambique, however, this was not the case. Ten days after the signing of the AGP, the Mozambican Popular Assembly, at the time controlled by the FRELIMO party, suddenly passed a law that left no room for second thoughts regarding either post-civil war politics and the possibilities for criminal trials or any other accountability measure. Law No 13/92 promulgated by the Mozambican Popular Assembly gave legal recognition to the AGP; it was followed by the approval of Law No 15/92 that granted unconditional amnesties for crimes committed between 1979 and 1992.[22]

Huntington suggests that the purpose of the amnesty law was simply to secure long-term legal impunity for those who had been directly and indirectly involved in the commission of serious crimes up to the date of the peace agreement.[23] The enactment of this law can also be interpreted as part of FRELIMO's struggle to maintain political power and control. Anne Pitcher, writing on the related topic of the FRELIMO-driven politics of forgetting that was its response to the socialist era in Mozambique, suggests that 'the articulation and projection of organized forgetting by the ruling party is an important element in its retention of power'.[24]

Within the context of the post-civil war politics of impunity and the abandonment of ordinary war survivors, we have to consider the following aspects: the Mozambican war survivors' painful memories of violence and abuse did not fade away simply because of the authorities' unwillingness to address them officially. It is therefore important to consider possible socio-cultural responses to the legacies of civil war violence. In order to understand the locally available socio-cultural approaches to dealing with the effects of extreme political violence, we have to analyse how the 'local world mediates between broader political forces and the responses of individuals'.[25] By focusing on the dynamics of local worlds that have been ravaged by civil wars we can acquire knowledge about the extent to which war survivors comply with or develop 'practices of rupture' from state policies that are aimed at dealing with the legacies of a violent past. However, to date, publications on transitional justice have paid little attention to the dynamics underlying the mediations of local experiences of violence.[26] Mainstream literature often suggests two possible outcomes to political violence and consequent amnesia and impunity: revenge or forgiveness.

Attitudes of revenge, which are frequently discussed in the literature, have been described as primary reactions to perceived or real injustices: it has been argued that 'the instinct for revenge is as elementary as thirst or sexual desire'.[27] In contexts of silence and the resulting political impunity, David Crocker suggests: 'Social amnesia fails to give either the perpetrators or victims of atrocities their due. Repressed emotions of rage, humiliation, and fear can be expressed in uncontrolled and harmful ways. Justified indignation gets transformed into irrational vengeance. Public virtue becomes private vice. The goal of forgetting turns into the goal of revenge.'[28] It has also been suggested that 'cycles of violence sometimes then make perpetrators and their supporters victims of new waves of vengeful responses. How those who survive understand and remember what happened can have real consequences for the chances of renewed violence.'[29]

From a cross-cultural perspective it is largely unclear to what extent in fact 'revenge is as elementary as thirst or sexual desire' or 'the goal of forgetting turns into the goal of revenge' and under what circumstances 'new waves of vengeful responses' may take place. In the wake of injustices the desire for revenge may indeed be present. What is intriguing and remains crucial is the extent to which, in the aftermath of political violence, vengeful feelings are expressed within different cultures. To what extent do official policies of transitional justice decisively shape the manner in which victims of abuse and grave injustice perceive and deal with their predicament?

Writing on the South African TRC, Richard Wilson indicates that there are indeed local forces that mediate between broader political forces and the responses of individuals. Wilson demonstrates that the official policies of transitional justice as enacted by the post-apartheid South African regime did correspond to the prevailing popular notions and feelings about how best to deal with the legacies of a violent past. Based on ethnographic research in some townships of Johannesburg, Wilson concluded that 'contra the established view within the TRC, retributive understandings of justice are much more salient in South African society than versions emphasizing reconciliation as forgiveness'.[30] In light of these discrepancies in expectations and options that existed between political elites and the ordinary victims of human rights violations, we still have to question whether there is a similar reaction across different cultures amongst victims of gross human rights violations and crimes. In order to determine whether political impunity generates similar reactions universally, we need to analyse particular case studies. For instance, is it always the case that abuse and injustice practised during war and the post-war impunity that follows lead to feelings and acts of revenge among victims? How do local cultures develop mechanisms to deal with the legacies of a violent past in ways that do not incorporate agendas of hatred and repetitive violence? To what extent are war survivors capable of repairing their devastated social world by using available notions of truth, justice and healing?

Forgiveness as a response to gross human rights violations and crime has received far less attention in the literature than revenge has. Forgiveness, wrote Hannah Arendt in *The human condition*, 'serves to undo the deeds of the past' and the dismissing of bitterness is necessary 'in order to make it possible for life to go on'.[31] Wole Soyinka, also writing on forgiveness, suggests:

> [T]here is something about the magnitude of some wrongs that transcends the feelings of vengeance, even of redress in any form. A kind of crimino-critical mass after which wrongs and suffering are transmuted into a totally different stage of sensibility from which can only derive a sense of peace, a space of Truth that overawes all else and chastens the human moral dimension. It is not a surrender to evil, not a condoning of wrongs.[32]

The conceptualisations of forgiveness by Arendt and Soyinka offer significant insights into the events that followed the end of the civil war in Mozambique, particularly in the communities that were directly ravaged by the violence and then experienced the effects of generalised political and legal impunity. Political impunity in Mozambique did not generate new cycles of hatred and vengeful violence at the community level. War survivors living in the former epicentres of the civil war violence did not fall into the trap of individual and collective bitterness and revenge; they unilaterally forgave and they engaged in *practices of rupture* from the formal political processes that attempted to promote either reconciliation without truth or reconciliation through amnesia. The rupture took the form of the development of effective community-based strategies to deal with the challenges of achieving both peace and justice. One meaningful strategy is enacted through the work of war-related spirits. This breaks with the prevailing silence about the grisly past in Gorongosa and forces people to engage actively in serious conversations about the deep divisions and bitterness fostered by the civil war.

MAGAMBA SPIRITS: POST-WAR AFFLICTIONS, JUSTICE AND HEALING STRATEGIES

The use of spiritual forces to make sense of the civil war violence in central Mozambique occurred in communities that already had cultural experiences of creative and resilient pluralism, that is, a set of adaptation practices that assimilates contradiction and encourages contestation and innovation. The model of 'creative and resilient pluralism' proposed by Terence Ranger suggests that African religions have always been multi-layered and dynamic, with a history of contradiction, contestation through appropriation, and innovation. Ranger argues that 'such a model helps to explain the remarkable adaptability of African societies and individuals during changes of colonial capitalism'.[33] Achille Mbembe argues as well that the reappropriation by Africans of the colonial rationality 'was not merely institutional; it also occurred in material spheres and in the sphere of the imaginary'.[34] In certain instances, the sphere of the imaginary was used as a mechanism to contest the colonial rationality.[35] These spirit possession practices can also reach the level of innovation by transferring violent aspects of the past into the field of medicine.

This chapter demonstrates that the model of creative and resilient pluralism is also useful for comprehending the effectiveness of the 'practices of rupture' adopted by many war survivors in the transitional process from civil war to peace and democracy in central Mozambique. These practices of rupture, whose agency is shared between spiritual and human forces, reveal the disjuncture that exists between the strategies applied by the Mozambican political elites and those adopted by the war survivors to address the legacies of the civil war. The rupture from the official strategies of silence allows war survivors in Gorongosa to reappropriate the past, that is, to bring the violent past to the present and to convene segregated family members who have not gathered together since the end of the civil war to count their deceased patrikin and engage in conversations about the divisions that may still prevail between them. The combination of these two aspects, that is, the embodiment of the violent past and family reunification, facilitates healing and the attainment of justice.

Gamba (*magamba* in plural) is the name of a spirit, an affliction and also the healer who specialises in *gamba* afflictions.[36] Generally *magamba* are spirits of male soldiers who died during the civil war. Their bodies were not properly buried and people living within the war zones and amid extreme conditions were said to have used pieces of the corpses of fallen soldiers to make protective medicines against the war violence. This was part of a historical belief that 'if you "eat" the dead you become immune to death'. 'Death' can mean either the end of life or a social death. Within this context *magamba* spirits return to the world of the living to fight for justice. The focal points of their struggle are principally (but not exclusively) the bodies of women whose relatives were allegedly involved in the use of protective medicines illicitly made from the corpses of fallen soldiers (known or unknown to them but not kin soldiers), or who were involved in the murder of the soldiers themselves.

Magamba spirits are believed to strike in order to address the post-civil war politics of denial and to fight for justice.[37] These goals are attained in two ways. Firstly, by causing afflictions among war survivors, *magamba* spirits possess the bodies of war survivors and usually impair their reproductive capacities until the needs of the *magamba* spirits are satisfied. The blockage of the reproductive functions of the war survivors constitutes a severe affliction to the host of the spirit, the relatives of the host and society in general.[38] Secondly, in order to deal with *magamba* spirits there is a need to bring some of the past scenes of the war violence into the present so that the process of truth disclosure can be initiated.

This transposition of the past to the present is done by means of discourse, embodiment and performance. During a diagnosis and healing session *magamba* healers and the participants sing songs that evoke war events, suffering and death. While they sing the *magamba* healers enter into a possession state and get hold of the bayonet (sacred instrument). The bayonet brings to the scene of the diagnosis the most violent instrument of war, since these bayonets are considered to be the ones fixed to the front of the Kalashnikovs that the soldiers used to stab and kill many people during the civil war. *Magamba* healers move around during the diagnosis, always carrying their bayonet, re-enacting different types of civil war events – crawling, firing weapons, fighting, aggressively manipulating their bayonets as if they were going to stab people, making strange movements, running, smoking *nbanje* (cannabis) and drinking alcohol.

The principal objective of these performances is to trigger fear in the patient in order to induce the possession state. The patient usually becomes hyper-excited, making uncontrolled body movements, and the participants, instead of singing, start screaming loudly to the spirit to manifest itself. Just before the spirit arrives the patient also gives a loud scream as if he or she is being hurt. During the state of possession, no matter whether the host is a young woman or man, *magamba* spirits are very strong and violent in all aspects: body movements, speech and staring. The local interpretation of the spirit's jostling acts is that the living people have been refusing to acknowledge the past wrongdoing and to assume their responsibilities. The *gamba* healer manages to appease the *gamba* spirit mainly through empathic identification and demonstrates this empathy by saying the following while in a state of trance: '*shamuale* [friend], I know what happened to you. I also suffered the same. Let us know who you are and tell us the truth about what happened to you, so that this family can hear.' The seething and jostling *gamba* spirit subsides and then starts disclosing what happened to him so that every participant can hear it.

When the *gamba* spirit is ready to make the indictments against the alleged perpetrator, these usually refer to the following acts: 'killing of one or more people', 'eating human body parts', or 'stealing the goods of dead people'. These indictments are not readily accepted. There are fierce disputes and the role of the *gamba* healer is to mediate in the proceedings. Since the *gamba* healer is also a survivor of extreme experiences and knows very well the politics of denial, he or she mediates the deliberations between the *gamba* spirit and the indicted person and kin, using as a starting point the principle that *não há fumo sem fogo* (there is no smoke without fire). In order to lead the people to feel and to see the fire that produced the smoke, the *gamba* spirit has to work very hard. Besides making the indictment the role of the *gamba* spirit is to provide more unknown clues that render the accusation indisputable. When this evidence is produced, the indicted person must assume his or her responsibilities. The way in which the evidence production unfolds conforms to the local notions of truth and the mechanisms necessary to disclose it. Truth is something that people can get hold of with their hands (*ku bata namadzai*, that is, to catch red-handed); truth can be invisible yet ordinary people can sense it; and through spiritual agency the truth can become logically accessible, materialised and visible to everyone. The truth of a wrongful act is both individual and collective, as the following case study illustrates.

A case study of assaults by magamba spirits: truth, justice and healing

The intimacy of the civil war violence seriously undermined the family bonding, mutual trust, solidarity and respect for taboos that for generations had offered protection and support to family members. In the aftermath of the war the victims unilaterally forgave one another and tried to move on in silence. The apparent silence was disrupted by the sudden emergence of the war-related spirits. The afflictions caused by *magamba* spirits denounce and verbalise what seems to lie beneath the surface: serious divisions and disputes among family members. Besides the suffering caused by the spirit, the possessed person has to struggle hard to mobilise the support required for healing. In most cases the patient is unable to find the requisite support, and the solution, as the following case of Maria illustrates, is to seek support among social and law and order forces that are available at community level, that is, from the association of traditional practitioners, the community courts and ultimately the police.

Maria is a 25-year-old woman living in a remote village in the middle of the Gorongosa mountains, located approximately 45 kilometres from the main village (Vila Paiva de Andrade). FRELIMO-led government soldiers extrajudicially killed her father during the civil war amid accusations that he supported the rebel movement, RENAMO. At the time of the killing Maria's mother was still pregnant with her. Maria's father was polygamous and although she has half-brothers and -sisters, Maria was her mother's only child. Some months after the death of her father, when Maria was still a baby and still in wartime, there was a family reunion in which the late father, through a medium healer, announced that his widow (Maria's mother) should leave his household and remarry elsewhere but she could not take Maria with her. Maria's mother was forced to abandon her daughter. She married another man and went with him to Barue (a neighbouring district). As a result of this premature separation from her mother Maria grew up in adverse circumstances, moving between her half-brother's and maternal grandparents' houses.

Maria survived the war and when she reached marriageable age she was married to a former RENAMO soldier. A year later she started suffering from spirit-possession episodes. She became pregnant three times and miscarried each time. She described her health problems thus: 'I feel tired, my heart beats fast, and I am in pain. Usually, after a possession episode I faint and only recover consciousness after two to four hours.' As part of her affliction Maria also revealed that she suffered from frightening dreams.

Her husband took her back to her patrikin (half-brothers' house). She asked her half-brothers for help but they steadfastly refused her desperate requests. Eventually she travelled to Barue to look for her mother. She found her mother after many years of separation but it was still not possible to perform *ku socera* (the diagnostic process consisting of playing drums and singing songs to call the spirit to come out). One particularity of *ku socera* is that it cannot be conducted without the presence of the paternal relatives of the sick person because when the sprit manifests itself to the public the relatives have to respond to the spirit's accusations and demands.

Maria's paternal relatives refused to co-operate in helping Maria to deal with the harmful *gamba* spirit. They said that Maria herself was responsible for whatever bad things she might have done during the civil war and for this reason they were not willing to take part in any *ku socera* session. Maria and her mother had no alternative but to go to the police station to report their case. Since most police officers share the same or similar beliefs, they do not hesitate to give official notification to force the relatives of a sick person to participate in a healing session. Maria and her mother obtained the official notice and the paternal relatives finally agreed to co-operate in the process of *ku socera* (the first step in the healthcare).

Maria, accompanied by her mother and her paternal relatives, took her case to the Mozambican Association of Traditional Practitioners (AMETRAMO). It is worth noting that this was the first time that Maria was able to reunite her patrikin and her mother after many years of traumatic separation. The presence of a *gamba* spirit created the possibility for Maria, even amid extreme adversity and fierce antagonism, to experience the feeling that she belonged to a family. Moreover, the *gamba* spirit was going to pave the way for repairing the prevailing family divisions.

The healers performed *ku socera* and Maria started making the usual uncontrolled and violent movements associated with possession by *magamba* spirits. From the apparently peaceful, depressed and gloomy Maria someone else emerged. Maria was gone: she was wheezing, her voice and language changed, her eyes kept rolling and the healers were treating her as a *seculo* (grandfather). Although the spirit that possessed Maria was not her grandfather, the healers used the designation of *seculo* as a way of showing respect and empathy for the spirit. The spirit manifested itself to everyone. The spirit in Maria's body was very aggressive towards Maria's family members and wanted to beat them; he demonstrated his strength by wanting to carry heavy objects and being insensitive to pain. He seemed to have great difficulty in breathing and he was screaming loudly. Everyone was afraid and the stronger men tried to hold him down.

The healers beseeched him, '*Seculo, seculo*, don't get annoyed; we are here to listen to your *micero* (problem) and solve [*ku tonga* – a judicial word for "to resolve"] it. Please, *seculo*, sit down, sit down and tell us who you are and your requests will be satisfied tonight.' When they finally managed to appease him (*ku gazikissa*), the spirit disclosed his identity. It was the spirit of a former RENAMO soldier.

The proceedings went on and the spirit, speaking through Maria's body, said that when he was still alive he had married Julieta (Julieta is Maria's half-sister and she was present during the session). The spirit continued narrating with the same wrath and recklessness. The spirit accused Julieta of having killed him during the war and cutting off his *mussuto* (penis) and *nguenje* (testicles) and eating them.

Julieta was confronted with this disclosure and initially adamantly refused to acknowledge it. She said that this was not the 'clone' of any of her previous husbands. She said that she had been married to a RENAMO soldier and had lived on a RENAMO military base but this spirit was not that of her deceased husband. For several hours there were heated deliberations, arguments and counter-arguments, shouting and protests among the family members because of Julieta's denials. The *magamba* healers tried to mediate the discussions while at the same time exert pressure on Julieta to accept the truth of what the spirit said. This pressure from the healers and the participants was based on the apparently irrefutable evidence that the spirit presented: Julieta's throat was occasionally swollen because sometimes his testicles, which she had eaten, moved from her stomach and took refuge in her throat. No one in the audience dared to contradict this evidence because from time to time Julieta did in fact suffer from a sore and very swollen throat.

Faced with this compelling evidence and mounting pressure from her relatives, Julieta had to change her position. She acknowledged the accusation and said that she was prepared to repair the damage. During follow-up sessions she told me in private that she had not been responsible for the possession and that she had only complied for the sake of the family, and Maria in particular. Yet Julieta revealed important facts about her life. She had been married more than four times, mostly to RENAMO military personnel, and she 'had thrown away many babies' (*ku tsay wana or zwi ntchia*), that is, she had lost many children to death. She also told me that she had lived on RENAMO bases where she had suffered a lot and had used sex to survive.

When the disclosure was finished the healers asked how the reparation should be done. The spirit said that he wanted back his *mussuto, nguenje, nfute* (weapon), military uniform, bag and *ntchorora* (bayonet). He also said that he wanted *nbanje* (cannabis), a red cloth and *folia* (tobacco leaves). The spirit ordered everyone to take these things to a tree in the bush so that he could leave everyone in peace. The relatives and the healer insisted on finding out if the spirit really would leave the family in peace if these objects were given back to him. The spirit confirmed that after the ceremony of returning his property had been performed, justice would have been attained for him and he would go back to his *dzindza* (family origin).

Some minutes later Maria recovered. As is usual in such cases Maria had complete *post facto* amnesia. She told me that she was very tired and was feeling a lot of pain in her body. Afterwards Maria's relatives and the healers started preparing everything that the *gamba* spirit had requested in order to perform the closure ceremony. The following day they managed to collect it all and in the late afternoon they went to the bush to worship the spirit and deliver his goods. The *gamba* healer ordered all kin members to spit on the goods of the spirit and to leave the goods in the bush near to a river. That marked the end of the reparation ceremony and the closure of the case.

The language of authority: Magamba *spirits and healers, truth and healing*

During healing ceremonies such as the one described above, the *gamba* healer is considered to be an authority on resolving conflicts, a *watongui* (authority or judge) rather than a *nahana* (healer). The nature of the problem that gave rise to *magamba* spirits transforms the role of the healer into one similar to that of a judge. This transformation also takes place at the level of the language, that is, different types of genre of discourse are used: indictment, conversation, revelation, inquisition, narrative and judgement. These different types of language (including the body language) used by *magamba* spirits increase the authority necessary for the *gamba* healing institution to produce healing and justice. In this respect, the work of the *magamba* healers could be compared to that of a legal institution, which can be defined as 'one by means of which the people of a society settle disputes that arise between one another and counteract any gross and flagrant abuses of the rules ... of at least some of the other institutions of society'.[39] The emergence of the *magamba* spirits bears witness to the gross violations of human rights that were perpetrated by both the FRELIMO-led governmental army and the RENAMO soldiers. It also illustrates the serious breaches of taboos regarding the care of corpses and the burial practices among the civilians who lived within the war zones in central Mozambique.

In the process of righting these wartime wrongs people believe the *magamba* healers embody a form of institutional authority that has the power to enforce certain types of truth that the state authorities and the institutions they represent have helped to produce but in the end have refused to deal with. In their turn, through possession by *magamba* spirits, the patients and the larger society get access to what Pierre Bourdieu refers to as 'the legitimate instruments of expression, and therefore the participation in the authority of the institution . . . .'[40] Another important aspect to consider is that '[m]ost of the conditions that have to be fulfilled in order for the performative utterance to succeed come down to the question of the appropriateness of the speaker'.[41] In post-civil war Gorongosa, the speaker becomes the appropriate person to enunciate the narrative and the indictment that carries the weight of authority when the *gamba* spirit possesses a person. The possession by the *gamba* spirit provides the host with a legitimate instrument of expression through which it can disclose the aetiology of the affliction, indict those responsible for the grave breaches of the rules that gave rise to the affliction and use the mechanisms of resolution. In turn the *gamba* healer, who represents the person specialising in war-related afflictions, possesses the power and authority that is necessary to create post-civil war healing and attain justice.

Magamba healers reiterate the authority of the *magamba* spirits' performative utterances. This is another dimension of the truth that is spurred on by *magamba* spirits, that is, truth as composed of complementary positions of authority. The *gamba* healer uses his or her position of authority to increase the validity of the spirit's narrative and to force the relatives of the patient to accept that the *gamba* spirit's disclosure is a solemn one. Inevitably the *magamba* spirits and healers are capable of swaying the relatives of the patient because '[t]he language of authority never governs without the collaboration of those it governs, without the help of the social mechanisms capable of producing this complicity, based on misrecognition, which is the basis of all authority'.[42] As Judith Butler later suggested, the 'power that at first appears as external . . . pressing the subject into subordination, assumes a psychic form that constitutes the subject's self identity'.[43] It is this process of identity formation which occurs during the ontogenesis that creates the complicity among the *magamba* spirits and healers, the hosts and their relatives, and society at large.

The nature of the truth as disclosed by *magamba* spirits on these occasions is neither factual nor about an individual past misdeed, nor is it perceived as an apocryphal story. It is a multi-dimensional and collective truth. The war generated multi-dimensional and extreme experiences and *magamba* spirits expose some of these many dimensions: there were soldiers as well as civilians; soldiers perpetrated extreme abuses and crimes; civilians had to commit abuses as well, albeit less frequently than the soldiers and for different reasons, that is, for survival. A crucial aspect of *magamba* spirits is that they expose only the truths concerning civilians; the *magamba* healers do not demand accountability from former soldiers or those who used to give them orders. The reason for this is that the generalised forgiveness that occurred at one level is the condition required for truth and justice at another level. The soldiers who return as spirits and as victims give only the political dimension and context of the family's problematic past: what happened to the families and their large collectives occurred in the context of the political violence that affected the region.

The strategy of the *magamba* spirits is to expose the violent past through a re-enactment of that past. The spirit presents himself as the dead victim of a particular individual. However, the individual does not represent a unit in itself; the individual is a member of a collective or family group. The spirit of the dead soldier represents the political dimension of the violence that escalated in the region and the indicted individual reflects the vicissitudes the family endured. Although the accusation of past misdeeds is levelled against only one individual it is the whole family that is expected to acknowledge the wrongdoing and engage in satisfying the demands of the *gamba* spirit, since, according to African beliefs, to a certain extent 'guilt is collective'.[44] It is not the accused person alone but the family group that looks for the goods for which the *gamba* spirit asks and it is through this cognate collective endeavour that the *gamba* spirit affliction subsides and the spirit is ultimately discharged. Only when the *gamba* spirit is gone does the patient begin the process of recovery.

Magamba spirits bear witness to a collective past that is saturated with shameful intrigues, amoral rejections, abuses and humiliation, and ultimately blood and murder. It is also useful to see *magamba* spirits as offering 'indices of truth', an essence and a reality that offers any people, however impoverished, a value in itself, a value that, especially when rooted in anguish and sacrifice, may dictate a resolve for redemption and strategies for social regeneration.

The value of social regeneration through the socio-cultural processes presented by *magamba* spirits must be spelled out. For instance, following the healing ceremonies performed for Maria, she stopped suffering from spirit possession; she became pregnant and gave birth to a baby boy. Two years later Maria's son remains healthy. However, there were two things the intervention did not seem to restore. First was the relationship with her half-brothers and sister, Julieta, for

295

although her relatives stated that they no longer had difficulties with Maria, it was she who made no effort to visit them regularly. Second was her quasi-nomadic life: although she had a stable relationship with her husband she moved constantly from one relative's house to the other, as she had during wartime. The side-effect of the intervention was that her half-sister, Julieta, got married and Julieta's husband built a house for Maria in her mother's yard.

CONCLUSION

The legal and political reforms initiated by the FRELIMO-led government in the mid-1980s represented a major shift in the internal political dynamics that led to the AGP, which also paved the way for the democratisation of the country.[45] These reforms, despite their paramount importance, fall short of offering to the war survivors transitional justice strategies that effectively address the extreme violence of the civil war. Nevertheless, the case of the *magamba* spirits in central Mozambique indicates that, following political violence and impunity, the result is not always the birth of new cycles of individual and collective hatred and revenge. In spite of the impunity spurred by the national political elites that negotiated the Mozambican peace agreement, it was through practices of rupture that war survivors in Gorongosa were able to devise a peaceful mechanism to deal with the legacies of the civil war. *Magamba* spirits employ a type of language that challenges the strategies of the national elites. It is through this language that the war survivors in Gorongosa have been able to dig up the grisly past legitimately in order to form a *determinate sense of justice*. From a comparative perspective the beliefs and practices evoked by *magamba* spirits demonstrate that the strategies available for dealing peacefully with the legacies of civil wars are not confined to retributive justice and formal processes of restorative justice. There are numerous everyday forms of settling accounts with the past in a way that actively engages with that terrible past yet at the same time takes into account the imperative need to preserve peace.

In fact, moving away from the prescriptive approaches that prevail in transitional justice literature, Alexandra Barahona de Brito and her associates analysed eighteen cases of democratisation and concluded: 'The key obstacle to theorizing about this topic is the enormous influence of the particular historical evolution of each country and various factors emerging therefrom, on policies of truth and justice in transition.'[46] One possibility for overcoming this obstacle and being able to grasp the dynamics of transitional justice at a local level could be through the application of broad definitions. For instance, Naomi Roht-Arriaza has recently suggested that a useful way in which to conceptualise transitional justice is through considering broad and narrow definitions. In its broadest sense transitional justice 'involves anything that a society devises to deal with a legacy of conflict and/or widespread human rights violations'.[47] Such broadness can enrich the study of both formal and informal peaceful strategies to deal with the legacies of civil war violence in countries undergoing transition.

This enrichment can be accomplished, for example, through the study of the everyday life of the communities and the positive and uplifting responses that war survivors develop regarding the past. Although it is clear that models of creative and resilient pluralism have been a cultural feature of many African societies,[48] empirical studies are needed in order to gain insight into the forms that creativity and resilience take in the face of catastrophic events that are triggered by civil wars. *Magamba* spirits and healers offer one example of the ways in which local worlds mediate between broader political forces and the responses of individuals. Politically, *magamba* spirits represent a rupture between the needs and interests of local communities and those of the central government on matters of justice, healing and peace in the aftermath of civil wars.

From a literary perspective the Angolan writer José Agualusa offers creative and imaginative insights about attempts to deal with personal biographies that are loaded with the commission of serious offences. He tells a story of a man who appears to be unaware of his magical powers but who is capable of transforming the past into a kind of commodity that can be sold. Particularly individuals with a very compromising and frightening past (to the extent that it impairs them from achieving peace and happiness) can buy a new past and bury the old one.[49] Such rituals of cleansing, which seem to wash hastily away past dirtiness, cannot be totally precluded from the range of possibilities that individuals and communities may imagine in order to deal with extreme legacies of civil war violence.

NOTES AND REFERENCES

1. A. Tusa and J. Tusa, *The Nuremberg trial* (New York: Cooper Square Press, 2003).
2. J. Elster, *Closing the books: Transitional justice in historical perspective* (Cambridge: Cambridge University Press, 2004).
3. S. Huntington, 'The third wave: Democratisation in the late twentieth century', in N.J. Kritz (ed.), *Transitional justice: How emerging democracies reckon with former regimes, vol. 1: General considerations* (Washington, DC: United States Institute of Peace Press, 1995), p. 70.

4. C. Sriram, *Confronting past human rights violations: Justice versus peace in times of transition* (London: Frank Cass, 2004), p. 2.

5. C. Geertz, *Local knowledge: Further essays in interpretive anthropology* (New York: Basic Books, 2000), p. 167.

6. Geertz, *Local knowledge*, p. 174.

7. C. Nordstrom, *A different kind of war story* (Philadelphia: University of Pennsylvania Press, 1997).

8. C. Hume, *Ending Mozambique's war: The role of mediation and good offices* (Washington, DC: United States Institute of Peace Press, 1994).

9. Author's interview with Don Jaime Gonçalves, Arcebispado da Beira, Mozambique, 16 August 2004 (author's translation).

10. S. Machel, 'Make Sofala and Manica provinces the grave of the armed bandits', *Notícias*, Maputo, 7 September 1985, p. 1.

11. For a definition of reconciliation as an event see W. Long and P. Brecke, *War and reconciliation: Reason and emotion in conflict resolution* (Cambridge, MA: MIT Press, 2003).

12. Joaquim Chissano, speech for the signature of the Mozambican peace agreement, Saint Egidio community, Rome, Italy, 4 October 1992.

13. Afonso Dhlakama, speech for the signature of the Mozambican peace agreement, Saint Egidio community, Rome, Italy, 4 October 1992 (author's translation).

14. J. Méndez, 'National reconciliation, transitional justice, and the International Criminal Court', *Ethics and International Affairs* 15(1), 2001: 25–44.

15. A. Boraine, *A country unmasked: Inside South Africa's Truth and Reconciliation Commission* (Oxford and New York: Oxford University Press, 2000), p. 7.

16. M. Minow, *Between vengeance and forgiveness: Facing history after genocide and mass violence* (Boston: Beacon Press, 1998), p. 5.

17. S. Cohen, *States of denial: Knowing about atrocities and suffering* (Cambridge: Polity Press, 2001).

18. B. Ackerman, *The future of liberal revolution* (New Haven: Yale University Press, 1992).

19. Elster, *Closing the books*.

20. P. Hayner, *Unspeakable truths: Confronting state terror and atrocity* (New York: Routledge, 2000).

21. Sriram, *Confronting past human rights violations*, p. 5.

22. Law No 15/92 states: 'Amnesties the crimes committed against the security of the people and of the popular State, foreseen in Law No 2/79, of March 1 and in Law No 1/83, of March 13, the crimes against the security of the state, foreseen in Law No 19/91, of August 16, and the military crimes foreseen in Law No 17/87, of December 21, and still those whose criminal procedures were not yet established by July 1 of 1988'. *Boletim da República*, I Série – Número 42, Quarta Feira, 14 de Outubro de 1992, Suplemento.

23. Huntington, 'The third wave'.

24. A. Pitcher, 'Forgetting from above and memory from below: Strategies of legitimation and struggle in post-socialist Mozambique', *Africa* 76(1), 2006: 88–111.

25. A. Kleinman, *Writing at the margin: Discourse between anthropology and medicine* (Berkeley: University of California Press, 1997), p. 183.

26. Exceptions are descriptions of practices of *mato oput* by the Acholi people in Northern Uganda, see T. Allen, *Trial justice: The International Criminal Court and Lord's Resistance Army* (London: Zed Books, 2006). Other examples can be found in rituals of reconciliation among Arab-Islamic cultures, see G. Irani and N. Funk, 'Rituals of reconciliation: Arab-Islamic perspectives', *Arab Studies Quarterly* 20, 1998: 53–73 (esp. p. 55).

27. W. Schivelbusch, *The culture of defeat: On national trauma, mourning, and recovery* (New York: Picador, 2003), p. 23.

28. D. Crocker, 'Transitional justice and international civil society: Toward a normative framework', *Constellations* 5, 1998: 492–517 (esp. p. 496).

29. M. Minow (ed.), *Breaking the cycles of hatred: Memory, law, and repair* (Princeton and Oxford: Princeton University Press, 2002), p. 15.

30. R. Wilson, *The politics of truth and reconciliation in South Africa: Legitimizing the post-apartheid state* (Cambridge: Cambridge University Press, 2001), p. 27.

31. H. Arendt, *The human condition* (Chicago: University of Chicago Press, 1958), pp. 237–40.

32. W. Soyinka, *The burden of memory, the muse of forgiveness* (Oxford: Oxford University Press, 1999), p. 68.

33. T. Ranger, 'The local and the global in Southern African religious history', in R. Hefner (ed.), *Conversion to Christianity: Historical and anthropological perspectives on a great transformation* (Berkeley: University of California Press, 1993), pp. 65–98 (esp. p. 73).

34. A. Mbembe, *On the postcolony: Studies on the history of society and culture* (Berkeley: University of California Press, 2001), p. 40.

35. I. Lewis, *Ecstatic religion: A study of shamanism and spirit possession* (London and New York: Routledge, 2003).

36. V. Igreja, 'Exploring the role of *gamba* spirits and healers in the post-war recovery period in Gorongosa', *Transcultural Psychiatry* 40, 2003: 459–487; R. Marlin, 'Possessing the past: Legacies of violence and reproductive illness in central Mozambique', Ph.D. dissertation, New Jersey, New Brunswick, 2001.

37. V. Igreja, B. Dias-Lambranca and A. Richters, '*Gamba* spirits, gender relations and healing in post-civil war Gorongosa, Mozambique', *Journal of the Royal Anthropological Institute* (forthcoming).

38. V. Igreja, W. Kleijn and A. Richters, 'Women's posttraumatic suffering after the war in Mozambique', *Journal of Nervous and Mental Disease* 194, 2006: 502–509.

39. P. Bohannan, 'The differing realms of law', *American Anthropologist* 67(6), 1965: 33–42 (esp. p. 35).

40. P. Bourdieu, *Language and symbolic power* (Cambridge, MA: Harvard University Press, 1991), p. 109.

41. Bourdieu, *Language and symbolic power*, p. 111.

42. Bourdieu, *Language and symbolic power*, p. 113.

43. J. Butler, *The psychic life of power: Theories in subjection* (Stanford, CA: Stanford University Press, 1997), p. 3.

44. Soyinka, *The burden of memory, the muse of forgiveness*, p. 60; I. Amadiume, 'The politics of memory: Biafra and the intellectual responsibility', in I. Amadiume and A.N. Abdullahi (eds.), *The politics of memory: Truth, healing and social justice* (London: Zed Books, 2000), pp. 38–55 (esp. p. 52).

45. H. Abrahamsson and A. Nilsson, *Moçambique em transição* (Mozambique in transition) (D. Leiria trans.) (Gothenburg: PDRI and Maputo: CEEI-ISRI, 1994); see also C. Manning, *The politics of peace in Mozambique: Post-conflict democratisation, 1992–2000* (Westport: Praeger, 2002), p. 94.

46. A. de Brito, C. González-Enríquez and P. Aguilar, *The politics of memory: Transitional justice in democratizing societies* (Oxford: Oxford University Press, 2001), p. 303.

47. Roht-Arriaza is sceptical about the broadening of the definition of transitional justice because accordingly it 'may make the effort so broad as to become meaningless', see N. Roht-Arriaza, 'The new landscape of transitional justice', in N. Roht-Arriaza and J. Mariezcurrena (eds.), *Transitional*

justice in the twenty-first century: Beyond truth versus justice (Cambridge: Cambridge University Press, 2006), pp. 1–16 (esp. p. 2).

48. Ranger, 'The local and the global in Southern African religious history'.
49. J. Agualusa, *O vendedor de passados* (The seller of pasts) (Lisboa: Dom Quixote, 2004).

15

Indigenous Justice or Political Instrument?

The Modern *Gacaca* Courts of Rwanda

Helen Scanlon and Nompumelelo Motlafi

INTRODUCTION

Recent debates concerning transitional justice in Africa have provoked discussions about whose justice is being served as well as the sources of the tools of justice that are used. These issues have led many local analysts to search for more indigenous models of justice. This is perhaps no more exemplified than in post-genocide Rwanda, where the much-extolled *gacaca* court system is considered to be a positive resurrection of the use of indigenous African understandings of justice and reconciliation. The need to find a more organic and local form of transitional justice in a country fractured by ethnically defined conflict has been starkly apparent. Although retributive justice mechanisms had been implemented in Rwanda to address the more than 800 000 deaths and the estimated 500 000 rapes that had been committed over 100 days in 1994, a major healing process was evidently still necessary in order to rebuild a country that remained severely divided by ethnic stereotypes and which had an inadequate judicial system unable to cope with the atrocities of its past. The arrest of almost 120 000 Rwandans charged with being complicit in the genocide and a beleaguered Rwandan judicial system post-1994, meant that the necessity to find alternatives was clear.[1]

In 2003, in an attempt to address this situation, Rwanda's President Paul Kagame issued a decree that granted the provisional release of over 50 000 prisoners who had been implicated in the Rwandan genocide, pending their trials in local *gacaca* courts.[2] *Gacaca* – in Kinyarwanda literally 'lawn-justice' or justice on the grass – were pre-colonial, community-based courts where respected male elders – known as *Inyangamugayo* or 'persons of honourable/exemplary conduct'

– acted as judges. These elders derived their authority from the *Mwami* (the Rwandan king in the pre-colonial and colonial eras) and gained their legitimacy through their election by community members. Their official resurrection under the authority of Rwanda's government was seen as a positive and expedient means of filling the gap between the need for justice and the need for reconciliation. The Rwandan government outlined five ambitious objectives for the *gacaca* system:

- to enable truth-telling about the genocide;
- to promote reconciliation among Rwandans;
- to eradicate the culture of impunity;
- to speed up the trial of genocide suspects; and
- to demonstrate Rwanda's own problem-solving capacity.[3]

The *gacaca* courts were thus established to enact justice for the genocide, and had an explicit mandate to emphasise the importance of confession and forgiveness as well as reparations for victims.

In 2007 there were some 12 000 *gacaca* courts in existence where, theoretically, ordinary citizens were able to try, convict and establish punishments for those accused of lesser crimes during the genocide.[4] By April 2007 more than 71 405 cases had been heard and the pink uniforms of those prisoners who had been sentenced to community service had become a common sight in Rwanda's rural areas.[5] Despite the honourable notion behind the *gacacas* they have nonetheless been marred both by the circumstances of their creation and the subsequent blurring of the line between what constitutes indigenous justice and what is in reality political expediency. This chapter maps the wider political context that surrounds the creation of the current *gacacas* as an attempt to heal the wounds of genocide, charts how the *gacacas* fit into the wider legal framework that exists to address the past in Rwanda, and analyses to what extent the *gacacas* have lived up to their promise of resurrecting indigenous justice. The chapter examines, in particular, the gender dimensions of the proceedings in Rwanda as well as the ways in which the form of *gacaca* that is currently being practised is distinct from its pre-colonial form.

RWANDA'S GENOCIDE AND THE SEARCH FOR JUSTICE

The history and background to the 1994 genocide have been well-documented elsewhere and are not the subject of this chapter. Rwanda's attempts to deal with issues of justice and peace are, however, pertinent to understanding the relevance of *gacaca* as a form of transitional justice and understanding to what extent it can be claimed that they are a truly indigenous process.

Since 1994, 72 key individuals who were implicated in orchestrating the genocide have been arrested and sent to be tried by the International Criminal Tribunal for Rwanda (ICTR) which was established by the United Nations (UN), in Arusha, Tanzania (see Chapter 13 in this volume). These individuals, who included the former Prime Minister Jean Kambanda, were therefore a minority who were deemed to have co-ordinated much of the genocide. Thus the vast majority of those who were accused of partaking in the massacres – an estimated 120 000 arrests were made and the detainees were held in prisons designed to hold a maximum of 15 000 prisoners – had to be processed through Rwanda's beleaguered criminal justice system. The Rwandan courts, which had been decimated by the conflict, faced the insurmountable task of dealing with the vast numbers awaiting trial. Some analysts noted that this process could take 150 years to conclude.[6]

As a result of the period of Belgian colonial rule, the Rwandan criminal justice system remains based largely on Belgian law, with the incorporation of a degree of Rwandan customary law.[7] Rwanda's criminal justice system has been historically weak due to limited resources and the dearth of qualified personnel. It has also been repeatedly criticised for its lack of independence from the executive branch of government.[8] The weakness of the judiciary in post-independence Rwanda is seen as a contributory factor in the creation of the culture of impunity that led to the 1994 genocide. As with most countries emerging from conflict, the genocide further weakened the justice system and since 1994 Rwanda's government has faced the serious challenge of rebuilding both the legal infrastructure and establishing adequate mechanisms to apply the rule of law. It was estimated that in the aftermath of the genocide as much as 95 per cent of the country's judicial personnel had been killed or gone into exile or been imprisoned for their involvement in the massacres.[9]

To resurrect the rule of law the judiciary had to be strengthened and the Rwandan penal codes had to be re-evaluated. Although Rwanda had been a signatory to the 1948 UN Convention on the Prevention and Punishment of Genocide, the country's penal code lacked the mechanisms necessary for prosecuting these crimes. As a result, in 1996, the Organic Law on the Organisation of Prosecution for Offences Constituting the Crimes against Humanity since

1990 was passed. This law outlined four categories under which individuals could be charged and tried for their involvement in the genocide.[10] The recruitment of judicial personnel also started in earnest and by 1996 some 700 new legal staff had been trained as prosecutors, judges and court clerks.[11] As of 2003, it was estimated that international donors had pumped more than US$100 million into Rwanda in an effort to rebuild the criminal justice system.[12] These funds came from various UN agencies, foreign governments such as Belgium, France and Germany, and non-governmental organisations (NGOs). This amount, however, is minimal when contrasted with the total amount spent on the ICTR, which is estimated to be in excess of US$1 billion.[13]

In spite of these reforms Rwanda still fell short of the structures and personnel that were necessary for a judicial system with its needs.[14] From 1996–2001 the Rwandan domestic courts delivered a mere 6 500 convictions for all genocide-related crimes, although this nonetheless compares favourably to the ICTR's 8 convictions during the same period (as of December 2007 only 33 cases had received judgment).[15] Accusations that the re-established judiciary was discriminatory and still tarnished with ethnic bias were rampant. Many Rwandan prisoners decried the fact that, while theoretically entitled to legal representation, the finances necessary for such were simply not forthcoming.[16] With inadequate penal facilities and an embryonic judicial system, observers viewed the slow pace of justice as critical. Thousands of prisoners remained in terrible conditions while awaiting an unfair trial and possible execution. The problems that were being encountered at both the national and the international level and that had been created by the vast numbers implicated in the genocide led to the search for inspiration from indigenous conflict-resolution mechanisms, specifically *gacaca*.

THE *GACACA* MANDATE AND REALITY

As already noted, *gacaca* courts are based on a pre-colonial system of justice whereby misdemeanours are tried by members of the (male) community. Traditionally, male elders mediated in intra- and inter-familial disputes as well as other disputes in the broader community. The matters upon which they mediated included issues such as land rights, inheritance rights, loans, minor attacks and damage to property.[17] *Gacaca* courts had no jurisdiction over serious crimes, such as homicide, which had to be taken directly to the *Mwami*.[18] Traditional *gacaca* courts were thus never equipped to deal with a crime of the magnitude of genocide. Their objective was simply to help parties to reach a mutual agreement, restore social order and – in instances where the wrongdoer was repentant – to reintegrate the perpetrator into the community.[19] The types of sanction varied but usually involved acts of contrition and reparations or compensation in kind. Corporal punishment or temporary banishment was reserved for more serious offences and imprisonment was not a factor of pre-colonial justice. *Gacaca* meetings relied on social pressure to ensure the compliance of the disputants. From the time of Rwanda's colonisation to the post-colonial era Western-style courts usurped the traditional form of *gacaca*. They nevertheless survived in the rural areas although they had been temporarily suspended during the genocide.

The modern *gacaca* courts officially came into being through Organic Law 40/2000, which established them as a permanent institution, in contrast to the ad hoc traditional *gacaca*.[20] Communities were to elect judges to the court from among persons 'of exemplary conduct'.[21] With the surviving victims and the community acting as an extended jury the accused was expected either to confess to the crimes with which he or she was charged or defend him- or herself against them.[22] As already noted, the Organic Law of 1996 stipulated four categories of genocide-related crime.[23] In 2004, these categories were reduced to three. Category One covers the organisers of genocide, genocide rapists and those who committed multiple homicides. The International Centre for Transitional Justice (ICTJ) and the Rwandan courts have sole jurisdiction over this category. A *gacaca* deals with Category Two and Category Three crimes, which cover physical assaults, including those that, intentionally or unintentionally, resulted in death, and property crimes. Thus *gacacas* can at most sentence perpetrators to prison terms but more generally to community service and/or order that compensation be paid to victims. They can also refer cases of rape and murder to the criminal justice system if clear evidence emerges.

There have been three stages in the *gacaca* process: information collection, categorisation and trials.[24] The first entailed collating information from the community about crimes committed and producing a list of all suspects. Judges were then tasked with categorising the crimes and transferring all Category One trials to the formal courts. The pilot information collection phase commenced on 19 June 2002 and concluded at the end of 2004. Trials commenced on 10 March 2005. Concurrently, the nationwide launch of the information collection *gacaca* sessions began on 15 January 2005 and nationwide trials commenced on 16 July 2006. The *gacaca* courts were initially expected to try up to an estimated 100 000 cases. However, this number swelled to more than 800 000 as more people were implicated through the testimonies of others.[25] The government nonetheless remains optimistic about the accomplishments of the *gacaca* courts, whose mandate ended in December 2007.[26]

The modern *gacaca* courts established a uniform system of punishment in an effort to create some sense of consistency but in practice this is rarely achieved.[27] Sentencing ranges from community service for Category Three crimes to imprisonment, ranging from one year to life, for Category Two crimes. There are two sets of possible sentencing based on whether the accused confesses prior to trial or not: those who confess before trial get a lesser prison sentence than those who confess once the trial has commenced. Up to half the prison sentence is convertible to community service or *travaux d'intérêt général* (TIG).[28] Many who were tried under *gacaca* have been released, having already served up to eleven years in prison, and have been given one to three years TIG for the remainder of their sentence. Prisoners have a right of appeal.[29]

As has occurred in other contexts, such as South Africa, the provision of reparations to victims has been seen as a symbolic gesture in the search for restorative justice. A Compensation Fund was established in Rwanda in 1999 to award damages to victims of the genocide,[30] and this is perhaps the most ambitious aspect of *gacaca*, proving, as it is, to be as problematic as it is controversial. The principle of reparations has always been enshrined in traditional *gacaca*, whereby reparations came directly from the perpetrator to the victim. However, bearing in mind that more than 50 per cent of all Rwandans live below the poverty line, it is clear that very few of the perpetrators are in a position to pay financial compensation. The fact that the Compensation Fund has been deemed the responsibility of the state has created a number of issues, such as where the financing will come from, as well as questions about the form and amount of compensation.[31]

TRADITIONAL VERSUS MODERN *GACACA*

The modern *gacaca* does try to respect the spirit of traditional *gacacas* but in practice is often quite different. The release of prisoners back into their communities represented both a political compromise and a gesture intended to facilitate the reintegration of prisoners into society. In the absence of both professional prosecutors and defence attorneys in *gacacas* the perpetrator symbolically puts himself at the mercy of the survivors and the greater community. Beyond this the similarities become increasingly blurred.

The first marked difference from traditional *gacaca* is the modern *gacacas'* legalised existence as part of a nationwide project of enormous ambition. A second significant variation is the make-up of the courts. Traditionally *gacacas* did not make provision for the participation of women and youths unless they were directly involved in a case.[32] Under the Organic Laws the criteria for eligibility as a *gacaca* judge include: Rwandan citizenship, being over 21 years of age in addition to being of good conduct, living a good life and espousing good moral standards, being honest, having no record of participation in the genocide or in crimes against humanity, and upholding a spirit of non-sectarianism and non-discrimination.[33] Judges are given basic legal training in implementing the Organic Law of *Gacaca*.[34] This means that, theoretically, the position of *gacaca* judge is open to all Rwandans, Tutsi or Hutu, men and women. In this respect it is notably different from the male-dominated structure of traditional courts. The current national representation of women in all the *gacaca* courts is 29 per cent and, at the national level, a woman holds the position of executive secretary of the *gacaca* system.[35]

The third distinctive feature of the modern *gacaca* is the vast number of related processes that are geared towards post-genocide recovery. The government-mandated National Unity and Reconciliation Commission (NURC) has been established at the grassroots level in order to facilitate *gacaca* and is intended to transfer the reconciliation process to the communities.[36] In addition, a number of traditional institutions such as *Ingando* have been revitalised. *Ingando* date back to pre-colonial times when the Rwandan military organised communal retreats/camps where ordinary people could partake in decisions on war and peace and on how Rwanda was governed, specifically during times of imminent national disaster, for example, during wars and famines. The NURC works at four levels to prepare accused perpetrators for participation in a *gacaca*:

- training prisoners before their release;
- organising *Ingandos* for newly released prisoners;
- working with perpetrators who have been sentenced to community service; and
- preparing survivors to receive perpetrators.

The fourth break from the traditional *gacaca* is the prevalence of international funding for modern *gacaca*-related organisations and activities. The European Union (EU) is among the major funders of these and other *gacaca*-related organisations. In 2002 the European Development Fund, in association with the Rwandan ministry of finance and economic planning, contributed €1.75 million to organisations such as the United Kingdom-based NGO, International Alert, working in partnership with the Rwanda-based *Profemmes Twesehamwe* (a collective of 40 women's organisations in Rwanda).[37] This partnership has been working towards increasing the participation of women in *gacaca* by training women to be judges and highlighting, from a gender perspective, the weaknesses in *gacaca* and other related laws amongst other projects.

A further departure is the creation of a Compensation Fund. In a proposal to the Belgian Secretariat of State for Development Cooperation, scholar Peter Uvin argued that even with a combination of funds from Rwandan state coffers, the confiscated monetary accounts from genocide leaders and the limited available funding from international donors, it would be impossible to financially compensate every surviving victim. Uvin proposed that international donors and the government of Rwanda could instead invest in social services that are targeted at surviving victims, such as the building of houses, schools and health centres.[38] He put a specific focus on increased and long-term funding for primary and secondary education for children, emphasising that it is the Rwandan government that should take primary responsibility for any long-term endeavours. Support of this type 'should possess the symbolic value of a society's commitment to make the future better than the past'.[39]

INDIGENOUS OR RETRIBUTIVE JUSTICE?

Amnesty International and a number of other international human rights NGOs have voiced alarm over the *gacaca* justice system, which, they argue, fails to meet international standards for fair trial and lacks independence, impartiality and transparency. It has been reported that the government is pressurising people to turn up to *gacaca* proceedings and that attendance is noted in their social service documents. If they fail to attend without good reason they may be turned away when seeking medical help at hospitals and clinics. Since 2000 there have also been an estimated 160 reprisal killings of genocide survivors, judges and witnesses who have been linked to the *gacaca* courts.[40] Although the government established a witness-protection programme in mid-2006, limited resources and a lack of political will have yielded few results.

The fear of implication and prosecution has reportedly led both to flights from the country and to people taking their own lives. National and international media have reported the flight of more than 3 000 individuals to neighbouring countries out of fear of appearing before the *gacacas*.[41] Between March and December 2005 alone it was estimated that 69 people due to appear before the *gacacas* committed suicide and a further 44 attempted to kill themselves. According to Rwandan officials, numerous attempted or successful suicides had also occurred in the months before they began to keep records.

Furthermore, the courts have been criticised for the fact that all the defendants have been Hutu, while atrocities and human rights violations that Tutsi Rwanda Patriotic Army (RPA) soldiers committed against both Hutu and Tutsi civilians are addressed in military tribunals and are therefore not accessible to the public. This promotes a public perception of an ethnically biased justice that many have come to criticise. This is further compounded by the fact that judges without any formal legal training are handing out sentences that range from community service to life imprisonment. In terms of programmes for the reintegration of surviving victims and prisoners, Rwanda's government has failed to create sufficient mechanisms and as a result national and international NGOs such as *Profemmes Twesehamwe*, International Alert and Oxfam have had to take on this role.

A number of dynamics determine the relative success of *gacaca* courts in some regions rather than others. These include the ethnic composition of the population in different regions; rural versus urban contexts; changes in the pre-genocide composition of communities due to internal displacement; and the creation of new communities through the government policy of villagisation known as *imidugudu*, implemented because of the need to resettle the internally displaced and former exiles.[42] These factors cannot be discussed in depth but what must be highlighted is that the *gacaca* process reflects the areas where the genocide was the most severe as well as where witnesses are more likely to give testimony against perpetrators or to hide them in a 'conspiracy of silence'.[43] While criticisms of the mandatory nature of *gacaca* may be valid, mandatory participation may not be entirely negative, as an opportunity to promote discussion and ideally reconciliation in the absence of any other official national reconciliation process.[44]

GENDERED DIMENSIONS OF THE *GACACA*: **PROBLEMS AND PROSPECTS**
The experiences of Rwandan men and women as both victims and perpetrators during the 1994 genocide have been well documented.[45] Comparative estimates of men and women killed are hard to come by but it is estimated that some 40 per cent of those killed were women. A census of the population of Rwanda

immediately after the Rwandan Patriotic Front (RPF) victory found 70 per cent of the total population to be female; 60 per cent of women who had been married at the time of the genocide were widowed.[46] Of the estimated 120 000 people imprisoned, 3.5 per cent were women.[47]

The rape of women was a tactic of war that was widely used by all parties during the 1994 genocide. Women became central to the propaganda and the so-called 'ten commandments' specifically targeted women in three of its directives. These included:

- Each Hutu man must know that Tutsi women, no matter whom, work in solidarity with their Tutsi ethnicity. In consequence, every Hutu man is a traitor:
  i. who marries a Tutsi woman;
  ii. who makes a Tutsi woman his concubine, or
  iii. who makes a Tutsi woman his secretary or protégé.
- Every Hutu man must know that our Hutu girls are more dignified and more conscientious in their roles as women, wives, and mothers. Aren't they pretty, good secretaries and more honest!
- Hutu women, be vigilant and bring your husbands, brothers, and sons to reason![48]

Based on calculations from the births of rape-conceived children, it is estimated that between 250 000 and 500 000 women were raped.[49] Women were often raped before being killed and many of those who survived such brutal attacks had been left for dead.[50] It has further been revealed that the interim government released patients known to be HIV-positive for the sole purpose of raping women. Some of the *génocidaire* militia also forced women to be their 'wives' in return for their lives; in mid-May 1994 the *génocidaire* leadership gave orders that Tutsi women and children were not to be spared.[51] Raped women suffered as a result of stigmatisation and were often unable to marry so the rapes also functioned as a way of ensuring that women survivors could not be reintegrated into society.[52] After their victory, soldiers of the RPA were implicated in the rape of Hutu women as revenge for the rape of Tutsi women.[53] Rwanda is a patrilineal society and the child is automatically deemed to be of the same ethnic origin as the father, no matter how contested these delineations may be, so some Tutsi soldiers were also implicated in the raping of women for the purpose of impregnating them and 'replenishing' the decimated Tutsi population.[54] Of those women who reported their rapes and consented to testing, 66 per cent tested HIV-positive.[55]

The *gacaca* process was intended to recognise both the victims and the perpetrators of the genocide and as part of the process there was an attempt to ensure gender sensitisation.[56] As discussed above, women were excluded from the traditional *gacaca* but they have become full participants in its current variant in both its formal structures and as witnesses to the genocide. Thirty per cent of the formal positions within the *gacaca* have been allotted to women. However, there are a number of impediments to women's full involvement in the process. For example, until 2007, rape and other gender-based crimes were classified as Category One crimes and testimony therefore had to be submitted to the formal courts.[57] Considering the consequences of the social stigma attached to being raped, there remain major impediments to encouraging women to testify about their experiences in front of their communities. Furthermore, although women of all ethnic groups suffered gender-based crimes, Hutu victim-survivors are not eligible for compensatory assistance.[58] It has been found that while the record of reintegration of prisoners is thus far unclear, women who have been incarcerated suffer additional stigma and their reintegration has proved especially difficult.[59]

The high percentage of widowed women has led to the prevalence of woman-headed households. In addition, there are many child-headed households and women who are virtually widowed because of the incarceration of their husbands. In many ways women bore the brunt of the war but still face social stigmatisation, economic disadvantage and psychological trauma. As a result, women prisoners and victims of gender-based violence have encountered more difficulties than their male counterparts in their attempts to resume a 'normal' life.

CONCLUSION

Has the Rwandan government facilitated the successful revival of indigenous justice or simply created its own vehicle to alleviate congestion in the criminal justice system? Post-1994 Rwanda faced insurmountable questions as to how to create a sense of reconciliation in the war-torn country, stem retribution and create circumstances that would encourage the return of refugees.[60] Through the *gacaca* courts ordinary Rwandans have been granted the opportunity to administer justice and be active agents in building a new nation. It should also be recognised that the *gacaca* courts are solving far more cases than the ICTR, or even the ordinary Rwandan domestic courts. There is therefore reason to appreciate some of the positive contributions made by the *gacaca* courts. Nevertheless, with their short mandate and the suspicions surrounding them, it is difficult to see how they could realistically achieve their aims, specifically that of the large-scale reconciliation of a nation. *Gacaca* have at best been a starting point in rebuilding the Rwandan nation but it still faces many challenges ahead.

NOTES AND REFERENCES

1 . See for example, J. Sarkin, 'The tension between justice and reconciliation in Rwanda: Politics, human rights, due process and the role of the *gacaca* courts in dealing with the genocide', *Journal of African Law* 45(2), 2001: 149.

2. The initial decision to set up *gacacas* occurred in 2000 but was officially launched after the 2003 elections.

3. F.K. Rusagara, '*Gacaca* as a reconciliation and nation-building strategy in post-genocide Rwanda', *Conflict Trends* 2(2), 2005: 22.

4. These 'lesser' crimes are: 'simple' murder, bodily injury and property damage.

5. Hirondelle News Agency, 'Rwanda/gacaca: The gacaca courts prepare to finish their mandate', 24 April 2007. http://www.hirondellenews.com/content/view/402/135/ (accessed 23 February 2009).

6. See, for example, Sarkin, 'The tension between justice and reconciliation in Rwanda'; P. Uvin and C. Mironko, 'Western and local approaches to justice in Rwanda', *Global Governance* 9, 2003: 219–231.

7. Idi T. Gaparayi, lecturer in the department of public law at the National University of Rwanda points out that in the colonial era Rwandan customary law could apply in certain situations provided that it did not supersede colonial law. See I.T. Gaparayi, 'Justice and social reconstruction in the aftermath of genocide in Rwanda: An evaluation of the possible role of the *gacaca* tribunals', *African Human Rights Law Journal* 1, 2001: 82.

8. Amnesty International, 'Rwanda: *gacaca*: A question of justice', AFR 47/007/2002, *Amnesty International Index*, 2002: 12.

9. Amnesty International, 'Rwanda: *gacaca*'.

10. Amnesty International, 'Rwanda: *gacaca*', p. 13.

11. Lawyers' Committee for Human Rights (LCHR), 'Prosecuting genocide in Rwanda: A Lawyers Committee report on the ICTR and National Trials', at http://www.humanrightsfirst.org/pubs/descriptions/rwanda.htm (accessed 23 February 2009).

12. Uvin and Mironko, 'Western and local approaches to justice in Rwanda': 223.

13. T. Cruvellier, 'Africa: The laboratory of justice', 2004, www.crimesofwar.org/africa-mag/afr_06_cruvellier.html (accessed 15 April 2007).

14. Cruvellier, 'Africa: The laboratory of justice'.

15. Uvin and Mironko, 'Western and local approaches to justice in Rwanda': 220, 223.

16. Amnesty International, 'Rwanda: *gacaca*': 14–15.

17. Gaparayi, 'Justice and social reconstruction in the aftermath of genocide in Rwanda': 81; A. Chakravarty, '*Gacaca* courts in Rwanda: Explaining divisions within the human rights community', *Yale Journal of International Affairs* 1(2), 2006: 133, www.yale.edu/yjia/articles/Vol_1_Iss_2_Spring 2006/Chakravarty223.pdf (accessed 15 January 2007).

18. N. Alusala, *Disarmament and reconciliation: Rwanda's concerns*, Occasional Paper 108, 2005, Institute for Security Studies.

19. A.E. Tiemessen, 'After Arusha: *Gacaca* justice in post-genocide Rwanda', *African Studies Quarterly* 8(1), 2004: 63. See also P. Clark, 'When the killers go home: Local justice in Rwanda', *Dissent*, Summer 2005: 14.

20. Organic Law 40/2000 of 26 January 2001 Setting up 'Gacaca Jurisdictions' and organizing Prosecutions for Offences constituting the Crime of Genocide or Crimes against Humanity Committed between 1 October 1990 and 31 December 1994, www.inkiko-gacaca.gov.rw/pdf/Law.pdf (accessed 27 November 2007).

21. Sarkin, 'The tension between justice and reconciliation in Rwanda': 164.

22. P. Uvin, 'The introduction of a modernized *gacaca* for judging suspects of participation in the genocide and the massacres of 1994 in Rwanda', discussion paper, 2001, p. 3, fletcher.tufts.edu/humansecurity/pdf/Bautmans.pdf (accessed 2 February 2007).

23. Organic Law 08/96 of 30 August 1996 on the Organisation of Prosecutions for Offences constituting the Crime of Genocide or Crimes against Humanity committed since 1 October 1990, www.preventgenocide.org/law/domestic/rwanda.htm (accessed 27 November 2007).

24. Organic Law 08/96 of 30 August 1996 on the Organisation of Prosecutions for Offences constituting the Crime of Genocide or Crimes against Humanity committed since 1 October 1990.

25. As of April 2004, 818 564 cases had been prepared, including 77 269 in the category of politicians and planners, 432 557 in the 2nd category of executors and 308 738 cases of looting.

26. W. Mugenzi, 'Rwanda: *Gacaca* courts on right track – *Gacaca* boss', *The New Times* (Kigali), 2006, allafrica.com/stories/200703150356.html (accessed 15 March 2007).

27. A. Chakravarty, '*Gacaca* courts in Rwanda: Explaining divisions within the human rights community', *Yale Journal of International Affairs* 1(2), 2006: 134.

28. Penal Reform International (2007) Community service (TIG), 'Monitoring and research report on the *gacaca*' (March 2007), www.penalreform.org/resources/rep-ga9-2007-community-service-en.pdf (accessed 20 January 2008).

29. Penal Reform International (2007) Community service (TIG), 'Monitoring and research report on the *gacaca*', p. 12.

30. Penal Reform International (2007) Community service (TIG), 'Monitoring and research report on the *gacaca*', p. 12.

31. See Uvin, 'The introduction of a modernized *gacaca* for judging suspects of participation in the genocide and the massacres of 1994 in Rwanda', p. 22. This is a dated article but there is evidence that the debate of the Compensation Fund is ongoing.

32. J. Mutamba and J. Izabiliza, 'The role of women in reconciliation and peace building in Rwanda: Ten years after genocide 1994–2004', study commissioned by the National Unity and Reconciliation Commission on Contributions, Challenges and Way Forward, May 2005, p. 32.

33. Sarkin, 'The tension between justice and reconciliation in Rwanda':164.

34. Gaparayi, 'Justice and social reconstruction in the aftermath of genocide in Rwanda': 91.

35. Mutamba and Izabiliza, 'The role of women in reconciliation and peace building in Rwanda', p. 32.

36. P. Nantulya, 'African nation-building and reconstruction: Lessons from Rwanda', *Conflict Trends* 1(1), 2006: 47.

37. International Alert, 'The EU's engagement with civil society in Rwanda: Justice after genocide', *Conflict Prevention Newsletter*, May 2003, pp. 7–8, www.gppac.org/documents/Newsletter/Newdletter_6=1.pdf (accessed 15 January 2008).

38. International Alert, 'The EU's engagement with civil society in Rwanda', p. 23.
39. International Alert, 'The EU's engagement with civil society in Rwanda', p. 23.
40. Human Rights Watch, 'Killings in Eastern Rwanda', 2007, www.hrw.org/backgrounder/africa/rwanda0107/ (accessed 25 February 2008).
41. Hirondelle News Agency (Lausanne), 'Villagers flee as genocide courts press on', 2005 (allAfrica.com), allafrica.com/stories/printable/200504260464 (accessed 30 January 2007).
42. Mutamba and Izabiliza, 'The role of women in reconciliation and peace building in Rwanda', p. 20.
43. Uvin, 'The introduction of a modernized *gacaca* for judging suspects of participation in the genocide and the massacres of 1994 in Rwanda', p. 10; P. Uvin and C. Mironko, 'Western and local approaches to justice in Rwanda', *Global Governance* 9, 2003: 227.
44. Uvin and Mironko, 'Western and local approaches to justice in Rwanda'.
45. African Rights, *Rwanda: Death, despair and defiance* (London: African Rights, 1995); African Rights, *Rwanda, not so innocent: When women become killers* (London: African Rights, 1995); L. Melvern, *Conspiracy to murder: The Rwandan genocide* (London and New York: Verso, 2006).
46. Melvern, *Conspiracy to murder*. Estimates from the NURC report are more modest, putting the number of female Rwandans at 53 per cent of the population. The NURC is report is more recent than the Twagiramariya and Turshen article and may take into consideration the returnees from Uganda, the DRC, Kenya and Tanzania.
47. International Alert, 'The EU's engagement with civil society in Rwanda, p. 8.
48. S. Adejumobi, 'Citizenship, rights, and the problem of conflicts and civil wars in Africa (Hutu Ten Commandments)', *Human Rights Quarterly* 23(1), 2001: 168.
49. Mutamba and Izabiliza, 'The role of women in reconciliation and peace building in Rwanda', p. 17; C. Twagiramariya and M. Turshen, '"Favours" to give and consenting victims: The sexual politics of survival in Rwanda', in M. Turshen and C. Twagiramariya (eds.), *What women do in wartime: Gender and conflict in Africa* (London and New York: Zed Books, 1998), pp. 103–104.
50. Mutamba and Izabiliza, 'The role of women in reconciliation and peace building in Rwanda', p. 17.
51. L. Sharlach, 'Gender and genocide in Rwanda: Women as agents and objects of the genocide', *Journal of Genocide Research* 1(3), 1999: 387.
52. Turshen and Twagiramariya, *What women do in wartime*, p. 104.
53. Turshen and Twagiramariya, *What women do in wartime*, p. 103. For details of the large-scale killing of Hutus upon liberation of certain regions and immediately after the civil war, see Uvin, 'The introduction of a modernized *gacaca* for judging suspects of participation in the genocide and the massacres of 1994 in Rwanda', p. 25.
54. Turshen and Twagiramariya, *What women do in wartime*, p. 104.
55. Mutamba and Izabiliza, 'The role of women in reconciliation and peace building in Rwanda', p. 17.
56. B. Ayindo, 'Retribution or restoration for Rwanda', *Africa News*, January 1998.
57. Turshen and Twagiramariya, *What women do in wartime*, p. 104.
58. Tiemessen, 'After Arusha: *Gacaca* justice in post-genocide Rwanda': 68–69. For a summary of the reparations provisions see H. Rombouts, *Victim organisations and the politics of reparation: A case study on Rwanda* (Antwerp and Oxford: Intersentia, 2004).
59. International Alert, 'The EU's engagement with civil society in Rwanda', p. 8.
60. In 2007 there were still some 57 000 Rwandan refugees hosted in 21 African countries (UNHCR Country Operations Plan 2007).

PART V

The International Criminal Court

Problems and Prospects

16

The International Criminal Court Africa Experiment

The Central African Republic, Darfur, Northern Uganda and the Democratic Republic of the Congo

Chandra Lekha Sriram

INTRODUCTION

While the International Criminal Court (ICC) only became operational in July 2002 with the coming into force of its Statute, it constitutes the culmination of the development of international justice over half a century. However, its creation and now its operation have not been without controversy. From the outset the Court faced a strong challenge from the United States, which first signed its Statute and then 'unsigned' it. Its early cases have also drawn some criticism on a number of grounds. There have been objections that the ICC has become an 'International Criminal Court for Africa'. There have also been concerns that prosecutions will hamper peace processes, or will be unnecessarily limited in cases where investigations are underway or indictments have been issued, in the Central African Republic (CAR), Uganda, the Democratic Republic of the Congo (DRC) and the Darfur region of Sudan.

This chapter discusses the background of the ICC and its current membership before turning very briefly to the objections of the United States and their ramifications. It then considers the Court's current case load as well as the two key criticisms of the Court that, to date, it has only selected cases from African countries, and that current practices hamper peacemaking or peacebuilding. Some responses to these criticisms follow.

A BRIEF HISTORY OF THE COURT

The ICC has built upon the concept of international criminal accountability that was inherent in the Nuremberg and Tokyo Tribunals that followed the Second World War, although proposals for a war crimes court date back at least to the nineteenth century.[1] Although the International Law Commission (ILC) drafted a statute for an international criminal court in the 1950s, the politics of the Cold War forestalled any possibility of international agreement on a convention. In 1989 Trinidad and Tobago revived the idea of the court, albeit because it sought a means to combat drug trafficking. The United Nations (UN) General Assembly thus asked the ILC to resume its work on a statute. The conflict in the former Yugoslavia and the genocide in Rwanda motivated the creation of two ad hoc international criminal tribunals in 1993 and 1994 respectively.[2] In 1994, the ILC presented its draft statute to the UN General Assembly, which in 1996 set up a preparatory committee to develop and refine the draft. In 1998 an international conference was convened in Rome to finalise the Rome Statute, which was completed in July 1998.[3] Of the states attending the negotiations 120 voted for the final draft, 21 abstained, and 7 voted against it, including the United States. The treaty required 60 ratifications to come into force and the sixtieth was deposited in April 2002. The Rome Statute came into force in July 2002. By January 2007, 104 states had signed and ratified the Statute, which now represented all regions of the world, with 29 African state parties, 22 state parties from Latin America and the Caribbean, 12 from Asia, 16 from Eastern Europe, and 25 from Western Europe and other states (including Canada and Australia).[4]

UNITED STATES' OBJECTIONS TO THE COURT

Although the United States was actively involved in negotiating the ICC treaty it ultimately voted against it in Rome. The Clinton administration signed the treaty in its final days but advised the Senate not to ratify it in its current form and the subsequent administration of George W. Bush 'unsigned' the treaty. The objections of the United States are well known and have been discussed extensively elsewhere. Consequently, I do not consider them in any detail but briefly address the impact of the United States's opposition to the Court.[5] This opposition has had, and may continue to have, a dramatic effect upon the role that international tribunals such as the ICC may play in Africa as well as upon the use of other mechanisms such as hybrid tribunals. The United States's threat to veto any referral of cases to the ICC not only long delayed the referral of the situation in Darfur but shaped that referral, which included an exemption from prosecution for peacekeepers from non-signatory states.[6] The debate over that referral also highlighted the ongoing promotion by the United States of ad hoc – particularly hybrid – mechanisms over and above the ICC. The United States insisted in its statement abstaining from the resolution that an ad hoc or regional court would be preferable, a position it maintained in supporting the Special Court for Sierra Leone (SCSL) as well.[7] The United States's objections to the ICC have at least two adverse effects upon its operation in response to crimes in Africa. Primarily these objections may generally undermine the Court's operation through the promotion of an alternative model, namely the hybrid court. Secondly, and more dangerously, United States's opposition may prevent dire cases from being referred to the Court, may delay their referral at great cost to human life or may limit the scope of referrals that do occur.

More generally, the United States's objections and the choice of the United States, China and a number of other powerful states to remain outside the regime, have raised concerns that the reach of the Court is unfair and that while the strong can shield themselves and their allies this leaves the ICC to handle cases from weak states only. The current case load, which involves only cases arising from African states, leads some critics to take the objection one step further and predict that the ICC will handle only cases from Africa.

THE ICC'S CURRENT CASE LOAD: THE CAR, NORTHERN UGANDA, DARFUR AND DRC

I briefly recount the status of the four cases under investigation by the Court. These have been undertaken through two of the means envisioned by the Statute: self-referral and UN Security Council resolution. There have to date been no instances of the prosecutor undertaking a case on his own initiative (*proprio motu*) or involving one state referring a situation in another state, subject to the Court's jurisdiction, to the Office of the Prosecutor.

In July 2005 the government of the CAR referred to the Court the 'situation of crimes within the jurisdiction of the Court committed anywhere on the territory of the state' since the Statute had come into force in July 2002. The prosecutor deferred investigation while the situation was considered internally, on the basis of complementarity.[8] The prosecutor revived consideration of an investigation following a decision by the CAR's *Cour de Cassation* in 2006 that the country's judicial system was unable to carry out effective investigations and prosecutions.[9]

In May 2007 the Office of the Prosecutor formally initiated an investigation in the CAR.[10] This investigation is not dealt with in detail here as it was initiated while this chapter was still being completed.

The other three cases reached the Court either through state self-referral or UN Security Council referral. In April 2004 the DRC formally referred crimes arising from its conflict and which fell within the Court's temporal jurisdiction. The first unsealed indictment was against the leader of the Union of Congolese Patriots, Thomas Lubanga Dyilo, who is now in the custody of the Court.[11] The government of Uganda referred the situation in Northern Uganda to the Court in December 2003 and the prosecutor formally opened an investigation in July 2004, with the first indictments being unsealed in October 2005.[12] In contrast, the situation in Darfur was referred by the UN Security Council in March 2005, with resolution 1593; as noted above, it included a clause exempting peacekeepers from non-state parties from the jurisdiction of the Court in order to prevent an American veto (see Chapter 17 in this volume).[13]

ARE AFRICAN CASES OVERREPRESENTED AT THE ICC?

Clearly the three active investigations and the one less active situation all relate to alleged crimes in African countries. There are no active investigations of such crimes committed in any other country in the world, although more than 1 700 communications were received by the Office of the Prosecutor throughout early 2006.[14] Ten cases have been closely analysed by the Office, while four active investigations have been undertaken. Two of the situations that have been analysed and rejected involve alleged crimes in Venezuela and Iraq. Given the current pursuit of exclusively African cases, there are suggestions that the ICC is really an international criminal court for Africa; that, more ominously, the ICC is using Africa as a guinea pig; and that the ICC is an expression of neo-colonialism.[15] I consider these claims carefully below, examining their merits as well as important counter-arguments.

The argument: African states are guinea pigs, or the Court is a tool of neo-colonialism

The claim that African states are being treated as guinea pigs, or that the ICC is in some sense neo-colonial, is a bit difficult to source because, while it is a concern that has been aired in conferences and in diplomatic circles, it is seldom articulated fully or in print. The Algerian representative on the UN Security Council when resolution 1593 was passed, referring the situation in Darfur to the Court, argued that justice needed to be done but that it could be better done through a process led by the African Union (AU). The Sudanese representative to the UN, who also spoke at the proceedings, made stronger claims, saying that it was hypocritical for some non-state parties to shield themselves from prosecutions while others could not. This was a clear challenge to the paragraph that had been inserted to alleviate the United States's concerns discussed above. He referred in his comments to colonialism and a new hegemony in order to challenge further the legitimacy of the referral.[16] These allegations echo concerns that have been raised in other quarters that the exercise of universal jurisdiction might be 'jurisdictional neo-imperialism'.[17] In other words, the allegation is that some states, largely ex-colonies and perhaps largely in Africa, will see their nationals prosecuted before the ICC while others, such as the United States or China, will not and that this constitutes either an invasion of sovereignty or an unfair violation of the principle of sovereign equality.

There are a number of counter-arguments that may be made to this.

There are many African signatories and many are or have been in conflict

A first counter-argument is that African cases are not overrepresented but rather that African countries present a disproportionate number of possible cases falling under the jurisdiction of the ICC. This response might proceed in two parts: firstly, that many African countries have signed and ratified the Statute and thus fall under its jurisdiction and, secondly, that many of these countries are in a state of conflict or emerging from conflict and therefore present crimes relevant to the Court. Conversely, many countries in other parts of the world that are engaged in conflict(s) have not joined the treaty, ranging from Myanmar to the United States.

When the Rome Statute was opened for signature in 1998 few expected that the Statute would enter into force so quickly or that it would attract so many state parties. It was perhaps even less predictable that so many state parties would come from countries in Africa that were experiencing internal conflict or emerging from conflict. By March 2009 there were 108 state parties, more than half the number of UN member states; more notably, more African states have become parties to the Statute than states from any other region in the world. Of the 53 members of the AU, 30 are parties to the Statute.[18] It is also true that many countries in Africa have experienced conflict and many of these conflicts have

321

engendered crimes that fall within the Court's personal and temporal jurisdiction. The Court can only consider cases where the accused is a national of a state party or is accused of a crime on the territory of a state party; where the crime is one of the three that can currently be considered by the Court (war crimes, genocide and crimes against humanity, aggression not yet being prosecutable); and where the Statute was in force for that territory/person at the time of the crime. This excludes a great number of crimes that either occurred prior to 2002 or were not committed by a state party or by a national of a state party. For example, this excludes crimes that may have been committed in Colombia prior to 2002, or in countries in conflict that have not signed or ratified the treaty, such as Sri Lanka, Nepal or Myanmar. A number of African countries, however, are not only among the most numerous groups of ratifiers but have also been engaged in serious conflicts since 2002. According to one count, there were twelve conflicts in Africa in 2002, seven in 2003, eight in 2004 and five in 2005. In comparison, while South and Central Asia, for example, have experienced as many or more conflicts during those years, only Afghanistan and Tajikistan are state parties.[19]

Cases have largely been referred by African states themselves

The argument that African states are being used as guinea pigs, or that prosecutions are imposed from the outside, ignores the actions of the states in question. With the exception of the situation in Darfur, which was referred by the UN Security Council, the cases being pursued have all been referred by the states in which crimes are now being investigated or prosecuted. They have, notably, not been pursued through the prosecutor's exercise of his power *proprio motu*, nor have they been pursued through the referral by one state of the situation in another. Referrals through either of these two means might have supported the claims of neo-colonialism, particularly if state referrals of others had been referrals by European states. Indeed, there has been only one non-voluntary referral, through the UN Security Council, where the absence of permanent African representatives might arguably be cause for concern. Nonetheless, African and other developing states that were seated on the Security Council might have abstained from or voted against resolution 1593. Of the three African states with rotating seats on the Security Council at the time, only Algeria abstained, making the objections noted above, while Benin and Tanzania voted in favour of the resolution.[20]

The government of Uganda referred the situation in the north of the country. The government of the DRC referred the situation existing in the entire country's territory. The CAR also referred its own situation to the Court, although a formal investigation was opened only several years later out of deference to that country's own internal legal process. Perhaps the question should be: 'Are the governments manipulating the Court?' rather than 'Is the Court manipulating states?' In the case of Uganda, the government sought to refer a narrow situation, that is, the crimes committed by the Lord's Resistance Army (LRA) in the north, and at the same time sought to shield from inquiry activities by the government and military across the country, including massive displacement and abuse of civilians in the north. The situation referred by the CAR emerged from an internal political struggle and may be driven by the government's desire to consolidate its political hold. The DRC referral may have been elicited with some coercion, but the Office of the Prosecutor had made it clear that the situation was under scrutiny and implied an investigation would follow, which may have pushed the government to refer the case first.[21]

One reason for the first referrals emerging from Africa may be to do with weak state capacity: many of the African states that have signed and ratified the ICC Statute have not passed implementing legislation and have weak or dysfunctional judiciaries. They may thus prefer the ICC to address difficult cases. Furthermore, they are prime candidates for referral cases under the principle of complementarity in the Statute, whereby the ICC will not hear cases where legitimate state-run proceedings are underway or have been completed.[22]

However, while these rebuttals may be convincing to a degree, it is worth considering whether the Office of the Prosecutor is pursuing the path of least resistance in the case of African countries with little state capacity. It has, as noted above, received a large number of communications seeking to refer cases. Two in particular were of such significance that the Office saw fit to publish responses to these calls for investigations: communications alleging serious crimes in Venezuela and Iraq. I turn now to the cases not taken.

The cases not taken: Venezuela and Iraq

The results of the Office of the Prosecutor's analysis of the Venezuela and Iraq communications partially support though also challenge any claim that investigations have focused excessively on Africa. In the case of the Venezuelan situation, following an analysis by the Office of the Prosecutor that there was either a lack of temporal jurisdiction or that the incidents alleged did not satisfy the elements of the crime alleged, the alleged crimes were not made the subject of a formal investigation. Firstly, the bulk of the incidents fell outside the ICC's temporal jurisdiction. The ICC Statute came into force in July 2002 and many of the crimes alleged related to a shortlived coup in April of that year. This meant that the ICC did not have jurisdiction over them. Secondly, however, the ICC did analyse a number of incidents within its jurisdiction and found that they would not fit the definition of the alleged crime, namely crimes against humanity. This was because, even should the alleged events be proven to have taken place, no evidence was presented that they had occurred as part of a widespread or systematic attack on the civilian population.[23]

The analysis of submissions relating to alleged crimes committed in Iraq after the United States-led invasion was somewhat more complex. In the first instance, the Court lacked territorial or personal jurisdiction over many alleged crimes and perpetrators as Iraq is not a state party to the ICC Statute and many who may have committed crimes are not nationals of state parties (for example, many are American). Thus the ICC has jurisdiction only over crimes committed in Iraq by nationals of state parties, reducing the range of cases it might investigate. However, a number of crimes were alleged to have been committed by nationals and the Office of the Prosecutor undertook an analysis of each, ultimately choosing not to prosecute. The first crime alleged was that of aggression, based upon claims that the war in Iraq was illegal. While aggression is a crime under the ICC's jurisdiction, the state parties were unable to agree on a definition of aggression; in the absence of such agreement the Court cannot investigate or prosecute this crime. Upon analysing claims that genocide and crimes against humanity had been committed, the Office of the Prosecutor found that the grounds for these claims did not satisfy the legal definitions for either. Specifically, evidence of the intent to destroy a relevant group (the definition of genocide) had not been presented. Evidence of a widespread or systematic attack on the civilian population (the definition of crimes against humanity) also had not been presented.

However, the Office of the Prosecutor did have occasion to consider allegations of war crimes. In particular, the complaints alleged that there had been targeting of civilians and clearly excessive attacks. Where the evidence presented in the complaints was insufficient the Office sought further evidence from other sources. Its analysis concluded that there was not sufficient evidence of actors under its jurisdiction either targeting civilians or engaging in clearly excessive attacks. It finally considered allegations of willful killing and mistreatment of civilians. Its decision about this is somewhat more controversial. The Office of the Prosecutor's analysis concluded that there was evidence that these crimes had been committed, involving between four and twelve cases of willful killing and up to twenty cases of mistreatment. However, the Office of the Prosecutor determined that these alleged crimes were not admissible as they failed to fulfil the gravity threshold in the Statute under article 8(1). This article provides that the Court has jurisdiction over war crimes committed as part of a plan or policy or committed as part of a wide-scale commission of the same crimes. The Office of the Prosecutor determined that these crimes therefore were not admissible, adding in its statement a reminder of the scale of crimes committed in the cases it did have under investigation, such as in the DRC.[24]

The case that could be: Colombia's paramilitaries

The ICC is not currently engaged in a formal investigation into crimes committed in Colombia but the prosecutor has indicated that he is monitoring the situation and has asked the government for information regarding a number of killings.[25] Colombia's internal conflict has raged for four decades, despite changing in form, parties and intensity.[26] The conflict between the government and a number of rebel guerrilla groups, most importantly the Revolutionary Armed Forces of Colombia (FARC) and the National Liberation Army (ELN), with the intervention of government-supported paramilitary groups – the United Self-Defense Groups of Colombia (AUC) – has killed tens of thousands and displaced anywhere from 1.8 to 3.5 million people, making Colombia second only to the Darfur region of Sudan in the number of internally displaced persons (IDPs). Most are fleeing violence that has largely targeted civilians, including extrajudicial killings, kidnappings, massacres and torture.[27] Colombia signed the ICC treaty and on 5 August 2002 deposited its instrument of ratification, meaning that many crimes committed in recent years would fall within the Court's jurisdiction.[28] However, Colombia has chosen to avail itself of article 124 of the Rome Statute, which allows member states to refuse to accept the Court's jurisdiction over war crimes for seven years.[29] Furthermore, the AUC leadership struck a deal with the government to demobilise in exchange for the suspension of arrest orders.[30] The government passed a Justice and Peace Law in July 2005 that granted amnesty or the promise of reduced sentences to former members of paramilitaries who demobilised.[31] The law was condemned by some European Union (EU) officials and human rights bodies, including the Office of the High Commissioner for Human Rights (OHCHR), and challenges to it were brought before the Colombian Constitutional Court, which revised it to ensure that top paramilitary leaders would face trial and moderate sentences if convicted.[32] Prior to these revisions, the ICC prosecutor expressed concern about the law as well; he has subsequently argued that the paramilitary leader, Carlos Castaño, agreed to demobilise out of fear of the reach of the ICC.[33]

The Office of the Prosecutor continues to monitor the situation. In the author's interviews in Colombia in August 2005 many sources suggested that all armed groups feared prosecution before the ICC but were split as to whether it would encourage them to keep fighting or to lay down their arms.[34] With trials of senior paramilitary leaders continuing in Colombia, the Office of the Prosecutor will refrain from exercising jurisdiction for the moment but could seek jurisdiction over other fighters, or over these individuals should the trials prove to be shams, which they do not appear to be. It would only be able to hear charges of crimes against humanity or genocide, as war crimes are excluded for seven years. Should the ICC take on a case arising from Colombia, this might serve to mitigate concerns about it being an International Criminal Court for Africa.

DOES THE COURT UNDERMINE PEACEMAKING OR PEACEBUILDING?

An interesting obverse of the objections addressed above, which is in essence that the Court is a political tool, is that the Court is apolitical, or improperly ignores politics, and does so at the cost of building peace in countries riven by conflict. The claim is made that, in pursuing its strictly legal mandate – investigating and seeking the arrest of individuals accused of committing crimes under its Statute – the Office of the Prosecutor is hampering peace negotiations. This is a serious accusation and one I believe may have merit, based upon past experience with international and domestic trials with at least one current ICC case.

This objection is heard most frequently in relation to the indictments issued for Joseph Kony of the LRA and four of his deputies, in the context of a revived peace process in Uganda. The prosecutor drew criticism first for accepting a referral that was crafted so as to exclude the possibility of prosecuting any person other than those who had committed crimes in northern Uganda, specifically members of the LRA. While he has publicly clarified that he is not constrained by the terms of the referral and can investigate crimes committed by the Ugandan army as well, those investigations have not proceeded, at least not publicly, and to date the only indictees have been LRA members. Critics were also concerned that he announced the investigation while standing next to Uganda's president, an act that appeared to endorse further the selectivity of the referral. Having initiated investigations, the Office of the Prosecutor has since been criticised for interfering in the peace process, unsealing indictments against Kony and others as peace talks were revived between the LRA and the Ugandan government in southern Sudan and the government offered amnesty to Kony and others. His insistence that he has a legal rather than political role has not lessened concerns that the pursuit of prosecutions may come at the cost of a peace process.[35] At the time of writing this chapter the lifting of indictments on Kony and others continues to be a key demand of the rebels before genuine talks can continue.[36]

There is mixed evidence regarding the impact of ICC investigations in other countries. In Sudan, the government has been resistant to allowing investigative teams into Darfur and has created a questionable alternative process for accountability, which by all accounts has never functioned and was intended as a smokescreen. Some interviews I have conducted suggest that a fear of ICC arrest warrants being executed has underpinned the resistance of the government in Khartoum to either a UN force or a hybrid UN–AU force in Darfur. This makes little sense given the 10 000-strong UN Mission in Sudan (UNMIS) force already present in the country.[37] As I have already noted, there is anecdotal evidence both that fear of ICC prosecution motivated paramilitary fighters (or at least their leaders) in Colombia to strike a deal, and that fear of prosecutions may mean a return to fighting or deter the two main guerrilla groups from negotiating.

CONCLUSION

Overall, the ICC has proven more robust or successful than its tortuous history and the vehement objections of the United States might have led us to expect. Its Statute entered into force very quickly; it has a majority of states in the world as members; and it has taken on three very serious situations for investigation and prosecution. The three cases are in Africa, which has given rise to concerns that Africa is being used as a guinea pig, or otherwise subject to neo-colonial control. While these concerns are not without merit, the self-referral of states and indeed the vast number of African state parties to the ICC Statute suggest that other dynamics are at play. A potentially more serious concern is that prosecutions, or prosecutorial strategy, may come into direct conflict with peace negotiations or peacebuilding, notably in the case of northern Uganda.

NOTES AND REFERENCES

Primary research carried out in Sudan and Colombia informed sections of this chapter, and was supported by Nuffield Small Grant SGS/01159/G (Sudan) and British Academy Small Grant SG-41812 (Colombia).

1. L.N. Sadat, *The International Criminal Court and the transformation of international law: Justice for the new millennium* (New Brunswick, NJ: Transnational Publishers, 2002); M. Arsanjani, 'The Rome Statute of the International Criminal Court', *American Journal of International Law* 93(1), 1999: 22–43; Coalition for the International Criminal Court, 'History of the ICC', www.iccnow.org/?mod=icchistory (accessed 11 March 2007).

2. See the websites of each court, www.un.org/icty/ (former Yugoslavia) and 69.94.11.53/ (Rwanda) (accessed 11 March 2007).

3. Rome Statute for the International Criminal Court (17 July 1998), www.icc-cpi.int/library/about/officialjournal/Rome_Statute_120704-EN.pdf (accessed 11 March 2007).

4. ICC, 'Assembly of state parties', www.icc-cpi.int/asp/statesparties.html (accessed 10 March 2007).

5. See, for example, J.R. Bolton, 'The risks and weaknesses of the International Criminal Court from America's perspective', *Law and Contemporary Problems* 64, 2001: 168; For a more nuanced account of the objections of the United States, see R. Wedgwood, 'The International Criminal Court: An American view', *European Journal of International Law* 10, 1999: 93–107; W.A. Schabas, 'United States hostility to the International Criminal Court: It's all about the Security Council', *European Journal of International Law* 15, 2004: 701–20; M. Morris, 'International humanitarian law: State collusion and the conundrum of jurisdiction', in T. Biersteker, P.J. Spiro, C.L. Sriram and V.I. Raffo (eds.), *International law and international relations: Bridging theory and practice* (London: Routledge, 2006), pp. 199–200; S. Zappala, 'The reaction of the US to the entry into force of the ICC Statute: Comments on UN SC Resolution 1422 (2002) and article 98 agreements', *Journal of International Criminal Justice* 1(1), 2003: 114–134; M. Weller, 'Undoing the global constitution: UN Security Council action on the International Criminal Court', *International Affairs* 78(6), 2002: 693–712.

6. UN Security Council Resolution 1593, UN Doc S/RES/1593 (2005), para. 6.

7. C.L. Sriram, 'Wrong sizing international justice? The Special Court for Sierra Leone', *Fordham Journal of International Law* 29(3), 2006: 472–506.

8. Under the principle of complementarity, where a genuine internal investigation or court proceeding is being held, or has been held and a judgment reached, the prosecutor of the ICC will refrain from pursuing a case.

9. Coalition for the International Criminal Court, 'Central African Republic', www.iccnow.org/?mod=car (accessed 21 March 2007); ICC, 'Central African Republic', www.icc-cpi.int/cases/RCA/s0105/s0105_doc.html (accessed 21 March 2007).

10. ICC, 'Prosecutor opens investigation in the Central African Republic', 22 May 2007, www.icc-cpi.int/pressrelease_details&id=248&l=en.html (accessed 26 September 2007).

11. ICC, 'Democratic Republic of the Congo', www.icc-cpi.int/cases/RDC.html (accessed 21 March 2007).

12. ICC, 'Uganda', www.icc-cpi.int/cases/UGD.html (accessed 21 March 2007).

13. UN Security Council Resolution 1593, UN Doc S/RES/1593 (31 March 2005). In Chapter 17 of this volume Dumisa Buhle Ntsebeza provides a closer examination of the role of the ICC in Darfur.

14. ICC, 'Update on communications received by the Office of the Prosecutor of the International Criminal Court', 10 February 2006, www.icc-cpi.int/library/organs/otp/OTP_Update_on_Communications_10_February_2006.pdf (accessed 10 March 2007).

15. This is of course in some ways the obverse of the criticism made following the Rwandan genocide and the slow start to the International Criminal Tribunal for Rwanda (ICTR) – that the international community is not concerned with either addressing conflicts in Africa or pursuing accountability for serious crimes there. On this topic, see M. Mutua, 'Never again: Questioning the Yugoslav and Rwanda tribunals', *Temple International and Comparative Law Journal* 11, 1997: 167–187.

16. Statements of H.E. M. Baali of Algeria and H.E. Mr Erwa of Sudan, in UN Doc S/PV.5158 (31 March 2005).

17. C.L. Sriram, *Globalizing justice for mass atrocities: A revolution in accountability* (London: Routledge, 2005), considers these allegations in more detail.

18. ICC, 'Assembly of state parties'. http://www.icc-cpi.int/Menus/ASP/ (accessed 23 February 2009).

19. Human Security Centre, 'Number of state-based armed conflicts (2002–2005)', www.humansecuritycentre.org/images/stories/HSBrief2006/figures/Figure1.2.pdf (accessed 11 March 2007).

20. See the record of the session, UN Security Council, 5158th meeting, UN Doc S/PV.5158 (31 March 2005).

21. See C.L. Sriram, and A. Ross, 'Geographies of crime and justice: Contemporary transitional justice and the creation of "zones of impunity"', *International Journal of Transitional Justice* 1(1), 2007: 45–65.

22. O. Bekou and S. Shah, 'Realising the potential of the International Criminal Court: The African experience', *Human Rights Law Review*, 2006: 499–544.

23. ICC, 'Venezuela response', 10 February 2006, www.icc-cpi.int/organs/otp/otp_com.html (accessed 10 March 2007).

24. ICC, 'Iraq response', 10 February 2006, www.icc-cpi.int/organs/otp/otp_com.html (accessed 10 March 2007).

25. Citizens for Global Solutions, 'ICC prosecutor discusses status of investigations', 22 August 2005, globalsolutions.org/programs/law_justice/news/ICC-Update.html (accessed 15 June 2007).

26. M. Chernick, 'Colombia: International involvement in protracted peacemaking', in C.L. Sriram and K. Wermester (eds.), *From promise to practice: Strengthening UN capacities for the prevention of violent conflict* (Boulder, CO: Lynne Rienner, 2003), pp. 233–266 offers a more extended historical account. See also I.O. Abad (*con la colaboración* A.D. de Aponte), *Combatientes, rebeldes, y teroristas: Guerra y Derecho en Colombia* (Bogotá: Instituto de Estudios Politicos y Relaciones Internacionales, Universidaed Nacional, 1992); E.P. Leongómez, *Colombia: Violencia y democracia: Informe Presentado*

Al Ministerio de Gobierno (Bogotá: Universidad Nacional de Colombia, 1998); E.P. Leongómez, *Insurgencia sin revolución: La guerrilla en Colombia en una perspective comparada* (Bogotá: Tercer Mundo Editores, 1996).

27. The low figure is the government figure while the high figure was generated by a Colombian non-governmental organisation. See report by Internal Displacement Monitoring Centre, 'Government "peace process" cements injustice for IDPs', 30 June 2006, www.internal-displacement.org/countries/colombia (accessed 15 June 2007). See generally J. Restrepo and M. Spagat, 'Civilian casualties in the Colombian conflict: A new approach to human security,' draft on file with author, 2004; J. Restrepo, M. Spagat and J.F. Vargas, 'The severity of the Colombian conflict: Cross-country datasets versus new micro-data', *Journal of Peace Research* 43(1), 2006: 99–115; J. Restrepo, M. Spagat and J.F. Vargas, 'The dynamics of the Colombian civil conflict: A new data set', *Homo Oeconomicus* 21(2), 2004: 396–428; Human Rights Watch, 'Colombia: Displaced and discarded', October 2005, hrw.org/reports/2005/colombia1005 (accessed 15 June 2007); 'Colombia gives militia ultimatum', 1 November 2005, news.bbc.co.uk/1/hi/world/americas/4397084.stm; J.A. Restrepo and M. Spagat, 'El conflicto Colombiano: Hacia donde va?', CERAC paper (2005).

28. On the status of Colombia's ratification, see the ICC website, www.icc-cpi.int/asp/statesparties/country&id=29.html (accessed 15 June 2007).

29. Reporters without Borders, 'Colombia follows France's bad example', 3 August 2002, www.rsf.org/article.php3?id_article=3615 (accessed 15 June 2007).

30. '*Acuerdo entre Gobierno Nacional y las Autodefensas Unidas de Colombia para la zona de ubicación en Tierralta, Cordoba*', 13 May 2004, www.reliefweb.int (23 February 2009).

31. La Ley de Justicia y Paz, Ley no 975 de 2005. http://www.altocomisionadoparalapaz.gov.co/justicia_paz/documentos/Ley1_975.pdf (accessed 23 February 2009); 'New Colombia law grants concessions to paramilitaries', *New York Times*, 23 June 2005, www.nytimes.com/2005/06/23/international /americas/23colombia.html; Á.U. Vélez, 'Hay que esperar para medir la ley y sus resultados', *INDEPAZ*. Interrogantes Sobre la ley de justicia y paz 28 (July–August 2005), *Punto de Encuentro*, pp. 17–19 and 20–22; Fundación Ideas Para La Paz, '¿En qué va la ley?' (1 July 2006).

32. L.C.R. Ramirez, 'Estado de la desmovilización de las AUC', *Punto de Encuentro*, 36, May 2006: 7–12; Centro por la Justicia y el Derecho Internacional, *Justicia y paz en Colombia: El Derecho a la verdad, la justicia, y la reparación* (San Jose, Costa Rica, 2006), on file with current author; International Crisis Group, 'Colombia: Towards justice and peace?' *Latin America Report* 16(1), 2006: 17.

33. E. Rubin, 'If not peace, then justice', *The New York Times*, 2 April 2006.

34. Author's interviews with a range of actors, not for attribution, Bogotá, Medellín, and Huila, Colombia, August 2006.

35. Sriram and Ross, 'Geographies of crime and justice'; A. Ross and C.L. Sriram, 'Catch-22 in Uganda: The LRA, the ICC, and the peace process', *The Jurist*, 17 July 2006, jurist.law.pitt.edu/forumy/2006/07/catch-22-in-uganda-lra-icc-and-peace.php (accessed 23 February 2009). See also A. Branch, 'Uganda's civil war and the politics of ICC intervention', *Ethics and International Affairs* 21(2), 2007: 179–197.

36. P. Clottey, 'Uganda peace talks enter new phase today', *Voice of America*, 14 June 2007, www.voanews.com/english/Africa/2007-06-14-voa2.cfm (accessed 15 June 2007).

37. Author's interviews, not for attribution, Khartoum, July 2006.

17

The International Criminal Court in Darfur

Dumisa Buhle Ntsebeza

INTRODUCTION

The concerns of all societies in transition from repression to democracy are issues of justice, truth, peace, reconciliation, human rights, nation-building, recon-struction of society and the elimination of a culture of impunity.[1] Truth, justice, peace and reconciliation sometimes find themselves at odds with one another. Those who would prefer criminals to be prosecuted run the risk of never discovering the truth of what happened because, by all accounts, criminal courts are not the best mechanism for discovering the truth.

I am in the fortunate and privileged position of having served as one of the commissioners appointed by President Nelson Mandela to the Truth and Reconciliation Commission (TRC) of South Africa in 1995. The report of that commission is replete with case studies that show that truth, or as near as one can come to it, was revealed to some victims only through the amnesty process. In the past, criminal justice processes in South Africa dismally failed to grant the victims a clearer understanding of what had happened to those who had disappeared or been murdered in suspicious circumstances. The TRC process succeeded where the criminal justice system had failed, albeit, as a quid pro quo, in a way that meant the perpetrators, in return for volunteering full disclosure of their crimes, escaped criminal prosecution and civil liability.[2]

In transitional societies incoming regimes are sometimes loath to prosecute because of a number of constraints that may include a lack of political will, a lack of capability and resources, the length of time that prosecutions would take, the threat of rebellion by former security personnel if they are still powerful and the regime's own capacity to delay prosecutions. These constraints apply even in post-conflict situations where there are 'clear victims'. In Rwanda, for example, the constraints on the process include some of the factors mentioned above. Whether the prosecutions are in the International Criminal Tribunal for Rwanda (ICTR) or in the domestic courts in Kigali, there are also other problems, which include, although they are not limited to, costs, ineptitude, the slow pace, corruption, ethno-racism, the lack of a real infrastructure and no jurisprudence to inform legislation to try genocides. Prosecutions in these circumstances may also undermine the criminal justice system principle of 'justice delayed is justice denied', the flouting of the principle of presumption of innocence in so far as suspects are kept in extremely poor and overcrowded detention facilities for endless periods of time without having the opportunity to appear before a tribunal or a court, and so on.

Prosecutions may also eliminate all chances of reconciliation. Perpetrators may well take the view, after prosecution and sentence, that they no longer have a debt to pay and that there is no need for them to be reconciled with their victims. If – as those accused sometimes argue – they believed in the 'rightness of their cause' in the perpetration of heinous crimes, they may well be filled with such resentment at having been prosecuted that no chance of reconciliation is possible, let alone opportunity for national unity, peace and the reconstruction of society.

By contrast, some victims may well justifiably feel that prosecutions are absolutely necessary. In Rwanda, for example, prosecutions were justified on the basis that they provide justice to the victims. Even with all the constraints prosecutions have had a symbolic value: they have reduced the potential for a culture of impunity to take root.[3] It is against this background that I look at the subject of peace and justice in the context of the role played by the International Criminal Court (ICC) in the crisis in Darfur, and make observations as to whether that situation calls for either a TRC or criminal prosecutions by the ICC, or a hybrid of both these attempts at promoting peace while achieving justice.

THE ICC

The idea of a permanent international criminal court gained impetus after the establishment of the Rwanda and Yugoslav Tribunals, which had been set up to try crimes such as war crimes, genocide and crimes against humanity. These crimes fuelled the widespread belief that a permanent international criminal court was desirable. Consequently, delegates convened in Rome in 1998 and drafted a statute for a permanent international criminal court. This was adopted on 17 July 1998 by an overwhelming majority of the states attending the Rome conference. By 31 December 2000, 139 states had signed the treaty, which came into force upon 60 ratifications. Sixty-six countries had ratified the treaty by 11 April 2002. To date, the Rome Statute has been signed by 139 states and ratified by 108, of which a very significant percentage is African.[4]

The ICC, as John Dugard notes, achieved ratifications far sooner than was generally expected. For this reason it stands as a working model for the international criminal justice system in which an international criminal forum applies rules of international law, is staffed by independent prosecutors and judges and holds persons individually responsible for crimes against humanity, war crimes and genocide, once they have allowed them a fair trial.[5]

Africa seems to be high on the Court's agenda. The prosecution of the Ugandan rebel leaders of the Lord's Resistance Army (LRA) was apparently the Court's first objective; this was in response to the alleged kidnapping of thousands of children who were used as soldiers or sex slaves. It appears that the recent crimes committed in the Central African Republic (CAR) and the territory of the Democratic Republic of the Congo (DRC) have also received the urgent, priority attention of the Court. In addition, the United Nations (UN) Security Council recently passed resolution 1593, which referred the prosecution of identified perpetrators for numerous atrocities committed in the Darfur region in western Sudan to the ICC.[6] This chapter is concerned with the ICC's response to events in Darfur.

BACKGROUND

On 18 September 2004 the UN Security Council, acting under Chapter VII of the UN Charter, adopted resolution 1564 in terms of which Secretary-General Kofi Annan, was mandated to 'rapidly establish an international commission of inquiry in order immediately to investigate reports of violations of international humanitarian law and human rights law in Darfur by all parties, to determine also whether or not acts of genocide have occurred and to identify the perpetrators of such violations with a view to ensuring that those responsible are held accountable'.[7]

In October 2004 I was honoured to be appointed as a member of the UN Commission of Inquiry on Darfur (UNCOI) together with Antonio Cassese (chairperson), Mohamed Fayek, Hina Jilani and Therese Striggner-Scott. UNCOI was requested to report on its findings within three months and was supported in its work by a secretariat and support staff that included a legal research team, investigators, forensic experts, military analysts and investigators specialising in gender violence, all of whom had been appointed by the office of the UN High Commission for Human Rights (UNCHR).[8] Throughout its mandate UNCOI consulted the government of Sudan in meetings in Geneva and Sudan itself, as well as through the work of the investigators. During UNCOI's time in Sudan it held extensive meetings with government representatives, governors of the Darfur states and other senior officials both in the capital and at provincial and local levels. It also interviewed members of the armed forces and the police, leaders of rebel forces, internally displaced persons (IDPs), victims and witnesses of violations, national government officials and UN representatives.

FINDINGS OF UNCOI

On 25 January 2005 UNCOI reported to the UN secretary-general. It had found, *inter alia*, that from February 2003 to mid-January 2005 grave human rights violations had been committed by all the parties to the conflict. In particular, in Darfur the armed forces of the Sudanese government and militia under their control, the Janjaweed, had attacked civilians and destroyed and burned down civilian villages, and that rebel forces had done the same albeit on a much smaller scale; that unlawful killing of civilians by both the Sudanese government armed forces and the Janjaweed had taken place; and that the killings had been widespread and systematic.

UNCOI found that the Sudanese government armed forces and the Janjaweed had committed rape and other forms of sexual violence in a widespread and systematic manner and had also inflicted torture and inhumane and degrading treatment as an integral and consistent part of attacks against civilians. In addition, they had forcibly displaced the civilian population in a widespread and systematic manner.

The Janjaweed had abducted women, and the government security apparatus had arrested and detained persons in violation of international human rights law, again as part of widespread and systematic attacks against civilians. Victims of attacks by the Sudanese government armed forces and the Janjaweed belonged mainly to the Fur, Zaghawa and Massalit tribes and therefore the discriminatory nature of the attacks might constitute persecution.[9]

Based on a thorough analysis of the information gathered in the course of its investigations, UNCOI established that the government of the Sudan and the

Janjaweed were responsible for serious violations of international human rights and humanitarian law that amounted to crimes under international law. In particular, it found that the government forces and the militia had conducted indiscriminate attacks throughout Darfur, which included the killing of civilians, torture, enforced disappearances, the destruction of villages, rape and other forms of sexual violence, pillaging and forced displacement. UNCOI was particularly alarmed that the attacks on villages, the killing of civilians, rape, pillaging and enforced displacement had continued during the course of its mandate. It was for this reason that UNCOI advocated that urgent action should be taken to end these violations. Even though UNCOI did not find that genocide had been committed – because it was of the view that the government authorities had not pursued and implemented genocidal policy in Darfur either directly or through the militias under their control – it was at pains to emphasise that that finding should not detract from the gravity of the crimes perpetrated in that region, notably crimes against humanity and war crimes, as these crimes were in reality no less egregious and heinous than genocide.

On the basis of a reliable body of material that was consistent with other verified circumstances that tended to show that a person or persons might reasonably be suspected of having been involved in the commission of the crimes, UNCOI also identified certain key individuals. It made no more than an assessment of likely suspects, since, given its modus operandi, it could not have made a final judgement as to criminal guilt. For example, certain government officials as well as members of the militia forces were named as possibly responsible for joint criminal enterprise in committing international crimes. Others were identified for their possible involvement in planning and/or ordering the commission of international crimes or of aiding and abetting the perpetration of such crimes. UNCOI also identified a number of senior government officials and military commanders who could have been responsible, under the notion of command responsibility, for knowingly having failed to prevent the perpetration of crimes. UNCOI strongly recommended that the UN Security Council should immediately refer the situation in Darfur to the ICC in terms of article 13(*b*) of the Rome Statute. Its view was that the situation in Darfur was a threat to international peace and security and given that serious violations of international human rights law and humanitarian law were continuing in Darfur even during the course of UNCOI's own investigations, the prosecution by the ICC of persons allegedly responsible for the more serious crimes in Darfur would contribute to the restoration of peace in that region. It was clear that there was an internal armed conflict in Darfur between the government authorities and organised groups, and a body of reliable information indicated that war crimes may have been committed on a large scale and at times even as part of a plan or policy.

UNCOI became convinced that the Sudanese authorities were unable to deal with the situation through their own criminal courts because the Sudanese criminal laws did not adequately proscribe war crimes and crimes against humanity such as those that were being committed in Darfur. UNCOI also felt that there was an unwillingness on the part of the authorities in Darfur to address the serious situation that had arisen in that region and that the perpetrators could never be brought to book for the serious crimes through the instrumentality of the national justice system. Measures that had been taken by the Sudanese authorities convinced UNCOI that only the ICC was competent to deal with the situation. It came to this conclusion after it considered and rejected the idea of recommending to the UN either that the matter be referred to the Rwandan Tribunal in Arusha (in terms of which the mandate of that Court would have had to be expanded to accommodate offences also committed in the Sudan) or that another special court such as the one in Sierra Leone be established, whereby a mixed court that would sit in Khartoum, Sudan, would be set up in which local judges and one or more international judges would sit as members of the trial court.

For reasons that need not detain us here UNCOI came to the conclusion that the ICC was the most appropriate institution to deal effectively with the crisis that had arisen in Darfur.[10]

REFERRING THE SITUATION IN DARFUR TO THE ICC

The clarity with which UNCOI's recommendations were expressed and the reasoned conclusions as to why the matter should serve in the ICC, must have weighed heavily with the UN Security Council when it met and eventually adopted resolution 1593 on 31 March 2005. This was the Security Council's 5 158th meeting. Acting under Chapter VII of the UN Charter, the Security Council adopted resolution 1593 (2005) by a vote of eleven in favour, none against, with four abstentions. The abstentions were Algeria, Brazil, China and the United States. The council also decided that the government of the Sudan and all the other parties to the conflict in Darfur should co-operate fully with the Court and the prosecutor, providing them with any necessary assistance. The council further decided that nationals, current or former officials or personnel from any contributing state outside Sudan which was not a party to the Rome Statute would be subject to the exclusive jurisdiction of that contributing state for all alleged acts or omissions arising out of or related to operations in Sudan that were authorised by the council or the African Union (AU), unless such exclusive jurisdiction had been expressly waived by that contributing state. This was clearly a clause inserted in the UN Security Council decision to accommodate the United States, which has never ratified the Rome Statute. The United States, however, strongly supported the idea of bringing to justice those who are responsible for the crimes and atrocities that have occurred in Darfur and of ending the climate of impunity there.

After the vote the United States spokesperson, Anne Woods-Patterson, stated that whilst the United States believed that a better mechanism would have been a hybrid tribunal, it was important that the international community spoke with one voice in order to help promote effective accountability. However, the United States fundamentally continued to object to the ICC's jurisdiction over its nationals and the nationals of those countries, including its government officials, which were not party to the Rome Statute (such as the Sudan). For this reason it could not agree to a referral of the situation in Darfur to the Court and abstained from the vote. The United States' representative stated in its comments on its abstention that it had not opposed the resolution because it understood the need for the international community to work together in order to end the climate of impunity in the Sudan. The resolution had protected from investigation or prosecution the United States nationals and members of the armed forces of non-state parties; the United States was therefore comfortable that it could, and would, be an important contributor to the peacekeeping and related humanitarian efforts in the Sudan.

The Chinese, speaking after the vote, explained that its abstention had been because it supported a political solution. The Chinese would have preferred the perpetrators to stand trial in Sudanese courts that the Sudanese claimed had recently taken action against people involved in human rights violations in Darfur. China did not favour the referral to the ICC without the consent of the Sudanese government. Since it also was not a party to the Rome Statute, China voiced reservations regarding some of its provisions and therefore found it difficult to endorse a UN Security Council authorisation of that referral.[11]

INVESTIGATION BY THE ICC PROSECUTOR

On 5 April 2005 the Office of the Prosecutor received more than 2 500 items from the commissioners of UNCOI, including a sealed envelope from the Secretary-

General that contained its conclusions. The Office of the Prosecutor also considered a report of the Sudanese National Commission of Inquiry, which the government of the Sudan had established on 8 May 2004 to investigate allegations of human rights violations committed by armed groups in the states of Darfur. The National Commission of Inquiry had reported to the president of the Sudan in January 2005 and on 29 May 2005 the Sudanese government made its report available to the Office of the Prosecutor. Incidentally, the National Commission of Inquiry had found, *inter alia*, that from 2003–2004 all parties to the conflict had committed grave breaches of human rights and that in each of the states of Darfur all parties to the conflict had committed the crime against humanity of murder. Many allegations concerning incidents of murder had been attributed to the Janjaweed, acting either alone or together with the armed forces. The Sudanese National Commission also found that members of a tribe called the Fur had been forcibly displaced in a part of South Darfur and that a large number of villages had been completely or partially razed during armed clashes in the Al Geneina, Cass and Wade Salih localities of the state of West Darfur.[12]

Having thoroughly evaluated UNCOI's conclusions and those of the National Commission of Inquiry, the Office of the Prosecutor analysed the evidence. The prosecutor determined that there was sufficient information to believe that there were cases that would be admissible. On the same day the prosecutor opened an investigation into the situation in Darfur. By 29 June 2005 the prosecutor had delivered the first report and statement to the UN Security Council, pursuant to resolution 1593, having been obliged to conduct an independent investigation, which, *inter alia*, would seek and consider evidence that might either corroborate or impugn information collected by other entities. The prosecution had to produce evidence capable of satisfying the relevant criminal burden of proof, namely, that of reasonable grounds to believe that the persons summoned had committed the crimes alleged in article 58(7). This is a standard lower than that required for the confirmation of charges – 'substantial grounds to believe'[13] and for conviction 'beyond reasonable doubt'.[14] The prosecution accordingly went ahead and collected statements and evidence, in conformity with the procedural requirements of the ICC, in 70 missions conducted in seventeen countries. After requesting co-operation from the Sudanese government the prosecution also conducted five missions to the Sudan where, with the agreement of the Sudanese government, it obtained information and accounts from senior officials of the government relating to events that occurred during the ongoing conflict in Darfur from July

2002 onwards, and relating to the national proceedings being conducted in the Sudan regarding crimes allegedly committed in Darfur.[15]

PROSECUTOR LAYS CHARGES

After the Office of the Prosecutor had completed its investigation into the crimes committed in Darfur, the prosecutor presented evidence to judges of the ICC. Consequently, on 27 February 2007, in terms of article 58(7) of the Statute, the Prosecutor Luis Moreno-Ocampo, applied to Pre-trial Chamber 1, to a panel of three judges (Judges Akua Kuenyehia [presiding], Claude Jorda and Sylvia Steiner), requesting the Chamber to issue summonses for Ahmad Mohammed Harun and Ali Mohammed Ali Abd-al-Rahman (also known as Ali Kushayb) to appear before the Court. Based on the evidence collected the prosecutor submitted to the judges that there were reasonable grounds to believe that Ahmad Harun and Ali Kushayb bore criminal responsibility for crimes against humanity and war crimes committed between 2003 and 2004.

The prosecutor submitted that the crimes alleged in the application were perpetrated during attacks carried out jointly by the Sudanese armed forces and Janjaweed upon four villages and towns in West Darfur: Kodoom, Bindisi, Mukjar and Arawalla. In the interests of protecting the identity of witnesses the prosecutor, in submitting to the judges his application, which necessarily becomes a public document, had redacted certain pages. The process of redaction was to ensure that the witnesses' identities were protected even though the general public had to know the facts that an application would reveal – facts conveyed by those victims that the Office of the Prosecutor had interviewed. The Office of the Prosecutor felt that it was in the interests of fairness and justice that the victims understood that the prosecutor was working to ensure that justice in Darfur was being done and that progress was being made.

The prosecutor further made the point that a characteristic of armed conflict in Darfur was that the majority of civilian deaths had been caused during attacks on towns and villages, carried out either by the Janjaweed alone or together with the Sudanese armed forces. The vast majority of attacks had been directed at areas inhabited mainly by the Fur, Massalit and Zaghawa tribes. However, the Sudanese armed forces and the Janjaweed did not target any rebel presence within these villages; rather, they attacked the villages based on the rationale that the tens of thousands of civilian residents living in and near the villages supported the rebel forces. This strategy became the justification for the mass murder, summary execution, mass rape and other grave crimes against civilians who were clearly known not to be participants in any armed conflict. The consequence of this modus operandi was that hundreds of villages in Darfur were pillaged and destroyed and two million people were forcibly displaced from their homes.

In its application the Office of the Prosecutor alleged that Ahmad Harun and Ali Kushayb bore criminal responsibility in relation to 51 counts of war crimes and crimes against humanity, including rape, murder, persecution, torture, forcible transfer, destruction of property, pillaging, inhumane acts, outrage upon personal dignity, attacks against civilian population and unlawful imprisonment or severe deprivation of liberty.[16]

INDIVIDUALS INDICTED BY THE ICC

The ICC has targeted the two individuals, Ahmad Harun and Ali Kushayb, for reasons that become apparent below.

Harun was state minister of the interior and responsible for the 'Darfur Security Desk'. The most prominent of the co-ordination tasks entrusted to him in this capacity was the management of, and personal participation in, the recruitment of the Janjaweed to supplement the Sudanese armed forces. He had recruited the Janjaweed with the full knowledge that these militia, often the motivating force behind joint attacks with forces of the Sudanese armed forces, would commit crimes against humanity and war crimes against the civilian population of Darfur. From April 2003 onwards Harun had visited Darfur on a regular basis. Witnesses have identified him as the official from Khartoum who was responsible for mobilising and funding the 'Janjaweed' or the 'Fursan'. Witnesses also stated that they used to see Harun meeting with or addressing leaders of the Janjaweed, including Ali Kushayb.

Ali Kushayb was the 'Aquid al Oqada' or 'Colonel of Colonels' in the ward in West Darfur. By mid-2003 he commanded thousands of the Janjaweed. He had led attacks on the villages of Kodoom, Bindisi, Mukjar and Arawalla and had also mobilised, recruited, armed and provided supplies to the militia, the Janjaweed under his command. The prosecution's stated case is that Harun and Kushayb joined each other and others in pursuing the shared and illegal objective of persecuting and attacking civilian populations in Darfur.[17]

CO-OPERATION OF THE SUDANESE GOVERNMENT

Paragraph 2 of the UN Security Council resolution 1593 (2005) requires the government of the Sudan and all other parties to the conflict in Darfur to co-operate fully with, and provide the necessary assistance to, the Court and the prosecutor. Other states and organisations have also been urged to co-operate fully. Consequently, in June 2006, the Office of the Prosecutor updated the UN Security Council on progress regarding the co-operation of the government of the Sudan with both the fact-finding process and the assessment of admissibility.

The participation of the government of the Sudan in the process is important in ensuring that the full picture of the events in Darfur is revealed. Consequently, the Office of the Prosecutor has made a number of requests to the government for assistance and for access to documentation and individuals that it wishes to interview. This includes a detailed and extensive request made in June 2006, in addition to earlier requests in 2005 and 2006. In June 2006 the Office of the Prosecutor reported to the UN Security Council that the requested interviews had not taken place but that the Sudanese authorities had agreed that the process could start in August 2006. When the interviews finally did take place, formal witness interviews were conducted with two senior government officials who, by virtue of their positions, were able to provide information in relation to the conflict in Darfur and the activities of government forces and other groups.

The Office of the Prosecutor met with officials in the ministry of justice and senior members of the judiciary to receive updates on national proceedings and the work of the Compensation Commission. The government of the Sudan also provided a limited amount of the documentation that the Office of the Prosecutor had requested. There are still several outstanding requests for documentation and interviews that remain an important feature of the fact-finding process and the Office of the Prosecutor is following up on these with the government of the Sudan. It would therefore appear that there has been noticeable, if not enthusiastic, co-operation with the ICC on the part of the government of the Sudan. In fact, in considering whether the Court should issue a summons or an arrest warrant to ensure the appearance of Ahmad Harun and Ali Kushayb in Court, if the Court were to grant an application, the prosecutor stated that 'a degree of co-operation [had] been forthcoming'. This included providing information required by the prosecution in respect of particular documents from the National Commission of Inquiry. The government's co-operation also entailed facilitating four missions to Khartoum during 2005 and 2006, as well as interviews, including that of the senior official under the procedures set forth in article 65(2). The government also assisted with organising a fifth mission to Khartoum in January 2007. The prosecutor told the Court that this last instance of co-operation occurred after the prosecution's announcement to the UN Security Council that it was completing its investigation and planning to submit its evidence to the judges in February 2007. In the light of this assistance and bearing in mind that this was a new phase of judicial proceedings, the prosecution stated that it foresaw the possibility of the government facilitating the appearance of those persons against whom a summons may be issued. Moreover, to the degree that compliance with summonses will depend upon the willingness of the persons concerned, Harun was a member of the government and Kushayb was a high-ranking official. Harun had in the past shown a willingness to co-operate with the UN Commission of Inquiry and the National Commission of Inquiry. It appeared, in any event, that Kushayb was in detention by order of a national jurisdiction rather than the ICC, under a distinct legal regime and for different charges. The prosecutor submitted, therefore, that it was only if the government of Sudan resisted or failed to comply with any decision of the Pre-trial Chamber that it would then apply for the issuance of a warrant of arrest for the two individuals in question.[18]

GENDER-BASED CRIME

In the very first application to the Court for the prosecution of the two named individuals, the ICC, through the Office of the Prosecutor, has taken a very serious view of gender-based violence. Rape is addressed in the summary of the case, starting on page 4, in eight counts of the charges referred against the two named individuals. In one count, for example, the count is rape constituting a crime against humanity. On or about 15 August 2003, Ahmad Harun and Ali Kushayb, as part of a group of persons acting with a common cause, are alleged to have contributed to the commission of a crime against humanity, namely, the rape of women and girls from primarily the Fur population of Bindisi town and surrounding areas. It is quite clear that because of the prevalence of this crime but more particularly because of its widespread and systematic perpetration, the prosecutor has correctly taken the view that it is a crime against humanity.[19]

A TRC VERSUS THE ICC

In its report, UNCOI considered whether a TRC would be appropriate in Darfur. It emphatically articulated that there is always a place for truth and reconciliation commissions that can play an important role in ensuring justice and accountability. As stated at the beginning of this chapter, this is because criminal courts by their very nature may not be best suited to revealing the broadest spectrum of crimes that took place during a period of repression, in part because they may convict only on proof beyond a reasonable doubt. In situations of mass crime, such as in Darfur, a relatively small number of prosecutions, no matter how successful, may not completely satisfy victims' expectations of acknowledgement of their suffering. In Sudan, what was important was a full disclosure of the whole range of criminality. However, UNCOI did argue that whether a TRC would be appropriate for Sudan and at what stage it should be established, were matters that only the Sudanese people should decide, through a truly participatory process. Those decisions should ideally occur only after the conflict has ended and peace has been re-established. They should also occur as a complementary measure to criminal prosecution. UNCOI also argued that the process of prosecution should be set in motion as soon as possible, even if the conflict was still underway, so that it might have a deterrent effect, that is, stop further violence. Furthermore, talks should ideally be held on the basis of an informed discussion among the broadest possible sections of Sudanese society and should take into account international experience. On that basis the likely contribution of a TRC to the Sudan could be assessed.

The commissioners of UNCOI therefore concluded that recent international experience indicates that TRCs are likely to have credibility and impact only when their mandates and composition are determined on the basis of a broad consultative process that encompasses civil society and victims' groups. TRCs established for the purpose of substituting justice with amnesties and producing a distorted truth should be avoided.[20]

I am obviously strongly supportive of the view that UNCOI took in this regard, having been one of the report's authors. In the case of Darfur it is clear that the ICC is not only the most appropriate but also the Court of last resort. The critical question is whether the Court can initiate proceedings. In terms of international criminal law the ICC may initiate a case only where there has not been any national investigation or prosecution of the case, or where there has been, or there is, such an investigation or prosecution but the state is unwilling or genuinely unable to carry out the investigation or prosecution.

On the basis of its own investigation and after five missions undertaken to the Sudan the prosecutor concluded that the Sudanese authorities have not investigated or prosecuted the case that is the subject of its application to the ICC Chamber. On that basis the prosecution has concluded that the case is admissible, an assessment which is not necessarily a judgement on the Sudanese justice system as a whole. In any event, the judges themselves will make a final determination if an issue regarding the case's admissibility is raised, now that a matter is before them for their consideration, at the insistence of the prosecutor.

On 27 April 2007 the same panel of three pre-trial judges issued warrants of arrest for Ahmad Harun and Ali Kushayb.

Having examined the request and evidence submitted by the prosecutor, the Chamber has concluded that there are reasonable grounds to believe that Ahmad Harun, by virtue of his position, had knowledge of the crimes committed against the civilian population and of the methods used by the Janjaweed, and that in his public speeches Harun had not only demonstrated that he knew the Janjaweed were attacking civilians and pillaging towns and villages but had also personally encouraged the commission of such illegal acts.

The Chamber has further concluded that there are reasonable grounds to believe that Ali Kushayb, the leader of the Janjaweed in the Wade Salih, enlisted fighters and armed, funded and provided supplies to the Janjaweed under his command, thereby intentionally contributing to the commission of the crimes. He personally participated in some of the attacks against civilians.

The Chamber also considered that there were reasonable grounds to believe that these two individuals would not voluntarily present themselves before the Court. Therefore, in order to meet the requirements of the Rome Statute, the Chamber decided to issue warrants of arrest. It ordered the registrar to prepare two requests for co-operation, seeking the arrest and surrender of Harun and Kushayb and containing the relevant information and documents, and to transmit such requests to the competent Sudanese authorities in accordance with rule 176(2) of the Rules of Procedure and Evidence. All state parties to the Rome Statute would also receive the information as well as the UN Security Council members that are not state parties to the Rome Statute. The information was also sent to Egypt, Eritrea, Ethiopia and Libya.

In a recent appeal to the UN Security Council, Prosecutor Ocampo passionately requested that body to put the necessary pressure on all states to ensure that these two individuals are arrested and surrendered to the ICC. He expressed his outrage that Harun is not only still in government but is a minister of state for humanitarian affairs. This, in my personal opinion, is indeed a sickening insult to the victims of the Darfur atrocities.

However, even though the victims of the international humanitarian tragedy in Darfur may feel that the pace of bringing perpetrators of the Darfurian atrocities to justice is tardy, they must take solace in the old adage that justice will eventually be done.

The wheels of justice may be grinding slowly but they grind exceedingly fine. Charging and eventually convicting and sentencing Harun and Kushayb, particularly because of their prominence in Sudanese society, will send a clear and necessary message to many that modern society will allow no one, however high their office, to get away with egregious crimes. The most recent testimony to the truism that the long arm of the law eventually catches up with perpetrators of heinous crimes, however long it may take to effect the arrest, is that of the arrest, detention and current trial of the former Liberian President Charles Taylor. It is hoped that his arrest, detention and possible conviction and sentence will not only contribute to peace in the region but will also translate into justice for those who were most affected by the war crimes and crimes against humanity committed under his presidency.

With respect to Darfur, I am personally saddened by the fact that in the more than two years since the submission of UNCOI's report no prosecutions have yet taken place and that only two individuals have been charged. At the same time I accept that the time may not be ripe for large-scale prosecutions or the prosecution of more high-profile individuals like Harun and Ali Kushayb. There is, however, no statute of limitations for war crimes and crimes against humanity. Justice and peace, even in Darfur, are still possible.

NOTES AND REFERENCES

1. See D.B. Ntsebeza, 'The relevance of transitional justice as a discipline', *Mthatha: Walter Sisulu University Law Journal* 2006: 95.
2. Ntsebeza, 'The relevance of transitional justice as a discipline'.
3. Ntsebeza, 'The relevance of transitional justice as a discipline': 96.
4. See www.iccnow.org/countryinfor/Ratifications-byUNGroups.pdf (accessed 15 April 2007).
5. J. Dugard, *International law: A South African perspective* (Cape Town: Juta, 2005), p. 178; A. Cassese, *International criminal law* (Oxford: Oxford University Press, 2003), pp. 340–347.
6. Dugard, *International law*; Cassese, *International criminal law*.
7. See UNCOI Report, p. 2, www.un.org/News/dh/sudan/com_inq_darfur.pdf (accessed 15 April 2007).
8. See UNCOI Report, p. 2.
9. UNCOI Report, paras 630–639, pp. 161–163.
10. UNCOI Report, pp. 3–6.
11. UN Press Release SC/8351, www.un.org/news/press/docs/2005/sc8351.doc.htm (accessed 15 April 2007).

12. See Prosecutor's application under art. 58(7) to Pre-trial Chamber 1: Case No ICC-02/05 (27 February 2007), paras 9–12, pp. 25–26, www.icc-cpi.int/library/cases/ICC-02-05-56_English.pdf (accessed 15 April 2007).

13. See Prosecutor's application.

14. See Prosecutor's application.

15. See Prosecution application for warrant of arrest, ICC-02/05/01 (27 February 2007), http://www.icc-cpi.int/menus/icc/situations%20and%20cases/situations/situation%20icc%200205/related%20cases/icc%200205%200107/darfur_%20sudan (accessed 25 February 2009).

16. See ICC, Office of the Prosecutor, Fact Sheet on the situation in Darfur ICC-02/05, 5 April 2007.

17. See Prosecutor's application, paras 29–37, pp. 31–34.

18. See Prosecutor's application, paras 29–37, pp. 31–34.

19. See Prosecutor's application, paras 29–37, pp. 31–34.

20. UNCOI Report, paras 617–621, pp. 156–157.

Conclusion

Suren Pillay

The need for 'justice' as a normative expectation frames much of our contemporary legal, political and ethical vocabulary. We inhabit a world in which justice itself has become normalised as a right enshrined in a cache of legal instruments. We also think of wrongs committed against us, as individuals and collectivities, through the prism of justice, framing these as forms of 'injustice'. Inherent to this sentiment is the almost naturalised view that when a wrong is committed, justice *has to be done or at least must be seen to be done*. The kind of justice to which we refer here concerns what might constitute the proper response to a wrong. The prevailing ethos that has shaped the 'proper' response to a wrong in the Western world has been influenced by the notion of *lex talionis*: 'an eye for an eye'. The genealogical origin of this response is, in turn, said to have metaphysical foundations of biblical lineage, in Exodus 21: 23–27. We can perhaps draw a certain amount of solace from the fact that the meaning of the phrase is no longer widely taken to prescribe a literal compliance to take an eye for an eye but rather has been integrated into the secular rationality of modern juridical discourse.

That said, many states around the world do still take a life for a life in the form of the death penalty. In recent decades, however, in conflicts within and between states there has been a shift away from 'victor's justice' and the encouragement of reconciliation between hostile parties. The Fourth Geneva Convention of 1949, for example, tries to ensure that those captured during and after a war are no longer treated as combatants who may be killed. Nevertheless, the lesson has been that losing parties tend to harbour hopes of revenge that undermine long-term peace. In early 2008, violence broke out in Kenya over disputed elections the year before, leading to numerous deaths. A commission of inquiry set up to investigate the violence compiled a list of names of perpetrators, which has been kept confidential. It recommended the creation of a special tribunal to try the perpetrators of the violence, and stipulated that names would be provided to the ICC should the tribunal not be created by the set deadline. However, political wrangling prevented the creation of the tribunal, and the deadline has been delayed. The political violence, its strong ethnic characterisation and the accompanying assaults and deaths, will in the years ahead no doubt shape the political and historical memory of Kenyans in many different ways. Addressing this legacy will mean finding ways to address the wrongs being committed now. The question of justice – while emphasising the need to rebuild a divided and fractured society in the future – is therefore the question of peace. Similarly, the conflicts in Chad, Sudan and Somalia will present such challenges. This brings to our attention the fact that Africa's turn to transitional justice tends to occur in the wake of a civil war or political conflict and not, as in the Latin American and East European experience, at the end of authoritarian rule. The case of Nigeria's Truth Commission, and the Ghanaian National Reconciliation Commission, as discussed in this volume, are possible exceptions to that trend.

Today the concept of *lex talionis* has a wider meaning in that it is more often used to refer to a set of legal categories of punishments proportionate to a crime committed, an approach described as 'retributive justice'.[1] The question posed here is the Kantian one of whether retributive justice is a categorical imperative. In other words, is justice-as-punishment something that must always be carried out when a wrong has been committed? Is it absolute? Are there conditions or circumstances that may arise whereby we are compelled to set aside the legal imperative to exercise justice as punishment?

In the trilogy of plays, *Oresteia*, the ancient Greek writer Aeschylus narrated three tales that focus on the events that followed the Trojan War.[2] The first story commences with the Greek King Agamemnon's victorious return from the battle for Troy along with his prize, the Princess Cassandra, and the unfortunate chain of events that this sets off. It is a compelling tale that sets out in staged dramatic form the generational intrigues that destroy the House of Atreus. In this famous story successive acts of injustice beget new acts of injustice and unleash a cycle of turmoil unforeseen by the central protagonists when they began their original quest for justice. The central lesson for Aeschylus is that the manner in which we right wrongs may impact on the future in ways that we might not have intended or desired. It is this dimension of the story that makes it one of the classics in the genre of Greek tragedy. Here we witness how the righting of a wrong through vengeance creates a new wrong, which in turn requires another act of vengeance to right, unleashing a delirious cycle of righteous violence until the very existence of the city is at stake. More than 2 000 years after the play was written the question posed by Aeschylus still haunts us: When does justice become revenge?

This question marks the intersection, and some might say the conflict, between law and politics. The modern rule of law is said to apply equally to all, regardless of time and place: we are all equal before the law, which means we are equal in access but also equally subject to it. It is this quality of modern legality that sets it apart from the unpredictability of monarchical whim or executive prerogative that is believed to have been a characteristic of feudal rule.[3] Yet, in this period of the modern rule of law, when might we set aside the rule of law itself? What conditions, if any, would present us with the conditions to invoke an 'exception' to the rule?[4]

Ruti Teitel has argued that this rule-of-law dilemma poses itself most forcefully during periods of political change, where 'a dilemma arises over adherence to the rule of law that relates to the problem of successor justice. To what extent does bringing the *ancien regime* to trial imply an inherent conflict between predecessor and successor visions of justice'?[5] The rule-of-law dilemma emerged acutely in the post-war period of the twentieth century, as a number of authors in this volume have noted (see Chapters 1, 2, 3 and 6). Victorious parties had to contend with the defeated pro-fascist leaders of Nazi rule in Germany. The Nuremburg (1945–1949) and Toyko (1946–1948) Trials were subsequently convened. Of paramount concern for many was the creation of a stable peace at the end of the Second World War while at the same time ensuring that justice was seen to be done. Could one have both the reconciliation of erstwhile enemies and the punishment of the vanquished by the victors? Would retributive justice have to be tempered for the sake of reconciling enemies who have to live together and create a single political community? In other words, would or should politics trump law in extraordinary times?[6]

'Transitional justice', as a form of justice that seeks to be a response to a wrong while at the same time seeking to be a form of justice which avoids the legal absolutism of retributive justice, emerged in response to this dilemma. The varied institutional forms and legal mechanisms of transitional justice that are available to us – truth commissions, war crimes tribunals, special courts, amnesties, reparations and indigenous or traditional processes – are the concern of the authors who have contributed to this book. Transitional justice has become central to the efforts of those who prioritise the need to end conflicts and wars because it allows for the consideration of instruments that simultaneously take note of wrongs committed and are amenable to 'principled compromises'[7] for the sake of peace and reconciliation. As a former South African minister of education and legal scholar, Kader Asmal, put it:

> We must deliberately sacrifice the formal trappings of justice, the courts and the trials for an even higher good: Truth. We sacrifice justice because the pains of justice might be to traumatize our country or affect the transition. We sacrifice justice for truth so as to consolidate democracy, to close the chapter of the past and to avoid confrontation.[8]

Critics, such as Kingsley Moghalu in this volume, are inclined, however, to suggest that an emphasis on reconciliation and peace can be an incitement to act with impunity if amnesty becomes something to which perpetrators feel entitled.[9]

The case studies in transitional justice mechanisms that have been discussed in this volume, and the insights of key 'insiders' in administering these mechanisms, has given us an acute sense of the challenges faced, while offering lessons which should be taken into account in the design of future peace and justice instruments. The vantage point of the African experience covers the entire spectrum of peace processes and mechanisms of transitional justice. We have contrasted attempts which emphasise judicial accountability for war crimes (Rwanda and Sierra Leone) with others that administered legal amnesty or societal forgiveness in exchange for truth-telling[10] (South Africa, Nigeria and Ghana), and still others that combined indigenous and international law processes (*gacaca* in Rwanda), or even embraced a policy of mutual amnesia and saw the local emergence of spirit medium reconciliatory practices (in Mozambique).

A further consideration to bear in mind when discussing the relationship between retributive justice and transitional justice is the role of international law. International law transcends national boundaries and exercises its juridical imperative above and beyond nation-states. International law has the jurisdiction to consider such injustices as 'crimes against humanity', 'war crimes' and 'genocide'. While these acts might be considered legitimate and therefore not criminal within the national legal regimes of certain countries under authoritarian rule, allowing perpetrators to escape accountability, they are nevertheless crimes under international law and subject to indictment. Questions and doubts have emerged: if international law denies the prerogative of states to consider whether to use retributive justice or not, will it undermine processes seeking a non-military solution to end wars and conflicts?

The International Criminal Court (ICC), the International Criminal Tribunal for Rwanda (ICTR) and the current trial of former Liberian President Charles Taylor as well as the case of Darfur, all addressed at length in this volume, speak to the potential and actual complications and innovations of international law in relation to transitional justice and the creation of longer-term peace.

The question of northern Uganda, taken up by Chandra Sriram in her discussion of the overwhelmingly African case load of the ICC, raises salient implications that are worth examining. The indictments of Joseph Kony, leader of Uganda's Lord's Resistance Army (LRA), and four deputies, have come under particular scrutiny in the context of an ongoing peace process there. The government of Uganda's referral of the matter to the ICC and the same government's perceived manipulation, in the eyes of some, of the Office of the Prosecutor could have serious implications both for the ICC and for the transitional justice process underway in northern Uganda. The noted Ugandan scholar, Mahmood Mamdani, in an open letter urged Ugandan President Yoweri Museveni to consider amnesty for the LRA rebels. Echoing the lessons of Greek writer Aeschylus discussed above, Mamdani asked Museveni: '[W]hen does the pursuit of justice turn into revenge-seeking? . . . Our response to these issues will shape both your legacy and the political future we bequeath to the next generation.' He went on to question the role of the ICC in Uganda:

> The conduct of the northern war has become more complicated by the entry of the International Criminal Court. The ICC was created to hold governments accountable, especially concerning large-scale atrocities against civilians, defined in law as 'crimes against humanity'. This is why the internment of a million plus civilians in armed camps in the north, without adequate provision of security or food or medicine, should have been a prime concern for the ICC. But the ICC has chosen to focus its apparatus of justice on just one side of the conflict, the LRA. By providing impunity for the government while seeking to bring the rebels to justice, the ICC is contributing to the continuation of the northern war, rather than its resolution.[11]

In Mamdani's view the entry of the ICC also potentially removes the prerogative of the government to make the political choice of giving amnesty to the LRA, taking away a key option from its repertoire of instruments available for ensuring peace. By contrast, in Chapter 17, we have seen the potential utility of having recourse to the ICC, particularly as regards the decision to refer the situation in Dafur to the United Nations (UN) Security Council. In his revealing account of the case, as a member of the UN Commission of Inquiry on Darfur (UNCOI), Dumisa Ntsebeza notes that while the commission did not arrive at the conclusion that genocide had taken place in the region, as had been pronounced in certain quarters, it did find that war crimes transgressions had transpired. Yet UNCOI did not feel that the government of Sudan would or could take the necessary actions to end these transgressions and hold those involved accountable: 'UNCOI became convinced that the Sudanese authorities were unable to deal with the situation through their own criminal courts because the Sudanese criminal laws did not adequately proscribe war crimes and crimes against humanity such as those that were being committed in Darfur' (see Chapter 17 in this volume). The role and effectiveness of the ICC in these two cases may be quite different and present landmark opportunities to shape its efficacy in the long term.

The richness of each case study in this book quickly makes it apparent that as much as all law might aspire to universalism, all politics might ultimately be local. The decision about the kind of transitional justice approach to be used must take local needs into account and learn from other experiences. The South African Truth and Reconciliation Commission (TRC), as has been noted before in this volume, has left an indelible mark in the imagination of other Africans as a model to be followed. Both Matthew Kukah and Kenneth Attafuah recall the powerful imprint of the South African model on the commissions set up in Nigeria and Ghana, yet both authors discuss the experience of having to learn to reshape the commissions to local dynamics. This point is borne out in the chapters by Alex Boraine, the deputy chairperson of South Africa's TRC, and by Charles Villa-Vicencio, its former head of research. Both caution against replicating the template of the TRC elsewhere without reshaping it to the new landscape. What all the case studies reveal is the need for a careful assessment of the particular 'wrong' that is being addressed in each country. Solutions are shaped by their problems. We need to understand what the problem is before reaching out for solutions. Solutions are often multiple and require careful consideration of the appropriate timing and mechanisms that can draw on lessons learnt elsewhere but these solutions must be tailored and reframed. Simply put, there can be no a priori rules about what would be an inappropriate instrument or procedure to use.

That local dynamics should shape the form of the mechanism is also highlighted in Villa-Vicencio's call for the importance of 'conversation' and 'truth-telling' in the transition process, placing emphasis on reconciliation rather than justice. If justice and reconciliation are in tension then the balance between the two is best judged according to the criteria of what most effectively creates lasting peace and stability in a divided political community. The main goal is to recreate a political community from a fractured historical experience. This may require a more nuanced understanding of both justice and peace. Justice can take many forms and can either be redistributive and restorative or retributive. A restorative or redistributive approach might enable the creation of lasting peace by addressing the material discrepancies and psychological legacies of conflict while a retributive approach might dissuade the repetition of human rights violations. Peace itself is not simply the absence of war but should be thought of as a process of creating a lasting harmony. Ending the fighting between warring parties may create only a short-term peace if the animosities, mistrust and bitterness that are produced during conflict are not addressed but instead are allowed to linger into the future, often overshadowing the everyday practices of social and political life after the conflict. This situation would then mean that both the symbolic realms of memory and identity as well as what Norwegian scholar Johan Galtung called 'structural violence',[12] would then need to be addressed in order to reduce the conditions which allow animosities to endure over time and manifest into actualised violence.

A recurrent regret and concern that emerges from the experiences with truth commissions in Africa is that agreements and undertakings made to victims and perpetrators, with respect to either material or psychological support, have been characteristically slow in the offering. The South African experience with reparations and similar experiences in Sierra Leone and Ghana underscore the seeming reluctance with which these commitments are fulfilled. Reparations often compete with other pressing demands and sometimes concerted pressure from victims on political leaders is required before such commitments are honoured.[13] As Thelma Ekiyor explains in Chapter 7, in the case of the Sierra Leonean TRC:

Amidst other issues, the TRC report makes recommendations for the implementation of a reparations programme. These recommendations call for measures to address the needs of victims on issues of health, pensions, education, skills training and micro-credit. Specifically, the commission recommends free lifetime healthcare for categories of victims, for example, amputees, the war-wounded and victims of sexual violence. Monthly pensions are also recommended for all adult amputees. Free education until senior secondary school level is recommended for children who are amputees or who had been abducted or conscripted and for those who are orphans of war.

However, Ekiyor also notes that these laudable recommendations require significant resources that are currently unavailable. In the case of Ghana, Kenneth Attafuah laments that the financial compensation for victims recommended by the commission took a couple of years to reach the beneficiaries (see Chapter 9 in this volume).

In order to maintain the future credibility of a process such as a truth commission, as a first consideration, the commitments made to those who participate should be fulfilled. Secondly, lasting peace is derivative of lasting interventions in the livelihood of people. These include investments in education, skills development and other social investments that address the concerns of those who commit to disarmament programmes, including child soldiers and women in particular. Thirdly, it is apparent that although some of the mechanisms are feasible, innovative and potentially effective, the necessary resources are required to ensure success. The examples of the Sierra Leone Truth Commission and the Rwandan *gacaca* process are cases in point in which good ideas and processes were potentially undermined as a result of the lack of funds. The stark difference in the funding given to criminal tribunals and to truth commissions is remarked on in Chapters 7 and 15. A concerted effort will have to be made to provide the necessary funding to ensure the functioning of the institutional arrangements, the efficacy of the processes and the ability to fulfil the recommendations made with regard to redress and reparations.

The case studies also suggest that reconciliation and peace – as goals realised over time rather than single events – require more than material reparations. There have been important indications that indigenous forms of reconciliation in the form of symbolic gestures, memorials, monuments and heritage sites can be particularly effective for recognition of past injustices suffered by sections of the population. For example, in Ghana the National Reconciliation Commission

(NRC) made the decision to honour women with a monument, in recognition that they had been the main victims of human rights abuses during the periods of military rule. In Mozambique the political leaders decided at the end of the war in 1992 to grant a mutual amnesty for any abuses committed by either the Liberation Front of Mozambique (FRELIMO) or the Mozambique National Resistance (RENAMO) forces. In Chapter 14, Victor Igreja argues that in the absence of a state-led reconciliatory process, local spirit media and cleansing rituals emerged through which women could be reconciled to their communities. Both Igreja's example of the *magamba* spirits in Mozambique and the *gacaca* courts discussed by Helen Scanlon and Nompumelelo Motlafi, suggest the need to rethink notions of justice and accountability in Africa in relation to the efficacy of indigenous practices.[13] Does 'justice' and 'accountability' take different cultural forms shaped by location and historical specificity? Should these shape mechanisms for dealing with human rights abuse, war crimes or crimes against humanity? How do we reconcile different conceptions of rights and responsibilities and how do the local, national and international actors converse with each other in a meaningful and coherent manner?

An important insight that may be drawn from the African experience is the need to consider widening the responsibility for the creation of lasting peace, justice and reconciliation in two ways. Firstly, it is best that justice, peace and reconciliation are not thought of as the sole responsibility of legal instruments or the central state. The Ghanaian experience of working closely with organisations of civil society proved crucial in providing a wider platform for organising and publicising the NRC. The use of partnerships also assists in promoting transparency, consultation and accessibility. In Ghana a citizen's handbook was developed, in which the workings of the commission were explained in accessible language, and this proved highly successful. The Nigerian and South African models used widespread access to the print and electronic media. The case of indigenous practices administered by spirit media in Mozambique, according to Igreja's account, suggests a successful process of social integration that takes place outside the ambit of the state. Secondly, the responsibility for peace, justice and reconciliation in African cases suggests the need to develop regional mechanisms to deal with the post-conflict peacebuilding efforts that follow wars. This observation follows the realisation that a number of African conflicts are regional in nature. The war that has raged since 1997 in the Democratic Republic of the Congo (DRC) demonstrates this dramatically.

Similarly, the conflict in West Africa involving Liberia and Sierra Leone since the 1990s had a strong regional dimension. The 1994 genocide in Rwanda and the massacres in Burundi since 1993 also took on a multi-state form as neighbouring countries Uganda, the DRC and Tanzania became important sites for refugees and militia regrouping. The current conflict in northern Uganda also involves Sudan, and the conflict in Darfur has spilled across borders into Chad and the Central African Republic (CAR). If conflicts in Africa are regional in scope and dynamic, the institutions to solve them are already becoming regionalised, through the African Union (AU), the Economic Community of West African States (ECOWAS), the Southern African Development Community (SADC) and other similar bodies. If this is the case, should the mechanisms to address questions of justice and reconciliation in the post-conflict phase not also be regional?[14]

These are important questions that are posed and answered in a number of chapters in this volume, both by scholars and participants who were actively involved in translating the ideals of peace and justice into a more usable reality. As the case studies demonstrate, the translation of the will to build a political community out of a violent and traumatic past is fraught with complexities, some of which can be anticipated and planned for. Others present themselves quite unannounced, reminding us that the process and institutional design must always be ready to anticipate the unexpected. Finally, the African experience with truth commissions, war crimes tribunals and peace processes demonstrates the resilience of the human spirit in the face of the most horrendous violations to life, dignity and wellbeing. Amidst tales of despair and folly there are also incredible displays of humanity as the processes of truth-telling, justice and the slow and arduous work of rebuilding communities in countries across the continent continues. This unique volume – written largely by a Pan-African group of scholars and practitioners and spanning all major cases of truth commissions and war crime tribunals on the continent – represents a modest contribution to supporting such efforts.

NOTES AND REFERENCES

1. B. Barry, *Theories of justice: A treatise on social justice* (Berkeley: University of California Press, 1989), p. xiii.
2. Aeschylus, *Oresteia: Agamemnon, the Libation Bearers, the Eumenides: the complete Greek tragedies* (Chicago: The University of Chicago Press, 1969).

3. A key text in social contract theory, seen as foundational to the modern liberal democratic state, which makes this argument for the philosophical basis of the state is J. Locke, *Two treatises of government* (Cambridge: Cambridge University Press, 1988).

4. The notion of the 'exception' in law is discussed more recently in G. Agamben, *Homo Sacer: Sovereign Power and Bare Life* (Stanford, CA: Stanford University Press, 1988).

5. R. Teitel, 'Transitional jurisprudence: The role of law in political transformation', *The Yale Law Journal* 106(7), 1997: 2018; see also E. Sklaar, 'Truth commissions, trials: Or nothing? Policy options in democratic transitions', *Third World Quarterly* 20(6), 1999: 1109–1128; and D. Pankhurst, 'Issues of justice and reconciliation in complex political emergencies: Conceptualising reconciliation, justice and peace', *Third World Quarterly* 20(1), 1999: 239–256.

6. R. Mani, 'Rebuilding an inclusive political community after war', *Security Dialogue* 36(4), 2005: 511–526.

7. J. Allen, 'Balancing justice and social unity: Political theory and the idea of a truth and reconciliation commission', *University of Toronto Law Journal* 49(3), 1999: 324–326.

8. Kader Asmal quoted in W. Verwoed, 'Justice after apartheid: Reflections on the South African Truth and Reconciliation Commission', paper presented to the 5th International Conference on Ethics and Development, Madras, India, 2–9 January 1997.

9. For a concise elaboration of these criticisms, see C.L. Sriram, 'Truth commissions and political theory: Tough moral choices in transitional situations', *Netherlands Quarterly of Human Rights* 18(4), 2000: 471–492.

10. C. Jenkins, 'They have built a legal system without punishment: Reflections on the use of amnesty in South Africa's transition', *Transformation* 64, 2007: 27–64.

11. J. Namutebi, 'Mamdani urges reconciliation', *New Vision*, 5 December 2005. Mamdani has, however, also been critical of the use of amnesty in the South African case. See M. Mamdani, 'Amnesty or impunity? A preliminary critique of the report of the Truth and Reconciliation Commission of South Africa', *Diacritics* 32(3&4), 2002: 33–59.

12. J. Galtung, 'Violence, peace, and peace research', *Journal of Peace Research* 69(3), 1969: 167–191.

13. See D. Ntsebeza and T. Bell, *Unfinished business: South Africa, apartheid and truth* (London: Verso, 2003).

14. For a more detailed discussion of this point, see C.L. Sriram and A. Ross, 'Geographies of crime and justice: Contemporary transitional justice and the creation of "zones of impunity"', *International Journal of Transitional Justice* 1, 2007: 45–65.

Contributors

Dr Mireille Affa'a Mindzie

Mireille Affa'a Mindzie is currently a Senior Project Officer for the Centre for Conflict Resolution's (CCR's) Conflict Intervention and Peacebuilding Support Project in Cape Town, South Africa. She works on the Human Rights and Conflict Management Project and specialises in the African Union's human rights frameworks and in children's rights. Dr Affa'a Mindzie holds a Ph.D. in international law from the University of Strasbourg. Before joining CCR, she worked as a Legal Officer for the Gambia-based Institute for Human Rights and Development in Africa where she co-ordinated the organisation's Child Rights Project. She was also involved in capacity-building, research and publications, as well as legal advocacy and litigation before the African Commission on Human and People's Rights.

Professor Kenneth Agyemang Attafuah

Kenneth Agyemang Attafuah was the United Nation's (UN's) International Advisor to Liberia's Truth and Reconciliation Commission. Prior to this he served as Executive Secretary of the National Reconciliation Commission in Ghana. He was a Commissioner for Human Rights in the Province of British Columbia, Canada, from 1992–1997, and an Adjudicator with the Canadian Immigration and Refugee Board. He has also been an Associate Professor of Governance and Leadership in the Graduate School at the Ghana Institute of Management and Public Administration (GIMPA). He previously served as Director of Anti-Corruption and Public Education, and Chief Investigator at Ghana's Commission on Human Rights and Administrative Justice (CHRAJ). Professor Attafuah is a private legal practitioner with Kulendi Law, Barristers and Solicitors specialising in human rights, constitutional law, and commercial and criminal litigation. He also doubles as Executive Director of the Justice and Human Rights Institute in Accra, which offers skills-based training and consultancy services in human rights, conflict resolution, corporate governance, crime prevention, investigations, and lobbying and advocacy.

Dr Alex Boraine

Alex Boraine was Deputy Chairperson of the South African Truth and Reconciliation Commission. In March 2001 he was appointed President of the International Centre for

Transitional Justice (ICTJ), based in New York, and became Chair of the Board of the ICTJ in June 2004. He opened a South African office of the ICTJ Justice in Cape Town in June 2004. He has been a Professor of New York University's School of Law since 1999. He has also been elected Fellow of the Centre for International Affairs at Harvard University, Fellow of Mansfield College, Oxford University; awarded honorary doctorates from Drew University, General Theological Seminar, Oregon University and Lafayette College in the United States; awarded an Honorary Doctorate of Laws from Rhodes University and of Social Sciences from the University of Cape Town, South Africa; awarded the Harvard Peace Prize and Paul Harris Fellowship by Rotary International; awarded Medal of the Presidency of the Italian Republic; and Distinguished Visiting Scholar at Columbia University, United States.

Ms Thelma Ekiyor
Thelma Ekiyor is the Executive Director of the West Africa Civil Society Institute (WACSI), based in Accra, Ghana. She was previously Senior Manager for Conflict Intervention and Peacebuilding Support at the Centre for Conflict Resolution, Cape Town, South Africa. She has also served as Director of Programmes at the West Africa Network for Peacebuilding (WANEP). At WANEP, Ms Ekiyor founded the Women in Peacebuilding Network (WIPNET), a regional women's network aimed at promoting the participation of women in peace processes. She also worked on a team that helped to strengthen the Economic Community of West African States's (ECOWAS's) early warning system. Ms Ekiyor served as Executive Director of Connect Synergy, a consultancy firm that provided capacity-building expertise to Shell Petroleum Company and the US Agency for International Development in early warning in the Niger Delta region of Nigeria. She has served as training consultant to the Forum for Early Warning and Response (FEWER) and has facilitated early warning training workshops across Africa. Ms Ekiyor also served on a team of experts that developed early warning training tools for Africa for the UN (UNIFEM, UN Department for Economic and Social Affairs and UN Institute for Training and Research), the African Union, and regional economic communities (specifically ECOWAS, InterGovernmental Authority on Development, and the Economic Community of Central African States), and has developed a variety of modules aimed at mainstreaming gender into peacebuilding and conflict prevention in Africa. A lawyer by training, Ms Ekiyor specialises in Alternative Dispute Resolution.

Ambassador John L. Hirsch
John L. Hirsch is Senior Adviser for the Africa Program at the International Peace Institute (formerly International Peace Academy [IPA]), Adjunct Professor at the School of International and Public Affairs at Columbia University, and Adjunct Professor of Diplomacy and World Affairs at Occidental College and Director of its United Nations Programme. From 1998–2005 he held appointments at the International Peace Academy, including as Vice President, and then as Senior Fellow, serving as Acting Director of the Africa Programme.

Before joining IPA he served as United States Ambassador to the Republic of Sierra Leone from 1995–1998. Ambassador Hirsch's extensive African experience in the Foreign Service includes assignments in Somalia from 1984–1986, and subsequently as Political Adviser to the Commander of the United Nations Transitional Assistance Force, General Robert Johnston, and as Deputy to President Bush's Special Envoy, Ambassador Robert Oakley (1992–1993). Ambassador Hirsch served as Consul General in Johannesburg, South Africa, from 1990–1993.

Dr Victor Igreja

Victor Igreja is a Post-Doctoral Fellow at the Australian Centre for Peace and Conflict Studies at The University of Queensland, Brisbane, Australia. Prior to that he was a research fellow at the Netherlands Institute for Advanced Study in the Humanities and Social Sciences, of the Royal Netherlands Academy of Arts and Sciences. He was also affiliated at the Leiden University Medical Center (LUMC), Research School of Asian, African, and Amerindian Studies and the Africa Study Centre in the Netherlands. He is trained in the fields of Psychology, Pedagogy and Medical Anthropology. Before that he was a Programme Officer, Senior Researcher and community activist in the Mozambican NGO *Associação Esperança para Todos*. His research interests lie in healing and reconciliation in post-war Mozambique. He has served as a facilitator in a conflict resolution training programme in Luanda, Angola, and as a visiting lecturer at the University of Hamburg in Germany.

Father Matthew Kukah

Father Matthew Kukah served as a member of the Human Rights Violations Investigation Commission in Nigeria, otherwise known as the Oputa Panel. He also served as Secretary of the Catholic Bishops Conference of Nigeria and as Secretary-General of the Nigerian National Political Reform Conference. Nigerian President Olesugun Obasanjo chose him to act as facilitator in negotiations between the transnational petroleum company Shell and the minority activist group, Movement for the Survival of the Ogoni People (MOSOP) and other Ogoni leaders. He is a member of the Electoral Reform Committee. Father Kukah is Vicar-General of the Catholic Archdiocese of Kaduna, Nigeria. He is also a member of the International Governing Council of the Centre for Democracy and Development. He received his Ph.D. from the University of London. He was a senior Rhodes fellow at Oxford University and spent a sabbatical at the Kennedy School of Government, Harvard University.

Dr Abdul Rahman Lamin

Abdul Rahman Lamin is Senior Lecturer in the Department of International Relations at the University of the Witwatersrand in Johannesburg, South Africa. Dr Lamin has also served as expert adviser to the Pan African Parliament (PAP) International Relations Ad-Hoc Committee on Africa-Europe Relations, where he assisted the Committee in drafting the Joint European Parliament (EP)-Pan African Parliament Declaration on the Joint EU-Africa

Strategy, presented by the Presidents of the EP and PAP at the EU-Africa Heads of State Summit in Lisbon, Portugal, in December, 2007. In 2003 and 2006, Dr Lamin was a Distinguished Visiting Scholar at the Solomon Asch Center for Study of Ethnopolitical Conflict at University of Pennsylvania, in Philadelphia. He is a regular guest lecturer on issues of governance, political leadership, human rights, peacekeeping, transitional justice and the political economy of post-conflict societies in Africa and is widely published on these subjects in academic and policy journals. Dr Lamin is also a prominent political commentator on African politics and international relations in the South African and international electronic and print media. Educated in Sierra Leone and the United States, Lamin holds a Ph.D. from Howard University in Washington, DC, an MA from Ohio University, in Athens, and a BA (Honours) from the University of Sierra Leone.

Professor Sheila Meintjes

Professor Sheila Meintjes has lectured in Political Studies at the University of the Witwatersrand in Johannesburg, South Africa, since 1989. She has a BA from Rhodes University, an MA in African Studies from the University of Sussex, and a Ph.D. in African History from the School of Oriental and African Studies. She teaches African politics, political theory and feminist theory and politics. Her research interests are gender violence, post-conflict transformation and gender politics in South Africa. She was a full-time Commissioner in the Commission on Gender Equality between May 2001 and March 2004, where she led the Commission's governance programme, and was responsible for the Commission in the province of Gauteng. She is the Chairperson of Tshwaranang Legal Advocacy Centre against Violence against Women and of Women'sNet. She has published widely on the politics of gender and on gender violence, including three co-edited books: *The aftermath: Women in post-conflict transformation* (2002); *One woman, one vote: The gender politics of elections* (2003); and *Women writing Africa: The southern volume* (2003).

Dr Kingsley Chiedu Moghalu

Kingsley Chiedu Moghalu is Head of Global Partnerships at the Geneva-based Global Fund to Fight AIDS, Tuberculosis and Malaria. At the invitation of the UN Secretary-General, Dr Moghalu served from January to July 2006 as a member of the high-level Redesign Panel on the UN Administration of Justice System, based at UN headquarters in New York, as part of the reform of the UN. Dr Moghalu joined the UN in 1992 and has served in political, legal, external relations and management positions at duty stations on four continents, including as Special Counsel and Spokesman of the International Criminal Tribunal for Rwanda in Arusha, Tanzania.

Ms Nompumelelo Motlafi

Nompumelelo Motlafi is a Masters student in International Relations at the University of Cape Town. She joined the Centre for Conflict Resolution in late 2006 as a Research Intern in the Policy Development and Research Unit and completed her internship in June 2007. Her contribution is the result of the mentoring provided by the internship programme offered at the Centre for Conflict Resolution.

Ms Wambui Mwangi

Wambui Mwangi is a Kenyan lawyer and is currently a legal officer at the Office of Legal Counsel at the UN in New York. Prior to this she worked in the Office of the Prosecutor at the International Criminal Tribunal for the Former Yugoslavia in The Hague and at the International Criminal Tribunal for Rwanda where she was both a Legal Officer in Chambers and the Special Assistant to the Deputy Registrar. She has practised as a criminal and immigration barrister in London and as a Capital Defence Attorney in New Orleans. She has also taught International Humanitarian and International Criminal Law at the University of Bristol. She has trained lawyers in specialised areas, in both the United Kingdom and United States, on issues such as the use of international human rights law in domestic capital cases, violence against women, immigration practices, and the relationship between gender and capital punishment.

Advocate Dumisa Buhle Ntsebeza, SC

Dumisa Buhle Ntsebeza is a Senior Counsel of the Republic of South Africa. In 1995 he was appointed as a Commissioner on the South African Truth and Reconciliation Commission. He became the Head of the Commission's Investigative Unit and also Head of its Witness Protection Programme. In 2002 he was a visiting distinguished Professor of Political Science and Law at the University of Connecticut. He has served as a consultant to numerous private and federal organisations and assisted in the establishment of a commission to investigate human rights violations in Nigeria. In 2004 Advocate Ntsebeza was one of five international legal and humanitarian rights experts appointed by then UN Secretary-General Kofi Annan to the Commission of Inquiry on Darfur.

Mr Suren Pillay

Suren Pillay is a Senior Lecturer in the Department of Political Studies at the University of the Western Cape and a Senior Research Specialist in the Democracy and Governance programme of the Human Sciences Research Council of South Africa. His areas of research include the relationship between violence and state formation; the ways in which race, culture and identity politics intersect in the fashioning of political communities, and developments in democracy, justice and citizenship in post-colonial Africa. Mr Pillay's publication record spans the authoring of a number of local and international journal articles and chapters in edited collections, and local and international conference presentations on youth and political violence in South Africa, death squads and state terror, the relationship between combatant and civilian deaths in wars, and the relationship between race, culture and minority rights in liberal democracies.

Dr Helen Scanlon

Helen Scanlon is Africa Co-ordinator of the Gender Programme at the International Centre for Transitional Justice (ICTJ) office in Cape Town. She was previously Senior Researcher at the Centre for Conflict Resolution and before that worked at the University of Cape Town's African Gender Institute. Between 2002 and 2004 she was a Research Fellow in the University of Cape Town's Department of Historical Studies and taught on a number of undergraduate courses within the university's humanities faculty.

Ms Yasmin Louise Sooka

Yasmin Louise Sooka practised as a human rights lawyer until 1995 and has been Executive Director of the Foundation for Human Rights in South Africa since January 2001. Prior to joining the Foundation, Ms Sooka was a member of the Truth and Reconciliation Commission in South Africa, serving first for three years as Deputy Chair to the Human Rights Violations Committee and then as the Chair of the committee. During 2002 and 2004 she was appointed by the UN as an international commissioner for the Truth and Reconciliation Commission of Sierra Leone. She has consulted and assisted the governments of Ghana, Nepal, Afghanistan, Burundi and Liberia in setting up truth commissions. She also serves on The Board of Trustees for Black Sash Trust, International Coalition of Historic Site Museums of Conscience, and is an Executive member of the Niwano Peace Foundation as well as an Advisory member for Leuven Centre for Global Governance Studies and Institute for International Law.

Professor Chandra Lekha Sriram

Chandra Lekha Sriram is Professor of Human Rights at the United Kingdom's University of East London School of Law. She was previously Senior Associate at the International Peace Academy (IPA) in New York, directing IPA's conflict-prevention project 'From Promise to Practice: Strengthening UN Capacities for the Prevention of Violent Conflict'. She is the Chair of the International Studies Association Human Rights Section and consults on issues of governance and conflict prevention for United Nations Development Programme. In 2006 she founded the Centre on Human Rights in Conflict, an interdisciplinary research centre, which is conducting research on the rule of law in post-conflict countries in Africa under the auspices of a British Academy grant, and on building just and durable peace with support from the European Union. She is the author of various books and journal articles on international relations, international law, human rights and conflict prevention and peacebuilding.

Mr Abdul Tejan-Cole

Abdul Tejan-Cole is the Commissioner of the Anti-Corruption Commission of Sierra Leone. Before that he was the Deputy Director of the International Centre for Transitional Justice's South African office. Mr Cole was a Human Rights Teaching Fellow at Columbia University in New York and a Yale World Fellow. He worked as a Trial Attorney and Appellate Counsel in the Special Court for Sierra Leone and taught law at the University of Sierra Leone. He has written extensively on human rights and transitional justice issues.

Dr Charles Villa-Vicencio

Charles Villa-Vicencio is presently a Senior Research Fellow at Georgetown University. Prior to that he was the Executive Director of the Institute for Justice and Reconciliation, based in Cape Town and, before that, the National Research Director in the South African Truth and Reconciliation Commission. A regular contributor to debate in South Africa, his present work is largely in the area of transitional justice and social transformation in South Africa. He has written and edited a range of books on transitional justice, truth and reconciliation commissions and the South African TRC in particular.

Index

365